LEARNING TO TEACH MUSIC IN THE SECONDARY SCHOOL

This fourth edition of *Learning to Teach Music in the Secondary School* has been thoroughly revised to reflect the latest changes, initiatives, research and scholarship in music education. By focusing on overarching principles, it aims to develop reflective practitioners who will creatively and critically examine their own and others' ideas about music education.

The new edition seeks to prioritise understandings of young people's musical lives—including their cultural experiences, digital competencies and individual needs—as the context in which to reflect on teaching and learning within and beyond the music classroom. Providing an overview of contemporary issues in music teaching and learning from a range of perspectives, this book focuses on teaching music musically and enables the reader to:

- place music education in its historical and social context;
- consider the nature of musical knowledge and how teachers can facilitate young people's musical learning;
- critically analyse the frameworks within which music teachers work;
- develop an understanding of composing, performing and responding to music, as well as key issues such as creativity, individual needs and assessment;
- examine aspects of music beyond the classroom and how effective links can be made between curriculum music and music outside school.

Including a range of case studies, tasks and reflections to help integrate the theory and practice of music education effectively, this new edition will provide valuable support, guidance and challenges for teachers at all stages of their careers, as well as being a useful resource for teacher educators in a wide range of settings.

Anthony Anderson is Associate Professor in Music Education and co-lead of Birmingham Music Education Research Group at Birmingham City University.

Carolyn Cooke is Senior Lecturer in Education at The Open University.

Victoria Kinsella is Associate Professor in Arts, Creativity and Education and Director of the Centre for the Study of Practice and Culture in Education (CSPACE) at Birmingham City University.

Elizabeth MacGregor is Teaching Fellow in Music Education and Performance at the University of Leeds.

LEARNING TO TEACH SUBJECTS IN THE SECONDARY SCHOOL SERIES

Series Editors: Susan Capel and Marilyn Leask

Designed for all students learning to teach in secondary schools, including those on school-based initial teacher education programmes, the books in this series complement *Learning to Teach in the Secondary School* and its companion, *Starting to Teach in the Secondary School*. Each book in the series applies underpinning theory and evidence to address practical issues to support student teachers in school and in higher education institutions in learning how to teach a particular subject.

Learning to Teach History in the Secondary School, 4th Edition
Edited by Terry Haydn, Alison Stephen, James Arthur and Martin Hunt

Learning to Teach ICT in the Secondary School, 3rd Edition
Edited by Marilyn Leask and Norbert Pachler

Learning to Teach Mathematics in the Secondary School, 4th Edition
Edited by Sue Johnston-Wilder, David Pimm and Clare Lee

Learning to Teach Physical Education in the Secondary School, 5th Edition
Edited by Susan Capel, Joanne Cliffe and Julia Lawrence

Learning to Teach Religious Education in the Secondary School, 3rd Edition
Edited by L. Philip Barnes

Learning to Teach in the Secondary School, 9th Edition
Edited by Susan Capel, Marilyn Leask and Sarah Younie

Surviving and Thriving in the Secondary School: The NQT's Essential Companion
Edited by Susan Capel, Marilyn Leask and Sarah Younie with Elizabeth Hidson and Julia Lawrence

Learning to Teach Business in the Secondary School
Edited by Limara Pascall

Learning to Teach Psychology in the Secondary School
Edited by Deborah Gajic and Jock McGinty

Learning to Teach Science in the Secondary School, 5th Edition
Edited by Lindsay Hetherington, Luke Graham & Darren Moore

Learning to Teach Art and Design in the Secondary School, 4th Edition
Edited by Nicholas Addison and Lesley Burgess

Learning to Teach Music in the Secondary School, 4th Edition
Edited by Anthony Anderson, Carolyn Cooke, Victoria Kinsella and Elizabeth MacGregor

LEARNING TO TEACH MUSIC IN THE SECONDARY SCHOOL

A Companion to School Experience

Fourth Edition

Edited by
Anthony Anderson,
Carolyn Cooke,
Victoria Kinsella
and
Elizabeth MacGregor

LONDON AND NEW YORK

Cover image: Lisa Dynan

Fourth edition published 2026
by Routledge
4 Park Square, Milton Park, Abingdon, Oxon, OX14 4RN

and by Routledge
605 Third Avenue, New York, NY 10158

Routledge is an imprint of the Taylor & Francis Group, an informa business

© 2026 selection and editorial matter, Anthony Anderson, Carolyn Cooke, Victoria Kinsella, and Elizabeth MacGregor; individual chapters, the contributors

The right of Anthony Anderson, Carolyn Cooke, Victoria Kinsella, and Elizabeth MacGregor to be identified as the authors of the editorial material, and of the authors for their individual chapters, has been asserted in accordance with sections 77 and 78 of the Copyright, Designs and Patents Act 1988.

All rights reserved. No part of this book may be reprinted or reproduced or utilised in any form or by any electronic, mechanical, or other means, now known or hereafter invented, including photocopying and recording, or in any information storage or retrieval system, without permission in writing from the publishers.

Trademark notice: Product or corporate names may be trademarks or registered trademarks, and are used only for identification and explanation without intent to infringe.

First edition published by Routledge 2000
Third edition published by Routledge 2016

British Library Cataloguing-in-Publication Data
A catalogue record for this book is available from the British Library

ISBN: 978-1-032-95108-9 (hbk)
ISBN: 978-1-032-95107-2 (pbk)
ISBN: 978-1-003-58322-6 (ebk)

DOI: 10.4324/9781003583226

Typeset in Interstate
by Apex CoVantage, LLC

CONTENTS

List of Figures ix
List of Tables xi
List of Boxes xii
List of Tasks xiv
List of Contributors xviii
Acknowledgements xxi

INTRODUCTION 1
ANTHONY ANDERSON, CAROLYN COOKE, VICTORIA KINSELLA
AND ELIZABETH MACGREGOR

PART 1 MUSICAL LIVES 5

1 THE PLACE OF MUSIC IN THE SECONDARY SCHOOL 7
JOHN FINNEY AND ELIZABETH MACGREGOR

2 CULTURE, SOCIETY AND MUSICAL LEARNING 22
GARY SPRUCE

3 DIGITAL MUSICAL LIVES 40
ANTHONY ANDERSON AND NICK HUGHES

4 INCLUSIVITY IN THE MUSIC CLASSROOM 55
PHIL MULLEN, VICTORIA KINSELLA AND CAROLYN COOKE

5 COLLABORATION FOR MUSICAL LEARNING 74
ANNA MARIGUDDI

CONTENTS

PART 2 MUSICAL TEACHING — 91

6 THE WHAT, HOW AND WHERE OF MUSICAL LEARNING AND DEVELOPMENT — 93
CHRIS PHILPOTT

7 WHAT IS A MUSIC CURRICULUM? — 115
CAROLYN COOKE WITH GARY SPRUCE AND ANTHONY ANDERSON

8 PLANNING FOR MUSICAL LEARNING — 134
ELIZABETH MACGREGOR AND GARY SPRUCE WITH VIVIENNE JOHN, JAMES O'NEIL AND ALYS WILDING

9 BEHAVIOUR FOR MUSICAL LEARNING — 154
CAROLYN COOKE

10 ASSESSMENT IN CLASSROOM MUSIC — WHAT, HOW, AND WHY — 170
MARTIN FAUTLEY

PART 3 MUSICAL LEARNING — 185

11 LANGUAGE AND LEARNING IN MUSIC — 187
CHRIS PHILPOTT WITH KEITH EVANS

12 CREATIVITY — 200
CHRIS PHILPOTT, KEITH EVANS AND VICTORIA KINSELLA

13 COMPOSING — 220
KIRSTY DEVANEY AND KELLY DAVEY NICKLIN

14 PERFORMING — 241
ELIZABETH MACGREGOR

15 LISTENING — 257
GARY SPRUCE

References — 273
Index — 288

FIGURES

3.1	Critical pedagogy for digital technologies in operation in the music classroom	43
3.2	When TPCK and critical pedagogies meet in facilitating digital music technologies	45
4.1	The teaching continuum	63
4.2	A model for differentiation	64
5.1	Situational roles of a collaborating music educator and young person	80
5.2	Interwoven model of collaboration	82
5.3	Episodic model of collaboration	84
5.4	Parallel model of collaboration	86
5.5	Hierarchical model of collaboration	88
6.1	Traditional song (to be sung as a round)	97
6.2	A model for musical learning	105
6.3	Formal, informal and non-formal contexts for music learning	107
7.1	Understanding curriculum	121
7.2	Interactions leading to an emerging curriculum	124
8.1	A framework for lesson planning	148
9.1	Learning behaviour conceptual framework	158
10.1	Who is the assessment for?	175
11.1	Intuition, analysis and technical vocabulary	191
12.1	Some tensions in the concept of creativity	204
12.2	A musical "feature": Wagner's "Trauermusik"	212
12.3	Question and answer	214
12.4	The blues in D with an F pentatonic improvisation	214
12.5	Riff and break	215
12.6	Some other ideas for improvisation	215
12.7	"Auguries of Spring": ritornello	217
12.8	"Auguries of Spring": chord structure of episodes	217
13.1	A composing process flow chart	227

FIGURES

13.2	A worksheet for a group composition beginning with an image of a haunted house	230
13.3	A worksheet for a group composition beginning with an image of a police car chase	231
13.4	A template for notating a *slendro* or *pelog* melody	233
14.1	The interconnection between the five principles of Green's (2008) informal learning	248
14.2	Extract from Riley's *In C*	250
14.3	Extract from devised material in the Aeolian mode	250

TABLES

4.1	Adapted Universal Design for Learning framework (CAST 2018)	58
4.2	Teaching and learning with young people with ADHD	68
6.1	The knowledge types in action	97
6.2	Some tensions in debating the "how" of musical learning	100
6.3	The types of and contexts for musical learning	108
6.4	Some models of musical and artistic development	111
7.1	The music curriculum as content and product	118
9.1	Learning capabilities	164
10.1	Summarising assessment in the music classroom	181
11.1	Worksheet idea: a grid analysis of music	193
15.1	Applying the principles: an example	269

BOXES

3.1	Using digital technologies to recontextualise music	48
4.1	Gender and music education	61
5.1	A collaborative entrepreneurial project	82
5.2	A collaborative school transition project	83
5.3	Collaborating with an instrumental teacher	85
5.4	Collaborating with a higher education institution	88
7.1	Teachers' statements about curriculum	119
7.2	Curriculum as lived experience	127
7.3	Curriculum as contextually connected experience	128
7.4	Curriculum decision-making	129
7.5	Musical learning and musical interactions	129
7.6	Young people as shapers of curriculum experiences	130
8.1	Lesson planning for recognising musical knowledge (Vivienne John: Wales)	137
8.2	Lesson planning for immersive musical activities (James O'Neil: Scotland)	141
8.3	Lesson planning for integrating musical experiences (Alys Wilding: England)	144
9.1	Good learning behaviours (PEEL 2013)	156
9.2	Classroom rules (Didau 2012)	156
9.3	Examples of learning behaviours	163
10.1	Questions for thinking about assessment	173
11.1	Possible confusions when talking about musical "elements" or "dimensions"	193
12.1	Some ideas about creativity	202
12.2	Models of creativity	207
12.3	Expressive problems	210
12.4	An illustration of continuity and progression in the concept of "musical variations"	216
12.5	*The Rite of Spring* (1913) by Stravinsky	217
14.1	Individual performing using multitracking	252

14.2	Exploring grime through small-group performing	253
14.3	Adaptation and inclusion in large-group performing	254
14.4	Performing and competing through whole-class singing	255
15.1	Valuing musical knowledge and understanding	261
15.2	Analysing musical elements and structures	262
15.3	Managing emotive and embodied responses to music	265
15.4	Interpreting and rehearsing a cover song	267

TASKS

0.1	An initial statement	3
1.1	What kind of subject is music?	9
1.2	Music as a civilising influence	10
1.3	Enduring principles?	11
1.4	How was it for you?	11
1.5	Creativity and imagination in music	13
1.6	Music and the arts	14
1.7	Dominant ideologies	15
1.8	Justifying music	18
1.9	Music and the expressive arts: discipline-specific requirements	19
1.10	Defining legitimate musical knowledge	20
1.11	Music's role in preparing young people for life and work	20
2.1	Your own musical studies	24
2.2	Young people and "their" music	26
2.3	Musical value and musical meaning	27
2.4	Talking about music?	27
2.5	Music and morality	31
2.6	The diversity of musical notations	33
2.7	Teaching without recourse to notation	34
2.8	Applying a social and cultural perspective	36
2.9	Adopting a praxial perspective to plan for music learning	38
3.1	Considering digital music technologies	42
3.2	Planning a music technology task	45
3.3	Creating and teaching with DAW templates	48
3.4	Overcoming technophobia in the music classroom	49
3.5	Adapting and recontextualising digital technology activities	50
3.6	Digital music learning across the school community	52
3.7	Questions for reflection	53
4.1	Thinking about principles of inclusion	57

TASKS

4.2	Barriers in a musical environment	58
4.3	Applying UDL to music learning contexts	59
4.4	Your own experience	61
4.5	Observing young people as musicians	62
4.6	The forms of differentiation	64
4.7	Auditing adaptive instruments and assistive technologies in your context	66
4.8	Supporting young people with ADHD in music lessons	69
4.9	Meeting young people's psychological needs	71
4.10	Evaluating inclusive practices	72
5.1	Existing collaborations	75
5.2	Collaboration opportunities	76
5.3	Young people at the centre of collaboration	76
5.4	Reflection on experience and identity	77
5.5	Interdisciplinary collaborations	81
5.6	The interwoven model	82
5.7	The episodic model	84
5.8	Collaboration with feeder primary schools	84
5.9	The parallel model	86
5.10	Reflection	87
5.11	The hierarchical model	89
5.12	Collaborative curriculum design	89
6.1	Types of musical knowledge	94
6.2	Musical knowledge "that," "how" and "of"	96
6.3	The knowledge types in action	97
6.4	Swanwick's (1979) hierarchy	98
6.5	Knowledge priorities at your school(s)	99
6.6	Encultured and instructional learning	100
6.7	Social learning	102
6.8	Informal self-directed learning	104
6.9	Formal and informal learning	105
6.10	Contexts for musical learning	107
6.11	The types of and contexts for musical learning	108
6.12	Musical development	109
6.13	The transfer of learning	112
6.14	Interdisciplinary learning	113
7.1	Your own experiences of music curriculum	117
7.2	Exploring curriculum as content and product	118
7.3	Talking with young people about curriculum	122
7.4	Interactions within a lesson	123
7.5	Identifying interactions that lead to emergence	126
7.6	Reviewing curriculum statements	130
7.7	Planning for an emergent curriculum	130
7.8	Developing and evaluating curriculum thinking	132

TASKS

7.9	Reviewing your understanding of music curriculum	133
8.1	Identifying musical knowledge	136
8.2	Identifying musical knowledge during lesson planning (Vivienne John: Wales)	139
8.3	Finding immersive musical learning through "border-walking" (James O'Neil: Scotland)	143
8.4	Evaluating the use of integrated musical activities (Alys Wilding: England)	146
8.5	Accounting for prior learning	149
8.6	Planning learning intentions and outcomes	150
8.7	Auditing musical activities	151
9.1	Recognising musical learning behaviours	155
9.2	Critiquing learning behaviours	157
9.3	Reflecting on Powell and Tod's (2004) model	157
9.4	Young people's learning behaviours	162
9.5	Identifying learning dispositions	165
9.6	Promoting effective learning behaviours	168
10.1	Exploring formative and summative assessment	172
10.2	Exploring assessment in your context	175
10.3	Observing assessment in practice	177
10.4	Assessment statements	178
10.5	Others' marking and grading practices	179
11.1	Describing music	188
11.2	Using adjective groups in worksheets	189
11.3	Comparing music	190
11.4	Introducing concepts musically	192
11.5	Confusions and misconceptions when using language about music	192
11.6	Grid analysis of a piece of music	194
11.7	Listening to student talk	195
11.8	Musical education as musical criticism	196
11.9	Responding to music in different ways	197
11.10	Notation	198
12.1	Creativity and education	200
12.2	What is creativity?	203
12.3	Recognising creativity and giving it value	206
12.4	The process of creativity	207
12.5	Creating the conditions for creativity	209
12.6	Using expressive problems to design a teaching activity	211
12.7	Musical features	212
12.8	Extra-musical ideas	213
12.9	Developing and using improvision	215
12.10	Creative musical approaches to teach at post-16 level	218
13.1	Composing in the curriculum	221

13.2	Reflecting on your own experiences of composing	222
13.3	Opportunities for composing	223
13.4	Composing myths	224
13.5	Defining composing	224
13.6	Identifying the different stages of composing	226
13.7	Supporting the composing process	227
13.8	Cross-curricular composing opportunities	234
13.9	Group planning	235
13.10	Creative blocks	236
13.11	Creating class guidelines for composing	237
13.12	Role models	238
13.13	Asking questions	239
14.1	Participatory performing in the community	243
14.2	Bringing the community into the classroom	244
14.3	Policy context for performing in the classroom	245
14.4	Individual performing on keyboards	247
14.5	Using informal, small-group approaches for performing in the classroom	248
14.6	Large-group performing	251
14.7	Individual performing and digital technology	252
14.8	Experimenting with small-group performing	253
14.9	Accessible opportunities for large-group performing	254
14.10	Creating cultures and structures for whole-class singing	255
15.1	Your own experience of listening and responding in school	258
15.2	Musical meaning and "high-status" musical knowledge	261
15.3	Musical meaning and musical materials	262
15.4	Adopting a holistic approach to traditional listening and responding tasks	264
15.5	Thinking about different ways in which people respond to music	265
15.6	Finding out how young people use listening to support performing and composing	268
15.7	Applying the principles of this chapter	269

CONTRIBUTORS

Anthony Anderson Birmingham City University, UK
Anthony Anderson is Associate Professor in Music Education and co-lead of Birmingham Music Education Research Group at Birmingham City University. He is fascinated by the many diverse aspects and ways of understanding music curricula and has presented, written and published on this subject widely. He is a former head of music and performing arts in secondary schools and worked as a classroom music teacher for sixteen years.

Carolyn Cooke The Open University, UK
Carolyn Cooke is a Senior Lecturer in Education. Following completion of her PhD thesis, *"Troubling" Music Education: Playing, (Re)making and Researching Differently* (2020), she is actively writing and presenting in the areas of transdisciplinarity, sound and the materiality of music education, sustainable pedagogies, appreciative inquiry and posthumanism.

Kirsty Devaney Royal College of Music, UK
Kirsty Devaney is a Lecturer in Music Education at the Royal College of Music and teaches composition at Royal Birmingham Conservatoire. Her practice centres on breaking down barriers to creative music-making and she has run the Young Composers Project at Royal Birmingham Conservatoire for over ten years. Kirsty is a co-author of *The Routledge Companion to Teaching Music Composition in Schools*.

Keith Evans University of Greenwich, UK
Keith Evans taught music in schools for over twenty-five years before moving to higher education to lead the PGCE Musicians in Education programme at the University of Greenwich in collaboration with Trinity Laban Conservatoire (2006-19). He has contributed to key music education texts including *A Practical Guide to Teaching Music in the Secondary School* and *Debates in Music Teaching*.

Martin Fautley Birmingham City University, UK
Martin Fautley is Emeritus Professor of Music Education at Birmingham City University. He researches assessment, classroom composing and creativity,

CONTRIBUTORS

policy in the English education system, and understandings of musical learning and progression. He has authored ten books and over sixty journal articles and chapters, and is co-editor of the *British Journal of Music Education*.

John Finney University of Cambridge, UK

John Finney taught music in secondary schools before leading the PGCE in Secondary Music at the University of Cambridge. John's research has focused on the relationship between public policy and classroom practice, with an enduring interest in ethical approaches to music education found in the relationship between pupil, teacher and what is being learnt.

Nick Hughes Robert Smyth Academy, UK

Nick Hughes is the Head of the Performing Arts Faculty at Robert Smyth Academy in Leicestershire. He has over twenty years of experience teaching music and music technology at secondary level and also works for Pearson as a principal examiner on the GCE music technology specification. He has a master's degree in teaching and learning focusing on composing using technology and has presented at numerous national conferences and events.

Vivienne John Cardiff Metropolitan University, UK

Vivienne John is a Senior Lecturer within the Cardiff Partnership for Initial Teacher Education at Cardiff Metropolitan University. She moved into higher education after many years as a secondary classroom music teacher working in England and Wales. Her research interests include the pedagogic beliefs and behaviours of early-career music teachers.

Victoria Kinsella Birmingham City University, UK

Victoria Kinsella is Associate Professor in Arts, Creativity and Education and Director of the Centre for the Study of Practice and Culture in Education (CSPACE). She has served as principal investigator on a substantial number of research projects. Her work notably focuses on music education, creativities, the arts and engaging with young people at risk of educational exclusion, including those with Special Educational Needs and Disabilities (SEND).

Elizabeth MacGregor University of Leeds, UK

Elizabeth MacGregor is currently Teaching Fellow in Music Education and Performance at the University of Leeds and has previously held posts at the University of Oxford and Birmingham City University. Her research into care and inclusion in music education has been published widely—including in her recent monograph, *Musical Vulnerability*—and she is also the assistant editor for *Research Studies in Music Education*.

Anna Mariguddi Edge Hill University, UK

Anna Mariguddi is a Senior Lecturer in Education (music specialist) in the Department of Primary and Childhood Education and is a Fellow of Advance

CONTRIBUTORS

Higher Education. Her research interests include informal learning pedagogy, qualitative methodology, and linking theory with practice. Anna worked as a secondary school music teacher prior to joining higher education.

Phil Mullen
Phil Mullen has worked for forty years developing music with people who are socially excluded. He specialises in working with young people at risk. Phil has a PhD from Winchester University, and his book, *Challenging Voices: Music Making with Young People Excluded from School*, is published by Peter Lang.

Kelly Davey Nicklin Birmingham City University, UK
Kelly Davey Nicklin is a composer and Senior Lecturer in Music Education with over twenty years' experience as a teacher and a head of faculty for performing arts. At Birmingham City University, Kelly has been the subject leader for the PGCE Secondary Music course, and she is also an experienced examiner for the International Baccalaureate Music Diploma and for teacher education programmes.

James O'Neil University of Aberdeen, UK
James O'Neil is a Lecturer and Lead Tutor for the PGDE Secondary Music at the University of Aberdeen. A former principal teacher of music in both urban and rural island settings, he continues to teach music in both primary and secondary schools alongside his work in initial teacher education.

Chris Philpott University of Greenwich, UK
Chris Philpott is Emeritus Reader in Music Education at the University of Greenwich where he was Dean of Education. He had previously been a music teacher and teacher educator with a musical background in the brass bands of east Kent. He has written widely for teacher education programmes in the United Kingdom and is an experienced school trustee.

Gary Spruce Birmingham City University, UK
Gary Spruce is a Visiting Lecturer in Music Education at Birmingham City University. He was previously subject leader for the Open University's PGCE Music course. He has written widely on music education, particularly around teacher professional development and music education and social justice. He is a practising musician with a particular interest in musical theatre.

Alys Wilding Birmingham City University, UK
Alys Wilding is a Senior Lecturer in Music Education and leads on the PGCE Secondary Music course at Birmingham City University. She has seventeen years of experience of classroom music teaching, many of them as a head of department. She has also taught singing and classroom music in primary schools across Birmingham.

ACKNOWLEDGEMENTS

The current editors would like to thank the editors and authors of the previous three editions of this book. Their work, much of which remains integral to this edition, continues to shape and inform the key ideas and nature of this book, and we are very much indebted to their support and guidance.

INTRODUCTION

Anthony Anderson,
Carolyn Cooke,
Victoria Kinsella and
Elizabeth MacGregor

THIS BOOK

This book is intended as a companion and resource to those who are learning how to teach music in secondary schools. Each chapter aims to provide support, guidance, ideas and challenges for beginning teachers and teacher educators, wherever they may find themselves. The multitude of routes into teaching, and the variety of contexts in which learning to teach music can occur, mean that beginning teachers and teacher educators all have very different needs. It is our hope that this book will prove useful to learning how to teach music across diverse routes and contexts. We also hope that qualified music teachers are able to use the content and tasks to extend and refresh their ongoing professional development.

Many aspects of learning how to teach are covered in the generic book (*Learning to Teach in the Secondary School: A Companion to School Experience*–Capel et al. (2022), 9th edition) and do not necessarily need a musical perspective here. For example, some aspects of behaviour management have cross-subject implications and are covered more than adequately in the generic book. We concentrate here on those aspects of learning how to teach that have unique implications for the music teacher.

This book does not take you stage by stage through the process of learning how to teach music (even if this were possible); instead, it is intended to be used after you have "audited" your own particular needs in your own specific circumstances. For example, the chapters can be read in preparation for, or as a response to, learning inside or outside the classroom, and the tasks can be used as part of a "development plan" by tutors, mentors or beginning teachers. The text covers knowledge and skills that will allow you to develop varied musical pedagogies, and, although not specifically designed to do so, will facilitate your progress towards the standards for Qualified Teacher Status or the equivalent in your context.

Many of the tasks ask you to share your thoughts and findings with other beginning teachers, colleagues or mentors. However, while engaging with a community of practitioners will be important to your learning, it can be difficult for music teachers to meet face to face, especially if working in a single-teacher department. It is here that we encourage you to develop your own community of practitioners through whatever combination of face-to-face and online opportunities are available to you, to enable you to share and obtain feedback from others working in different music education contexts. These tasks, and the conversations you have as a result, are a critical space for reflecting on your practice.

Learning how to teach any subject involves a willingness to engage in reflection and evaluate theory and practice. The cycle of *plan-act-reflect-evaluate* is important in the development of teachers in all contexts. Indeed, all teachers have a professional obligation to the young people they teach to become better practitioners, and it is the aim of this book to contribute to that developmental cycle. In this sense, learning to teach music is a lifelong process. The questions and activities throughout this book allow you to respond to the themes and issues presented at a variety of different levels, supporting you to synthesise, innovate, evaluate and critique in ways that develop skills necessary for undergraduate and postgraduate study.

Primarily, this book aims to identify musical and pedagogical principles that underpin effective music teaching and learning. In doing so, we have intentionally avoided details of particular curricula, policies or syllabi (for these often change), although there are times when we use such details as examples or case studies when making broader pedagogical points. This means the book can be used across a wide range of learning contexts, age groups and national frameworks, provided that you reflect on how the principles that are introduced could apply to your own context and statutory responsibilities. Nevertheless, we believe that the pursuit of a "musical" music education should transcend published standards and curricula.

Some of the chapters in this book are unashamedly theoretical in outlook. We believe that theory and practice are inextricably linked, for theory always underpins practice. We do not use the concept of theory here to mean anything distinct from practice, but as the evidence base for practice. All teachers have theories about the development of young people, the importance of their subject and the nature of learning, upon which they build their everyday work. These theories are often intuitive, since,

> no human mind is free from the impulse towards theorising, any more than human physiology can get by for long without breathing–[teachers] are implicitly working to theories about music and educational processes, whether or not they declare them publicly.
>
> (Swanwick 1988: 6-7)

INTRODUCTION

Different chapters in this book expound different theories of music education, adopting a variety of positions on musical meaning, musical knowledge, musical learning and musical development. These contrasting positions will confront you with the problems, difficulties and issues that surround the complex job that is music teaching and require that you reflect on your developing practice. You may not agree with every position explored in this book, but it is important that you evaluate what you do believe. This process will help to underpin your beliefs with a strong philosophy of music education. This is significant, for experience suggests that the best music teachers are those who have developed for themselves well-reasoned positions on teaching and learning music. The strength of such teachers is enhanced if, at the same time, they are receptive to the theories that underpin the good practice of others.

There are at least three important reasons for developing a personal philosophy of music education. First, your theories underpin the successful planning and teaching of your lessons. Second, having an individual philosophy of music education empowers you to critique and take reasoned decisions about education policy, curriculum design and young people's musical experiences. Such empowerment is critical in ensuring that different policies and agendas have a positive impact on musical teaching and learning in your classroom, rather than inadvertently diminishing it. Third, having a reasoned philosophy informs your ability to advocate the value of making music in school and its importance in wider society.

A valuable starting point for any personal philosophy of music education is your own experience as a learner or teacher. It is likely that your biography will be an important influence on the way you think about music and the teaching of music. Task 0.1 helps you to reflect on your own music education.

Task 0.1 **An initial statement**

From your experiences as a learner and teacher of music, answer the following questions:

1. What makes a good teacher?
2. What makes a "musical" music lesson?

On the basis of these reflections, write an initial statement that identifies the sort of music teacher you would like to become. If you are already a teacher, outline the areas of your practice you would like to develop further.

THIS EDITION

This fourth edition of *Learning to Teach Music in the Secondary School* builds on the valuable content of the previous edition, which was published at a time when significant changes were occurring in the social and political landscapes surrounding music education across the United Kingdom and the wider world. Since the publication of the third edition, discourse around teaching and learning music has continued to develop, and this is what we aim to address in the present edition.

There are significant similarities between the content of the third and fourth editions, such as in the chapters concerning key discussions and debates around the justification of music in the curriculum, the place of performing and appraising, and the role of assessment. However, in the fourth edition we have re-ordered and reframed some chapters to reflect current music education discourse. We have sought to prioritise understandings of young people's musical lives—including their cultural experiences, digital competencies and individual needs—by placing these chapters within the first section, "Musical lives." The issues discussed thereafter, in the sections "Musical teaching" and "Musical learning," should be read in light of these opening chapters.

The fourth edition marks the first version of *Learning to Teach Music in the Secondary School* to have been overseen by a new editorial team. We are grateful to Keith Evans, Chris Philpott and Gary Spruce for their much-valued work on the previous editions and hope that this edition meets the high standards they fostered in their roles as authors and editors. As a new editorial team, we have taken the opportunity to broaden the authorship of the chapters in the fourth edition, drawing on the expertise of professional practitioners in varied settings to help beginning teachers think about music education from diverse perspectives. We hope that this serves to make this edition both thought-provoking and useful in the classroom. We suggest that it is best read alongside its companion volume, *A Practical Guide to Teaching Music in the Secondary School* (Cooke and Philpott 2023), which offers further support and suggestions for exploring different pedagogical approaches, listening and responding, musical literacy, improvising, singing, composing, performing and cross-curricular learning.

FURTHER READING

Cooke, C. and Philpott, C. (eds) (2023)
A Practical Guide to Teaching Music in the Secondary School, 2nd edn, Abingdon: Routledge.

This volume can be used alongside *Learning to Teach Music* as a valuable source of practical prompts and ideas for classroom teaching.

Elliott, D.J. and Silverman, M. (2015)
Music Matters: A Philosophy of Music Education, 2nd edn, New York: Oxford University Press.

Swanwick, K. (1988)
Music, Mind and Education, London: Routledge.

In the early chapters of both of these books the authors make a strong claim for the importance of theory in music education and also the need for a coherent philosophy to underpin and inform our practice.

PART 1

MUSICAL LIVES

THE PLACE OF MUSIC IN THE SECONDARY SCHOOL

John Finney and Elizabeth MacGregor

INTRODUCTION

This chapter sets out to stimulate thought about the place of music in the secondary school, to consider what role it might play within a general education, and to do this within a historical perspective. Particular attention will be paid to some of the beliefs and ideologies that continue to shape current thought and practice. This in turn will lead to a consideration of the kinds of justification made for music as a subject of the curriculum.

> **Objectives**
>
> By the end of the chapter you will be able to:
>
> - discuss with other beginning teachers, music teachers, and school administrators the value placed on music education in the secondary school;
> - examine critically the validity of arguments supporting the place of music in the secondary school;
> - distinguish between justifications made for music education and music education advocacy;
> - read with insight policy documents defining the place of music in school and its contribution to the whole curriculum;
> - create in outline the case you would want to present in support of music education, whether in a job application letter, interview, or meeting of parents or governors.

A MORAL AND POLITICAL QUESTION

Writing in the fourth century BC, the Greek philosopher Plato saw music as educating the soul and shaping the personality (Plato 1982). Music could be of good and bad character. Music's modes and rhythms were to be selected with care: some were vulgar, some sentimental, and not all were equally civilising. After all, the modes had been named after tribes of people, some of whom were to be admired and others of whom were not. Modes were constructed out of musical proportions: some able to bring about the harmony of mind, body, and soul, and some not; some able to bring about perfection, and some not. This being the case, music education required careful regulation (Plato 1982).

Plato's ideal state required men of courage who were disciplined in war, reflective in peace, physically agile, and politically adroit. Thus, the character of boys was to be developed through modes that were modest, simple, and masculine rather than fickle, violent, or effeminate (Plato 1982). Music, like the other arts, touched emotion, affected mood and character, and—in Plato's theory of knowledge—had low status. Music was perceived to be less cognitively demanding than other subjects and therefore overly sensuous, seductively arousing, and potentially dangerous. A music education, then as now, was wholly implicated in the moral and political life of society and of greater or lesser interest to those who wished to educate, govern, and manipulate. Music was recognised as a medium through which to induct and socialise each new generation into the norms, values, and aspirations of a society. However, that this process should take place in schools attended by all young people was a novel idea. Only as nineteenth-century Europe embraced the idea of mass education was music—in the form of singing—officially sanctioned in schools across the United Kingdom.

The idea of music as having a distinctive contribution to make towards general education was one that was believed to have emerged from antiquity. One form of this conception, frequently referred to, was what became known as the Seven Liberal Arts (Rainbow and Cox 2006). Here, the curriculum was divided into lower and higher divisions: the trivium (grammar, logic, and rhetoric) and the quadrivium (arithmetic, astronomy, geometry, and music). The trivium was concerned with the arts of language, leading to the mastery of self-expression and understanding of the human mind. The quadrivium, on the other hand, entered into the world of ideas and abstractions (Bernstein 2000). Music—placed alongside other mathematical arts—was given high status, to be engaged with by the select few initiates thought qualified enough to probe the mysteries of the universe and search for ultimate truths.

Within the Seven Liberal Arts, interconnections between disciplines were sought through searching for common patterns and analogies. This concern for overall coherence was matched by the counterbalancing features of the two divisions: the trivium's sacredness and the quadrivium's secularity; the trivium's reaching inward and the quadrivium's reaching outward; the trivium's linguistic nature and the quadrivium's concern with the numerical, spatial, and temporal. As explored in Task 1.1, music was given high status as an abstract natural science, rather than as an artistic source of self-expression. Music was conceptualised as a temporal art bringing time and space to order: to be and become musical required organising time, and a musician's craft required playing with time as well as playing in time.

THE PLACE OF MUSIC IN THE SECONDARY SCHOOL

> ### Task 1.1 **What kind of subject is music?**
>
> How do you view music as a subject of study? Meet with another beginning music teacher. Decide on one of the following talking points and, through discussion, find arguments for and against the statement selected:
>
> - Music is a subject that enables self-expression;
> - Music is a subject with a strong mathematical orientation;
> - Music is by its nature an exclusive subject;
> - Music is a subject that orders time and space like no other;
> - Music is not a subject but an activity to participate in.
>
> Revisit this task at the end of the chapter.

The Seven Liberal Arts proved to be a prototype of what came to be thought of as liberal humanism: a philosophical stance that posited that education was able to bring about understanding of ourselves and the world in which we live. In this view, education—and with it, music education—had intrinsic worth, with the potential to open the mind to creative possibilities and meetings with the unexpected. This was an education that, through its rigour, discipline, and training, was thought to be liberating, while serving the common good.

The aim of Plato's regulation of music to preserve the state, ensure social order, and establish and sustain a common culture was one that was reiterated as music education found its place in schools during the nineteenth and twentieth centuries. By the turn of the twentieth century, the debate around the role of music education focused on which musical repertory was taught in the classroom. In suggestions made to music teachers by the English Board of Education in 1927, the following recommendation was made:

> As a rule the music first learned by children should be drawn from our Folk and Traditional songs. These are the true classics of the people, and form the foundation on which a national love of music can be built up . . . a pupil whose memory is stored with these songs from his earliest school days has the best protection that education can give against the attractions of vulgar and sentimental music when school days are over; and it is not always realised how strong and vital a tie between the members of a school, a college, or even a nation may be formed by their knowledge of a common body of traditional song.
>
> (Board of Education 1927: 253)

Here was the age-old conviction that, through singing, shared identities would be formed and a national community of common values created. Music education was, in this way, conceived of as an education in citizenship, to be regulated in the way that Plato had proposed. As discussed in Task 1.2, vulgarity, sentiment, and excess in music was to be avoided for the sake of "good taste," while respectable, rational, and disciplined training in music was to be lauded as symbolic of civility and morality (Bull 2019).

Task 1.2 **Music as a civilising influence**

Based on your in-school observations:

- To what extent do you consider music's "civilising effects" to be relevant in light of what you have observed in school?
- To what extent do you think the task of music education is to educate "good taste"?

TENTATIVE BEGINNINGS: MUSIC IN THE CURRICULUM IN THE UNITED KINGDOM

By the 1950s, curricula in the United Kingdom had evolved into what His Majesty's Inspectorate referred to as "singing plus." Group singing, musical appreciation, and the acquisition of clearly defined skills, techniques, and repertories were the common fare of music classrooms following the Second World War. However, in practice this often resembled a very narrow course of musical training, since overemphasis on skill and technique frequently got in the way of musical experience and enjoyment. While the English Board of Education (1927) had called for careful management of repertory, in 1955 the Scottish Education Department called for concession (Task 1.3). Writing of the choice of music for instruction in listening, music teachers were given the following advice:

> At first it should not be too unlike that which the pupils are accustomed to hear in the cinema or at home. The lively polkas and graceful waltzes of Strauss, for example, are a means of capturing the interest of the pupils who may not respond so quickly to the music of Bach and Beethoven. The simple classics should remain the foundations of good musical training, but the interest of the pupils in contemporary popular music should not be ignored. When they leave school—indeed, while they are still at school—the pupil's interest is drawn towards this very attractive, although perhaps ephemeral, music, which forms so large a part of their musical experience. The school's obligation is not to dissociate itself entirely from this kind of music but to teach some discrimination in sorting out the good from the bad.
> (Scottish Education Department 1955: 218)

However, despite decreasing censorship and increasing concession within classroom music education in the United Kingdom, a patronising attitude to

> **THE PLACE OF MUSIC IN THE SECONDARY SCHOOL**

Task 1.3 **Enduring principles?**

The statement made by the Scottish Education Department (1955) is carefully crafted and offers helpful principles that can continue to be commended:

- Recognise the interests of young people;
- Acknowledge their prior knowledge and experience beyond school;
- Move from the known to the unknown;
- Nurture critical judgement and discrimination.

Through your observations in school, note down ways in which these principles work in practice. Discard the one principle that you consider least relevant to a music education today. Replace it with one of your own.

Task 1.4 **How was it for you?**

Contact somebody who was at school in the 1960s or 1970s. Find out what they remember most about their music lessons in school. What long-term influence has school music had on their lives?

Use the following prompts to help the process of determining positive as well as negative responses:

- Did lessons leave you feeling musical?
- Did you create your own music?
- What music did you listen to during lessons?
- Are there songs from school days still in your head?
- What was your most memorable music lesson?

---

the value of popular music in the curriculum began to emerge. As considered in Task 1.4, as the 1960s and 1970s unfolded, young people were not slow to recognise this. A survey of the attitudes of young school leavers showed music given lowly status as a school subject (Schools Council 1968). One young person reflected:

> It was 1965 and our music teacher tried some experimental lessons when we got to Year 9. We were invited to bring our favourite records to the lesson. I brought Bob Dylan's *She Belongs to Me*. I remember thinking this was a really worthy piece of work because both the words and music had been created by Dylan. This encapsulated my ideal of individual expression and what I considered to be authenticity. The piece connected with my interest in surrealism too. The teacher noted the harmonica playing with some disdain: "it's just suck-blow, suck-blow." We seemed to be in parallel

universes. The teacher always kept a tight lid on discussion to avoid tribal warfare.

(Interview with first author 2004)

By the 1970s, the curriculum on offer was experienced as increasingly irrelevant by the young people for whom it was designed. A gap had grown between policy makers, teachers, and young people. Children were changing faster than schools, and new technologies provided young people with the means of organising their own music education (Bunch and Bickford 2022). The terms "good music" and "good taste" became problematic. Music in secondary school was experienced by the majority of young people not as liberating but rather as a training in skills and techniques largely considered to be unnecessary. Like the rarefied notion of music in the medieval quadrivium, the subject was in danger of becoming exclusive. Yet this crisis of confidence in fact became instrumental in forging fresh ideologies and competing visions of the role of music in the secondary school.

THE CREATIVE TURN: TOWARDS AN AESTHETIC EDUCATION

The most influential of these new ideas came from the composer-educator Paynter, who began drawing on innovative classroom practice as he worked on a major curriculum development programme at the University of York. He noted, for example, that teachers following the principles of Orff commonly used small-group music-making in the classroom, and, while taking care to teach instrumental techniques, they nurtured improvisation and composition and were willing to build on the ideas of young people (Finney 2011). The York Project, as it came to be known, developed the slogans "Music for the Majority" and "All Kinds of Music." Paynter fought against "Music for the Minority," in which training in skill and proficiency dominated, to the exclusion of imagination and creativity. Instead, Paynter brought composition, improvisation, and interpretation to the fore, thereby raising the status of music as a central element within creative secondary education (Paynter and Aston 1970). He also posed difficult questions, challenging the role of reading and writing staff notation and proposing the dissolution of the theoretical-practical divide for the integration of technical and expressive matters: "children need the creative stimulus of 'using' the skills they have acquired *as* they acquire them. We must try, therefore, to provide opportunities for interpretive decision-making even at the most elementary levels" (Paynter 1982: 123).

In Paynter's vision, emphasis was placed on the development of young people's ability to grow in discernment and in the capacity to make informed judgements of their own. In particular, giving young people freedom to make decisions about "how music should go" in the context of composing music provided them with the opportunity to know music from the inside. In this view, nurturing creativity and imagination was essential to the notion of being musically educated (Task 1.5).

> ## Task 1.5 **Creativity and imagination in music**
>
> Compare your responses to these questions to those of another music teacher:
>
> - In what situations do you consider yourself to be most musically creative?
> - When is it that you feel most musically alive?
> - To what extent have you gained knowledge of music from the inside through your performing, improvising, listening, and composing?

THE ARTS: A COMMON PURPOSE

The creative banner was taken up by others, and notably by Ross, an arts educator who declared a common purpose for the arts: the education of feeling (Ross 1980). For Ross, as for Paynter, music lagged hopelessly behind the way other arts subjects were conceived and taught (Ross 1995). The music classroom was either a dusty museum or a hallowed concert hall, the music teacher either the expressionless curator or the demanding Kapellmeister. In Ross's view this was not how it was in art, drama, dance, or English lessons, which engaged at a feelingful level to explore creativity, subjectivity, and self-expression. If music were to share a common purpose with the other arts, it needed to move beyond notions of great canonic works, rigorous technical training, and literacy in staff notation (Bate 2020). Instead, the music classroom needed to be reconceptualised as an experimental laboratory, a place privileging hypotheses, activities, and investigative impulses—"at once deeply unstable and nonauthoritative, webbed and webmaking" (Allsup 2016: 86-87).

The move towards more explorative classrooms at the end of the twentieth century saw the growing argument that the feelingful nature of the arts existed to provide an antidote to scientific subjects defined by rules and right answers, and where knowledge was "impressed" on the learner. An aesthetic education of emotion and expression was considered fundamental to general education for fostering individual flourishing and democratic society (Reimer 2003; Woodford 2012). Here was the conviction that before people could cooperate effectively with other people, they must understand themselves. Involvement in the arts demanded exploration of personal ideas, feelings, and artistry—and all young people had the potential to be "artists." This "child-centred," "progressive" approach placed existing norms and values, as well as heritage and tradition, in a supportive (even subordinate) rather than a leading role (Finney 2011).

These kinds of developments in thinking had the potential to bring the arts closer together. Indeed, the growing belief that the arts formed a coherent area of the curriculum was marked by the proliferation of terms such as "combined arts," "integrated arts," "expressive arts," "creative arts," and "performing arts." Yet—as discussed in Task 1.6—just precisely how teachers of the arts were to forge closer relationships within the classroom was to prove problematic,

> **Task 1.6 Music and the arts**
>
> In school, observe lessons across a range of subjects. Using the following table, note down the similarities and differences between the teaching and learning in music, other arts subjects, and non-arts subjects.
>
> | | Similarities | Differences |
> |---|---|---|
> | Music | | |
> | Arts | | |
> | Non-arts | | |
>
> Now reflect on the following questions:
>
> - Can a case be made for strongly distinguishing the arts from the rest of the curriculum?
> - To what extent do the different arts subjects share common values?
> - What opportunities are there for young people to engage in music in other arts subjects?
> - What opportunities are there for young people to engage in other arts subjects in music lessons?
> - How could cross-disciplinary learning across the secondary school be improved?

for while the arts in broad terms might share a common purpose and support each other in providing for a creative-aesthetic education, they were not interchangeable. Music could not be learnt by studying art or drama—but at the same time, it thrived in the artistic amalgamations and visual spectacles of musical theatre, opera, rap, dance, film, and video.

SOCIAL PRACTICE AND CRITICAL THEORY: TOWARDS A PRAXIAL EDUCATION

For some music educators, the idea of "aesthetic education" and "creative music"—whether in conjunction with the arts or not—failed to recognise music as socially located, arising from interpersonal structures affecting the conditions of its practice. In their eyes, conceptualising music education as aesthetic education would continue to perpetuate a patronising attitude to popular music, as "serious" high culture took precedence over "trivial" popular culture (see Chapter 15). Arguments for the transcendent qualities of art music enabled specific works to be moved to a special realm of aesthetic contemplation and beyond the social milieu of everyday life. An individual's inner life could therefore be enriched, safe from the contradictions and injustices of the social world.

THE PLACE OF MUSIC IN THE SECONDARY SCHOOL

Task 1.7 **Dominant ideologies**

Look back on your own past music education. To what extent did it value certain musical genres and practices over others? Using the pyramid that follows, construct a hierarchy representing the music that was considered to be of most and least value and reflect on how this has affected the way you relate to music today.

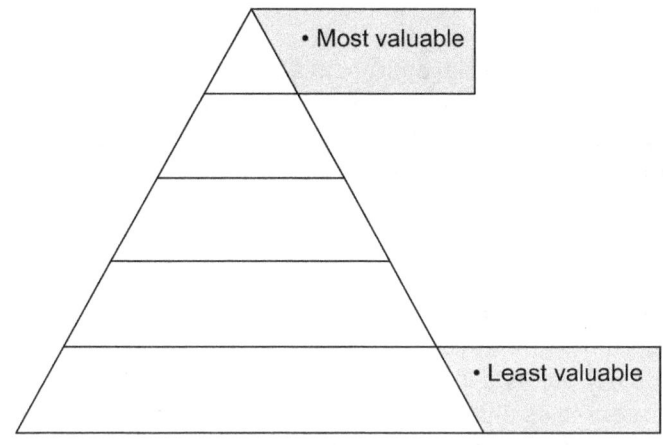

Over time, the dominating ideology of aesthetic and creative education, with its roots in the liberal humanist tradition, came under scrutiny from critical theorists, whose task was to expose taken-for-granted ideas that served to legitimise sociocultural hierarchies and hegemonies (Gibson 1986; Spruce 2012). Concurrently, new sociologies of knowledge raised questions about what "counted" as knowledge and, in particular, why some knowledge was given higher or lower status (Task 1.7). In the case of music, this knowledge came most obviously through the western art music canon, instrumental mastery, and reading and writing staff notation. As such, it was unable to account for the diverse musical traditions and contemporary practices valued by many young people (Vulliamy 1978): how was the music teacher to value young people imitating the vocal inflections of popular singers, for example, if value had to be derived from the western art music tradition?

In this view, music education needed to free itself from the long-established formalities of European high art cultures. Proponents of music as social practice, such as Shepherd (1991) and Elliott (1995; Elliott and Silverman 2015), argued that staff notation, for example, obstructed real musical experiences that were socially constructed. Pop, rock, and blues—as well as music from "unsung" subcultures and diverse ethnic groups—were the means by which to liberate the structures of schooling and change society. It was an illusion to suggest that music had innate meaning or value that existed in a vacuum, separate from the conditions that brought it into existence or the circumstances in which it continued to be practised. Furthermore, such practices could be understood as "praxes," actions undertaken with an ethical concern for alleviating exclusion and alienation and fostering inclusion and flourishing (Bowman 2014; Spruce and Matthews 2012).

VOICES OF ADVOCACY: JUSTIFYING MUSIC IN THE CURRICULUM

While both aesthetic and praxial approaches to music education had proponents and opponents, among some educators there remained a legitimate concern that the arts would become devalued in schools through an insistence on their subjective natures. Instead, music needed to be understood as part of the objective world—as a form of discourse:

> Music maintains its foothold in formal education not because it gives some kind of direct sensory pleasure, or enhances the public image of a school, or because some few students may eventually earn a living in music-related occupations. It persists in our educational systems because it is a form of human discourse as old as the human race, a medium in which ideas about ourselves and others are embodied in sonorous forms, ideas that may be simple or complex, obvious or enigmatic. And insight into these ideas—as into any significant idea—can be intrinsically rewarding.
>
> (Swanwick 1997: 4)

Swanwick (1997, 1999) was opposed to thinking of music as a social symbol and unconvinced by loosely defined ideas about creativity and self-expression. He advocated a carefully argued model of music education in which the processes of performing, composing, and listening gave direct access to individual aesthetic understanding (Swanwick 1979). This understanding—arising from the human capacity to animate the physical properties of sound as expressive shapes—built on music's symbolic and metaphorical meaning and subsequent engagement with personal and cultural histories (Swanwick 1999). In presenting music as "a great symbolic form" and "a discourse as old as the human race," Swanwick (1997) sought to strengthen the place of music in the secondary school, giving it the kind of significance that could be attached to other "great" symbolic forms such as linguistics and mathematics. Swanwick reminded music educators that every known human culture has valued music as a form of expression universally inherited, experienced, and passed on.

Valuing music in such a way sought to go beyond so-called soft, instrumental, or utilitarian justifications that have proliferated throughout the history of music education (Philpott 2012b). From the earliest debates around music's character-building and civilising effects, these justifications have drawn upon the seemingly extra-musical capacity of music to bestow benefits relating to academic achievement, social development, and health and wellbeing. They remain prevalent within the twenty-first century, with numerous publications devoted to collating research evidence for "the power of music" (e.g., Fancourt and Finn 2019; Hallam and Himonides 2022). Music has been shown to impact language and literacy skills, numeracy and reasoning performance, aural and visual memory, social and emotional development, mental health and wellbeing, and intellect and attainment. Yet the benefits of such impacts are always contingent upon particular circumstances and conditions, and in the same way in which music can encourage inclusivity, enjoyment, and healing, it can also contribute towards exclusivity, hatred, and harm. While music can encourage social bonding, it can also cause tribalism; while it can break down barriers, it can also enshrine prejudice and propaganda; and while it can be accessible, fun, and relaxing, it can also shape manipulative, solipsistic, and violent behaviours (MacGregor 2022; Philpott 2012b).

While claims for the power and potential of music undoubtedly form strong advocacy for engagement in music education, they simultaneously fabricate an unrealistic and naïve conception of what music is in the world (Philpott 2012b). But through understanding music as having power both for healing and hurting, helping and harming, it can be appreciated as socially situated, living in the world within complex webs of meanings that are continually being interpreted and reinterpreted, imagined and reimagined. In extending Swanwick's (1997) idea of music as a great symbolic form, music can be conceived of like language (Philpott 2012b). This is not to see in music the properties of speech that communicate shades of meaning, such as tempo, pitch, and intonational contour; nor is it to see in music grammar, syntax, or dialect; but it is, more fundamentally, to see music as characterised by an openness to acquired and multiple interpretations where value is determined by use in particular contexts. Music, rather than simply offering a source of enduring comfort, becomes yet more powerful when thought of as a subject that engages critically with ideological meaning and affects our embodied humanity. When we conceptualise music in such a way we find we are vulnerable to it: that it impacts our self- and social identities through its associations and delineations, and that it causes us to physically respond–singing, dancing, shaking, aching–whether we like it or not (MacGregor 2022). Music is no longer a soft, therapeutic subject, but a critically alive, ideologically loaded education that thrives on suspicion and critique (Philpott 2012b). To think of music as simply a source of wellbeing–whether that be for character building, civilising society, or academic outcomes–serves to undermine the most important justifications for its place in the curriculum (Task 1.8).

MUSIC EDUCATION NOW

Although appeals to the instrumental and utilitarian values of music education do not necessarily offer an accurate portrayal of music's power and potential, to date, they have been successful at ensuring that music education enjoys a relatively secure position in curricula across the four nations of the United

LEARNING TO TEACH MUSIC IN THE SECONDARY SCHOOL

> ### Task 1.8 **Justifying music**
>
> In light of the preceding discussion, examine the following statements taken from the Welsh National Plan for Music Education (Welsh Government 2022) and the English National Plan for Music Education (DfE and DCMS 2022). Identify and evaluate the different justifications used in each statement to advocate for music education.
>
> > Whether we were born here or live in Wales, music has been a strong influence in all of our lives. Music has been, and continues to be, one of the most inclusive ways to communicate and celebrate our culture and language. We can be proud that our communities across Wales have long produced music renowned across the world. We have all learned music in some form from a young age. Whether it is from our family and friends or schools and settings, these tenets are a vital part of . . . the many benefits music can play in the life and well-being of children and young people.
> >
> > (Welsh Government 2022: 1)
>
> > This country has a proud history of music-making. Down the generations, music has enriched our national identity, our community and our economy. Music education is essential to safeguarding and extending the musical life of our country for generations to come. Excellent music education opens opportunities, but it is not simply a means to an end: it is also an end in itself. It gives children and young people an opportunity to express themselves, to explore their creativity, to work hard at something, persevere and shine. These experiences and achievements stay with them and shape their lives. That is why music is an essential part of a broad and ambitious curriculum for all pupils.
> >
> > (DfE and DCMS 2022: 2)

Kingdom. In England, Wales, Scotland, and Northern Ireland music remains a statutory aspect of national curricula for young people until the age of 14.

However, throughout the United Kingdom the contexts, justifications, and aims for classroom music differ substantially. In both Scotland and Wales, music is one strand within curricula for "expressive arts." They explore how, collectively, experiences in art and design, film and media, music, dance, and drama "involve creating and presenting and are practical and experiential. Evaluating and appreciating are used to enhance enjoyment and develop knowledge and understanding" (Education Scotland 2010: 1). Music is considered to be one way of "developing artistic skills and knowledge," "responding and reflecting, both as artist and audience," and creating work that draws upon "the senses, inspiration and imagination" (Welsh Government 2020: n.p.). But, as explored in Task 1.9, music is also considered to have some discipline-specific requirements.

In contrast to Scotland and Wales, in England the National Curriculum (DfE 2013) considers music as a discrete subject. It links its purpose of study to the development of young people's self-confidence, creativity, and sense of achievement:

> Task 1.9 **Music and the expressive arts: discipline-specific requirements**
>
> In the Curriculum for Wales (Welsh Government 2020), the discipline-specific considerations for the subject of music indicate that young people should cover:
>
> - concepts of pitch, melody, dynamics, texture, tempo, timbre, rhythm, metre, form and structure, tonality, musical devices (e.g., repetition, ostinato, sequence), harmony, and intonation;
> - binary, ternary, rondo, round, minuet and trio, strophic, theme and variation, through-composed, and sonata forms;
> - performing (including vocal, instrumental, and using technology, e.g., DJ-ing), improvising and composing (including vocal, instrumental, acoustic, electric and digital, and editing and production), and listening (including analysing, evaluating, and appreciating a range of musical forms and styles across genres and periods of time).
>
> Do you agree that these features set music apart from the other expressive arts? What would you add to the list? What would you remove from the list?

> Music is a universal language that embodies one of the highest forms of creativity. A high-quality music education should engage and inspire pupils to develop a love of music and their talent as musicians, and so increase their self-confidence, creativity and sense of achievement. As pupils progress, they should develop a critical engagement with music, allowing them to compose, and to listen with discrimination to the best in the musical canon.
>
> (DfE 2013: 257)

Although the curriculum framework document itself refrains from defining exactly how teachers should engage with concepts such as "the best in the musical canon" (Bate 2020), subsequent publications including the Model Music Curriculum (DfE 2021) and the National Plan for Music Education (DfE and DCMS 2022) illustrate a growing trend towards a "neoconservative attempt to gain strong control over legitimate music knowledge" (Young 2023: 150) through prescribed skills and repertoires (Task 1.10).

Northern Ireland, like England, also addresses music as a distinct subject area. As explored in Task 1.11, the Northern Irish National Curriculum aims to justify how each discipline relates to its overall objectives of preparing young people for life and work as individuals, as contributors to society, and as contributors to the economy and the environment (CCEA 2007a: 38). It specifies that:

> Music has a significant role to play in this. The fundamental aim of the music curriculum is to develop pupils' musical ability. All pupils are potentially musical and should be provided with learning experiences which

LEARNING TO TEACH MUSIC IN THE SECONDARY SCHOOL

Task 1.10 Defining legitimate musical knowledge

Reconsider the conceptualisations of musical knowledge put forward by the aesthetic and praxial approaches to music education discussed earlier in this chapter. Based on the excerpt that follows, how do these contrasting approaches relate to the musical knowledge fostered by England's Model Music Curriculum (DfE 2021)?

By the end of Key Stage 3 (Year 9) [age 14], pupils will have:

> gained an aural knowledge of some of the great musical output of human civilisation;
>
> engaged with creative processes through improvisation and composition;
>
> built an understanding of how musical elements work and discussed how these interact with subjective and objective models of musical meaning;
>
> developed knowledge of a wider range of notes and improved their fluency in music notation. Notation can grant access to a lifelong passion for music-making if this skill is nurtured.

(DfE 2021: 37)

Task 1.11 Music's role in preparing young people for life and work

Consider the Northern Irish curriculum requirements (CCEA 2007a) to prepare young people for life and work,

- as individuals;
- as contributors to society;
- as contributors to the economy and the environment.

How do you think classroom music education contributes to each of these goals? List the justifications you would use to advocate for music's place in the curriculum according to these objectives. Exchange your answers with those of another beginning music teacher and together look at how your answers compare to the justifications given in your own national curriculum documentation.

---

develop their knowledge, understanding and skills in making and responding to music through active engagement in the core musical activities of composing, performing and listening.

(CCEA 2007b: 3)

SUMMARY

This chapter has addressed the ways in which music education has been understood and validated over time. We have seen that the justification for music in education:

- has a long and winding history tied to social and political systems;
- has been influenced by dominant ideologies around aesthetic value and challenged by notions of social praxis;
- has been conceived of as a shaper of character, a marker of the educated citizen, a great symbolic form—or indeed as a valuable influence upon academic achievement, social development, and health and wellbeing.

Whatever the justification, there remains a call to every secondary school music teacher to ask, "why music?" Our responses can quickly resort to enthusiastic rhetoric and vague advocacy or draw upon too many diffuse claims and arguments. We should take time to rehearse our case and be able to defend it in theory and practice.

FURTHER READING

Bate, E.H. (2020)
'Justifying music in the National Curriculum: The habit concept and the question of social justice and academic rigour', *British Journal of Music Education*, 37, 1: 3-15.

Philpott, C. (2012b)
The justification for music in the curriculum: Music can be bad for you, in C. Philpott and G. Spruce (eds) *Debates in Music Teaching*, 1st edn, Abingdon: Routledge, pp. 48-63.

Pitts, S.E. (2019)
A Century of Change in Music Education: Historical Perspectives on Contemporary Practice in British Secondary School Music, 2nd edn, Abingdon: Routledge.

These readings offer wider perspectives upon the history, ideology, and justification of music education in the United Kingdom from the early twentieth century to the present day.

CULTURE, SOCIETY AND MUSICAL LEARNING

Gary Spruce

INTRODUCTION

The relationship between music, society and culture has attracted considerable attention over recent decades. Among others, Blacking (1987), Leppert and McClary (1987), Shepherd (1991), Martin (1995), Small (1977, 1998), DeNora (2000), Laughey (2006) and Street (2012) have published important work in this area. Small (1977), Green (1995, 1997) and Woodford (2005) have adopted a specific educational focus: Small (1977) examining the disjuncture between young people's experiences of music inside and outside school; Green (1997) publishing significant research on the relationship between music, gender and education; and Woodford (2005) exploring the links between music education and democracy. More recent literature includes a multi-authored volume examining the links between music education and policy (Schmidt and Colwell 2017) and substantial handbooks addressing the relationships between social justice and music education (Benedict et al. 2015) and the sociological underpinning of music education (Wright et al. 2021). The premise of all these publications is that taking into account the social, political, cultural and economic factors that impact upon music's production, dissemination and reception is an important part of fully coming to understand it. It follows, therefore, that a sociocultural understanding of music is critical to teaching it effectively.

> **Objectives**
>
> By the end of this chapter, you should be able to:
>
> - understand how culturally constructed assumptions about the nature of music have influenced the development of the music curriculum and the way in which it has been taught;
> - explain how music has been used to create and sustain social divisions;

- consider how cultural and social perspectives can inform the music curriculum and its teaching, leading to a wider range of musical styles, skills and understandings being valued and celebrated, and thus to the music curriculum becoming more inclusive.

CONTEXT AND BACKGROUND

Parallel with the development of a sociological perspective on music and music education was the emergence in the late 1980s and 1990s of what came to be called the "new musicology." This sought to challenge the assumed and seemingly self-evident "greatness" of western art music through showing that such greatness is historically and socially constructed and sometimes retrospectively applied. For example, DeNora (1996) persuasively demonstrated how, in the case of Beethoven (arguably the paradigm of the "great composer"), "the very notion of greatness was tailored to 'fit' the forms that Beethoven produced" (169). Drawing on ethnomusicology and the emerging discipline of music sociology, the new musicology sought to move beyond traditional analytical approaches to understand western art musics as more than simply the products of individual genius. Instead, it aimed to view these musics in relation to the values, conventions and practices of the societies within which they were created and from which they emerged.

This approach generated considerable controversy among musicologists, since it challenged what Regelski (2005: 221) calls the "aesthetic ideology" of musical study: a broadly formalist belief that musical meaning and value is contained within, and articulated exclusively through, the sounds (sonic materials) of music. This ideology has had a significant impact upon music education, particularly through musical "reification" (or objectification), where meaning is understood as fixed within music's objectified form—typically "the score." Reification reinforces beliefs in music's transcendency and autonomy, where musical meaning is understood as transcending time and place. Such beliefs maintain that a performance of a Beethoven symphony in early nineteenth-century Vienna, for example, has the same musical meaning as a performance of the same work at a youth orchestra concert in 2025. The impact of this aesthetic ideology upon music education has resulted in a focus on the study of the sonic materials of music (the ubiquitous "musical elements") and on the musical score as an autonomous entity—a kind of musical text or vehicle for carrying musical meaning.

Within the field of music education, one of the most significant outcomes of the sociocultural perspective was the reaction against aesthetic ideology resulting in a "praxial" approach to teaching and learning. Originating in the work of Elliott—particularly in his seminal book *Music Matters* (1995), but also developed by music educators such as Regelski (2015)—"praxialism" challenges "aesthetic" understandings of music by arguing that musical meaning is created not only through the organisation of sonic materials, but also (and arguably primarily) through the ways in which people use it and the value they ascribe to it; in other words, through musical *practices*. Music, praxialism argues, does not have an autonomous existence or possess autonomous value, but rather its existence and value derive from the contexts in which it takes place and the purposes for which it is practised.

A praxial approach to music education is embedded in the belief that musical understanding is developed not solely through the examination, exploration and appreciation of the "objects" of music, but through an understanding of the "practices" of music—of the ways in which people engage with it. This approach argues that conceptions of musical "excellence" are situated within and specific to particular musical contexts, practices and traditions. For example, conceptions of excellence in blues music are underpinned by different musical values from conceptions of excellence in western art music or gamelan music.

Praxial philosophies of music have had a significant influence on music education, and their impact can be observed in approaches such as informal learning. However, praxialism has also been subject to significant critique, not least for the danger that it can result in the "freezing" of musical practices at an arbitrary point in time in order to make them teachable, thus negating their essential dynamism and sociality and slipping back into reification (Allsup 2016). Furthermore, in Elliott's conception of praxial music-making, performing is privileged over other activities such as composing and improvising, which maintain an important part in music education across the United Kingdom.

It is important to note, therefore, that in critiquing the impact of aesthetic perspectives on music education and promoting a more praxial approach, this chapter too promotes a particular ideology which is open to critique. In the final activity of this chapter you will be invited to make such a critique. We want you to begin, however, by reflecting on your own musical studies from a social and cultural perspective by completing Task 2.1.

> ### Task 2.1 **Your own musical studies**
>
> Think about your own musical studies, perhaps through focusing on a musical work that you have studied in detail for an examination. Note down the aspects of the music that were considered to be important and the kinds of questions that were asked in the examination. Was the focus of study just on analysing the music, or was any attention paid to the sociocultural contexts and practices through which it was created and performed? What do you feel is to be gained (if anything) from exploring music's social and cultural underpinnings?

WHY IS A SOCIOCULTURAL PERSPECTIVE IMPORTANT IN MUSIC EDUCATION?

At the outset, it is important to ask how an understanding of the links between society, culture and music might help music teachers meet the challenges of teaching music in the twenty-first century. First—and most obviously—music permeates almost every aspect of everyday life. It is present as we do our shopping, eat in restaurants or cafés, drink in bars, watch television or films, work out in the gym and await an encounter with a dentist. All kinds of music can now be instantly downloaded to or streamed from a multitude of mobile technologies, meaning that, if we wish it to be, music can be an almost permanent presence in our lives. This is almost certainly the case for many of the young people whom we teach. Music is, therefore, a central part of most young people's lives, and its centrality needs to be recognised in and through the way in which we teach it in schools.

Restaurants, nightclubs and bars also employ particular types of music to create atmosphere, and music is used to enhance state, religious and sporting occasions. DeNora (2000) has pointed out that there is a natural tendency on the part of humans to comply with expectations created by the use of particular music in specific social contexts; think, perhaps, of music at a funeral or wedding. Such compliance is rooted in our formal and informal musical enculturation, where we learn to associate certain musical gestures with particular ideas, emotions or occasions. Music can also affect patterns of consumption, either through the association of specific music with a product, or, more significantly, when a musical style is used to express group identity for those with shared dispositions and beliefs, along with, for example, choice of clothing or lifestyle. Consequently, "control over music in social settings is a source of social power; it is an opportunity to structure the parameters of action" (DeNora 2000: 20). Given that most encounters with music take place in such social settings, it is important that we develop an understanding of how music operates in these situations and how our actions can be influenced by it. For young people, their understanding of and engagement with music will be about much more than simply the sound it makes—and this needs to be acknowledged within the classroom.

Second, society is not a homogeneous entity, but rather a collection of disparate social groupings based commonly on class and ethnicity but also involving religion, gender, and family and peer relationships. Given that a person is typically a member of more than one social group, how their different groups use and practise music is one means by which they create and express identity: "social groups can be identified partly in terms of their different musical production, distribution and reception practices" (Green and O'Neill 2001: 26). An important part of music education is supporting young people in understanding how these production, distribution and reception practices impact on how music makes its meaning. Through gaining an understanding of the musical values and preferences of these different social groupings, teachers can also begin to address one of the key reasons given for the low esteem in which curriculum music is held by some young people: that it makes so few connections with the music they encounter outside school. As you will explore in Task 2.2, a key element of successful and inclusive music teaching is that music in school takes account of young people's musical experiences beyond school, but, importantly, is not restricted simply to reflecting these encounters but takes young people to hitherto unexplored musical understandings.

> ### Task 2.2 **Young people and "their" music**
>
> Construct a list of questions that could form the basis of a discussion with young people about their musical tastes and preferences. These questions might include:
>
> - the types of music they listen to;
> - what they find attractive and interesting about that music;
> - how (if it does) their chosen music enables them to identify as members of a particular social group;
> - whether they make other lifestyle choices related to this music (e.g., in the clothes they wear, the food they eat or the media they consume).

Third, schools are social arenas within which particular values and norms are transmitted. Certain social groups are best positioned to influence the organisation of schools and what is taught within them, therefore ensuring that the values that serve their interests are those that are promulgated and come to be seen as self-evidently good. Formal education is a means by which young people are enculturated into the values and norms of the dominant culture, and music has traditionally been an important means of reflecting and articulating these values and norms. Green (1997), for example, has demonstrated how school reinforces gendered stereotypes and assumptions about musical practices that are rooted in the traditions of western art music:

> [School] takes part in the perpetuation of subtle definitions of femininity and masculinity as connotations of musical practices, linked to musical styles in which pupils invest their desires to conform, not . . . to the school only, but to the wider field of gender and sexual politics.
>
> (192)

An important part of music education, then, is to develop young people's (and perhaps our own) understandings of how music can perpetuate potentially undesirable stereotyping and sustain oppressive hegemonies (Philpott 2012b). Freire refers to this as the process of conscientisation, whereby learners come to understand and develop their awareness "of the power relationships that impact their lives and those of others" (Spruce 2015: 299).

Finally, and arguably most importantly from an educational perspective, the way in which we actually think about music—the way in which we construe and construct its meaning—is culturally and socially rooted. At a very basic level, our recognition of music as sad, happy, martial, romantic and so on, although often seemingly natural and self-evident, is *learnt* as part of our

CULTURE, SOCIETY AND MUSICAL LEARNING

(often informal) enculturation into society. More significantly, the music that is typically and unquestioningly assumed by many to have the highest status—that of the western art music tradition—has attained this hegemonic status through its association with a dominant cultural order and has come to be one means by which such hierarchy is maintained. Whereas the overt dominance of western art music in the curriculum is, for the most part, a thing of the past, we remain to a great extent held in its thrall. It still exerts its influence through the assumptions we hold about music: about the way in which music's quality is best evaluated, about the way in which it communicates its meaning and about how it is best experienced. Such assumptions inevitably influence the way in which music is taught in schools, and it is important that we recognise, understand and are aware of them so that we control them, rather than they us. As explored in Task 2.3, this is part of our own conscientisation as teachers.

Task 2.3 **Musical value and musical meaning**

Note down your thoughts about:

- the criteria by which you evaluate the quality of a piece of music;
- how you feel music communicates its meaning;
- the way in which music is best experienced.

As you read through the rest of the chapter, refer back to your responses, noting whether or not your initial thoughts change.

THE IDEOLOGY OF AUTONOMOUS MUSIC

The language we use to describe music tells us much about the way we think about it. With this in mind, complete Task 2.4 (which in any other context is not recommended as a model of good teaching!).

Task 2.4 **Talking about music?**

Insert the missing word to complete the following sentences.

- Please _____ all your music to next week's rehearsal.
- Compose a _____ of music for the opening of the new school music building.
- Buy a _____ of Beethoven's *Moonlight Sonata* from your local music shop.
- Listen to as many musical _____ by Elgar as possible.

It is likely that the words you inserted into the sentences were, respectively, "bring," "piece," "copy" and "works." This is the way we tend to talk about music—or at least about western art music. We speak of *bringing* music to a rehearsal, of playing or composing a *piece* of music, of buying a *copy* of a musical score and of hearing a musical *work*. The use of such terms suggests that we think of music (at least subconsciously) as a kind of imaginary "object"—something we can "hold," like a jug. Now, clearly music is not the same as a jug, as the essence of it—sound—cannot be "held" in the same way as one can hold an object. However, the fact that we tend to think of music as an object reveals our underlying assumptions concerning the nature of music, the way in which music articulates its meaning and—perhaps most importantly—the criteria we instinctively use to apportion musical value. This then influences the way in which we interact with music and, of course, *teach* it.

So, how did we end up thinking and talking about music in this arguably rather odd way? And, perhaps more importantly, why does it seem so natural to do so? Certainly, we have not always thought of music like this. Until the late eighteenth century, music was thought of as a *performance* art rather than a *productive* art. Composers created a performance to fulfil the needs of a particular social occasion, often within the context of the court or church. They did not think they were engaged in producing an object.

However, during the late eighteenth century there developed the notion of "fine art." Fine art drew a distinction between art and craft: the latter was valued in terms of how well it fulfilled a primarily utilitarian function, while the former was evaluated in terms of its aesthetic merit. It was, essentially, the beginning of the ideology of "art for art's sake." Here, the art object is understood and valued not in terms of its usefulness, or for its accuracy as a representation of something external to it, but as an autonomous creation to be valued in terms of the success with which it organises its basic materials into a formally satisfying and beautiful whole. The distinction between fine art and craft was replicated in music through the division of music that was of sufficient quality to enjoy an *autonomous* existence and music whose function was essentially social: the music of the streets, fields and coffee houses (Goehr, 2007).

Art music reflected the object arts, in that meaning was understood to be articulated exclusively through the relationship and interaction of its musical materials. Consequently, the objectification process—the codification of music into a score—took on much greater significance towards the end of the eighteenth century. Prior to this period, the score had acted only as a general guide to performance, but it now came to be seen as definitive, encapsulating the musical meaning: the "score" and the "music" were perceived as virtually synonymous. Musical practice was now thought of as something that must naturally and inevitably result in a product: an object in the form of a score. This conception of music—this musical reification—has since informed the teaching of music for almost two centuries.

Musical autonomy and social stratification

The development of the ideology of autonomous music coincided with the emergence of a middle class seeking a cultural and social identity that would mark them out from the labouring classes—a cultural identity that through its inherent "sensitivity" and "sensibility" could be drawn on as a justification for the unequal distribution of wealth and power (Bull 2019). Autonomous art music—and particularly the score—provided one particularly effective means of articulating this distinctive identity.

A score, like any other object, could be traded and access to it controlled through the application of market forces. Once music had been objectified, it could act, as memorably described by Everitt (1997: 26), like a pre-cooked frozen meal, capable of being reconstituted at any time and in any place. Having control of the time and place at which a performance would take place made it possible to exclude the "hoi-polloi," so that identification with this music could be reserved exclusively for the middle classes. Performances of art music therefore took place at pre-arranged times, in venues often specifically constructed for the purpose, where access could be controlled—often by levying a fee for entry. Brewer (1997) notes how:

> Concerts . . . were organised as a series for which one had to pay a full season's subscription. . . . Grand musical occasions, such as St Cecilia's Day concerts held in Salisbury Cathedral . . . charged entrance prices in excess of the seasonal fee to a subscription series.
>
> (535)

Simply put, the working classes were charged with not being sufficiently sensitive to appreciate autonomous art music but economically barred from proving otherwise. Art music, its forms, procedures, modes of production and dissemination, became intrinsically linked to middle-class sociocultural identities and thus became a potent tool for constructing and sustaining social stratification and cultural hegemony.

Maintaining social hegemony: music education in the early twentieth century

Allsup (2003) argues that "for a ruling class to survive or reproduce it needs to pass down its culture through some form of education" (8). It naturally follows that western art music has traditionally been seen as the most appropriate music for the school curriculum—and in some schools this remains so. Where other music was admitted into schools (such as traditional music), it served primarily as a stepping stone to engagement with "high" art music. The basic premise was that all music could, and should, be evaluated according to the principles, practices and procedures of autonomous art music, irrespective of the music's genesis and original intended function.

The music that working-class children experienced outside school and which was part of their cultural identity—typically the music of the streets and music halls—did not meet the criteria of value as predicated by autonomous art music and was therefore seen as unworthy and even degenerate. In *Class-Singing*, Whittaker (1925) wrote that:

> It would seem incredible that the head mistress of a kindergarten should use the sentimental rubbish of a well-known popular contralto for a school repertoire, that one should find a music-hall song which runs, "Strolling round the town, Knocking people down, We all got drunk", etc., used as a marching tune, yet these are actual examples of what is perpetrated in the sacred name of education.
>
> (105)

At the time, Whittaker's outrage would have seemed quite justified. During the late nineteenth and early twentieth centuries, the Platonic notion of the power of "good" music to have a positive impact on the moral character of the nation's youth came to be seen as one of the main purposes of music in schools. The editorial of the first edition of the *School Music Review* in 1892 stated, "the beneficial influence an early taste of music might exert upon the choice and character of the amusements of the people cannot seriously be disputed" (Russell 1987/97: 52). Likewise, Cringen (1889), in *The Teacher's Handbook of the Tonic Sol-fa System*, wrote that, "progressive teachers . . . are now fully alive to the beneficial effects of the study of Music as a refining, moral influence in the schoolroom and the home" (3). Singing was seen as particularly beneficial in that it not only provided "the most valuable means we know of introducing children to music of sterling value and of forming taste" (Whittaker 1925: 106), but that it was also essential "for the education and character-building value of the stirring words that are sung" (Crowe 1996: n.p.).

As considered in Task 2.5, refined taste and moral rectitude were defined as reflecting middle-class values and norms and consequently reinforced the predominating social order. The potential, particularly of songs, to affirm the social and cultural status quo was not lost on those who developed music materials for schools. Crowe (1996), for example, quotes from a songbook used in Canadian schools in the early part of the last century, words and music from *Three Part Songs* by one Mr Henry Sefton (1868):

> My hands how nicely they are made, To hold, to touch and do:
> I'll try to learn some honest trade; That will be useful too;
> My eyes, how fit they are to read, To mind my work and look;
> I ought to think of that, indeed, And use them in my book.

> ### Task 2.5 **Music and morality**
>
> Some forms of young people's music-making or musical preferences continue to excite disapproval. This can be because of negative perceptions of certain genres (e.g., rap) or associations between music, lyrics or artists with, for example, misogynistic or violent views and beliefs.
>
> How might you address the issues surrounding such music in the context of a curriculum for 13- and 14-year-olds? What are the pedagogical approaches you would adopt which might raise young people's critical awareness of the issues surrounding this music where the values expressed are damaging and harmful? Similarly, how might you support them in articulating why they think music that others disapprove of is of value to them?

A SOCIOCULTURAL PERSPECTIVE ON CONTEMPORARY MUSIC EDUCATION

One of the most significant changes in school music over the past thirty years or so is the broad range of musical traditions and styles that most young people now encounter as part of the music curriculum. Popular musics and music from around the world, as well as traditional music and western art music, are an important part of the music curriculum in most schools, and young people's entitlement to a broad and balanced offering is enshrined within curriculum documents such as the English National Curriculum for Music (DfE 2013).

In most schools, western art music therefore takes its place in the curriculum alongside music from many other styles and traditions. However, in England, a concern that this has resulted in the marginalisation of western art music and its associated theoretical underpinnings has resulted in the reassertion of its importance through statutory and quasi-statutory policy and guidelines. For example, the most recent version of the National Curriculum for Music in England includes the stipulation that young people "listen with increasing discrimination to a wide range of music from great composers and musicians" (DfE 2013: 259).

Philpott (2022), in an analysis of political and epistemological shifts in music education over the last ten years, demonstrates that despite the recent entry of a range of musical styles into the curriculum, the ideological values of western art music continue to exert a hegemonic presence. He suggests that this occurs through three distortions. First, the reification of curriculum as content (see Chapter 7) can easily privilege facts about music over the musical learning to be gained from direct experience of listening to or making music. Second, a reified curriculum as content privileges the forms, procedures and values of western art music even where the focus is on music of other traditions (such as when music from popular or non-western traditions is studied using the lens of western art music theory or nomenclature). Third, the implicit privileging of western art music results in the restriction of musical meaning and renders the relationships between musical and sociocultural structures invisible. These reifications, Philpott (2022) contends, lead to pedagogies which marginalise the construction of musical meaning—"the reason why we engage with music in the first place" (5).

In the final section of this chapter, we therefore analyse different aspects of music education to identify further distortions rooted in the reifications that Philpott (2022) identifies. We suggest, however, that through adopting a sociocultural perspective, these distortions might be addressed with the consequence that music education in school might become more relevant, inclusive and, above all, musical.

Musical literacy

A philosophy of music education predicated upon the western art music tradition inevitably places great importance on the "score." To understand the score is to understand the meaning of the music, so the argument goes. Kendall (1977) espouses such a view when he writes:

> The child who cannot read music is in a very similar position to the child who cannot read words. He simply does not know what a wonderful world exists beyond the barrier of the symbol—the secret code which he cannot crack. Between him and incredible spiritual wealth stand five lines and some dots with tails.
>
> (31)

A similar sentiment was expressed in a 2013 inspection report into music education in English schools. Here, once again the lack of theoretical understanding is perceived as inevitably presenting a barrier to musical understanding:

> The Year 3 cohort [aged 7 to 8], as their final lesson in a singing unit, sang in three part harmony to the whole school. The teaching was expert and encouraging and the quality of the pupils' performance truly excellent and uplifting. But, as the teacher and the hub leader recognised, the pupils had not seen the notation of the song, learning to sing it by copying the teacher. The pupils were in the dark about the chord sequence, time signature and melody that they had sung so beautifully.
>
> (Ofsted 2013: 26)

The belief that musical meaning resides within the notated form of music (its objectification) and that the key to that meaning lies through the decoding of this notation has exerted an almost hypnotic power over music education. It has often caused us to ignore the fact that musical knowing is, primarily, embodied knowing: we demonstrate musical understanding through responding to music as composers, improvisers and performers, but also through listening to music and discussing what it means to us. Views such as those expressed earlier have

CULTURE, SOCIETY AND MUSICAL LEARNING

sometimes led to notation being taught as an abstract concept separated from any musical context, since it is perceived as having intrinsic value with no need to be linked to a particular musical practice.

A further consequence of this focus on notation is that we have come to think of musical literacy in very narrow terms: the ability to read staff notation. The emphasis on reading staff notation as a process of decoding pre-existing musical scores has led us to ignore, and consequently to fail to teach, the many other ways in which notation is used in the musical world. Task 2.6 will help you think about this in light of Fautley's (2013) description of the role that different forms of notation played in his musical life:

> I also learned alternate notations–guitar chords, and like hundreds of other children of the third quarter of the twentieth century, I learned to play the electronic organ using guitar chord symbols. Simultaneously doing "academic" music the translation of chord symbols into roman numerals was straightforward, and, later, figured basses seemed to me to be built on the same sets of premises. At the time I played in orchestras using notation, dance bands using a hybrid of staff notation and chord symbols, and in the pit for shows from charts entirely consisting of chord symbols. But I've also played in acoustic folk bands, rock bands, and, for a brief while in the wacky '80s, kraut-rock inspired synth multitracking, with none of the above. Many of these non-formal musickings were undertaken with musicians far better than me who could "just do it", some of whom were kids in my classes.
>
> (n.p.)

Task 2.6 **The diversity of musical notations**

Think of the ways in which you have worked with different forms of notation or with staff notation in ways other than simply realising a score. What kinds of musical learning and skills did these engender?

Take one of the examples that you have identified and work this up into an activity or lesson for the young people you teach. Share your ideas with colleagues or other beginning teachers.

Over the past two decades a more nuanced and inclusive understanding of musical literacy has developed which acknowledges that musical literacy can manifest and be demonstrated in many ways and which rejects the idea that those who don't read staff notation are musically illiterate. As Kwami (2001) points out:

> For the majority of the world's people, musical literacy does not involve the ability to read and write music. . . . For many, musical literacy operates as the ability to communicate with others through music in a practical way.

One factor, internalisation, is a process that characterises this type of musical literacy. . . . A second factor is improvisation. . . . Other facets of this musical literacy involve dance, movement and language which feature to a greater extent elsewhere than in the Western classical tradition, the main currency of the school curriculum.

(144)

Mills and McPherson (2015) make a similar point about the multiple ways in which "musical literacy" can be demonstrated. Drawing on the example of a 13-year-old flautist who does not read music but plays a key role in her father's folk band, they note how her musical literacies include the ability to play by ear, musical memory and an acute awareness of the "characteristics and timbral possibilities of the instruments available to her" (1790). They also note the damaging impact of pedagogies which separate musical literacies from music-making, and where an over-emphasis on staff notation stifles musical creativities. Likewise, Evans and Philpott (2023: 29) identify the following attributes in a set of musical literacies:

- Technical literacies on instruments, voices or technologies;
- Analytical literacies in relation to being able to name and describe technical musical features;
- Perceptual literacies in "understanding how music works and is put together";
- Cultural literacies in discerning the place of music in society–literacies which this chapter seeks to develop and support;
- Digital literacies;
- Notational literacies.

The point that all these authors make is that, in developing a curriculum that is inclusive, music educators need to adopt a broad view of what constitutes musical literacy and to draw on appropriate pedagogies to support its development. Task 2.7 asks you to consider what a broader view of musical literacy might mean in practice.

Task 2.7 **Teaching without recourse to notation**

Imagine that you are teaching the first lesson in a sequence of lessons on the blues. The first lesson has within it aspects of listening, performing and composing. You have decided to teach the lesson without recourse to notation. Drawing on the list of literacies preceding this task (Evans and Philpott 2023), outline the activities you might ask the class to do and the teaching strategies you would employ.

Then think how you might introduce appropriate notation into a lesson on the blues. Adopting a more praxial approach, find out about the ways in which blues and jazz musicians use notation (when they do) and use this to inform your teaching. What do you think young people will gain from engaging with notation in this way?

Set works

The tradition of "set works" is rooted in the idea of musical meaning being exclusively contained within the score. Let us think for a moment about the way in which set works—such as a movement from a symphony—are usually taught. The teacher typically focuses on the music's thematic content, the way in which instruments are used and combined, the harmony and rhythm and how these relate to each other; thought is given to relationships between tonalities, harmonic functions and large-scale structures. Even where the production of the symphony is closely related to contemporary events (say, the depiction of Stalinist terror in Shostakovich's *Tenth Symphony*), consideration of these aspects is usually peripheral to analysing the interrelationships of the musical elements. Such an approach is predicated on an understanding that musical meaning resides, essentially, within the score as an objectification of the music. Little attention is paid to the social context of its composition, performance and reception or the extent to which the music articulates any extrinsic message.

Let us consider now a different way in which set work might be approached—one that takes into account the social context of its creation. Here the set work is Bach's *Fifth Brandenburg Concerto*. At the end of the first movement there is a long cadenza for the harpsichord. This cadenza is notable for two reasons: first, its length in proportion to the rest of the movement; and second, the way in which an instrument that normally plays a supporting role is suddenly brought to the fore. Clearly, this music can be analysed in terms of the autonomous working out of its materials. However, conventional analysis only tells us the "what" of the music, not the "why." Why did Bach choose, at this time, in this place and in this piece, to compose a cadenza that is disproportionate to the rest of the movement, modulates to keys that are well beyond the expectations of the period and focuses on an instrument that (in orchestral music, at least) had hitherto been kept well in the background? Such questions are not answerable simply through analysing the music as an autonomous object and cannot be wholly explained as Bach "intuiting the way to new modes of expression, opening up musical vocabulary, simply as a result of his genius" (Gaines 2004: 133). A different perspective is required: one that is provided by looking beyond the musical object to the social context of the music's composition.

In a seminal text of the new musicology, "The blasphemy of talking politics during Bach Year," McClary (1987) suggests that what Bach is doing in this movement is challenging the social norms, conventions and hierarchy of the Brandenburg Court. In her analysis, the flute and violin (the main solo instruments) represent the conforming members of society who are allowed limited freedoms within the tightly drawn parameters of courtly society. However, the harpsichord "hijacks" the music and, in doing so, directly challenges both musical and courtly conventions and the social hierarchy that underpins them:

The flute and violin drop out, inconclusively, one after another, exactly in the way an orchestra would if one of its members started making up a new piece in the middle of a performance. They fall silent in the face of this affront from the ensemble's lackey.... Certainly, social order and individual freedom are possible but only as long as the individuals in question abide by the rules. What happens when a genuine deviant (and one from the ensemble's service staff yet!) declares itself a genius and takes over?

(40)

This cultural perspective potentially tells us more about the revolutionary nature of this cadenza than any amount of abstract analysis of its "autonomous" form. It provides an explanation of *why* Bach breaks conventions so dramatically *in this work*, *at this time* and *in this place*. In other words, it links the music to its social context. This is not to suggest that analyses like this should be used exclusively, any more than one should rely wholly on traditional analysis of the musical object. One perspective does not exclude the other. Instead, they go hand in hand, enriching our understanding of the music. Complete Task 2.8 to explore the social and cultural contexts of the creation of one piece of music and their potential for developing young people's musical understanding.

> Task 2.8 **Applying a social and cultural perspective**
>
> Choose a piece of classical music that you know well. Briefly analyse it in terms of its structure, key relationships, harmony and rhythm. Now research the background to its composition, performance and reception, focusing not on biographical details of the composer but on the social milieu in which it was created. Finally, decide how you might use your research to develop young people's understanding of the music.

Non-western musics

Asked why music from other cultures should be included in the music curriculum, music teachers might reply that it enables young people to gain an understanding of other cultures and an awareness of and respect for ethnic and cultural diversity. However, although this is an assumption that often underpins the rationale for including musics from a range of cultures in the curriculum, there is limited research to demonstrate how or if this happens. Indeed, it is questionable whether coming into contact with music of other cultures (simply brushing against it) really has any significant impact on young people's knowledge and awareness of cultural diversity.

It might also be argued that taking music from a different cultural context and then engaging and evaluating it purely in terms of dominant musical norms (those of western art genres) is little more than cultural imperialism and will inevitably result in the music being perceived as inferior or primitive. Indeed, as noted previously, Philpott (2022) suggests that the inclusion of traditions other than western art music does not guarantee that the curriculum becomes more inclusive. Sometimes their inclusion is simply tokenistic and "can be evidence of prejudicially 'othering' and trivialising musics from other cultures and traditions" (5).

Developing young people's cultural awareness and understanding through music therefore involves integrating into the curriculum and its teaching not just the musical artefacts of other cultures, but also their practices, procedures and processes—adopting a praxial approach. The musical practices of these cultures are often radically different from those of western art music. Many musical cultures have different conceptions of musical time, space, beat and pulse. The temporal organisation of most western art music is "linear": we think of music as progressing through time, as in a sonata form. However, other musics (such as American minimalism, Hindustani and Carnatic classical music, and Javanese gamelan) operate on cyclical principles. Western music's typical emphasis on the first and third beats and its predilection towards a regular pulse is not reflected in, for example, reggae styles where the emphasis is on the second and fourth beats, or "in African traditions [where] what we have may be closer to a medieval scenario of tempus perfectum and imperfectum—of 'twos and threes'" (Kwami 2000: n.p.).

Providing opportunities for young people to engage with music on its own terms means that they are able to demonstrate their musical knowledge and understanding through means other than the skills exemplified through western art music practices. Those who learn best through aural imitation and improvisation (skills exemplified in most popular and non-western musical styles) are then given the opportunity to excel, while those who are skilled in western art musics are given the chance to develop other ways of understanding music and being musical. Restricting the curriculum to one that is underpinned exclusively by the western, aesthetic ideology can result in a curriculum that is narrow and over-specialised and within which many young people "fail." This leads inevitably to disillusionment with curriculum music.

In contrast, adopting a praxial approach to music teaching, which takes into account music's original mode of production, dissemination and reception, can help young people develop a deeper understanding of other cultures. Young people who are given the opportunity to work with music in ways similar to its originators may develop an understanding of the diverse approaches through which music is created, played and shared. This may then lead to greater empathy with both the music and the culture from which it has emerged. Such teaching is, we would argue, more inclusive as it recognises and celebrates both musical and cultural diversity.

Focusing on musical practices, the values that underpin them and their modes of production, distribution and reception—adopting a praxial approach—allows for conscious links to be made between different musical practices on an equal footing. This approach also allows for different kinds of musical learners to succeed, as musical achievement can be demonstrated across a much wider musical canvas. At the same time, non-western and western musics are granted equal status in the classroom, not simply through asserting it to be so, but by integrating into the curriculum the different ways in which those cultures communicate musically.

The opportunities offered by a music curriculum that is cognisant of the cultural and social genesis of music are less about inducting young people into a specific set of musical and cultural norms and values and more about facilitating entry into a range of musical practices. Such a curriculum is, as Kwami (2001) puts it, about "trying to understand the music in a manner similar to that of the people from whom it originates or belongs" (145). For as Small (1999) says, in order to really understand what music's meaning is, we should not ask, "what does this musical work mean?" but rather, "what does it mean when this performance takes place at this location at this time, with these people taking part, both as performers and listeners?" (19). This, in a sense, is the essence of a praxial approach to music education (Task 2.9).

Task 2.9 **Adopting a praxial perspective to plan for music learning**

Imagine that you are going to use popular or non-western music as the basis for a sequence of lessons. Research the social and cultural background of the music. Plan an outline for these lessons that shows how you will develop young people's musical skills, knowledge and understanding through activities that reflect the ways in which the music is created, disseminated and received.

A praxial approach to music education offers the potential to far exceed aesthetic, analytical ideologies:

> For music educators, the message is that we in music do far more than merely teach skills and techniques. Music cannot speak its profound message about the society it lives in merely from the sound. The sounds of music can only become valuable in education when they are explained in terms of the belief and knowledge systems of society which alone enables us to endow them with meanings.
>
> (Walker 2005: 15)

However, to achieve this means revisiting what we consider as musical norms. It means casting a critical gaze over beliefs that we may hold dear and which have served us well, aware of the possibility that the musical beliefs and values that young people bring to our lessons may be different but equally legitimate.

Music teaching then, at least in part, becomes about bridging the gaps between these different sets of beliefs in a spirit of mutual respect—which is not without its challenges.

SUMMARY

In this chapter we suggest that:

- a too narrow conception of what music is can lead to an impoverished model of music teaching and learning;
- music teaching that is informed by a sociocultural and praxial perspective has the potential to be more inclusive—to celebrate and value a wider range of musical genres, musical skills and musical understanding;
- adopting a wider definition of musical literacies and focusing on appropriate pedagogies for developing musical literacies will lead to a more inclusive curriculum;
- musics from outside the western art music tradition have their own unique practices and values that can be integrated into teaching and learning to allow for diverse understandings of musical meaning.

FURTHER READING

Cheetham, J. (2013)
An after school rock school investigated: Why are they here?, in J. Finney and F. Laurence (eds) *MasterClass in Music Education: Transforming Teaching and Learning*, London: Bloomsbury, pp. 151-156.

Cook, N. (2023)
Music: Why It Matters, London: Polity Press.

Mantie, R. (2023)
'What should one expect from a sociology of music education?' *Action, Criticism, and Theory for Music Education*, 22, 1: 112-138.

The chapter by Cheetham and article by Mantie helpfully contextualise the issues and ideas underpinning a sociocultural perspective on music and music education. Cook's short book provides an engaging update on contemporary musicological thinking in relation to the role of music in society and why it matters to us and to the young people we teach.

DIGITAL MUSICAL LIVES

Anthony Anderson and Nick Hughes

INTRODUCTION

Young people experience music both inside and outside the classroom, and their musical experiences and exposure are diverse and eclectic. The means by which young people access and engage with music are increasingly digital, and their digital musical lives need to be acknowledged in any discussion of what music teaching means today. What follows is an attempt to navigate these complex waters and to consider how the intricacies of digital music technologies might connect with how music is taught and experienced in the classroom. We begin by contextualising contemporary music teaching within this digital world, before attempting to theorise digital technology and pedagogies for digital musical learning. We then discuss practical considerations for classroom teaching, before thinking about what a digital future might mean for music in schools.

> **Objectives**
>
> By the end of this chapter, you should be able to:
>
> - reflect on the place of digital technologies in the lives of the young people you teach;
> - consider your role as a music teacher in the context of constantly developing digital musical possibilities;
> - understand some theoretical approaches to planning for embedding digital technologies in the music classroom;
> - think creatively about connecting and enabling digital technologies beyond the classroom.

CONTEMPORARY MUSIC TEACHING

The contemporary music teacher is required to draw from a wide portfolio of skills. Alongside general musicianship, instrumental facility, directing and rehearsing capabilities, and advanced teaching skills in the classroom, music teachers are also often required to be audio engineers, software developers, and sound technicians. Young people also bring a wide range of differing skills, backgrounds, experiences, and attitudes to their use of digital technologies in the music classroom. Some will be active music technologists, others perhaps more reticent, but all are likely to engage with digital forms of music in one way or another. Thinking about and engaging with digital dimensions of music is therefore an important area of development for the beginning teacher. Setting aside time to think about how digital technologies might be realised and actualised in the music classroom is time well spent. Digital technologies are continually emerging, developing, and transforming and can prove challenging for teachers. This chapter will not be able to keep pace with such changes, but it will seek to give a reasoned pedagogical grounding through which to approach digital teaching and learning, alongside examples of how this might feature in the music classroom. We hope this will build your confidence as a music teacher and present a range of possible approaches from which to build learning experiences for the young people in your classes.

In identifying and facilitating musical growth through digital technologies, music teachers need to adopt inclusive practices which embrace the wide range of musical backgrounds through which young people have experienced music in digital forms (see Chapter 4). Enabling young people to access digital technologies matters, and it is essential to be aware of potential digital poverty and lack of opportunity. Music teachers therefore need to blend their teaching and thinking about digital technologies with a mindfulness that young people in their classes have different technological backgrounds to their own. Outlining curriculum rationales and purposes and how to present a learning environment which is accessible for all, whilst encouraging and allowing for digital musical development, therefore requires careful reflection. Advanced understandings of technological details are not necessary, but an open disposition to learn from young people and spot and utilise digital approaches within an informed and reflective pedagogy is, however, important. Without a thinking approach—in which the use and development of digital practices are constantly re-evaluated and re-designed—the incorporation of music technologies in the classroom will be resigned to annexes, additions, or afterthoughts. This will be, at best, pedagogically unsettling for the music teacher, and, at worst, damaging for the young people, creating unsatisfying musical experiences that could impede their developing musicianship. As encouraged in Task 3.1, thinking about and tracing out discerning approaches to facilitating digital learning, considering the aesthetics of music technology software, and deciding how to use it musically, are therefore critical activities.

> Task 3.1 **Considering digital music technologies**
>
> Write a series of statements which set out:
>
> a. how you feel about digital music technologies, thinking about your own confidence, experience, and skills;
> b. the range of digital musical lives you think young people may have;
> c. how you are currently embedding digital technologies in your teaching, or how you think that you might in the future.

THEORISING THE USE OF DIGITAL TECHNOLOGIES FOR THE MUSIC CLASSROOM

As we turn to consider how to embed digital music technologies in classroom spaces, we now outline some theoretical foundations which we hope will support you in thinking and developing your own classroom practices. Notions of equity and access for all young people form a starting point, followed by how digital musical pedagogies might be experienced and the place of technology in a pedagogical outlook. These three strands provide a coherent context for justifying teaching using digital music technologies. Our approach here is therefore one of surveying the ground before beginning, and in doing so providing space for you to reflect on your own understandings of digital music technologies and how these might influence your teaching.

When thinking about digital technologies in the music classroom, it is helpful to first consider the pedagogical stance we are adopting, because how we think about digital music technologies will be influenced by our beliefs about education more generally. Thinking about pedagogies is therefore important, so that we are choosing technologies that align with our teaching dispositions and philosophies. This ensures we don't start from the capabilities and features of a particular piece of hardware or software, but instead start from the questions, "in what musical learning do we want our young people to engage?," "how do we want them to engage?" and, therefore, "what technologies might assist them to do so?" Using technology musically, but also in a pedagogically informed manner, will help to enable young people in the classroom to learn musically *and* digitally.

Critical pedagogy

The notion of *critical pedagogy* is helpful when working both technologically and pedagogically. Critical pedagogy refers to when your work as a teacher critically interrogates the framing you are using when making decisions about how best to enable young people to learn—and in this case, to develop their musicianship through digital technologies. Freire and Macedo (1987)

DIGITAL MUSICAL LIVES

advocate a critical pedagogy that interrogates barriers and limitations to learning, arguing for an acknowledgement of "the word and the world" (35), thereby enabling young people to link their lived experiences with their learning. Where musical learning is connected with creative acts (McCarthy 2000)—which is often the case in digital music (such as in sequencing, recording, and composing, for instance)—critical pedagogy offers an opportunity to link experiences in the music classroom to experiences beyond, and thus to create more cohesive musical development. In this way, young people can be reflective as they create (Abrahams 2005), and digital learning becomes not merely something that is presented to young people but something that is instead an interactive social process leading to transformative, educative experiences (Hess 2019).

Critical pedagogies for using digital technologies in the music classroom might be experienced as a wrap-around process (see Figure 3.1), where young people's digital experiences are surrounded by the digitally creative environment of the music classroom. During this process, young people bring their digital music experiences within the supportive environment of the classroom, create music together and with their teacher, whilst reflecting, continuously interacting, and musically responding to each other. This enables musical development and the integration and use of music technologies to occur in the manner of co-creation between young people, teachers, and resources, rather than relying solely on all-knowledgeable teachers (an increasingly challenging expectation!). The iterative process of critical pedagogy, which is continuously open to collaboration and co-construction, therefore allows for greater flexibility and a range of learning responses.

Technological Pedagogical Content Knowledge (TPCK)

How and why music teachers enact digital pedagogies extends to considering how we transform subject knowledge, through and with digital technologies, into what Shulman (1986) describes as Pedagogical Content Knowledge (PCK). Simply put, PCK is the knowledge needed for transforming *subject knowledge* into *teaching activity*. As Shulman (1986) explains, PCK asks the question, "how do teachers decide what to teach, how to represent it, how

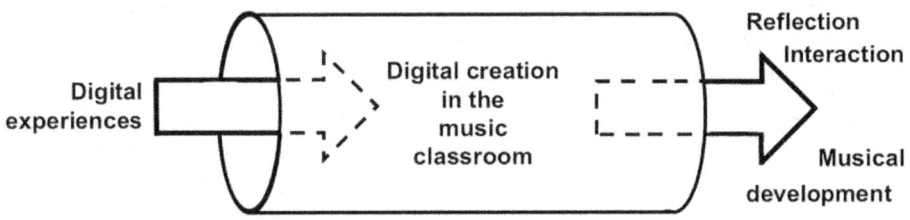

Figure 3.1 Critical pedagogy for digital technologies in operation in the music classroom

to question students about it and how to deal with problems of misunderstanding?" (8). When technology is introduced into this frame, the question of pedagogy becomes a little more complex still. The question might now be, "how is music technology positioned within pedagogy, how does it impact teaching and learning approaches, and how do teachers recognise and appropriately deploy it as part of their teaching practices?" It has been argued that Shulman's model should be expanded to include technology (Mishra and Koehler 2006), which has led to the Technological Pedagogical Content Knowledge (TPCK) model. This helps us to think about why and how we enact digital pedagogies in the music classroom. Mishra and Koehler (2006) highlight that in the past, looking at characteristics of technologies, rather than how they are put to use, has led to a lack of "theoretical grounding" (1018), meaning that technology drives learning rather than being part of a more considered approach. They see content knowledge, pedagogical knowledge, and technological knowledge as each revealing a layer of understanding for the teacher, with technological pedagogical content knowledge sitting at its heart.

Thinking about technology, how we understand it, and how to apply our knowledge to digital learning is an important starting point for music teaching, where questions sometimes arise over the use of digital technology versus traditional acoustic instruments. In this vein, Gall (2016) suggests that musical knowledge should sit within the three different types of knowledge that Mishra and Koehler (2006) outline. She further conceptualises "Pupils' Technological Knowledge," "Pupils' Music Technological Knowledge," and "Pupils' Musical Preferences" as interconnecting circles, emphasising how young people's musical identities are highly influential in teaching and learning. Reflecting on how you think about pedagogies for digital music technologies, how they might intersect, and why you include digital technologies in the classroom at all is therefore important and will guide your teaching preparation.

Combining reflective starting points with the notions of critical pedagogy discussed earlier should allow you to consider how young people's digital music knowledge from outside the classroom might connect with the notions of pedagogy in the TPCK model. Trying to separate these young people's differing worlds outside and inside the classroom can be problematic, since pedagogy is closely interconnected with young people's digital and musical identities. We therefore suggest the pedagogical model in Figure 3.2 for understanding digital music technologies. This representation illustrates how the digital identities with which young people enter school relate to the pedagogies at play in the music classroom space. These two aspects are entangled and inseparable and cannot easily be teased apart. Before coming to your own use of technology in the music classroom, it is therefore helpful to reflect on your own thinking about these pedagogical approaches. Task 3.2 will help you with this.

■ ■ ■ ■ DIGITAL MUSICAL LIVES

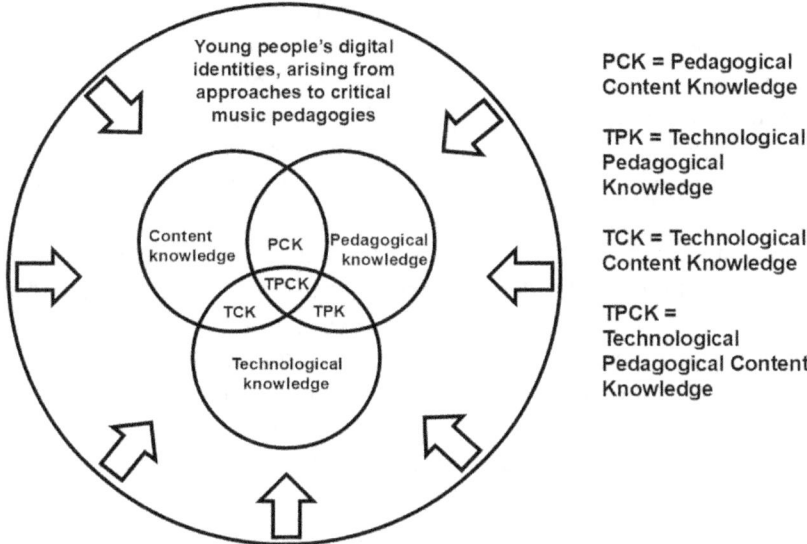

■ **Figure 3.2** When TPCK and critical pedagogies meet in facilitating digital music technologies

Adapted from Mishra and Koehler (2006)

Task 3.2 **Planning a music technology task**

Working with your mentor or colleague, plan a simple music technology activity together.

1. Reflecting on your activity, and using Figure 3.2 as a model, how do PCK, TCK, TPK, and TPCK interact?
2. Drawing from notions of critical pedagogy, how could you structure your music technology task to reduce barriers for young people?

PEDAGOGICAL APPROACHES FOR DIGITAL TECHNOLOGIES

Before designing curriculum programmes of study (something we discuss in Chapter 7), it is helpful to think about how to embed the digital tools prevalent in today's musical world into classroom-based musical learning. Without this careful reflection from the outset, digital tools may appear as tokenistic gestures in secondary curricula. This can arise from lack of teacher confidence in using digital technologies or uncertainty about how such tools can support and enable musical development. If this is the case, a conversation with senior leaders in your setting about subject-based continuing professional development might be one place to start. This is especially important for beginning music

45

teachers, who may be thinking for the first time about how to translate their digital know-how into pedagogical practice. Developing your own understanding of relevant hardware and software and connecting this to other aspects of your teaching might be a useful starting point. This will help you to make curriculum links and facilitate musical development for the young people with whom you are working. This may emerge with time, but it also needs deliberate thought to ensure it is more than a chance happening.

With all instruments, the aesthetics and/or mechanics of the instrument need to be understood before the development of more advanced musical ideas. For instance, where do your hands go? When do you press down your fingers and in what patterns? If necessary, how do you coordinate your breathing? Even more elementally, how do you play a note and how do you sustain it? These ideas are no different when working with a digital tool. Time needs to be spent learning and then teaching the software aesthetics, and curricula need thoughtful sequencing so that new skills build on what has previously been taught. For example, within particular programs or apps, you might need to explain the linear nature of the "arrange" window; where "stop" and "play" are; where the bar numbers are; or where the "zoom" function is so that note values become clear. Facility with these features takes time to develop but is invaluable for supporting other musical dimensions you may be teaching.

There is a considerable amount of foundational knowledge to be taught when learning the aesthetics of digital tools. Using pre-existing music is one way to ease potential learning stress. Some young people may like to record their own musical ideas immediately, while for others, a more bespoke approach will be required. These differences can make learning in digital formats challenging at times, but the richness of opportunities that they offer and the potential for realising musical ideas in diverse dimensions mean that these challenges are ones that are worth tackling.

We think in more detail about assessment in Chapter 10. However, it is important to state at this point that assessing young people's use of digital tools tends to be centred in assessing what you, as the beginning teacher, want them to learn. Creating a suitable approach which values both musical and technological capabilities is important, and there is no one way to achieve this. It could be as simple as listening to young people's "live" work-in-progress or asking them to submit their digital work to you via digital means. Live, in-the-moment, formative feedback might have more instantaneous impact, but the submission of digital work may allow for a greater depth of learning conversation. There are therefore a variety of assessment aspects which will require careful thought. For example, the clarity of verbal feedback could be combined with depth by adding pre-recorded feedback made using screen-recording software or an audiovisual recording of a computer display. Whatever the latest technological advancement is, the question you will need to ask—as a beginning or experienced teacher—will be how such technology can be used to enable the increasingly musical assessment of young people's work.

DIGITAL AUDIO WORKSTATIONS (DAWS)

Digital technologies are multi-faceted and multi-modal tools that encapsulate and can enable holistic experiences of music. They can be used for composing, improvising, critical listening, and performing, and combine all these activities together, often simultaneously. During the 1980s and 1990s, the Musical Instrument Digital Interface (MIDI) sequencer was the digital tool of choice to create music, and as computer-processing power rapidly increased around the turn of the twenty-first century, sequencers could store and manipulate large amounts of digital audio. Such tools therefore became known as Digital Audio Workstations (DAWs). DAWs are now the cornerstone of all recorded music and are commonplace in musicians' homes and on their computers as well as in professional recording studios, where they are used to record performances, sequence compositions, and produce industry-standard outputs. Although there are many other digital instruments available to musicians, this chapter will primarily focus on the integrated nature of the DAW. The rest of this section will consider ways to use DAWs to support young people's musical development, suggest how recontextualising music using technology can reveal important musical learning opportunities, and finally explore how DAWs can create equitable learning opportunities for young people with diverse learning needs.

Encouraging musical development through digital technologies

To include technology as a standard musical *practice*, rather than as a musical *product*, can be a helpful way to proceed in music lesson planning. Due to the inherently multi-modal nature of DAWs, they can be used to teach most musical concepts in a classroom and can help realise young people's musical expectations by removing, muting, and even deleting music instantly. Spending one or two lessons exploring a musical idea or composing technique provides parameters, and therefore structure, within which young people can explore and helps to reduce anxiety around creating new music. They can then save their different ideas as DAW or notation files to create a rich resource for stimulating further creativity. This approach acts like an artist's sketchbook, and the teacher can embed different stimuli at different points in setting and assessing young people's work, placing value on fragmented activities which combine organically over time to create something more complex. Much like the discussions about different approaches to listening in Chapter 15, this organic approach to building musical ideas through technology is very different from treating music as a mathematical problem with a definitive answer. Such a question-and-answer dynamic is not always helpful for giving young people confidence in their digital development. Instead, the gradual mosaicking of fragmentary activities allows young people to build a library of different files that explore chord extensions, textures, structures, sound effects, melodic phrases, instruments, or genre-specific techniques. Such a library can become a treasure trove of musical ideas for young people to explore and develop, and Task 3.3 gives you an opportunity to try initiating one in your own planning.

LEARNING TO TEACH MUSIC IN THE SECONDARY SCHOOL

> ### Task 3.3 **Creating and teaching with DAW templates**
>
> Break down your thinking about digital learning into two stages:
>
> 1. Create a simple DAW template that enables young people to develop a melodic motif. Think about how you could display the MIDI regions (blocks) so that they are easily manipulated and can stimulate musical development.
> 2. Consider what you would need to teach young people in order for them to access this template. Reflecting back on Task 3.2, what digital pedagogies could you use in preparation?

Using digital technologies for recontextualising music

When using a DAW, transferring musical ideas into new contexts can cause previously unappreciated characteristics to be revealed. For instance, a piano piece when arranged for orchestra or a pop song riff recontextualised into a leitmotif for a character in a film may reveal fresh musical potential and opportunities to explore new musical features. In this way, digital tools afford us the opportunity to learn about music in a contrasting manner by seeing it, using it, hearing it, and manipulating it in different ways, or experiencing it in different contextual settings. An example of how this might work is set out in Box 3.1.

> ### Box 3.1 **Using digital technologies to recontextualise music**
>
> Many small-scale composing tasks that are designed for notating on a stave or performing on an instrument can easily be adapted to work using technology. Doing so often enables young people to refine and extend more sophisticated ideas in their creative work.
>
> One possible scenario with 14- to 16-year-olds could be working together on a "composition consequences" activity, where they rotate around the classroom adding a new element to each other's composition on another computer. This is an adaptation of an activity which may be more familiar using manuscript paper, but there is no reason why this approach should not be equally—or perhaps more—successful in digital formats. It is a fun and creative activity that can be incorporated into a lesson as a way of preparing young people for their first individual compositions.

Listening to and thinking about music in different contexts can provide young people with new ways of understanding musical concepts that may previously have been obscured by more immediately striking musical features. In this sense, musical expression can benefit from repeated recontextualisation within digital technology frameworks. Creating, performing, and critically engaging with music are no less important, but they can be formulated in a different manner in which digital technologies constitute the vehicle for musical expression and communication. Thinking about this different approach to music can bring its own challenges, both for you as a teacher but also for different young people. While DAWs can be a great way of "levelling the playing field" for young people who have differing degrees of previous musical experience, we will now consider how to model and structure DAW learning experiences to support young people who might be more reluctant to engage with technology.

Technophobia

As long ago as the late 1980s technophobia was recognised as a problem for music teachers, since fear of technology could inhibit the potential for digital engagement in the classroom (Kassner 1988). Technophobia can embody a range of trepidations, including a fear of jargon, a fear of feeling de-skilled, or a fear of vulnerability. Fear of technology is not limited to teachers, however, and can affect young people too. Beginning a new DAW session can feel like a blank canvas and cause anxiety for some young people. Preparing templates that reference existing musical knowledge is one way to create scaffolds and steps for young people to better understand different elements of music and reduce learning anxiety around music technology. Such templates could be where the teacher creates different textural interpretations of a well-known chord sequence in a song, to highlight the textural variation or help a young person learn how to create different accompaniment styles. An example is shared for you to try out in Task 3.4.

Young people have been programming musical parts to create backing tracks for live performances in schools for decades, and a DAW offers an accessible

---

Task 3.4 **Overcoming technophobia in the music classroom**

Using a genre which requires digital engagement can be one way to encourage young people to overcome their digital music anxieties.

Try encouraging a class of 13- and 14-year-olds to write an electronic four-to-the-floor beat, by enabling them to use loops to create bass lines and chords that surround the beat after they have programmed or played it. If any young people are reticent to explore music in its digital form, try:

- supplying them with half a sequence of a simple song and asking them to record or quantise another part against it;
- providing multi-track stems of well-known pop songs in a DAW so that they can learn to balance, pan, and discover what layers exist within a pop song that they know.

approach for musicians to create additional performance parts for their ensembles. This can make approaching digital music technologies less daunting, putting young people's agency at the heart of their musical experiences, developing their aural acumen, and building their confidence. Learning to listen critically is at the heart of this kind of approach to developing musicality, and digital technologies have an important role to play in this respect. As explored in Chapter 15, learning to listen with criticality has a significant impact not only on composing and producing, but on musical understanding more widely. Learning to re-create parts of pre-existing music can further unlock musical understanding beyond formulaic composing (which can also be fear-inducing), thereby enhancing notions of what it means to develop music and to realise creative ideas. Task 3.5 will help you think about what technophobia means in the music classroom and puts this in the context of the digital planning we have already thought about in this chapter.

> Task 3.5 **Adapting and recontextualising digital technology activities**
>
> 1. Look again at the technology activity you planned for Task 3.3 and the activities you tried out in Task 3.4.
> 2. List some ideas for how you would *adapt* your plan from Task 3.3 for young people's varied experiences and confidence levels using digital music technologies.
> 3. Add some ideas for how you could *recontextualise* your plan from Task 3.3 for young people who are more willing to engage with digital technologies.

Connecting digital technologies to musical learning in and beyond the classroom

With a little careful thought, work that uses a DAW as a digital music interface can also become embedded into school culture as part of a recontextualising approach. This moves musical learning beyond the music classroom and allows it to become part of young people's experiences in other contexts. Facilitating and preparing young people to learn outside the classroom matters because, as we saw in the discussion of critical pedagogy towards the beginning of this chapter, music-making continues in other areas of school life and beyond school spaces. Teaching approaches which encourage young people to keep thinking and developing their digital musicality enable learning to grow significantly.

To encourage this kind of learning continuum, music teachers can develop young people's awareness of using current digital tools for musical purposes such as listening and responding. This may begin by showing young people the affordances and constraints of software they use in the classroom, which tend to offer a linear composing process as well as a default starting tempo of 120bpm and a simple quadruple metre. Reminders for young people to think consciously regarding tempo, metre, and composition structure are integral interactions for a secondary school music teacher. Digital technologies present young people with a variety of approaches to each dimension of musical learning. For example, when learning about chord extensions, a teacher may demonstrate how to use western staff notation, but this can be enriched with the use of a piano roll view on a DAW, or through a visualiser displaying the same chord on a keyboard or guitar. The choice of how to use these tools will depend on the young person and the musical learning being developed.

When encouraging young people to think about the musical choices they are making through DAWs, it is worth emphasising to them that critical listening skills are at the forefront of any musician's learning, no matter the extent of their experience. Reverse-engineering is a term used to describe the process of trying to determine a piece of music's effects: the approach to sound-creation, the recording method, and, ultimately, breaking down the music into its constituent parts. Listening alongside young people whilst reverse-engineering a piece of music, and allowing them time to re-create individual musical features in a DAW, for example, can open their ears through musical learning via digital tools. This can support them in listening to and dissecting the music that they engage with away from the classroom, so that they can evaluate the sum of its constituent parts.

When thinking about music outside school, young people need to have a similar awareness of the boundaries of software design as they do within the classroom, even though such limitations may be presented differently. Software that is now commonly available includes free-to-access cloud-based sequencers, which can appear to be simple DAWs. The user can sequence and manipulate basic MIDI loops but only where there is a simple sonic palette, standard metre, and relatively static tempo. This may lead young people to develop musical misconceptions or lack contextualised musical experiences. Where it is more successful, software and hardware used outside school can facilitate more rounded criticality through focused listening with a simple graphic user interface that does not limit young people's metrical and tempi choices. There is therefore a need for music teachers to connect and explore the digital musical experiences young people are accessing in their home environments and to build on these in school settings. Such approaches can also be blended into school experiences, where appropriate, through careful selection of materials, as well as identifying moments of synergy between the music curriculum, the broader school curriculum, and young people's sound exploration beyond the classroom.

For instance, with some well-considered framing, listening and responding to music can become part of young people's school experiences at other parts of the school day. Sending hyperlinks to musical excerpts to tutor groups (which are often very diverse in secondary schools), for example, could prompt thought-provoking discussion between non-music teachers and young people during tutor sessions. These could be connected with wider social and personal development themes already being explored across the school. A similar approach could be utilised for making cross-curricular links with young people's other subject lessons, therefore allowing musical learning to become embedded throughout school. This can allow for young people's digital musical experiences to be discussed across contexts, give teachers an opportunity to further develop digital pedagogies, and encourage attitudes to music to be free-flowing rather than compartmentalised. Spend some time thinking about how this outward-looking approach to music might work in your own school context using the starting points in Task 3.6.

> Task 3.6 **Digital music learning across the school community**
>
> Think about how sharing music across tutor groups might work. Experiment with the following procedure:
>
> 1. Think about what piece you would choose and why.
> 2. Write one question that you might ask a non-music teacher to discuss with their group after they have listened to the music.
> 3. Show your question to a friend or colleague who teaches another school subject. How do they interpret what you have written?
> 4. Revise your question if you need to in light of their feedback.
> 5. Identify some other parts of school life where music could be shared and discussed in this way (e.g., between subject classes, with young people at other schools, or in work with visiting community groups).

It is important to remember that whilst we work with classes in school and seek to inspire musical learning, young people's digital musical lives are also developed outside school. For the final section of discussion, we now think about how teachers can continue to think about their digital musical practices and keep pace with this continually developing field.

THINKING DIGITALLY INTO THE FUTURE

Integrating and thinking about digital approaches to music in the classroom requires a continuing focus and purposeful review and evaluation. Reflecting on current developments in digital technologies and emerging digital pedagogies is therefore important, and these aspects of music teaching will quickly fall out of view without conscious and determined effort. What approaches music teachers choose from the digital pedagogical palette that they and their young people bring to the classroom, and how these blend together into a canvas of musical activity, is an aspect of classroom practice that requires an evaluative and critical ethos. As previously discussed, allowing classroom decisions to be dominated by technological capabilities can inhibit musical learning. It needs to be acknowledged that the digital resources music teachers use in their lesson design, and how these are embedded in classroom music-making and creating, reflect teachers' own digital and musical identities. Thinking about how these approaches fit with young people's experiences, progression routes, and overarching curricula will need continual attention.

Further to critical evaluation of the digital classroom, thinking and teaching digitally in music will require continued horizon scanning, connectivity with the wider world of digital music technologies, and networking with other teachers and musicians. Keeping practices current is one of the most challenging aspects of embedding digital technologies within a meaningful music curriculum and with this in mind, we have included some reflective questions to guide you in Task 3.7. This chapter is limited by the time in which we have written it, but your thinking as a music teacher will need to continue to develop. We hope the ideas we have set out are useful starting points, acting as a framework against which to evaluate and re-evaluate your teaching practices. Reviewing the technology you are using in your music teaching, thinking about how you are implementing and applying it, and considering how you are identifying and including young people's digital experiences is likely to require revision more often than annually. Digital technologies in music rapidly shift and develop, and teaching approaches which not only notice these developments but consider how to embed them into rewarding learning experiences for young people in classroom contexts make for well-framed pedagogy and responsive curriculum design.

Task 3.7 **Questions for reflection**

1. How will you think about digital music technologies differently as a result of reading this chapter?
2. When planning for the inclusion of technologies in your lessons, what key principles will you ensure underpin your teaching?

Perhaps unlike some other aspects of music teaching, teaching through the medium of digital music technologies will be a continually shifting landscape. It is difficult to predict the shape of future developments, as history shows that these are not always those which we can anticipate. In addition to thinking critically and keeping practices current, it may also be helpful to adopt a teaching disposition that seeks to look ahead and search for emerging technologies, especially considering their potential application to the music classroom. Aim to ask what new developments in digital technologies will mean for introducing fresh dimensions in music lessons and enabling young people to have a dynamic and informed musical experience. Whilst teaching in this way is challenging, it is also rewarding in helping young people to achieve their musical potential, and we hope that this chapter will be a helpful starting point in doing so.

SUMMARY

This chapter has introduced the role of digital music technologies in young people's lives and considered the implications this has in the music classroom. It has introduced ideas about how digital music pedagogies might be framed, both conceptually and in practical terms, and suggested the importance of adopting reflective and responsive perspectives in a field which is constantly developing. It has outlined the need for digital thinking and suggested approaches which give value to technology in the classroom irrespective of teachers' and young people's backgrounds and prior experiences, arguing that developing skills in using digital music technologies is an important aspect of musical understanding.

FURTHER READING

Purves, R. and Himonides, E. (2026)
Towards environmentally sustainable practices for teaching music with technology, in C. Philpott and G. Spruce (eds) *Debates in Music Teaching*, 2nd edn, Abingdon: Routledge, pp. 310–327.

Hughes, N. (2023)
'Impacts of sequencing existing music using a Digital Audio Workstation on creating original music', *Journal of Popular Music Education*, 7, 3: 241–267.

INCLUSIVITY IN THE MUSIC CLASSROOM

Phil Mullen, Victoria Kinsella and Carolyn Cooke

INTRODUCTION

The concept of inclusion in the classroom and within music education has gained significant prominence in recent years, both in the United Kingdom and internationally. This is reflected in policy developments and institutional frameworks that emphasise equitable access to education for all young people. Inclusive education is now widely recognised as a means of ensuring that young people, regardless of background or ability, receive high-quality learning experiences that are supportive of their individual needs. The United Nations Educational, Scientific and Cultural Organization (UNESCO) states that:

> Inclusive education is not a marginal issue but is central to the achievement of high-quality education for all learners and the development of more inclusive societies. Inclusive education is essential to achieve social equity and is a constituent element of lifelong learning.
>
> (UNESCO 2009: 4)

This chapter will talk about what inclusion is, why it is important, and how to begin to apply it in the secondary music classroom. We will also consider what inclusion looks like for specific groups of young people. While the topic of musical inclusion is vast, we hope this chapter will cover some important fundamentals and get you thinking more deeply about musical inclusion as a starting point to your own reflections and inquiries into how best to support the young people in your classes.

> ### Objectives
>
> By the end of this chapter, you should be able to:
>
> - understand what inclusion means in the secondary music classroom and why it is important;

- reflect on how key ideas in musical inclusion can inform the design of teaching and learning;
- understand how to use differentiation to overcome barriers to musical learning;
- understand how creative and musical interactions with young people can support and extend the learning of those with additional needs;
- consider how adopting inclusive approaches will shape your teaching practice.

WHAT DO WE MEAN BY INCLUSION?

In the United Kingdom, several legislative frameworks have reinforced the commitment to inclusive education by establishing legal protections and structured support for young people with diverse needs. The *Children and Families Act* (2014) introduced reforms for young people with Special Educational Needs and Disabilities (SEND), including the implementation of Education, Health, and Care Plans (EHCPs), which provide an individualised approach to learning support. Similarly, the *Special Educational Needs and Disability Code of Practice: 0 to 25 Years* (DfE and DHSC 2015) offers statutory guidance to local authorities, schools, and colleges on how to support young people with SEND. Alongside these, the *Equality Act* (2010) mandates that educational institutions work to eliminate discrimination, advance equality of opportunity, and foster inclusive practices, reinforcing the legal obligation to provide an education that makes provision for all young people.

Alongside policies applying across the United Kingdom, each devolved nation has introduced legislation to support inclusive education within their own contexts. These include Scotland's *Education (Additional Support for Learning) Act* (2004), Wales's *Additional Learning Needs and Education Tribunal Act* (2018), and Northern Ireland's *Special Educational Needs and Disability Act* (2016), which further strengthen protections against disability and discrimination in schools.

While many governments and institutions have revised and expanded their approaches to inclusivity, a key international reference remains the *Salamanca Statement* (UNESCO 1994). Developed during a UNESCO-organised conference in Salamanca, Spain, this landmark document brought together over 300 participants from ninety-two governments and twenty-five international organisations to reaffirm the commitment to education for all. The statement outlines several fundamental principles:

- Every child has a fundamental right to education and must be given the opportunity to achieve and maintain an acceptable level of learning;
- Every child has unique characteristics, interests, abilities, and learning needs;
- Education systems should be designed, and educational programs implemented, to accommodate the wide diversity of young people;
- Children with special educational needs must have access to regular schools that adopt a child-centred pedagogy capable of meeting diverse needs;
- Inclusive schools are the most effective means of combating discrimination, fostering welcoming communities, and building an inclusive society.

Individual needs

While some of the principles of the *Salamanca Statement* (UNESCO 1994) speak to large-scale, system-wide actions, underpinning all of them is a commitment to understand, respect, and support the broad range of individual needs that there are in our classrooms. An accessible music curriculum recognises the right of every young person to teaching and learning that inspires and motivates them to be the best musician they can be, in a way that is relevant to them. While each curriculum will have its own approach to inclusion, it is important for you to know your own national guidance. For the purposes of the next task, we focus on the underpinning principles of the National Curriculum for England (DfE 2013). Task 4.1 provides you with an opportunity to explore your understanding of these principles and compare them to your own context's requirements.

Task 4.1 **Thinking about principles of inclusion**

1. Consider the following statements adapted from National Curriculum for England (DfE 2013) and O'Brien (1998). For each statement note down an example of how this might be enacted in practice. You can draw on your own experiences or imagine scenarios in which they might be important.

    a. Setting suitable challenges for all young people (addressing common needs);
    b. Responding to young people's diverse needs (addressing individual and unique needs);
    c. Overcoming potential barriers for individuals and groups of young people (addressing exceptional shared needs).

2. Seek out the inclusion guidance provided in your own national curriculum and school setting. Compare the documents, noticing what is similar and different. Why are there differences? Would those differences change how you approached the scenarios or examples you considered in Question 1?

The social model of disability

While being aware of individual needs and responding to them is important, the traditional "medical" model viewed disability solely in terms of personal needs or deficits, leading to both physical and attitudinal discrimination. More recently, the "social" model of disability has shifted the focus from individual deficiency to societal disablement, taking the view that,

> People are disabled by barriers in society, not by their impairment or difference. Barriers can be physical, like buildings not having accessible toilets. Or they can be caused by people's attitudes to difference, like assuming disabled people can't do certain things. The social model helps us recognise barriers that make life harder for disabled people.
>
> (Scope 2024: n.p.)

Removing these barriers creates equality and offers disabled people more independence, choice, and control. Therefore, the challenge for us as teachers is *both* to consider the individual needs of all our young people, *and* to be critically aware of and work to reduce disabling barriers within our pedagogy. This approach—reducing barriers and ensuring all young people can access and succeed within the curriculum—is known as "inclusive pedagogy," which you can explore in Task 4.2.

> Task 4.2 **Barriers in a musical environment**
>
> Make a list of ten barriers (both physical and attitudinal) that could occur in a music learning environment for a diverse range of young people. By creating this list, you will be developing your critical awareness of the types of issues that an inclusive pedagogy might need to address.

Inclusive approaches to teaching and learning

Inclusive pedagogy promotes the idea that all young people can learn, progress, and achieve when given the right support. Teachers should focus on "what students *can* do rather than what they cannot" (Florian and Spratt 2015: 92), fostering a classroom environment that values diversity as a strength. A key principle of inclusive pedagogy is the normalisation of opportunities, ensuring all young people, regardless of ability, can fully participate in learning experiences. Inclusion should therefore be an integral part of music education, rather than an afterthought. This includes identifying and removing barriers to learning, whether physical, emotional, cognitive, financial, or geographical.

Inclusive pedagogy has been shaped by several key ideas embedded in educational policy and practice. One of the most significant is Universal Design (UD), which originally focused on the physical accessibility of amenities and facilities such as community spaces and public toilets. Over time, Universal Design for Learning (UDL) extended these principles into education, emphasising flexible teaching approaches that accommodate diverse needs. As Florian and Black-Hawkins (2011) note, adopting such an approach "involves the development of a rich learning community characterised by learning opportunities that are sufficiently made available for *everyone*, so that all learners are able to participate in classroom life" (814; emphasis added). At the centre of UDL are the ideas shown in Table 4.1, which you will explore in Task 4.3.

Table 4.1 Adapted Universal Design for Learning framework (CAST 2018)

Provide multiple means of representation	Provide multiple means of action and expression	Provide multiple means of engagement
Offer options and supports to stimulate motivation and sustained enthusiasm for learning	Present information in different ways to support access and understanding	Offer options and supports to all so everyone can create, learn, and share

■ ■ ■ ■ **INCLUSIVITY IN THE MUSIC CLASSROOM**

> ### Task 4.3 **Applying UDL to music learning contexts**
>
> Think of a music lesson you have either taught or observed recently. Consider each of the three principles of UDL in Table 4.1. Consider how the music lesson already was, or could have been, adapted to provide:
>
> - multiple ways of representation;
> - multiple ways of action and expression;
> - multiple ways of engagement.

Ensuring all young people have equitable opportunities to participate in musical learning requires adaptations to teaching and learning that promote accessibility and inclusion. This means, for example, ensuring young people can enter the classroom, use suitable or adapted instruments, and engage with a flexible, differentiated curriculum. As Florian and Spratt (2015) note, "difficulties students experience in learning should be considered dilemmas for teaching rather than problems with students" (92). This perspective encourages us not only to adapt our pedagogical approaches but also to expand our communication skills and create inclusive learning environments where all young people can flourish.

AN INCLUSIVE MUSIC EDUCATION

Having considered what we mean by inclusion and some key underpinning principles, it is important to acknowledge broader structural issues that impact how inclusive or exclusive music education might feel for young people. These include the diverse musical backgrounds that young people bring into the classroom (see Chapter 2) and challenges such as gender stereotypes and representation. While much of the rest of this chapter focuses on how to plan and differentiate for young people's needs, these systematic issues continue to influence inclusive musical learning.

Diverse musical backgrounds

The increasing diversity of our young people, their access to a broad range of musics and musical practices, and the recognition of how in the past, particular ways of learning music have been valued and prioritised over others, have all increased our awareness of how important it is to embrace and celebrate young people's diverse musical backgrounds. Therefore, a core responsibility in the classroom is to be sensitive to and proactive around issues of musical diversity, where "music is a powerful means of defining heritage, developing intercultural understandings, and breaking down barriers between various ethnic, racial, cultural and language groups" (Campbell 2018: xvi).

Since the 1980s, there has been a temptation to address this increasing musical diversity by "adding" different musics to a curriculum understood as "curriculum as content" (see Chapter 7). While representation can be an important factor, Philpott (2022) argues that "while well intentioned, the inclusion of a wide range of musics can take on the appearance of things to be 'ticked off' and 'delivered'" (4). Indeed, the addition of,

> Other musics can be patronising, inaccurate and less than authentic. For example, the prevalence of units of work in UK classrooms on "African music" or "Indian music" can be evidence of prejudicially "othering" and trivialising musics from cultures and traditions outside of Western art music.
> (5)

This approach of "adding" diverse musics into curricula, described by Hess (2015) as a "touristic" approach, can inadvertently re-emphasise the "privileging of Western classical music [where it] marginalizes all 'Other' musics, effectively arranging them around the Western classical center in such a way that affirms and reinforces racial hierarchies" (339).

To be critically aware of the potential for tokenistic responses to musical diversity, Chapter 7 of this book argues that we need to shift our attention from "curriculum as content" to curriculum encounters as a site for making meaning together. This stance repositions diverse musics as a site for exploration, co-construction of knowledge, and an openness to critical engagement and interpretation. Hess (2015) suggests a comparative approach that,

> Emphasizes the interconnectedness between the musics and the contexts of the musics. . . . Teaching and thinking comparatively and relationally allows us to think broadly *across* categories, thinking through power relations as they pertain to the musics of the world and as they relate to bringing those musics into an elementary school classroom. Understanding musics relationally also allows students and teachers to come to know themselves relationally, as thinking in this manner facilitates the analysis of all relationships.
> (341)

Gender and music education

For some time, there has been concern expressed over the underachievement of boys in our education system (Younger and Warrington 1996; Francis 2000). In addition, a growing body of research in music education (Green 1996; Hallam 1998; Wright 2001; Bain 2019; Bull 2019; Bull et al. 2022) has highlighted the importance of understanding gender differences and the broader social influences that affect the relationship between gender and achievement in music. It is important that teachers embrace these issues and devise appropriate learning strategies to address them.

INCLUSIVITY IN THE MUSIC CLASSROOM

The following are some of the issues that have been identified by research into gender and society, gender and music, and gender and music education:

- The general underachievement of boys in music at school;
- The apparent paradox that boys are disproportionately over-represented in the music profession;
- The stereotypical patterns of achievement and attitude among boys and girls at school;
- The gendered meanings placed on music, which are determined by the structure and nature of society;
- The "loss" of a female history of music.

These issues are amplified by the quotations in Box 4.1, before Task 4.4 offers you the opportunity to reflect on your own experience.

Box 4.1 **Gender and music education**

Rehearsal processes shape the embodied dispositions of young musicians to cultivate a mode of restraint and gendered control, which is congruent with a particular classed identity.

(Bull 2015: 3)

Boys have traditionally been underrepresented among those learning to play an instrument. Approximately twice as many girls play instruments as boys. Girls also do better in school music examinations. Despite this there appear to be no gender differences in measures of musical ability on music tests.

(Hallam 1998: 55)

A great deal of music by women composers has been denigrated for its effeminacy: other music has been more favourably received as displaying positive feminine attributes such as delicacy or sensitivity; a tiny amount of music by women has been incredulously hailed as equal to music by men.

(Green 1996: 127)

Task 4.4 **Your own experience**

Think about your own experiences as a musician and music teacher. Consider the following questions:

- Have you observed any gender patterns to those who adopt various roles in the music industry: teachers, composers, conductors, instrumentalists (e.g., drummers, flautists, guitarists)?
- Do you perceive there to be differences in achievement between girls and boys across the different areas of the music curriculum: performing, composing, and responding?

- Is there a gender difference in the uptake of music in school for young people aged 14 to 16?
- Have you used or experienced the use of the work of female musicians and/or composers as examples in music lessons?

KNOWING YOUNG PEOPLE'S MUSICIANSHIP

The previous section explored large-scale structural inclusion issues for music education. Whether addressing these structural issues, responding to individual needs within your class, or planning differentiated learning for small groups, you need to know the young people you are working with and understand them as musicians. As outlined in Chapter 2 and elsewhere, this will include observing what knowledge, preferences, and experiences they bring to the classroom. One of the best ways (indeed, perhaps the only way) to get to know your young people and their needs is to watch them participating *in music*, paying attention to the ways in which they create and respond (Task 4.5).

Task 4.5 **Observing young people as musicians**

During a music lesson in which a class are actively engaged in performing, composing, or listening, observe a small group of young people, noticing how they participate and paying attention to their musical choices, interactions, and responses.
After the lesson, reflect on the following:

- Which young people were most engaged? Why?
- Did any of them seem disengaged or excluded? Why?
- What choices did the young people make as to *how* they engaged in activities? Did they follow the teacher's instructions or develop their own approaches?
- What barriers to participation were evident, and how did the teacher plan to overcome them?

As illustrated in Figure 4.1, understanding young people as musicians involves a continuous cycle of planning, observing, and assessing. It is important to allow yourself time during every lesson to stand to one side and observe a class working, so that you can use this information to plan future lessons. This will also involve the assessment of learning, which includes:

- gathering and interpreting evidence about young people's learning;
- using that evidence to decide where young people are in their learning and where to go next.

INCLUSIVITY IN THE MUSIC CLASSROOM

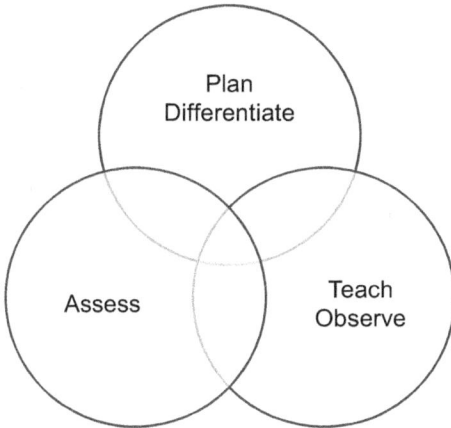

Figure 4.1 The teaching continuum

Knowing our young people as musicians, monitoring their developing musicianship, and planning for individual needs and an inclusive environment requires us to continually listen to their verbal reflections and musical contributions. This responsivity informs how we make in-the-moment decisions according to young people's experiences (see Chapter 7) and tailor learning to their individual needs.

The process of differentiation

All young people should have opportunities to experience success and progress in their musical learning. This requires content and tasks suited to their developmental levels and individual needs—a process known as differentiation. In this chapter, we define differentiation as identifying the most effective teaching and learning strategies for individual young people or groups of young people. As part of UDL, such differentiation strategies should be embedded within planning, not considered as an afterthought.

The goal of differentiation is to recognise and respond to young people's differences in order to promote achievement, build self-esteem, and sustain motivation. As Green (1997) states, "in addressing differentiation, we are recognising and celebrating the range of different strategies that young people use in order to learn, as well as the different rates at which they might learn" (9). Dickinson and Wright (1993) offer a model for planning differentiation, which has been adapted in Figure 4.2. Implementing differentiation is central to inclusive education, and the rest of this section explores its implications for teaching and learning in music.

It is not always appropriate for all young people to study the same content at the same time, and national frameworks across the United Kingdom do not require this. Offering varied lesson content can better address young people's needs. Although managing such an approach may seem complex, music is well suited to this flexibility through composition and performance activities. This is particularly effective in post-14 qualifications, where smaller groups allow for more individualised work.

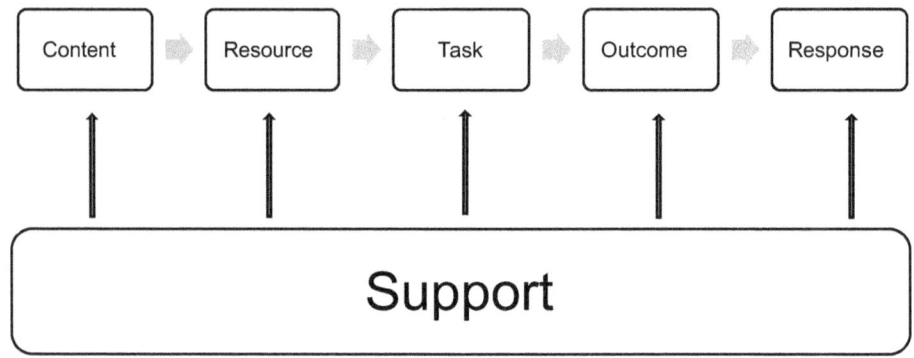

Figure 4.2 A model for differentiation

Differentiation requires a range of resources. Recorded music, for example, should offer authentic experiences to help young people engage meaningfully. Resources also play a role in overcoming barriers to learning. For example, technology can enable all young people, including those with SEND, to develop and demonstrate their creativity.

Providing activities matched to young people's developmental stages, interests, and aspirations is also important. When performing, roles can be assigned based on skill and attainment, ensuring all activities have musical value. Composing tasks can also be adapted by modifying briefs, stimuli, or structures. Questioning techniques (both verbal and written) can further differentiate learning, with probing questions deepening understanding.

Music naturally differentiates itself through engagement (Swanwick 1988), particularly when young people interact with materials in varied ways through composing and listening. Support can be tailored intuitively, but differentiation can also involve teaching assistants, instrumental staff, and outside music organisations. Peer learning and support can also be effective. As shown in Task 4.6, understanding and being able to draw on these forms of differentiation is critical for enacting inclusive pedagogy.

> ### Task 4.6 **The forms of differentiation**
>
> Evaluate the forms of differentiation you have observed or used in the classroom. Map each form against the headings in the model in Figure 4.2. For each form of differentiation, note down further musical examples or activities to which it could be applied. Discuss your reflections with another beginning teacher, colleague, or mentor.

WORKING WITH YOUNG PEOPLE WITH ADDITIONAL NEEDS

Young people with additional needs (including SEND) have historically faced exclusion from music education. An inclusive approach highlights their right to equitable participation in a high-quality music education. This section considers three specific approaches for working with those with additional needs as a starting point for your own, contextually informed, teaching.

Sounds of Intent

Sounds of Intent (2015) is an assessment framework designed for those working with young people with learning difficulties, including profound and multiple learning disabilities, severe learning disabilities, and autism spectrum conditions. It provides a structured approach to understanding musical engagement and development by categorising responses into three domains:

- Reactive—listening and responding to sound and music;
- Proactive—actively making sound and music;
- Interactive—engaging with sound and music in a social context.

The framework helps teachers and parents observe and interpret a young person's musical activity by aligning their musical behaviours with specific developmental levels. These levels range from basic awareness of sound to mature artistic expression, offering a structured path for musical progression. The framework outlines six levels of musical engagement. Level 1 (confusion and chaos) reflects unstructured responses to sound, while Level 2 (awareness and intentionality) shows deliberate engagement. Level 3 (relationships, repetition, and regularity) introduces pattern recognition, and Level 4 (sounds forming clusters) involves organising sounds meaningfully. Level 5 (deeper structural links) demonstrates an understanding of musical relationships, leading to Level 6 (mature artistic expression), where individuals engage in intentional and creative music-making.

Sounds of Intent (2015) offers teachers a basis for musical planning and assessment when working with young people with complex needs and is both grounded in valid observation and theoretically coherent. Recognising young people's musical engagement using the six levels enables teachers to plan activities that will support progression. You may find this framework useful when identifying and planning for the development of young people's musicianship.

Adaptive instruments

Young people with physical disabilities often participate in mainstream classrooms and should always be given appropriate support to access music. Frequently, this support involves using adaptive instruments or assistive technology. Adaptive instruments are widely used to assist young people "who may have differing levels of abilities such as decreased muscle control, impaired vision, diminished hearing, or loss of a limb" (Chapin 2020: 1). These instruments are specially designed or modified to suit different needs: for example, some can be played with the opposite hand (like a trumpet adapted for the left hand); others can be adjusted for one-handed playing; and digital options, like tablets, can allow young people to touch screens to create music (Snedeker 2005).

External organisations and charities play a crucial role in supporting inclusive music education and can often be accessed through regional music organisations, educational networks, or arts councils across the four nations of the United Kingdom. These organisations can provide a range of resources, including adaptive instruments, assistive technology, and specialised training to ensure that all young people, including those with physical disabilities, can actively participate in music-making. Some ideas for adapting instruments include:

- dots or colours on guitars and pianos to indicate which notes to play;
- open tuning for guitars—such as (from the bass string upwards) D-A-D-F#-A-D;
- using Velcro to hold instruments;
- gaffer tape on drum beaters to give added grip;
- using chime bars in ensembles to help create chords;
- providing ear-defenders when playing loud instruments.

Assistive technologies

Some music technology is easy for young people to operate and therefore doesn't require a long period of learning before they can create or perform their own music. Given the disaffection of some young people from their own sense of themselves as musicians, this "instant" and accessible factor can help retain their engagement: "technology has smashed down the barriers to accessing music—music that is technically complex and rewarding" (Hewitt 2013: 105).

Assistive technology—technology that is designed to increase access to music-making, especially for disabled people—has been helpful in creating real equality for disabled musicians. From single sound switches through to SoundBeams and intuitive music apps, all have helped increase access. Many teachers now use GarageBand, Clarion, and other forms of accessible technology, some of which are listed at the end of this chapter. You can think about your own use of adaptive instruments and assistive technologies in Task 4.7.

Task 4.7 **Auditing adaptive instruments and assistive technologies in your context**

1. Make a note of the different instruments, technologies, and apps that you have access to in your context which you think could be used to support young people with additional needs.
2. Download the *Take It Away* guide to adaptive instruments (Creative United 2020) or do some online research on adaptive instruments and assistive technologies. Note down additional instruments and technologies that you feel would make a substantial difference to the inclusivity of your classroom.
3. Research your local music charities, cultural organisations, or library board to see if they have an accessible instrument lending library and what is in it.

■ ■ ■ ■ INCLUSIVITY IN THE MUSIC CLASSROOM

Working with neurodivergent young people

The term "neurodiversity" refers to the naturally occurring variation in neurocognitive functioning across populations (Walker 2021). For those who are "neurodivergent" (as opposed to "neurotypical"), their cognitive, affective, or perceptual experience may differ from the norm, often because of SEND such as autism spectrum condition or attention deficit hyperactivity disorder. While teaching neurodivergent young people can often be approached using the same underpinning principles of inclusion and differentiation outlined earlier in this chapter, there are specific barriers to overcome within music classrooms for some of these young people.

Autism spectrum condition (ASC)

Many autistic young people experience music differently from their peers. With appropriate support, they can develop deep engagement in music that aligns with their interests (McLachlan 2016). However, certain challenges around social interaction and sensory processing may affect their participation.

Recognising that autism is a spectrum condition, and experienced very individually, the principles of observing young people, knowing them as musicians, and creating open dialogue with them about their learning are vital for fostering inclusion. However, there are some particular approaches which can be useful when thinking about young people with autism. One issue to address in planning is how to create a classroom environment that isn't sensorily distressing. Many autistic young people experience heightened sensitivity to sound, which may mean that unpredictable or sudden noises can be overwhelming. To support them, consider introducing volume changes gradually over a lesson or series of lessons, allowing them to build their tolerance at a comfortable pace. Providing young people with control over the volume of their instrument, ear-defenders, or access to a quiet space outside the classroom can also be helpful. A key element in this approach is open communication: encouraging young people to express their preferred strategies for managing their auditory environment is essential for ensuring that teaching and learning is responsive to their needs.

To support musical engagement, teachers can also adopt structured and predictable approaches which may help some autistic young people regulate their thoughts and develop their skills. These might include:

- using a consistent rhythm vocabulary (e.g., boom, rocka, rockachicka);
- maintaining a regular, fixed routine to provide familiarity;
- designing pieces around young people's interests to encourage motivation;
- incorporating repetitive musical patterns (e.g., ostinati, riffs) to support engagement;
- making use of drones for grounding and focus.

Many autistic young people have exceptional musical perception, and with the right support, they can become highly skilled musicians (Ockelford 2013).

Attention deficit hyperactivity disorder (ADHD)

Attention deficit hyperactivity disorder (ADHD) is a complex neurodevelopmental condition that is subject to ongoing research. Maté (1999) has written of the differences in motivation, attention, emotional intensity, and behaviour that can come with ADHD, noting that those with ADHD can often exhibit restlessness, trouble concentrating, and impulse behaviours. Some challenges young people with ADHD may face include:

- having a short attention span and being easily distracted;
- making careless mistakes;
- appearing forgetful or losing things;
- being unable to stick to tasks that are tedious or time-consuming;
- constantly fidgeting;
- excessive talking;
- being unable to wait their turn;
- acting without thinking.

Table 4.2 suggests some strategies that may be helpful for supporting young people with ADHD in music lessons, which you can reflect on in Task 4.8.

Table 4.2 Teaching and learning with young people with ADHD

Break down instructions	Give one step at a time, ensuring clarity and avoiding cognitive overload
Leverage hyper-focus	If a young person is fully engaged, allow them time to immerse themselves in the task, as this can lead to highly productive sessions
Use consistent positivity	Offer appropriate praise to reinforce engagement and effort
Encourage flow (Csikszentmihalyi 2002)	Minimise interruptions and give space for the continuation of ideas
Be flexible with time management	Praise young people's effort rather than penalising unfinished work if they struggle to complete work on time
Support organisation	Work with a young person to help them develop a simple, structured system for managing their musical equipment
Acknowledge limitations	Be patient and provide ongoing support when young people are forgetful
Allow extra time for setting up	Offer assistance with setting up equipment if needed
Avoid blame	Recognise that certain behaviours, such as disorganisation or time-blindness, are not intentional

Task 4.8 Supporting young people with ADHD in music lessons

Review the strategies in Table 4.2 for working with young people with ADHD in the music classroom. Consider how you might implement these approaches in your own teaching by reflecting on:

- which of these strategies you already use;
- which you could implement more in your teaching;
- the potential implications of implementing these strategies.

Social, emotional, and mental health difficulties (SEMHD)

The term social, emotional, and mental health difficulties (SEMHD) was introduced in England in the SEND *Code of Practice* (DfE and DHSC 2015) to describe young people who experience multiple risk factors and may lack the protective resilience necessary for good mental health. Young people with SEMHD may face some of the following challenges:

- Difficulty in recognising, regulating, or de-escalating their emotions;
- Becoming withdrawn or isolated;
- Displaying challenging, disruptive, or disturbing behaviour;
- Deep sensitivity to perceived rejection.

Establishing trust and ensuring that young people feel at ease, respected, and not pressured into participation is important when working with young people with SEMHD. Part of the process of creating a comfortable and safe environment can be the co-creation of whole-class ground rules in an initial lesson. These could even be arranged into a song and then recorded, to help foster a sense of ownership.

Since the COVID-19 pandemic, the number of young people experiencing SEMHD has increased significantly (NHS Digital 2021). Given its benefits for improving mental wellbeing (Hallam and Himonides 2022), music both inside and outside the classroom can be one way for these young people to affirm their identity and regulate their emotions.

Trauma-informed practice

Trauma-informed practice acknowledges that many young people may have experienced adverse life events that could have lasting negative effects. As teachers, we may not always be aware of these histories, but we can adopt a mindful and supportive approach that aligns with trauma-informed principles.

These practices aim to minimise re-traumatisation, which occurs when an individual re-experiences thoughts or emotions linked to past trauma.

Key principles of trauma-informed practice (DfE 2024) include:

1. *Safety*—ensuring that young people feel physically and emotionally secure by fostering a supportive environment, implementing safeguarding measures, and working to prevent re-traumatisation;
2. *Trustworthiness*—maintaining transparency by clearly explaining actions and expectations, following through on commitments, and building consistent, predictable relationships;
3. *Choice*—providing young people with agency in decision-making, recognising that those who have experienced trauma may struggle with feelings of powerlessness, which can impact their ability to build trusting relationships;
4. *Collaboration*—encouraging peer support and mutual self-help, working alongside young people to create shared learning experiences that promote connection and inclusion;
5. *Empowerment*—actively listening, validating emotions, and supporting young people in developing confidence and autonomy.

The American National Association for Music Education (NAfME) have also published guidance on trauma-informed music practices (Van Klompenberg 2022), including recognising the power of music-making as an affective experience allowing young people the space and means to explore and develop their emotional responses. They suggest allowing space for emotions within the classroom, validating emotions that are expressed, and recognising the collective power of emotional response within a larger group to create safety and belonging.

Self-determination theory (SDT)

In an inclusive music classroom, fostering motivation, engagement, and wellbeing is essential to ensuring that all young people feel valued and capable of participating meaningfully. One further way to achieve this is through considering the implications of self-determination theory (SDT), a psychological framework that explores how we develop intrinsic motivation when our fundamental psychological needs are met. A key principle of inclusive education is creating a learning environment where young people feel competent, autonomous, and connected to others. SDT, developed by Deci and Ryan (2017), identifies these three needs—competence, autonomy, and relatedness—as essential to psychological flourishing and suggests that failing to meet these needs can diminish wellbeing.

When applied to music education, the principles of SDT can enhance young people's engagement, support individual growth, and promote a sense of belonging within a group. This might occur through:

INCLUSIVITY IN THE MUSIC CLASSROOM

- a commitment to mutual goal setting, realisation of targets, and positive feedback to develop a sense of individual and collective competency;
- a focus on group music-making which honours each young person's contribution, developing a strong sense of relatedness;
- shared ownership, coupled with the importance of individual and group creativity, together encouraging a sense of autonomy.

An opportunity to consider meeting young people's psychological needs is given in Task 4.9.

Task 4.9 **Meeting young people's psychological needs**

Design a lesson for a specific class, focusing on the psychological needs of the young people in the group. Plan for each of the psychological needs outlined in SDT:

- *Competency*: helping young people develop confidence and mastery, creating opportunities for positive feedback;
- *Relatedness*: strengthening connection and collaboration, encouraging group work, peer support, and shared musical experiences;
- *Autonomy*: promoting independent decision-making, allowing young people to take creative ownership of their learning through self-directed composing or improvising.

BECOMING AN INCLUSIVE TEACHER

Inclusive music teachers tend to work in a relational way, communicating with young people as they would with fellow musicians. They use their leadership to build shared musical experiences, setting (or suggesting) activities which they know will be engaging and supporting and celebrating young people's achievements. Working inclusively with young people may look like:

- *Shared ownership*. Using a shared ownership approach engages young people because it is tied to their sense of self. It gives them the responsibility to develop (with support) their own musical identity. This can start with asking young people to choose what music to work on, to lead warm-up activities, to direct small groups, to conduct, to write songs, and so on;
- *Relational working*. Regularly (but unobtrusively) checking in, being positive and supportive, and showing interest and empathy is especially important when young people find things difficult;
- *Flexibility*. Inclusive music-making tends to be immersive, responsive, and in-the-moment. Although planning is important, following young people's

interests and enthusiasms are more so. This requires flexibility, being able to follow and explore young people's ideas without losing sight of the backbone of the lesson;
- *Groupings*. Having different group combinations in different parts of a lesson (e.g., whole class, two halves, small groups, pairs) can help create variety in approach, power dynamic, and degree of individual contribution;
- *Inclusive structures*. These might include developing a group contract on how to work together, balancing contributions equally from each participant, offering support rather than issuing commands, articulating a non-coercive approach, allowing young people to exit and re-enter the group without sanction, or creating a positive quiet or time-out space.

Evaluating and reflecting to support inclusivity

Reflective practice—a key aspect of inclusive teaching—involves the ability to critically examine experiences and understand their implications. This process enables us to evaluate what has happened during learning to identify potential barriers for young people and strategies to foster inclusivity in the classroom. In classrooms where young people have widely differing needs, it is vital that we evaluate our own practices (Task 4.10) to ensure we are maintaining our commitment to inclusivity.

Task 4.10 **Evaluating inclusive practices**

Take one lesson plan for a class that you have taught or observed, plus any reflections you have already made upon it. Evaluate which aspects of the lesson were successful in creating an inclusive musical learning environment, by considering:

- the young people with specific SEND;
- the broader needs of all the young people in that class, whether social, developmental, musical, or otherwise;
- the differentiation strategies that were planned into the lesson;
- the barriers that were overcome within the planning of the lesson;
- the barriers that still existed within the lesson;
- the young people's engagement and achievement in the lesson;
- how you would plan the lesson differently to make it even more inclusive.

As well as personal reflection and evaluation of your practices, it is essential in working with young people with specific needs to understand their experiences from their own perspectives. Arguably, this is imperative for all good teaching. Group reflections that are built into lessons can provide a good space for gathering ideas from young people to improve the inclusivity of your classroom. To create spaces for reflection and dialogue you could begin with gathering verbal feedback at the end of a section of work or at the close of a lesson. This could include the following questions:

1. How did you feel about what we did?
2. What did you like or dislike and why?
3. What would you like to do that is different and why?

Try not to be overly defensive if young people have criticisms; try to find ways to change things that don't work for them and keep on seeking their contributions.

SUMMARY

In this chapter we have looked at what inclusion means and how it can tackle exclusion. We have looked at classroom strategies such as accommodating young people's diverse musical backgrounds, being sensitive to structural inequalities, and implementing differentiation. We have touched on theories including the social model of disability and self-determination theory, and offered ideas for working with young people who are disabled, neurodivergent, or have social, emotional, and mental health difficulties. Though we have barely scratched the surface of inclusive education, you will hopefully have gained some idea of the importance of the field and some ways in which you can begin to make your contribution.

FURTHER RESOURCES: USEFUL MUSIC APPS FOR TEACHING AND LEARNING

Bloom: 10 Worlds: a generative music app that allows the creation of patterns and melodies using a simple touch interface. Available on Apple and Android devices (https://generativemusic.com/bloom10worlds.html).

The Clarion: a tablet-based musical instrument that is both expressive and accessible (https://theclarion.uk/).

Chrome Music Lab: web-based educational games and experiments for exploring music and related disciplines such as science, art, and dance. Available on all web browsers (https://musiclab.chromeexperiments.com/).

GarageBand: a Digital Audio Workstation with an accessible and simple-to-use interface. Available on Apple devices (https://www.apple.com/uk/mac/garageband/).

iKaossilator: a synthesiser app allowing the creation of expressive sounds and visual effects through an intuitive touchpad. Available on Apple devices (https://www.korg.com/uk/products/software/ikaossilator/).

LaunchPad: a grid-based app for making and remixing electronic music. Available on Apple devices (https://novationmusic.com/software/launchpad-ios).

ThumbJam: an app with samples from over forty high-quality instruments that can be played using touch, tilt, and shake. Available on Apple devices (https://thumbjam.com/).

COLLABORATION FOR MUSICAL LEARNING

Anna Mariguddi

INTRODUCTION

Collaboration is essential for widening the scope and diversity of possibilities for musical learning. Effective collaboration can facilitate the flourishing of all involved, including teachers and young people. This is because collaborations "provide opportunities to create something bigger than ourselves, and through the creative-collaborative processes, become *more*" (Bresler 2018: ix). Collaborations can result in valuable learning experiences, enhance the musical participation and engagement of young people, and nurture the development of supportive collegial relationships. Collaborations can be formed between secondary school music teachers, young people, and a variety of other educators, bringing different practices and cultures into the classroom and developing new ways of working. Yet collaborations can be complex and challenging, requiring careful navigation and thoughtful interaction in order to succeed. It is therefore important to gain increased awareness and understanding of collaboration during your time as a beginning teacher—by embracing practical experiences (observing and becoming directly involved in existing collaborations), critically engaging with relevant literature, and beginning to plan your own future collaborations.

> **Objectives**
>
> By the end of this chapter you should be able to:
>
> - understand the meaning of collaboration and be able to explain some of the benefits and challenges of collaboration;
> - understand the range of collaborations that can be developed with others, within and beyond the school;

- critically reflect upon your own teacher identity, skills, and knowledge, and consider what type of collaborations you would like to develop to enhance musical learning for young people;
- establish conditions that allow for collaborations to thrive, drawing upon the suggestions and examples shared in this chapter.

COLLABORATION—WHAT IS IT?

Collaboration can be understood as a type of partnership "in which two or more organisations [or individuals] collaborate over events or programmes. They jointly plan the nature and content, and identify targeted groups" (Hallam 2011: 158). This definition can be broadened to encompass more than just events and programmes within the context of education and can include smaller-scale activities and experiences. The terms "collaboration" and "partnership" are sometimes used interchangeably, but a partnership tends to be recognised as a more formalised arrangement.

Collaboration is a key aspect of a teacher's role. Daily collaborations occur between teaching and non-teaching staff to ensure the effective running of the school: between teachers and teaching assistants, technicians, teaching colleagues, pastoral staff, senior leadership, and those with specific support responsibilities, including for Special Educational Needs and Disabilities (SEND). This chapter will consider these in-school collaborations but also extend our understanding to include those that can occur with outside organisations and educators.

Collaboration in your own context

Consider your own music education context. What collaboration opportunities already exist and what can be expanded upon? Tasks 5.1, 5.2, and 5.3 will help you engage with this process.

> Task 5.1 **Existing collaborations**
>
> Find out about any previous or existing collaborations in your school and gain insight into the planning of these collaborations and how they are facilitated.
>
> Explore the strengths and limitations of the collaborations and what can be learnt from them. This may involve talking with a wide range of people, including young people themselves.

After having reflected upon previous or existing collaborations in your context, you can now begin to consider the opportunities upon which you could expand.

> ### Task 5.2 **Collaboration opportunities**
>
> Note down potential collaboration opportunities that you can identify within your own context that could expand upon the current offer. These might include music teacher colleagues in different schools (including those you have met during teacher education), local professional or amateur musicians, charitable music organisations, regional orchestras or bands, higher education institutions, and personal musical contacts. Consider the expertise of your collaborator, the purpose of the collaboration, and the potential positive outcomes for all involved.
>
> | Name of collaborator | Role/expertise | Purpose of collaboration | Positive outcomes |
> |---|---|---|---|
> | | | | |
> | | | | |
> | | | | |

Perhaps most importantly, you will need to consider the young people at the heart of any future collaborations (Zeserson 2012). This will enable you to decide which of the potential collaborations will be most relevant for your local context. Task 5.3 provides a framework for you to do this.

> ### Task 5.3 **Young people at the centre of collaboration**
>
> Consider the young people at the centre of any potential collaboration. Use the following questions as prompts to reflect upon your knowledge as their teacher:
>
> - What do the young people seem to enjoy about their current school music lessons?
> - To your knowledge, what music do the young people enjoy engaging with outside school?
> - Do any of the young people sing or play musical instruments?
> - What music would be culturally relevant and authentic for the young people in your context?
> - Are there any areas of the curriculum that could be developed to extend the skills, knowledge, and experience of the young people?
>
> Use your responses to these questions to add further ideas to the table you created in Task 5.2.

By comparing your notes from Tasks 5.2 and 5.3, you will begin to identify matches between what a potential collaboration might be able to offer, and the perceived needs and interests of the young people in your context. Knowledge gained from Task 5.1 can begin to inform your ideas of how a potential collaboration might be approached in practice.

■ ■ ■ ■ COLLABORATION FOR MUSICAL LEARNING

IDENTITY, VALUES, INFLUENCES, AND EXPERIENCE

To develop fruitful collaborations, other important factors must be considered. Teacher identity, the values a teacher holds, and the experiences they have had throughout their own music education and time as a music educator will impact upon the skills, knowledge, and practice they bring to collaborations. These factors will shape a teacher's "habitus": the way they perceive and respond to the world, and their patterns of disposition within the classroom (Bourdieu 1977). Of equal importance are the identities, influences, and experiences that young people bring into the classroom. Facilitation of young people's voices is key in this process. It is important to reflect upon these elements, as reflection can raise awareness of any potential strengths, limitations, and assumptions that they will bring to a collaboration (Zeserson 2012). Inclusion of the interests and expertise of young people can lead to increased motivation but are factors which are sometimes overlooked by teachers. Task 5.4 builds on Task 5.3 by encouraging deeper reflection upon these elements.

Task 5.4 **Reflection on experience and identity**

1. Reflect upon your own previous experiences that have had an impact upon your musical skills, knowledge, values, and pedagogical approach. This could include the influence or inspiration of your past music teachers, opportunities you were offered as a musical learner (inside or outside school), something you have read, or any other personal musical experiences that you can recall. Draw a timeline and map these experiences out along your own musical journey. Try to identify the impact of these experiences on your teacher identity and practices.
2. At the start of the school year, set a task for the young people in your class to reflect upon their own musical identities, influences, and experiences. Ask the young people to share any particular musical expertise that they have, of which you might not have been aware. This could also form the starting point for you to facilitate peer-to-peer collaborations.

Once you have completed Task 5.4, compare the musical identities of the young people in your chosen class to your own teacher identity, values, influences, and expertise. Identify how collaborations might act as a "bridge" between contrasting aspects of your teacher musical identity and expertise, and a young person's musical identity and expertise. Refer back to your answers for Tasks 5.1, 5.2, and 5.3, to reconsider which wider collaborations might be the most fruitful in light of your own strengths and limitations, and your increased understanding of the young people in your context. This will allow you to make a more informed decision about why and with whom you would like to collaborate.

POLICY CONTEXT

Collaborations are not immune from or independent of policy. After all, "partnership, collaboration and musical learning are heavily incorporated into, and influenced by, political agendas" (Kinsella et al. 2022: 308). Perhaps one of the most ambitious plans for partnership and collaboration in policy in England comes in the form of the National Plan for Music Education (DfE and DCMS 2011, 2022), which established the formation of local music hubs. Similarly, the Welsh National Plan for Music Education called for the formation of a national music service to complement school music provision (Welsh Government 2022). Yet despite the publication and enactment of these policy documents that seek to enhance music education, literature suggests that provision remains patchy and inequalities prevail, particularly in England (Savage 2020; Henley and Barton 2022; ISM 2022). Stakelum (2024) echoes this view by pointing out the difference between policy and reality, where challenges include disrupted practice caused by the global pandemic restrictions or strike action, risk-averse teaching that errs towards the familiar, and the difference in nature between the role and accountability expectations of the practice of instrumental teachers in comparison to school teachers. Such adversities emphasise the importance of classroom teachers themselves actively seeking opportunities to collaborate, in light of the benefits that collaboration is able to offer.

Benefits of collaboration

There are many benefits of collaboration. These include:

- the welcoming of diverse cultures, musics, and practices into the classroom—where teachers can act as facilitators and co-learners, rather than "doorkeepers of learning" (Gaunt and Westerlund 2013: 1);
- the potential enhancement of young people's progression in music, the broadening and deepening of provision, and benefits for the wider community when collaborations stretch beyond the school (Henley and Barton 2022);
- the development of teaching practice (Ofsted 2012).

These benefits are key to enhancing the quality, diversity, and inclusivity of music education, which is explored further in Chapter 4. Collaboration is particularly relevant given the prevalence of single-teacher departments, where secondary school music teachers sometimes work in isolation. Being part of a collaboration has the potential to build a community for teachers and musicians alike, providing an important sense of belonging to a professional support network (Mariguddi 2026).

Each collaborator can bring with them a variety of complementary skills, knowledge, and expertise. For this reason, collaboration can be understood as a "marriage of insufficiencies" (Shulman 2004: 476). The plethora of different musical styles and practices, each characterised by different types of skills and knowledge, is underpinned by an abundance of social complexities. It is therefore impossible and undesirable for an individual music teacher to be well-versed in all such styles and practices, but collaboration can be a fruitful way of providing a wider offer in music education. Such complementary collaborations also have the potential to develop, update, and refresh the practice of the educators involved.

Challenges of collaboration

Nevertheless, as Barrett (2014) admits, "collaboration is not easy—it is fraught with disagreements, tensions and contradictions" (8). Some of the challenges include:

- potential lack of alignment between a collaboration and a school's day-to-day provision;
- possible breakdown of professional relationships where contributors do not work together successfully, and a lack of appropriate monitoring by school leaders;
- facilitating collaborations across differing locations, particularly when funding or competitive elements are involved (Henley and Barton 2022).

Thus, collaboration requires careful, thoughtful, and sensitive navigation. When a collaboration occurs between a school setting and an out-of-school setting, there can be differences and complexities in the sense of purpose and function of the collaborators (Kinsella et al. 2022). This often stems from a dichotomy between school methods of evaluation (attainment and progression recorded through a system of grading), in comparison to out-of-school evaluations of the music produced (engagement, performance, or composition, for example).

There can also be specific formal and informal pedagogies associated with different sectors. In the context of music education in England, this is attributed to "school music education . . . [being] highly controlled, which differs greatly from the largely unregulated world of informal learning and teaching" (Kinsella et al. 2022: 301). The work of Green (2002, 2008) can provide a useful theoretical framework to understand informal learning pedagogy, where learning is less structured and involves increased choice and autonomy for young people. It is worth noting that formal and informal learning "should not be seen as primarily physical" settings (Folkestad 2006: 142), since informal ways of learning can indeed occur within formal settings and vice versa. Therefore, it is important to remember that informal learning pedagogies can play a valuable role within formal school settings and collaborations. A key influence that will inform the pedagogic approach to be adopted often relates back to an important decision that teachers make between wanting to "confine the learning discourse to a specific goal [or] how far to allow it to range freely according to students' questions and experiences" (Zeserson 2012: 213). Indeed, young people's increased choice,

LEARNING TO TEACH MUSIC IN THE SECONDARY SCHOOL

autonomy, and ownership are elements of informal learning pedagogy that have been associated with greater motivation for learning (Green 2008; Mariguddi 2021). However, a balanced approach between informal and formal approaches should be advocated in order to support young people to navigate both musical worlds (Hess 2020).

COLLABORATION—WITH WHOM AND HOW?

To broaden your understanding of collaboration, the following sections provide some examples of with whom and how collaborations can be formed. For such collaborations to prove successful, it is also important to consider the role expectations of all involved. The role of each collaborator will vary according to their level of involvement, expertise, and experience. Expectations will need to be established as to who is responsible for which aspect of the collaboration. The holistic act of planning the collaboration is likely to be a shared pursuit, but responsibility for specific actions might be designated to individual contributors. A project timeline can therefore be a useful tool to ensure that various actions are carried out as planned.

Zeserson (2012) offers a structure to aid understanding of the various situational roles that a music educator can adopt during a collaboration, which include those of a guide, facilitator, knowledge provider, animateur, ally, trainer, beacon, role model, and manager. In addition to these suggested roles of music educators, the role of the young person should also be considered in light of the development opportunities and democratisation of knowledge that collaboration encourages. An adapted representation of Zeserson's (2012) model is presented in Figure 5.1.

Before entering a partnership or collaboration, Kenny (2016) notes that "every community of musical practice exists within certain local, national and international contexts. Each one has particular norms, rules, structures,

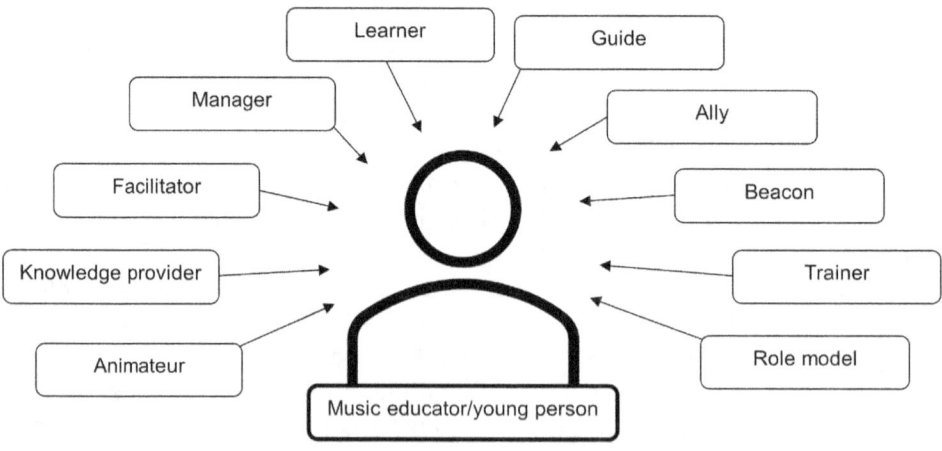

Figure 5.1 Situational roles of a collaborating music educator and young person

COLLABORATION FOR MUSICAL LEARNING

interactions and 'practices' distinct to their collective situations" (45). Thus, it is important to find out about the other person's existing role, what they do each day, how they work, and what they can offer as part of a musical collaboration.

Collaboration within your school

In-school collaborations can be within or between subject teams and can also occur between teachers and young people.

Collaboration between subject teams

Collaborations with colleagues can be cross-curricular in nature and involve both a music teacher and a teacher from a different subject area. Such collaborations can be interdisciplinary, where links between different subjects are identified and utilised to address a common purpose, or transdisciplinary, where traditional subject-specific boundaries are transcended to address a particular issue. Interdisciplinary project-based learning is a common way to realise a collaboration during curriculum time, with a shared focus on a particular theme. Each subject should remain distinct and establish "clear, appropriate, subject-based learning objects" (Barnes 2011: 207). Progression should occur within each subject area (Barnes 2011). For this to work in practice, it is best to involve only two or three subjects to ensure the collaboration is appropriate and manageable. Task 5.5 encourages you to develop an idea for a future interdisciplinary project within your school.

Task 5.5 **Interdisciplinary collaborations**

When planning an interdisciplinary collaboration,

- what topic would you choose to focus on?
- what other subject areas could you collaborate with?
- how would you ensure that the collaboration is appropriate and manageable?
- what could be the benefits and challenges of this collaboration?
- how could the collaboration extend young people's learning in the topic?

Collaborations between teachers and young people

Some of the most important collaborations can occur between teachers and young people (for example, co-designing a curriculum or resource)–enhancing the autonomy, relevance, and ownership of learning for young people. Transdisciplinary collaborations can occur between teachers and young people as extra-curricular activities, such as in the entrepreneurial project presented in Box 5.1.

> Box 5.1 **A collaborative entrepreneurial project**
>
> A group of 14- and 15-year-olds wanted to raise funds for the music department by organising a music concert. An after-school organising group of music teachers and young people was established. Some young people were studying business and brought their knowledge and skills from this subject area to ensure that the project was well-managed. Ticket prices and refreshment costs were calculated (drawing upon skills and knowledge developed in maths), and a business case was developed to gain the support of (and financial contribution from) school leadership. An additional collaboration was formed with the art and design department to produce the marketing materials for the concert, involving additional young people and their teachers. The young people in the organising group developed the concert programme, recruited performers, arranged rehearsals, and ensured the smooth running of the event—with the support of the music teachers throughout. A music technician supported the event by setting up equipment, sound checking, and producing a recording of the event.

The case study in Box 5.1 offers an example of an interwoven model of collaboration (Figure 5.2), in which all collaborators work together in a fully integrated manner, making equal contribution and often without hierarchy. Use Task 5.6 to reflect how—like "weaving together threads" (Evans 2016a: 222-223)—this model allows music educators and young people to work together to develop a strong "fabric" of musical learning within a cross-discipline collaboration.

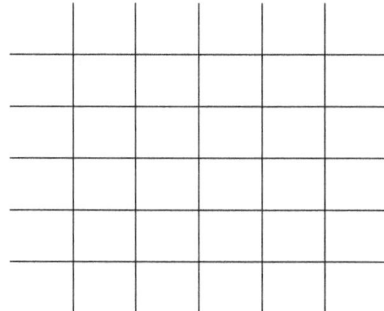

Figure 5.2 Interwoven model of collaboration
(Evans 2016a: 223)

> Task 5.6 **The interwoven model**
>
> In discussion with another teacher, identify the strengths and limitations of the interwoven model of collaboration, considering practicalities, potential for teacher development, and the experience and learning of the young people.

COLLABORATION FOR MUSICAL LEARNING

Collaboration with feeder primary schools

Collaboration with feeder primary schools can happen with any primary year group but is particularly important for supporting young people transitioning into secondary school—which can be an exciting but anxious time. When planning transition collaborations, including the voices of young people is valuable for developing an increased understanding of their needs, interests, and expectations (Kokotsaki 2017).

Collaboration with feeder primary schools can enable you to understand the knowledge and skills that young people bring with them from primary to secondary settings. They may have had a range of experiences in their primary schools that differ from one another, so understanding these can help plan learning. It is important to understand young people's instrumental learning experiences, their involvement in other activities like shows, choirs, and ensembles, and their perceived aptitude in music. Singing in primary schools is often a particular strength, so—as illustrated in Box 5.2—this could be an appropriate starting point when developing potential ideas for primary-secondary school collaborations.

Box 5.2 **A collaborative school transition project**

A primary school teacher and secondary school music teacher had planned a collaborative learning experience together, based upon a transition project developed by the Musical Futures organisation (Musical Futures 2022). The purpose of the collaboration was to engage young people who were about to leave primary school in popular music-making of the kind they said they enjoyed outside school. The secondary school teacher visited the primary school once per fortnight over a period of six weeks, facilitating chair-drumming and whole-class ukulele workshops based upon the rhythms and chords used in the song *Wellerman*. The Musical Futures resources were selected and adapted to suit the context and young people involved. In between these sessions, the primary school teacher developed singing and body percussion workshops using the same material and explored the topic of sea shanties with the young people. Young people were frequently asked for ideas about how they wanted to shape their learning experience. When the young people transitioned to secondary school after the collaboration had taken place, the secondary school teacher used this learning as the starting point for classroom music lessons, ensuring appropriate and fluent progression between schools.

In contrast to the case study in Box 5.1, Box 5.2 provides an example of an episodic model of collaboration. As shown in Figure 5.3, different music educators or classroom teachers are responsible for leading the project at different points.

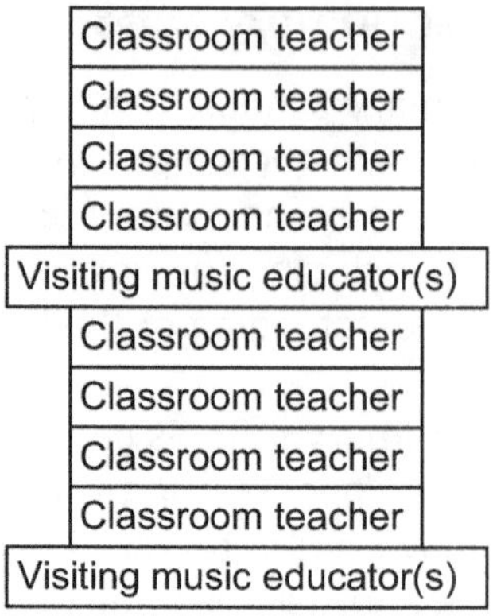

LEARNING TO TEACH MUSIC IN THE SECONDARY SCHOOL

Classroom teacher
Classroom teacher
Classroom teacher
Classroom teacher
Visiting music educator(s)
Classroom teacher
Classroom teacher
Classroom teacher
Classroom teacher
Visiting music educator(s)

Figure 5.3 Episodic model of collaboration

(Evans 2016a: 222)

During episodic collaboration, regular communication between the various learning episodes is key. This model allows for increased practicality, since if the visiting music educator(s) is not able to regularly attend the school setting (due to cost or other commitments), the classroom teacher is able to continue to facilitate the project as planned. Use Task 5.7 to reflect on further strengths and limitations of the episodic model of collaboration.

Task 5.7 **The episodic model**

In discussion with another teacher, identify the strengths and limitations of the episodic model of collaboration, considering practicalities, potential for teacher development, and the experience and learning of the young people.

It is worth considering and exploring your own ideas for a transition project with feeder primary schools using Task 5.8. Your project might adhere to an episodic model of collaboration or involve one of the other models presented in this chapter.

Task 5.8 **Collaboration with feeder primary schools**

Plan a musical activity or project for primary leavers in your local feeder schools, which can be developed and extended in their secondary school curriculum lessons. If possible, plan this collaboratively with the music coordinator or class teacher in the feeder primary school, to help deliver and evaluate the collaboration.

Collaboration with instrumental teachers

Instrumental teachers can either be employed by music services or as independent self-employed specialists that schools recruit directly. As shown in Box 5.3, ways in which collaboration between instrumental teachers and classroom teachers can enhance opportunities available include: the provision of specialist instrumental tuition; the provision of resources that would otherwise be inaccessible (for example, djembes or steel pans); the co-design of a curriculum; and the provision of access to live performance. Collaboration with instrumental teachers may also enable some young people to borrow adapted musical instruments, encouraging inclusion and participation for physically disabled young people and enhancing their musical learning (see Chapter 4).

Box 5.3 **Collaborating with an instrumental teacher**

Since beginning secondary school, Alex has received in-school instrumental lessons for half an hour each week. When Alex reached Year 8 (aged 12), they participated in a composition scheme of work during their curriculum music lessons. They were invited to bring their clarinet into their lessons (along with others in the class who played a musical instrument). The classroom music teacher and instrumental teacher were in regular contact with each other to share information about the young people's learning and progress. The classroom teacher communicated Alex's strengths and areas for development in relation to their performance of the composition, but also noted their interest in using different ranges of the clarinet for different effects. The instrumental teacher made connections between the composition experiences and music Alex was beginning to play in their lessons. This collaboration ensured that Alex's instrumental lessons were not disjointed from their wider musical learning during curriculum time.

The case study in Box 5.3 provides an example of a parallel model of collaboration in action. The parallel model of collaboration (see Figure 5.4) acknowledges that the collaborators working with young people have equal but different strengths that can be used to complement each other within the classroom.

Within the parallel model of collaboration, the classroom teacher and other music educator will often take it in turns to work with the young people, or one might be present within the classroom as a learner alongside the young people while the other is teaching. The classroom teacher may continue to facilitate the project during lessons when the other music educator is not due to attend and

LEARNING TO TEACH MUSIC IN THE SECONDARY SCHOOL

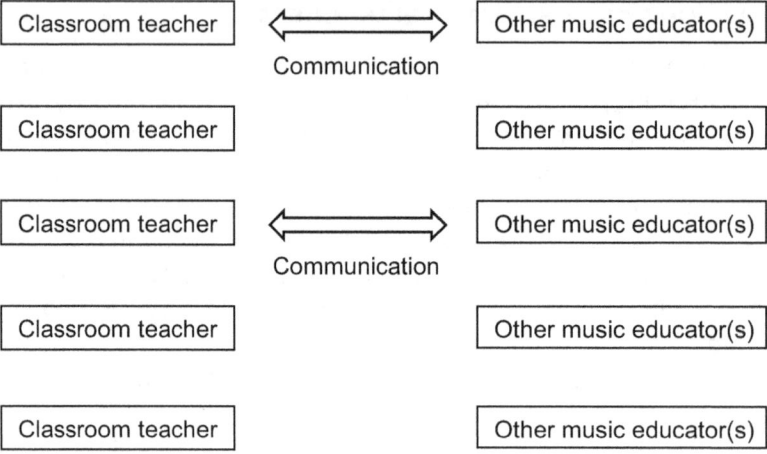

Figure 5.4 Parallel model of collaboration

(Evans 2016a: 220)

vice versa, but communication will be ongoing, either virtually or in-person. As you will consider in Task 5.9, continuous communication is important, to share information about the young people's progress, difficulties, and needs, and also to discuss any practicalities and next steps for the collaboration.

> Task 5.9 **The parallel model**
>
> In discussion with another teacher, identify the strengths and limitations of the parallel model of collaboration, considering its practicalities, potential for teacher development, and the experience and learning of the young people.

Collaboration with musicians

Collaboration with musicians (both amateur and professional) can provide access to a variety of genres and practices that a school music teacher might otherwise be unable to facilitate. This causes a positive shift to occur within the classroom where "a musician entering an educational setting 'alters' the space, potentially adding elements of surprise, tension, and/or interest ... new musical worlds can be discovered and accessed through such music-in-education initiatives" (Kenny and Christophersen 2018: 3). Collaboration with musicians also has the potential to improve links between classroom music and the music that young people are listening to out-of-school, therefore increasing relevance, authenticity, and motivation (Task 5.10).

> **Task 5.10 Reflection**
>
> Look back at the case studies in Boxes 5.1, 5.2, and 5.3. How could these collaborations be enhanced by widening the collaboration to involve external musicians? What opportunities would this create?

Outreach projects can include collaborations between young people and musicians. Outreach projects are planned schemes or activities through which organisations "reach out" to schools to provide experiences for young people that otherwise might be inaccessible. Outreach projects can improve teacher confidence and nurture the ethos that music-making is for everyone (Pitts 2014). Emotional, social, and creative benefits can also be gained for those involved (Henley 2021). Outreach project collaborations can include time-bound projects that are co-designed and facilitated between the teacher and musicians, visits to live rehearsals or performances, and joint music-making between young people and musicians. Such collaborations can vary in duration, but "when schools come into contact with different musical modalities, fresh thinking can produce new curriculum ideas" (Kinsella et al. 2022: 309) and ensure prolonged impact.

Collaboration with higher education institutions

Collaborations with higher education institutions are often underutilised. This can be due to geographical limitations (although collaborations can be virtual or in-person). Higher education institutions can bring many affordances to collaborations, including resources, expertise, and research-informed approaches. Henley and Barton (2022) advocate for collaborations to be established between secondary school teachers and universities and conservatoires, particularly in light of what higher education students might be able to offer. This could include those on music, music technology, performing arts, or teacher training programmes. Nevertheless, there are challenges of working with universities. These include the different reward structures and priorities in universities, a lack of transferability between university and school sites and cultures, and a reliance on funding for large-scale collaborations (Slater 2010). Effective communication and relationship-building can mitigate some of these issues. Collaborations with higher education institutions can either be for the purpose of facilitating or conducting research, music-making experience, or both. Box 5.4 provides an example where the purpose was to experience music-making as a collective endeavour.

LEARNING TO TEACH MUSIC IN THE SECONDARY SCHOOL

> Box 5.4 **Collaborating with a higher education institution**
>
> A learning and participation team from a conservatoire reached out to a local secondary school, as they had a performance opportunity for young people to participate in. The school teacher suggested that the opportunity could become a more collaborative pursuit, and a plan for a learning experience was developed between the music teacher and the lecturer at the conservatoire. Young people (aged 13 and 14) visited the conservatoire for a day and worked alongside conservatoire students in a composition workshop, led by the conservatoire lecturer. The conservatoire students then followed the lead of the young people, encouraging and nurturing their musical ideas to develop a composition by the end of the day. The school teacher supported the group as needed. The composition was then shared at a performance opportunity (which was the initial offer from the conservatoire), with parents and other schools in attendance.

The case study in Box 5.4 illustrates a hierarchical model of collaboration. Unlike in the parallel model, the university lecturer led the composition workshop as an "expert," the teacher supported the group as needed throughout the day, and the young people and students developed a composition together. The hierarchical model is presented in Figure 5.5.

The hierarchical model of collaboration is often used within school contexts. In this model, an individual is regarded as an expert (for example, a head of department), who disseminates knowledge and skills to other colleagues (for example, a beginning teacher of music) and to young people in a pyramidal fashion.

But hierarchical models can also be inverted, where the expertise of colleagues (for example, a beginning teacher of music) will be recognised within a department and their knowledge and skills disseminated to others. This can also be the case when recognising the expertise of young people, particularly in relation to their musical lives outside the classroom. A teacher can learn much from young people about topics such as beatboxing, DJing, and various contemporary

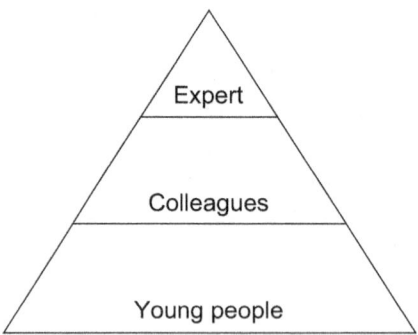

Figure 5.5 Hierarchical model of collaboration

(Evans 2016a: 219)

genres and artists. When an external "expert" (for example, a musician or instrumental teacher) visits the school to facilitate a collaboration, it is not uncommon for the head of department or music teacher to play a subservient role, allowing the external expert to take control. Use Task 5.11 to reflect on the potential role of hierarchical and inverted hierarchical models for collaboration.

> Task 5.11 **The hierarchical model**
>
> In discussion with another teacher, identify the strengths and limitations of the hierarchical model of collaboration, considering its practicalities, potential for teacher development, and the experience and learning of the young people.

For ethical reasons, it is important to reflect upon any hierarchies that might be present within collaborations and consider their impacts (Gaunt and Westerlund 2013). To democratise knowledge, allowing all to participate fully within collaborations, contributors should consider how any undesirable unequal power distributions might be mitigated. According to Westerlund and colleagues (2020), it is not new to acknowledge that "teachers have the power to not only include, but also exclude ideas, knowledge, agencies, communities and worldviews" (2). Inclusion and exclusion in music education can also impact upon pedagogy and curriculum design and must be approached in a socially just manner. You may wish to refer to Chapter 6, which explores curriculum design, to address Task 5.12.

> Task 5.12 **Collaborative curriculum design**
>
> - What might a collaborative curriculum design look like?
> - What types of skills and knowledge will be included and what will be excluded? Why?
> - How could you include the voice of young people in curriculum design and implementation?

THRIVING COLLABORATIONS

Collaborations have the potential to create a thriving secondary school music education. However, certain conditions are necessary. Hallam (2011) proposes that:

> Effective partnership working takes account of context; requires good communication, time, leadership, mutual trust, clarity of roles and responsibilities, and the support of senior management. Training needs must be identified and addressed. Planning, monitoring and evaluation are crucial and a shared ethos and sense of purpose are essential.
>
> (158)

All of these factors must be taken into account during the planning, action, and evaluation stages of each collaboration. Additional characteristics that are important for collaborators to demonstrate include commitment, flexibility, and resilience. Strong collaborative relationships are key for developing "an environment conducive to educational exchange. This include[s] listening to learners, developing safe spaces for peer-to-peer interaction, agency and independence" (Kinsella et al. 2019: 10). Young people should always be positioned at the centre of collaboration for musical learning.

SUMMARY

In this chapter we have:

- explored the concept and meaning of collaboration in the context of secondary school music education;
- presented the many affordances of collaboration to justify its value and place in schools;
- presented the challenges of collaboration, along with suggestions about how to mitigate potential issues;
- discussed the importance of reflecting upon the identities, values, influences, and experiences of music educators and young people throughout the collaborative process;
- explored the range of collaborations available to secondary school music teachers using examples and case studies;
- shared key models and theories of collaboration that can provide theoretical frameworks for the ways in which we approach and facilitate collaborations;
- described the conditions that allow collaborations to thrive, so that you are equipped to begin to plan and facilitate collaborations within your own context.

FURTHER READING

Christophersen, C. and Kenny, A. (eds) (2018)
Musician-Teacher Collaborations: Altering the Chord, New York: Routledge.

Henley, J. and Barton, D. (2022)
'Time for change? Recurrent barriers to music education', *British Journal of Music Education*, 39, 2: 203-217. https://doi.org/10.1017/S026505172200016X

Kinsella, V., Fautley, M. and Whittaker, A. (2022)
'Re-thinking music education partnerships through intra-actions', *Music Education Research*, 24, 3: 299-311. https://doi.org/10.1080/14613808.2022.2053510

Further reading is recommended to enhance understanding of collaboration in music education. The texts listed are useful as they share alternative perspectives, theoretical frameworks, wider contextual detail, and examples of collaboration.

PART 2

MUSICAL TEACHING

THE WHAT, HOW AND WHERE OF MUSICAL LEARNING AND DEVELOPMENT

Chris Philpott

INTRODUCTION

Musical learning is complex. However, it is important for the music teacher to formulate an understanding of the nature of learning in music if they are to plan lessons and units of work that enable young people to become progressively more accomplished composers, performers and responders to music.

In this chapter we address five related issues in order to help you build an understanding of the nature of musical learning:

- What is there to learn? What is the nature of musical knowledge?
- How do young people learn? How do they learn what there is to know?
- Where do they learn?
- How does their musical knowledge develop?
- What is the relationship of musical learning to other subjects and disciplines?

For the purposes of this chapter, learning is defined as having taken place when a change has occurred in the understandings, skills, attitudes or values of young people through the development of different types of musical knowledge. As we shall see, sometimes learning is intentional, where the learner sets out to learn and/or a teacher sets out to bring about learning. However, it is often the case that learning takes place that was not intended by the learner or teacher, for any musical experience can lead to the development of knowledge. Furthermore, there are many complexities surrounding musical learning (Hallam 2001), including:

- the learners' characteristics, i.e., their level of development, prior knowledge, age, gender, motivation and self-esteem;
- the learning environment, i.e., society, culture, school, home and peers;
- the teaching environment and teacher characteristics.

DOI: 10.4324/9781003583226-9

LEARNING TO TEACH MUSIC IN THE SECONDARY SCHOOL

Teaching constitutes the intentional strategies employed to create and sustain an environment of the optimum conditions to bring about learning. Given the complexity of musical learning, music teachers have a professional responsibility to make meaningful connections between their own teaching and the learning of the young people in their classes.

> **Objectives**
>
> By the end of this chapter you should know how:
>
> - music can be differentiated into several types of knowledge;
> - these knowledge types can inform your objectives for planning music lessons;
> - musical knowledge is learnt;
> - musical knowledge can develop in both formal and informal settings;
> - the learning of musical knowledge develops;
> - learning in music is related to wider learning in education.

WHAT IS THERE TO LEARN? THE NATURE OF MUSICAL KNOWLEDGE

What is there for learners to learn in music? What is the nature of musical knowledge? Answers to these questions are particularly important when you are setting objectives for learning in your classroom.

> Task 6.1 **Types of musical knowledge**
>
> What different types of musical knowledge have you needed to learn in order to become a successful musician? Think back to your own musical development and try to place your learning into categories or types of knowledge. Discuss your analysis with another beginning teacher and compare ideas.

Music teachers are always engaging with the question found in Task 6.1 (consciously or not) when deciding what to teach, how to frame learning objectives, how to bring about learning and how to "measure" musical learning. To some extent the learning you expect in your music lessons will be dictated by the intuitive assumptions behind your answers to this question.

As a model to structure our considerations, three different types of musical knowledge are introduced here, based on the work of Reid (1986) and, in particular, Swanwick (1979, 1988).

Knowledge "about"

This might be referred to as factual knowledge; that is, factual knowledge about composers, about style, about theory, about musical concepts. While developments in music education over the past fifty years have explicitly moved us away from an over-reliance on factual musical knowledge to practical engagement, "facts" have an important role to play in informing our understanding of music. Knowing *that* a song is in verse-chorus form or *that* Mozart was a prodigy or *that* a diminished seventh is a pile of minor thirds can enhance our understanding and enjoyment of music. However, facts about music are only "musical" in as much as they are derived from and related to the practice of music itself. Facts about music are only given meaning by real music, without which they are indistinguishable from historical or theoretical (albeit interesting) trivia.

Knowledge "how"

This could be termed "know-how" and is clearly an important dimension of musical knowledge. Musicians might have know-how in the following areas:

- Technical know-how (knowing how to do this or that on an instrument or digital system);
- Creative know-how (the skills of creative problem-solving);
- Discriminatory know-how (knowing how to aurally distinguish between sounds);
- Perceptual know-how (for example, knowing how to recognise a "drone");
- Presentational know-how (knowing how to present a piece to an audience);
- Notational know-how (the skills of reading and writing music);
- Craft know-how (knowing how to make music sound in a particular way).

Clearly some of these skills are closely linked; for example, an aural dictation exercise can test discrimination, perception and notational know-how. It is also clear that learning facts *about* music without the *know-how* to recognise their embodiment in music can be a sterile process. Furthermore, know-how can remain intuitive. For example, many young people immerse themselves in particular musics and while they may know how to recognise the main features, they may not necessarily have the desire or conceptual language to "name" what they hear.

Knowledge "of"

This form of musical knowledge is a knowledge "of" music by direct acquaintance (Reid 1986). It implies the building of an understanding relationship with the music, in the same way that we get to know a person or a face. We might not be able to say what we know or even demonstrate it, yet the relationship with "this" piece of music cannot be denied. Indeed, this is the only way that we can account for young people developing musically without any formal music education. Young people arrive at secondary school with a good deal of intuitive understanding (knowledge *of* music); in particular, they understand "their" music and use it to make sense of the world. Clearly our knowledge *of* music (our understanding relationship with it) is differentiated by *how* and *about*. Knowing *that* we are listening to an Irish rebel folk song and knowing *how* to identify the structural elements, of course, enhances our understanding of the work. However, formal know-how and factual knowledge are not essential to this understanding. Young people (and indeed us all) build significant relationships with pieces of music without any formal understanding about the music or how it is put together. This is not to say that their relationship–their knowledge *of* the music–is not underpinned by much intuitive know-how. Task 6.2 helps you begin to identify these different but interrelated forms of knowledge.

Task 6.2 **Musical knowledge "that," "how" and "of"**

Complete the following with examples from your own musical knowledge:

1. I know that (Eminem is a rapper) . . . .
2. I know that . . . .
3. I know that . . . .
4. I know how to (recognise a tritone). . . . .
5. I know how to. . . . .
6. I know how to. . . . .
7. I know (Wagner's *Ring* cycle in the same way I know a person). . . . .
8. I know. . . . .
9. I know. . . . .

Once you have completed this task, discuss the following questions with another beginning teacher. Is it possible to rank these types of musical knowledge in any order of importance? How are they related? Do we need to learn know-how before we can build meaningful relationships with music?

The knowledge types in action

Our observations on the different types of musical knowledge and their relationship are clearly important when planning objectives for music lessons and when understanding the potential strategies for achieving these. For example, the traditional song in Figure 6.1 can be used with young people to develop knowledge about music, knowledge of music and the know-how of music (see Table 6.1).

As can be seen from Table 6.1, you can develop young people's *technical* musical knowledge (factual and know-how) as well as their *intuitive* knowledge of the music as they build an understanding relationship with the expressive and structural character of the music. Task 6.3 asks you to consider these knowledge types in relation to your own teaching.

■ ■ ■ ■ **THE WHAT, HOW AND WHERE OF LEARNING**

■ **Figure 6.1** Traditional song (to be sung as a round)

■ **Table 6.1** The knowledge types in action

Knowledge *about*	Know *how*	Knowledge *of*
■ What a round is ■ What counterpoint is ■ What quadruple time is ■ Others?	■ To sing and recognise a round ■ To breathe in the right places ■ To sing in ensemble ■ To conduct in quadruple time ■ Others?	■ The expressive shape and character of the music ■ The expressive potential of the music (what would happen if we sang it as a strident march or as a lament?) ■ Others?

Task 6.3 **The knowledge types in action**

Using the example in Figure 6.1 and Table 6.1 as a model, take a musical activity of your own, such as the learning of a song, and try to analyse which aspects of the knowledge types can be developed when young people engage with this work. Try to turn this analysis into a lesson plan that addresses learning objectives in relation to all of the knowledge types. You might like to refer to Chapter 8 for further guidance.

Musical knowledge and objectives for the music lesson

Swanwick (1979) makes a strong case for placing knowledge *of* music at the centre of music education. He argues that our relationship with music is at the core of why we engage with music at all—because it means something to us! He does not deny the interplay of the knowledge types, yet believes that knowing about music and the know-how of music services our foundational knowledge of music. For this reason, he believes that developing relationships with music through immersion in listening, responding, composing and performing should be at the heart of the objectives of every music lesson. For Swanwick, it is impossible to imagine a "musical" lesson that deals only with knowledge about or technical know-how divorced from the context of making or listening to music. However, learning about and learning how can take place in parallel with building meaningful relationships with music.

When designing lesson objectives in relation to the knowledge types, Swanwick (1979: 67) suggests that the following priorities should be observed:

- Category 1 objectives: for young people to recognise, identify, understand and use expressive gestures and structures in a range of styles (primarily knowledge *of* music);
- Category 2 objectives: for young people to engage in skill acquisition and literature studies; to assemble and categorise information (mainly concerned with knowing *how* and knowing *about*);
- Category 3 objectives: for young people to develop skills in human interaction (cooperation and sharing).

Swanwick is quite clearly saying that, for him, developing knowledge *of* music underpins music education. While he recognises the interrelationships between the knowledge types, he believes that Categories 2 and 3 *service* Category 1 objectives; that is, those objectives that aim to develop young people's meaningful relationships with music. However, it is notoriously difficult to plan for Category 1 objectives in the classroom. While many music educators have placed knowledge of as an ultimate aim of music education, there has been less agreement on how to achieve it. Metcalfe (1987) has shown that while the history of music education is littered with good intentions, many music curricula have become reductionist about musical knowledge, assuming that the only way we can teach music is by breaking down the holistic experience into chunks of knowledge about and knowledge how. Writers such as Reimer (1989) have suggested that in order to plan for knowledge of music, we must return to the nature of music itself. He asks us to consider how we understand music: what do we mean when we say we know a piece of music? Clearly, such knowledge does not merely amount to knowledge about or knowledge how, for this would exclude the intuitive musical understandings that young people bring with them to the classroom. Task 6.4 asks you to reflect on Swanwick's hierarchy of objective categories.

Task 6.4 **Swanwick's (1979) hierarchy**

What are your thoughts about Swanwick's hierarchy? To what extent can Category 1 develop without Categories 2 or 3? Do we need to address objectives in Categories 2 and 3 before we can achieve Category 1? Is it possible to have Category 1 learning as your overriding priority?

As illustrated here and in Chapter 8, there are many other accounts of musical knowledge that you should explore to inform your understanding of music education. For example, while Swanwick's hierarchy offers one case study example, the work of Elliott (1995, and his subsequent writing) has also been influential in this regard. Elliott focuses his attention on what he calls a *praxial* philosophy of music education, where the central concept of musicianship is underpinned by procedural knowledge that is further differentiated into interrelated knowledge types such as formal, informal, impressionistic and supervisory knowledge (see Chapters 1 and 2).

McPhail (2022) gives another important contemporary account of musical knowledge that draws on the wider field of social realism. While McPhail recognises the primary importance of an intuitive knowledge of music, he argues for a curriculum that is built around progressively sequenced disciplinary concepts. He proposes a typology where, "'knowledge-that' (concepts and content) and 'know-how-to' (knowledge applied) need to be developed together so that deep learning can occur" (171). McPhail's view therefore contrasts with Swanwick in prioritising knowing that, about and how above the intuitive when designing a curriculum.

In Swanwick (1979), Elliott (1995) and McPhail's (2022) accounts, musical knowledge is seen as being at the core of music education, and the nature of musical knowledge is derived from the essential nature and practice of music itself. They each aim to answer the question: what is it that we need to know in order to behave as a musician when listening, responding, composing and performing? You will begin to consider how this question matters in practice through Task 6.5.

Task 6.5 **Knowledge priorities at your school(s)**

In relation to Swanwick (1979), Elliot (1995) and McPhail (2022), what are the priorities for musical knowledge in the school in which you work or where you have been on placement? Discuss these questions with colleagues, mentors or other beginning teachers.

HOW DO WE LEARN MUSICAL KNOWLEDGE?

We now turn our attention to how musical knowledge is learnt. There has always been controversy surrounding how young people learn musical knowledge, and the following questions have exercised music educators for many years:

- What is the relationship between informal, intuitive, encultured learning and formal training and instruction?
- What account should teachers take of informal, intuitive and encultured learning?

Whatever our answers to these questions, it is clear that the "how" of musical learning is as complex as musical knowledge itself.

LEARNING TO TEACH MUSIC IN THE SECONDARY SCHOOL

Enculturation and instruction

One of the main concerns for how we learn in music is the relationship between "encultured" learning and "instructional" learning. Enculturation happens without conscious effort. This is learning that is "caught" by being part of a culture, through the music that is always around us. For example, we might "catch" how rap works and even be able to create and perform it. The instructional aspects of musical learning take place as a result of the intentional efforts of teachers and/or learners. For example, we might be taught how to analyse the technical aspects of rap and how to develop our skills of performance in rap.

There is an ongoing debate that surrounds the relationship between enculturation and instruction, with some suggesting that enculturation and instruction are quite separate, and that the latter is essential to making sense of the former. Others believe in the necessary and parallel interplay between each, while some espouse the need to trust the encultured learning of young people as fundamental to how they learn. The tensions in the debate about encultured and instructional musical learning can be found in Table 6.2, while Task 6.6 asks you to consider these issues in relation to your own experiences of music education.

Table 6.2 Some tensions in debating the "how" of musical learning

Encultured learning	Instructional learning
Osmosis (caught)	Instruction (taught)
Led by the young person	Led by the teacher
Encounter	Instruction
Knowing of music	Knowing the about and how of music
Intuition	Technique and analysis
Informal	Formal

Task 6.6 **Encultured and instructional learning**

Using a four-point scale where one is closest to *encultured learning* and four is closest to *instructional learning*, rate:

- the music education at your school as a child;
- the music education in any group of your choice;
- the music education at your current school or placement school;
- the music education you would like to promote.

Where do you find the majority of your answers? What are the differences between your answers for each? What does this activity tell you about your views of music education in relation to your past and current experiences?

What is clear is that these complexities need to be understood by teachers and taken into account when facilitating musical learning. To not do so may cause the disjuncture between the various aspects and moments of musical learning and the consequent alienation and poor motivation of young people, a situation that has often dogged classroom music in the past. However, current effective practice suggests that formal instruction and informal enculturation *can* co-exist in the classroom where knowledge types develop alongside and in parallel with each other. The theoretical resolution of the tensions of how we learn can be found in the broad concept of constructivism.

Constructivism

Constructivism is a theory of learning that embraces both enculturation and instruction. This theory of learning assumes that learning takes place when existing knowledge interacts with new learning experiences. Learning is not seen as a passive process but one in which the learner actively engages in the construction of knowledge. Here young people need to feel responsible for their learning, and their teachers need to facilitate learning experiences that encourage ownership and the productive interplay of enculturation and instruction.

Sloboda (1985) refers to intuitive musical learning as enculturation, which he maintains happens in "waves" without conscious effort or instruction in the early years of life. The formal aspects of music education are, he maintains, concerned with training and skill acquisition where skills are formed out of habits which become automatic after repetition. Sloboda deals with these two aspects of musical learning quite separately. He embraces our knowledge *of* music through our intuitive enculturation, and skills (*know-how*) through training and instruction. Sloboda suggests that we cannot progress significantly from the encultured state unless we engage with high-level skill development and that the role of formal education is to provide this training at various levels. For Sloboda, a new type of learning needs to take place after initial immersion in the culture, and on this analysis formal instructional learning exists in a linear and sequential relationship to informal and encultured learning.

Swanwick (1988) has also developed a constructivist theory of musical learning in which the knowledge types are integrated into a spiral of musical development. For Swanwick, learning from enculturation and instruction takes place in tandem. He suggests that music lessons should contain a productive tension between musical encounters (enculturation) and instruction, where knowledge of music is at the centre of all musical learning. Progress in learning moves *from* encultured learning *to* instructional learning and back again. That is, we can only make sense of instructional know-how and knowledge about music by building meaningful encultured relationships with it.

Social learning

Implicit in the constructivist work of both Sloboda (1985) and Swanwick (1988) is the dimension of *social learning*, and this has important implications for music teachers. Clearly, much (but not all) learning takes place within specific social and cultural contexts, and we are subjected to models of musical practice as part of both enculturation and instruction. At the heart of social learning is what Elliott (1995) calls "procedural knowledge": how to behave musically within a particular culture. For him, this learning can only develop in conditions where "real" music is being made in "real" circumstances, and where "the heart of the music curriculum [is] a musical teacher inducting students into musical practices through active music making" (Elliott 1995: 285). Plummeridge (1991) also takes up this point when he maintains that:

> The central aim of music education is to engage youngsters in practical activities through which they will come to learn and internalise the procedures of the discipline. In this way they develop musical thinking. . . . Procedures have to be taught . . . but there is a sense in which they are "caught" . . . people come to understand the methods, or procedures, of music by working with others who are on the inside of that discipline.
>
> (29)

Indeed, in much community-based music education (see Chapter 14), such as brass bands and church choirs, learning is based upon a healthy mixture of formal induction into musical practices and the "catching" of musical learning by osmosis—just by being there! The implications of social learning for music teachers are significant, and Task 6.7 asks you to think about them in relation to your practice:

- The music teacher is a model for young people's learning;
- The models we provide need to be as musical and as authentic as possible;
- Young people bring much social learning with them (e.g., from social media communities where music is discussed and shared);
- Young people can also be musical models for the learning of others (e.g., their peers and their teacher);
- The school and classroom can be seen as communities of musical learning.

Task 6.7 **Social learning**

What are the implications of social learning for music education, and how might the theory influence the way you teach? Prepare some notes as the basis for a seminar or discussion with colleagues or other beginning teachers.

Informal and formal learning

Another dimension to the constructivist take on how we learn in music is the issue and debate surrounding informal and formal learning. As we have seen, some musical learning takes place by being immersed in culture, and this is known as enculturation. There is a sense in which we cannot help this happening to us and, as such, this learning is "informal": it is not based upon formal instruction.

There is, however, another notion of informal learning abroad, which is more intentional on the part of young people. For example, this can be found when young people play, sing and compose music by themselves and often in their own time. The nature of learning in these circumstances has come to be known as informal learning. While enculturation and what we have come to call informal learning are closely related concepts, the latter is more obviously intentional.

In many ways the tension between the formal and informal has been at the core of the history of music education in the United Kingdom for the past fifty years. Music has often been reported as the most unpopular subject in the school curriculum and yet paradoxically the most important to young people outside school (Schools Council 1971; Harland et al. 2000). Indeed, the history of music education in the late twentieth and early twenty-first centuries can be seen as a series of attempts to "heal" this alienation (Philpott 2010).

The pedagogy of self-directed or "informal" learning was developed as a possible solution to ongoing issues of young people's alienation from school music, although it would be fair to suggest that, at present, this has a diminishing influence in the current climate across the United Kingdom. It is exemplified in the work of Green (2008) and Musical Futures (www.musicalfutures.org). Green used her work on how popular musicians learn to research a classroom pedagogy that explores the informal processes that some popular musicians appear to employ when learning in music:

> Playing music of one's own choice, with which one identifies personally, operating both as a performer and a composer with like-minded friends, and having fun doing it must be high priorities in the quest for increasing numbers of young people to benefit from a music education which makes music not merely available, but meaningful, worthwhile and participatory.
> (Green 2002: 216)

Green (2008: 9-10) has developed five principles for self-directed, informal learning and pedagogy:

- Young people work with music chosen by themselves that they enjoy and with which they identify;
- Young people work mainly through listening and copying;
- Young people work with peers in groups chosen by themselves;
- Skills and knowledge are gained in a haphazard fashion with whole "real" pieces at the core;
- Listening, performing and composing are integrated throughout the learning process.

Crucial to developing this informal pedagogy is the role of the teacher. Self-directed approaches promote informal learning and thus aim to begin with the musical ideas and knowledge of young people themselves. The role of the teacher in the learning process is relatively non-interventionist—teachers are seen as facilitators and resources for the young people to draw on. They are expected to:

- establish ground rules for behaviour;
- remind young people of the ongoing task at the start of each session;
- stand back and observe what the young people are doing;
- empathise with the perspectives and goals young people set themselves;
- diagnose young people's needs in relation to these perceived goals;
- offer suggestions and models for them to achieve their self-set goals;
- be available for help but not for instructing in the "normal" way.

It is clear that this approach is in stark contrast to the "formal" notion that the teacher decides what needs to be learnt and then plans a set of instructional strategies to make this happen. While the results of the research have been encouraging in terms of achievement, increased participation, ownership of the learning and breaking the cycle of alienation from school classroom music, critics remain concerned about the reduced role of the instructional interventions from a professional music teacher (Cain 2013). You will now consider these issues in Task 6.8.

Task 6.8 Informal self-directed learning

How much of your own learning has been self-directed and informal? Can you identify which aspects of your musical learning have developed as a result of this?

How can constructivism provide a resolution to the apparent tension between formal learning (initiated by teachers) and informal learning (initiated by young people)? Folkestad (2005, 2006) has recognised that the relationship between the formal and the informal is immensely complex. He maintains that an understanding of the relationship between the formal and the informal is crucial to understanding all musical learning, and he proposes the following distinction: formal learning can be characterised as the intentional, predetermined sequencing of learning activities by "a person who takes on the task of organising and leading the learning activity" (Folkestad 2006: 141). Teaching is always part of the formal moment, whoever does it. Informal learning can be characterised as being "not sequenced beforehand" and occurs during "self chosen and voluntary activity" (141). Task 6.9 asks you to consider Folkestad's analysis in relation to practice.

THE WHAT, HOW AND WHERE OF LEARNING

> ### Task 6.9 **Formal and informal learning**
>
> Using Folkestad's (2006) analysis discussed earlier, list examples under the following headings:
>
> - Formal learning in school;
> - Informal learning in school;
> - Formal learning out of school;
> - Informal learning out of school.

For Folkestad (2006), the crucial issue is the intentionality of the learner. Formal learning is found when the minds of young people and teachers are directed towards learning *how to play* music. Informal learning is found when minds are directed towards *playing and making* music. Furthermore, "what characterises most learning situations is the instant switch between these learning styles and the dialectic interaction between them" (142).

We can characterise this switch as "flipping"; for example, when a band improvises over a riff but then stops while one member teaches the others how to play a chord (see Figure 6.2). Most musicians will have experienced flipping, although the formal moment is often so prioritised in music education that the informal experience can be buried (Finney and Philpott 2010). And so, for Folkestad (2006), the relationship of formal to informal is not a dichotomy but a continuum: "in most learning situations, both of these aspects of learning are in various degrees present and interacting" (143). In the current context, the ready availability of mobile and smart technologies facilitate flipping between formal and informal learning for individuals and groups alike. This is a strong and powerful phenomenon which for some young people is entirely intuitive and is ignored by music teachers at their peril.

In relation to the "how" of learning in music, flipping is another manifestation of constructivism. However, it is important to make the point that formal instructional learning (how to play) is most likely to be accepted when it is perceived to be needed by the young people themselves, arising out of their

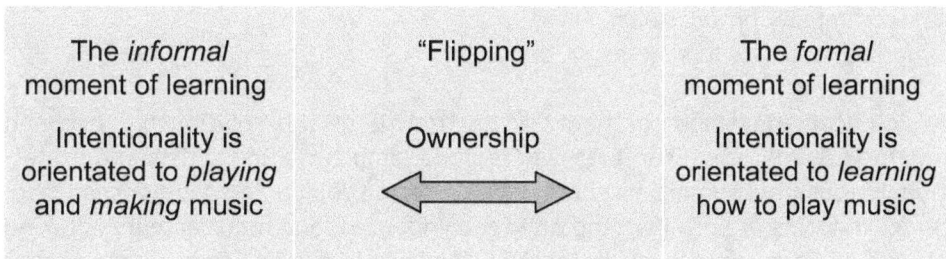

Figure 6.2 A model for musical learning

encultured, informal interests (focused on playing and making music) and thus *owned* by them.

WHERE DO WE LEARN MUSICAL KNOWLEDGE?

The "how" of musical learning is of course differentiated by "where" musical learning takes place, and it is to this that we now turn. There appear to be three interrelated contexts and settings for musical learning: formal, informal and non-formal, and yet these should not be confused with formal and informal learning.

Formal contexts

Formal contexts for musical learning include all of those settings where music education is planned as part of statutory provision. This includes schools and colleges delivering national curriculum frameworks and local music services offering tuition on a variety of instruments.

Informal contexts

Informal learning through both enculturation and self-directed learning often takes place in informal settings, individually or in groups outside institutional contexts. This can occur in-person and online. The use of a wider range of technologies (and especially mobile devices) and social media is a particularly significant context for informal learning that has important implications for young people's musical engagement. This is explored further in Chapter 3.

Non-formal contexts

Non-formal contexts for learning are an area of ever-increasing attention in music education. These include traditional community settings such as choirs and brass bands, but also:

- youth groups;
- local bands and choirs;
- music studios offering "clubs";
- community productions;
- visiting artists to schools.

A significant development here is the growth of the relationship between non-formal and formal contexts, where, for example, visiting artists and professional orchestras run either short- or long-term projects in schools (see Chapter 5). In terms of both learning and teaching, more and more activity is taking place in various contextual intersections and not in discrete formal, informal or non-formal sectors. The challenge for the secondary school music teacher is

THE WHAT, HOW AND WHERE OF LEARNING

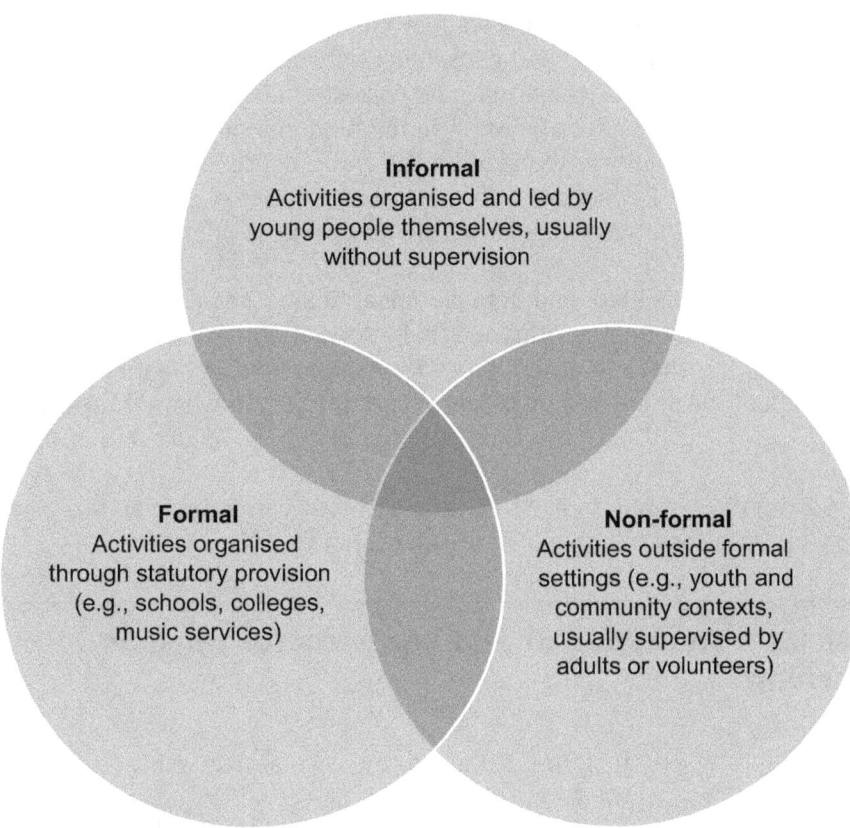

Figure 6.3 Formal, informal and non-formal contexts for music learning

to take account of these contexts and settings in their own planning for musical learning. Figure 6.3 aims to show this relationship, which you are asked to explore in Task 6.10.

Task 6.10 **Contexts for musical learning**

For each of formal, informal and non-formal music learning contexts:

a. Audit your own learning in each setting: what musical knowledge have you developed in each?
b. Identify ways in which the learning from one setting has informed or underpinned learning in another.
c. List three implications of this analysis for planning for musical learning in your classroom.
d. Have you observed any music teaching that has managed to take account of all three contexts?

While a setting often dictates *how* we learn (e.g., formal learning in formal settings), there is no necessary and causal link between the where and how (and indeed the what) of musical learning. As Folkestad (2005) has noted, the *how* is related to an intentional orientation to learning and not *where* we are learning. Young people might be engaged in all three contexts and bring learning from one to another. Formal and informal learning can take place in any physical space and are not limited to the school-home or school-community dichotomy:

> It is far too simplified, and actually false, to say that formal learning only occurs in institutional settings and that informal learning only occurs outside of school ... what are described as formal and informal learning styles are aspects of the phenomenon of learning regardless of where it takes place.
>
> (Folkestad 2005: 283)

Table 6.3 offers examples to illustrate how all types of learning can take place in all contexts. Use Task 6.11 to add your own scenarios.

Task 6.11 **The types of and contexts for musical learning**

1. Using a blank version of Table 6.3, try to fill in each section with an example of your own.
2. Using either Table 6.3 or your own version, outline how you would plan to integrate each example activity into your teaching. For example, if you were teaching a unit of work on the rondo, how might you integrate the learning and experience of the pop group or the cornet player?

Table 6.3 The types of and contexts for musical learning

		Context for learning		
		Formal context e.g., school music classroom	Informal context e.g., four friends form a pop group (online or face-to-face)	Non-formal context e.g., local brass band
Type of learning	Formal learning: An orientation to learning *how to* play music	A teacher leads a lesson on the nature and structure of rondo form.	One of the group asks a friend to teach her how to play two chords on a guitar to go with one of the songs.	An experienced cornet player begins to teach a child the rhythm of a part from a piece the band are studying.
	Informal learning: An orientation to *playing and making* music	Composing a rondo with a small group of peers.	The group learn a new tune together online and then at home after school.	A child sits in on a rehearsal even though they cannot yet play the part.

THE WHAT, HOW AND WHERE OF LEARNING

HOW DOES MUSICAL KNOWLEDGE DEVELOP?

We have explored the types of musical knowledge and how and where these might be learnt. We now turn to how young people develop musically. Why is a theory of musical development important to music teachers? You can use a theory of musical development to:

- recognise what it means to be musical;
- recognise that some young people are more or less musically developed than others;
- inform your short-, medium- and long-term planning, including that which occurs around transitions between key stages or phases in your curriculum;
- evaluate the impact of your teaching;
- help you assess musical learning both formatively and summatively.

We have identified that musical learning can be both intuitive and formal, encultured and instructional. Theories of musical development can provide us with a framework for understanding the role of both the formal and the informal in musical development. For example, the sequence of learning is vital to successful teaching, and thus a theory of development helps you to decide if you are "putting the cart before the horse." The wrong sequence of learning can demotivate and alienate young people.

Task 6.12 encourages you to engage with the notion of musical development, first through your own intuitive perceptions and then through some influential models of development. You will be asked to apply these to your practice in schools and to reflect on their usefulness.

Task 6.12 **Musical development**

1. Draw a table that shows your intuitive sense of how musical knowledge, learning and engagement will manifest itself in the development of 5-, 8-, 11- and 15-year-olds. Consider:

    a. the sorts of music they listen to;
    b. the sorts of comments they might make about music;
    c. what you might notice about their singing or performing;
    d. what their composing will be like.

2. Once you have done this, compare your answers to Table 6.4. This summarises some simplified models of musical and artistic development.

> 3. Using Table 6.4:
>
>   a. identify any similarities between the theories;
>   b. identify any contradictions between the theories;
>   c. do any of the theories confirm or contradict your own experience thus far?
>
> Share and discuss your answers with colleagues or other beginning teachers.

Despite the differences in emphasis between the theories shared in Table 6.4, it does seem that there is a broad sequence to musical development; it is not random. It is, however, important to emphasise that any ages attached to musical development need to be read with considerable caution. You are likely to find young people of vastly different developmental stages in the same class.

Musical development, assessment and transitions

Even if you do not have a fully worked out "theory" of musical development, Task 6.12 demonstrates that we all make intuitive assumptions about musical development that inform our everyday work as music teachers. This is especially the case in relation to assessment in the music classroom.

In our summative assessment *of* musical learning, different levels or stages of development will underpin the criteria we use to make judgements about compositions and performances. Models of musical development are inherent in the criteria that we use, whether they are derived from a national curriculum or examination assessment regime, or invented by teachers and classes in response to specific units and lessons. Every summative judgement in assessment of learning is a statement about the musical development of the young people involved. Levels or stages of musical development also underpin formative assessment *for* learning in the music classroom. When we ask questions, give feedback, provide models and set targets for young people, we intuitively engage with our sense of musical development as part of the formative discourse that is assessment for learning (Philpott 2009).

Furthermore, assessment of learning and assessment for learning are vital tools in planning for transitions between units of work, from one school year to the next and between key stages or phases of your curriculum framework. These tools provide us with ways of coming to know young people's developmental stages, such that we can support their musical learning and facilitate the development of their musical knowledge. While more detail can be found on these themes in Chapter 10 on assessment, you will need to be aware of both the implicit and explicit relationship between the development of musical knowledge and appropriate and timely assessment.

THE WHAT, HOW AND WHERE OF LEARNING

Table 6.4 Some models of musical and artistic development

	Ages 0–4	Ages 5–9	Ages 10–15	Ages 16+
Swanwick (1988)	Materials: being impressed by extremes of sound (e.g., dynamics, timbre); making rambling explorations of instruments or the voice	Expression: making gross musical gestures (e.g., loudness to express song words); later on, recognising musical conventions (e.g., metrical four-bar units)	Form: experimenting with structure (e.g., surprise and contrast); later developing a desire for empathy with authentic structures from immediate culture (e.g., pop songs)	Value: coming to value music as special, with personal significance; sometimes becoming discursive on own and others' music
Parsons et al. (1978)		Perceiving artistic objects in terms of their own experience	Understanding the "rules" of public use of artistic symbols	Understanding that a wide variety of traditions and styles exist
Shuter-Dyson and Gabriel (1981)	Very young children (0–1): reacting to sounds. Older children (2–3): reproducing bits of songs	Beginning to understand basic sound elements; discriminating pitch and rhythm	Improving in musical perception and skill (i.e., tonal and rhythmic); establishing harmonic sense	Increasing cognitive and emotional response to music
Sloboda (1985)	Enculturation: spontaneously acquiring musical skill; lacking self-conscious effort and explicit instruction	Enculturation: improving ability to pick up songs, without consciously aspiring to do so	Training: self-consciously engaging in training; participating in experiences specific to a subculture but based on the foundation of enculturation	Training: contributing to a depth of knowledge and accomplishment in a narrow skill area, developed through instruction
Ross (1982)	Engaging through sensory play; developing early relationships to the mood of music	Doodling and mastering sound patterns	Establishing emergent musical procedures, conventional competence and association with idiom	Expressing personality, embodying meaning, vision and significance

MUSIC AND WIDER EDUCATIONAL LEARNING

Finally, we turn to an aspect of musical learning that has taken on an increasing importance in advocacy for music in the curriculum: the relationship of learning in music to other areas of knowledge, skill and understanding.

The transfer of musical learning

One of the justifications for music in the curriculum is that learning *in* the discipline leads to a good deal of learning *through* it; in other words, there is transfer to other areas of the curriculum and to young people's general development. While you should exercise caution so as not to become over-reliant on justifying music in terms of its influence on learning in other subjects, there is some evidence for such effects (Hallam and Himonides 2022). It has been claimed that music education might have positive transferable effects in:

- aural perception;
- performance in mathematics;
- spatial reasoning;
- aural and visual memory;
- literacy skills;
- intellectual development;
- language skills.

Task 6.13 will help you reflect on the transfer of musical learning.

Task 6.13 **The transfer of learning**

(1) Can you add to the list of transferable learning?
(2) Have you experienced or observed any of these transferable effects of learning through your experience of music?
(3) How and why do you think this effect occurred? Try to give specific examples from your own learning or that of young people at your school. Record what you have noticed and discuss this with a colleague, mentor or another beginning teacher.

Research into the transfer of learning in music education is a strong theme for much current scholarship, where the outcomes are used to make a positive case for the extrinsic importance of music in the secondary school curriculum. However, the evidence needs to be read critically, especially where such justifications overshadow those for (a) the intrinsic value of music itself and (b) the deep relationships between all subjects.

Beyond transfer

The notion that music can be singly and uniquely responsible for learning in other areas of the curriculum has some potential drawbacks, not least that such

THE WHAT, HOW AND WHERE OF LEARNING

exceptionalism can isolate music from an understanding of its deep and equitable relationships with other subjects and disciplines. One way of thinking about the relationship of music to wider learning is not that it has a special and exceptional impact, but that music is deeply related to other disciplines and that this relationship has implications for mutually beneficial cross-curricular learning.

For music, cross-curricular learning has most commonly been associated with other arts, where there is rich potential for equitable collaboration between visual, aural, kinaesthetic, verbal and enactive artistic modes. Indeed, in the world beyond school these disciplines frequently work together in opera, ballet, musical theatre, film and so on. By the same token, this means that there are opportunities for collaborative arts projects in and beyond the classroom, which:

- reflect what happens in "real life";
- are consistent with the encultured and informal learning of young people;
- support the human mind in making connections that make sense of the world.

This last point is important when justifying cross-curricular work where it can enhance learning in the "home" subject, other disciplines and across young people's wider education.

Barnes (2023) argues that such learning is not just about relationships between the arts but also about relationships between all subjects. Amongst other things, cross-curricular learning can:

- introduce values that unite themes and concepts across subjects (e.g., critical thinking and cultural context);
- model multisensory learning and connections between different ways of understanding the world;
- develop open and flexible attitudes to problem-solving and decision-making;
- provoke a rich and diverse approach to creativity and imagination;
- exemplify diversity.

Task 6.14 will help you reflect on interdisciplinary learning.

Task 6.14 **Interdisciplinary learning**

1. In what ways are you conscious of having been part of cross-curricular or interdisciplinary learning during your education (not necessarily music specific)?
2. What are the commonalities between music and other arts subjects?
3. What is the potential for combining music learning with sciences and humanities?

Share your answers with other teachers. Then design a lesson or short unit of work that models an equitable and multidisciplinary approach to learning across a group of disciplines (see Barnes 2023 for further support on starting points).

Music learning, then, can be seen as part of wider learning both for its own sake as a subject and also in its deep relationship with all disciplinary modes.

SUMMARY

In this chapter we have seen that:

- musical knowledge can be differentiated into several types;
- knowledge "of" music is particularly important in a constructivist approach to musical learning, where young people build meaningful relationships with their own music and the music of others;
- musical knowledge is developed through the interplay between encultured/informal/intuitive learning and formal/instructional learning;
- the informal and formal musical learning of young people can be developed in many different contexts;
- an understanding of musical development is vital if you are to plan and assess musical knowledge in your classes;
- learning in music can have important transferable effects to learning in other areas of young people's development,
- we should, however, also consider the ways in which music is deeply related to other subjects in learning across the curriculum.

FURTHER READING

Barnes, J. (2011)
Cross-Curricular Learning 3–14, 2nd edn, London: SAGE.

This is a detailed account of the wider potential of cross-curricular learning.

Hallam, S. and Himonides, E. (2022)
The Power of Music: An Exploration of the Evidence, Cambridge: Open Book Publishers.

This is a comprehensive review of research on the impact of music on the intellectual, social and personal development of young people.

Hargreaves, D.J. (1986)
The Developmental Psychology of Music, Cambridge: Cambridge University Press.

Hargreaves offers a valuable overview of psychological issues that impinge on musical learning.

Swanwick, K. (1979)
A Basis for Music Education, Windsor: NFER-Nelson.

Swanwick, K. (1988)
Music, Mind and Education, London: Routledge.

Swanwick's seminal publications develop an influential theory of musical knowledge, learning and development.

WHAT IS A MUSIC CURRICULUM?

Carolyn Cooke with Gary Spruce and Anthony Anderson

> The school curriculum, construed as what is intended to be learned and what is actually learned, constitutes an important means by which educational transformations occur. This is the point where theory meets practices, where ideas and beliefs are actualized in the phenomenal world.
>
> (Jorgensen 2003: 72)

INTRODUCTION

As a beginning teacher going into school for the first time, perhaps as part of a course of initial teacher education, it is likely that you will be presented with some form of "curriculum document" for music. This might be a "programme of study" or a detailed "scheme of work." For classroom teaching at Key Stage 3 in England (11- to 14-year-olds), or in the Broad General Education phase of the Scottish Curriculum for Excellence, for example, a programme of study is a very popular approach with music teachers. It usually consists of a summary document outlining music topics, the sequence in which they are to be taught, their duration and their scheduling across the academic year for different year groups (Anderson 2021). Representative examples of these kinds of topics are headings such as "The Elements of Music," "The Blues," "Minimalism" or "Film Music." Alternatively, if you are working with a class preparing for an external examination, you might just be given the examination syllabus or specification to use as the basis for planning lessons or units of work. Your success as a beginning teacher, and how well you "fit into" the music department, may be dependent on how effectively your teaching is seen as reflecting the perceived intentions of that documentation.

This conception of curriculum as a *document* that specifies what teachers will teach (and sometimes how they should teach) and what young people will learn (e.g., a national, school or subject curriculum) is the way in which curriculum is typically understood within government policy and media and political discussions and debates. Consequently, this conception of curriculum has come to dominate educational discourse, such that it is difficult, perhaps, to contemplate other ways of thinking about what a curriculum might be or might do.

However, is such a document the sum total of a curriculum? If asked, "what is your school's music curriculum?" would it be sufficient to offer in response a copy of the national curriculum or the school's curriculum document or scheme of work? We suggest not. In this chapter we propose a much broader and richer conception of what is meant by a music curriculum. In doing so, we prompt some fundamental questions about the purposes, ideologies and values that underpin conceptions of a music curriculum and, in particular, who the music curriculum is for. We will suggest that a music curriculum is more than simply a fixed and static document that teachers use as a template to guide their teaching but rather has the potential to be a dynamic phenomenon that emerges from the interactions and interrelationships between teachers, learners and what there is to be learnt. We will argue that a curriculum conceived in such a way has the potential to empower teachers and to address some of the issues that cause many young people to become disenchanted with, and alienated from, the formal school music curriculum.

Objectives

By the end of this chapter you should:

- be able to examine critically your own views about the purposes and aims of a music curriculum;
- understand different conceptions of curriculum and the potential implications of these for music education;
- understand how young people experience curriculum and how they see their role within it;
- understand what an emergent music curriculum might look and sound like within the classroom and how it might be enacted.

YOUR BELIEFS ABOUT MUSIC CURRICULUM

Conceptions of what a music curriculum is—or should be—are inevitably underpinned by particular beliefs and values—and particularly *musical* beliefs and values. As Regelski (2005) says:

> The most basic curricular thinking involves the question: of all that can be taught, what is most worth learning? There is always more to teach than time and resources permit, and decisions concerning what to teach and for what ends involve important questions about the value of music and, hence, of music education.
>
> (220)

■ ■ ■ ■ **WHAT IS A MUSIC CURRICULUM?**

Before beginning to explore and critique different conceptions of curriculum, we want you to examine your own beliefs about what a music curriculum should be, what it should do and who it is for. A starting point for such thinking is to acknowledge that these beliefs almost inevitably, and legitimately, are rooted in your own previous experiences (both positive and negative) of music education and being a musician. These experiences will colour your evaluation of, and attitudes towards, different kinds of and approaches to music curricula. One can never uncouple oneself completely from one's previous experiences (and neither should one try to), but acknowledging their existence is an important first step towards reflecting critically upon them and being open to alternative visions of–in this case–what a music curriculum might be. These alternative visions will emerge, inevitably, from changes to official policy, but also from schools, other teachers, research and scholarship, and–perhaps most importantly–from young people themselves, if we are prepared to listen to what they have to say. As Task 7.1 illustrates, it is by understanding our existing views, where they stem from and actively researching and trying alternatives that we can develop music curricula to best support the young people we teach.

Task 7.1 **Your own experiences of music curriculum**

1. Construct a table like the one that follows. Then, thinking about your own experience of music curricula when you were a young person at school:

   a. in the *first* column, list the different contexts in which you learnt music. These might include a whole-class curriculum, an instrumental or vocal lesson curriculum or an examination curriculum;
   b. in the *second* column, note down the kind of learning that took place in these different contexts. What kinds of musical learning were developed in each one?
   c. in the *third* column, describe your experiences of these contexts. Were they positive or negative experiences for you, and why?

Musical context	Learning	Experiences

2. Now write a statement that outlines your current thinking about what is important for a successful curriculum, using the sentence stems:

   a. "An effective music curriculum for teachers should . . ."
   b. "An effective music curriculum for young people should . . ."

   Be clear about why you think you hold the views that you do and how your own experiences as a young person, musician and, if appropriate, teacher have influenced these views. Find an opportunity to discuss your views with other (beginning) teachers, either online, in seminars or in school. Where there are differences in your points of view, try to identify what these result from.

THE MUSIC CURRICULUM AS OBJECT – IMPLICATIONS OF CURRICULUM REIFICATION

At the beginning of this chapter, we suggested that "curriculum" is commonly understood as being synonymous with a "curriculum document." This document then acts as a template for what is to be taught and learnt (e.g., a national curriculum). In academic literature, this conception of the curriculum is typically referred to either as "curriculum as content," where the document limits itself to specifying the knowledge and skills to be learnt (e.g., examination specifications), or "curriculum as product."

"Curriculum as product" builds on "curriculum as content" in identifying not only what is to be learnt but also how learning content and experiences are sequenced (aspects of pedagogy) and how learning is recognised and evaluated (aspects of assessment). As its name suggests, "curriculum as product" is concerned primarily with the achievement of "some kind of desirable end product" such as "knowledge of certain facts, mastery of specific skills and competencies, and acquisition of appropriate attitudes and values" (Abie 2014: 153).

The characteristics of curriculum as content and curriculum as product and some of their manifestations in music curricula are described in Table 7.1 and explored in Task 7.2.

Task 7.2 Exploring curriculum as content and product

Go to the document or website for a post-16 specification that you are, or might be, teaching (e.g., A-level, Higher or Advanced Higher, BTEC). Analyse this in detail in terms of the characteristics of content- and product-driven curricula identified in Table 7.1. What particular musical values, knowledge and skills do you think are being promoted through the specification? To what extent do you feel that these priorities are able to accommodate and support the development of all young people?

Table 7.1 The music curriculum as content and product

Curriculum as...	Characteristics	Examples from music education
Content	Limited to specifying the knowledge to be studied and learnt.	■ Programmes of study ■ School music examinations (e.g., GCSE, A-level, International Baccalaureate, Scottish Highers) ■ Graded music theory examinations

(Continued)

WHAT IS A MUSIC CURRICULUM?

Table 7.1 Continued

		▪ Graded instrumental and vocal examinations ▪ National curriculum documents (e.g., English National Curriculum, Scottish Curriculum for Excellence, National Standards in the United States)
Product	Learning objectives are identified and set, a plan is devised for achieving these objectives, the plan is implemented, and the outcomes are measured. This "managerial" approach to education underpins the "performativity" agendas described above (Abie 2014).	▪ National curriculum documents as "delivered" through school curricula ▪ Commercial curriculum packages (e.g., Musical Futures, Charanga) ▪ Performance-based curricula (e.g., the American band method) ▪ Curriculum measured through "outcomes" such as the quality of a performance or accurate notation of a composition

Both curriculum as content and curriculum as product are what might be described as "reified" forms of curriculum. One of the ways in which reification can be understood is as a process whereby essentially abstract phenomena are treated or thought of as concrete objects. In music, reification occurs when we come to think of "the music" and "the score" as synonymous. A consequence of reification is that meaning is seen as being inherent in the reified form of the abstraction (the score or curriculum document) and consequently remains fixed in all times and places. As shown in Box 7.1, the unquestioning acceptance of this reified conception of the curriculum often comes across in the way in which music teachers talk about curriculum.

Box 7.1 **Teachers' statements about curriculum**

a. "The curriculum tells me what musical genres to teach and when."
b. "The curriculum is a document that helps me to plan lessons in the correct sequence so that the young people develop the skills and knowledge they need to work towards the end-of-term assessment."
c. "The curriculum outlines all the musical learning that takes place over the key stage."
d. "The curriculum tells me how to teach using the department's resources."
e. "The curriculum makes sure all young people achieve the stated outcomes by the end of the term."
f. "The curriculum has stayed pretty much the same for the past five years after a big rewrite we did to incorporate more group work."

What is evident in the statements in Box 7.1 is that irrespective of whether a music curriculum is *imposed upon* teachers (e.g., national curricula or exam specifications) or *created by* teachers, it is thought of in a reified way and carried out as a well-tested master plan to guarantee that young people learn and meet predefined outcomes. Teachers then become what Savage (2013), perhaps a touch tendentiously, describes as "a white-van curriculum delivery service, dropping off pre-ordained packages of curriculum content within a set timetable of deliveries" (85), with young people as "curriculum consumers" (Philpott 2012a: 154).

The attraction for teachers of thinking about curriculum in this reified way is that it allows for the curriculum to be prepared prior to its enactment within the classroom. Learning outcomes and teaching strategies can be identified and content selected and structured away from the immediacy of the classroom moment. Reified conceptions of curriculum are also attractive to commercial organisations, which can produce off-the-shelf curriculum "packages" to be purchased by schools for implementation in the classroom. Reified conceptions of curriculum are also powerful political tools (which is why this conception of curriculum typifies contemporary policy), as it allows for dominant social groups to exert direct influence over a curriculum's content, pedagogy and assessment and the learning dispositions it promotes.

In this reified form of curriculum, young people are treated simply as curriculum consumers and often come to see the curriculum as something in which they have little investment, as something that is "void of self" (Giddens in Schmidt 2005: 5). This lack of investment is further aggravated by the way in which reification promotes the idea that a music curriculum is only that which happens within school (where it can be controlled), as comes through clearly in the teacher statements in Box 7.1. However, we know that young people are active as listeners, performers and composers beyond the classroom during their teenage years (Hargreaves and Marshall 2003; Lamont et al. 2003; North et al. 2000) and that this has a significant impact on how they relate to music in the formal classroom setting. If young people come to believe that they have little investment in or ownership of a curriculum, and that it ignores their musical lives and identities outside school, this can easily result in alienation from curriculum realisations and from formal school music education.

CURRICULUM AS A LIVED EXPERIENCE

So, what is the alternative? Style (1996) introduces the idea of curriculum as both a mirror and window, reflecting a young person's identity and revealing the identities of others. She describes this as enabling young people to see themselves in a curriculum (mirror) and to understand others better by looking beyond (window). These ideas are powerful for music in the classroom, where musical discoveries through making and creating hinge on revealing and developing musical identities through reflective and interactive work.

■ ■ ■ ■ WHAT IS A MUSIC CURRICULUM?

Alternative framings propose that curriculum may be multi-dimensional, with different aspects operating in diverse ways at the same time. For instance, Pollard and Triggs (1997) suggest that curriculum can be conceptualised in four ways:

1. *Official curriculum*: this almost always exists as a document and sets out the knowledge to be acquired, the sequence of learning, assessment and so on. This is what we have called the "reified curriculum."
2. *Hidden curriculum*: everything that is learnt that isn't an explicit part of a curriculum but may have a profound impact on the young person's attitude towards education and learning.
3. *Observed curriculum*: what is observed happening in the classroom.
4. *Curriculum-as-experienced*: what the young people connect to—how they "live" the curriculum, both official and hidden.

What Pollard and Triggs (1997) are suggesting here is that a reified curriculum can only ever tell us part of the story of what goes on in the music classroom. To understand a curriculum, we need to triangulate how this curriculum is described in documents and conversations based on reified curriculum conceptions, with what can be seen to happen in the classroom, *and* with what young people actually experience (see Figure 7.1). Pollard and Triggs thus bring into the curriculum equation the hitherto missing element of the young people themselves. To understand their lived experiences of a music curriculum will involve careful attention to their musical responses to a curriculum but also to how they describe their experiences verbally. As a beginning teacher and throughout your career, conversations with young people like those suggested in Task 7.3 are an excellent starting point to begin to understand how they have "lived" curriculum.

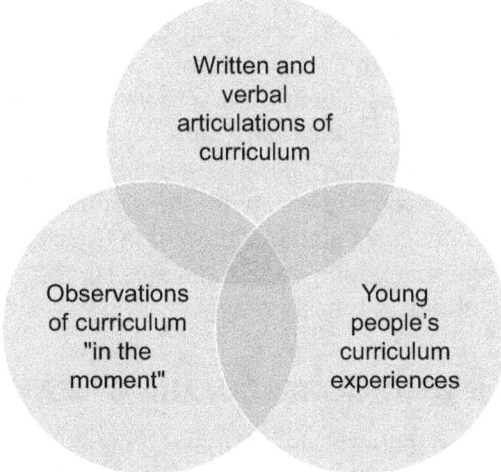

■ **Figure 7.1** Understanding curriculum

> ### Task 7.3 **Talking with young people about curriculum**
>
> Spend time with two young people in different year groups, talking to them about their curriculum experiences in your setting. You might ask questions such as:
>
> - Have they been given information about the music curriculum and, if so, what?
> - What information are they given at the start of a new unit about what they will be doing?
> - How do they see their role in the curriculum?
> - What types of experiences do they find positive and valuable?
> - What do these positive and valuable experiences have in common (if anything)?
> - What musical experiences do they have beyond class?
> - Do they feel connections between the musical experiences they have in and beyond the classroom?

Talking with young people about their lived experiences of curriculum provides a valuable insight into their views—but only into the issues that they can express verbally. Asking any young person to recall and describe accurately their musical experiences, using terminology that avoids ambiguity for either party, is a tall order. Moreover, such conversations still tell us little about the way in which curriculum is *enacted* within individual classrooms with individual teachers and individual young people. Curriculum comes alive only in the moment, and it is in that moment that we come to know what a curriculum actually involves and what those participating actually believe such a curriculum to be. We are not referring here to the moments spent deciding a curriculum map in a planning session, buying resources, writing curriculum documents for parents or young people, or even planning individual lessons. Rather, we are talking about the momentary, spontaneous, improvisatory interactions that happen with young people in the classroom each minute of a lesson.

As we begin to explore what a curriculum created "in the moment" might mean in practice, it becomes more obvious that reified conceptions of the curriculum are inadequate for describing what actually happens when a curriculum is enacted in the classroom. Reifications fail to take account of the complex, unique ways in which a music curriculum as a lived experience brings together different influences, and the resulting myriad of different personal encounters and outcomes that impact curriculum enactment in the classroom. In particular, it fails to recognise the role young people have as co-creators of a curriculum through their contributions to these moments.

YOUNG PEOPLE AND CURRICULUM CREATING

Central to a non-reified conception of music curriculum is the belief that young people play an active role in creating a curriculum. This is a radically different approach from the curriculum-as-content and curriculum-as-product

WHAT IS A MUSIC CURRICULUM?

approaches which tend to dominate educational policy and discourse. We are not suggesting here that young people are not already given the opportunity to do this in most, if not all, music classrooms. No matter how content- or product-driven a curriculum is, teachers' decisions, musical resources and social interactions within a class at any particular moment will inevitably mean that young people exert influence on what happens in the music classroom and are therefore active creators of their curriculum experiences. What we are arguing for here is a greater recognition of this influence and an approach to curriculum that deliberately promotes this kind of engagement and creates an environment in which young people explicitly recognise the role they play.

If young people are to play such a role in curriculum design and realisation, it requires us to rethink conventional conceptualisations of the role of the teacher and the learner, the nature of musical knowledge and the interrelationship between teacher, learner and what is learnt. Above all, it requires us to understand how complex social and contextual factors shape curriculum. In addressing this complexity, Cornbleth (1990) defines curriculum as "an ongoing social process comprised of the interactions of students, teachers, knowledge and milieu" (5). The milieu, or context within which curriculum is situated, might include, among other things, the learning environment, the classroom resources and the particular time and day (see Figure 7.2). But Cornbleth argues that none of these individual factors—or even all of them together—form a curriculum. She identifies an equal relationship between young people, teachers, knowledge and the broader context, and suggests that it is the *interactions between* these factors that create a curriculum through an ongoing, ever-developing *social process*.

Task 7.4 **Interactions within a lesson**

Think of a music lesson that you have taught or observed. Make a more detailed version of the diagram in Figure 7.2 showing the interactions that occurred during that lesson. You could include the following factors to help you start:

- The experiences and views of the music teacher about the topic (the knowledge and skills perceived as important);
- The prior experiences and views of the young people about the topic;
- The experiences of the young people during the topic;
- The musical experiences of the young people in and out of school;
- The resources available to the young people and the teacher;
- The influence of interpersonal relationships between young people in the class;
- The approaches of other teachers towards the topic;
- The time and place of the lesson.

Wegerif describes such social processes as forming "dialogic space" where there is a "dynamic continuous emergence of meaning" from the "interplay of two or more perspectives" (Wegerif in Spruce 2015: 297). Wegerif is suggesting here that the interplay between young people and the musical resources, young people and

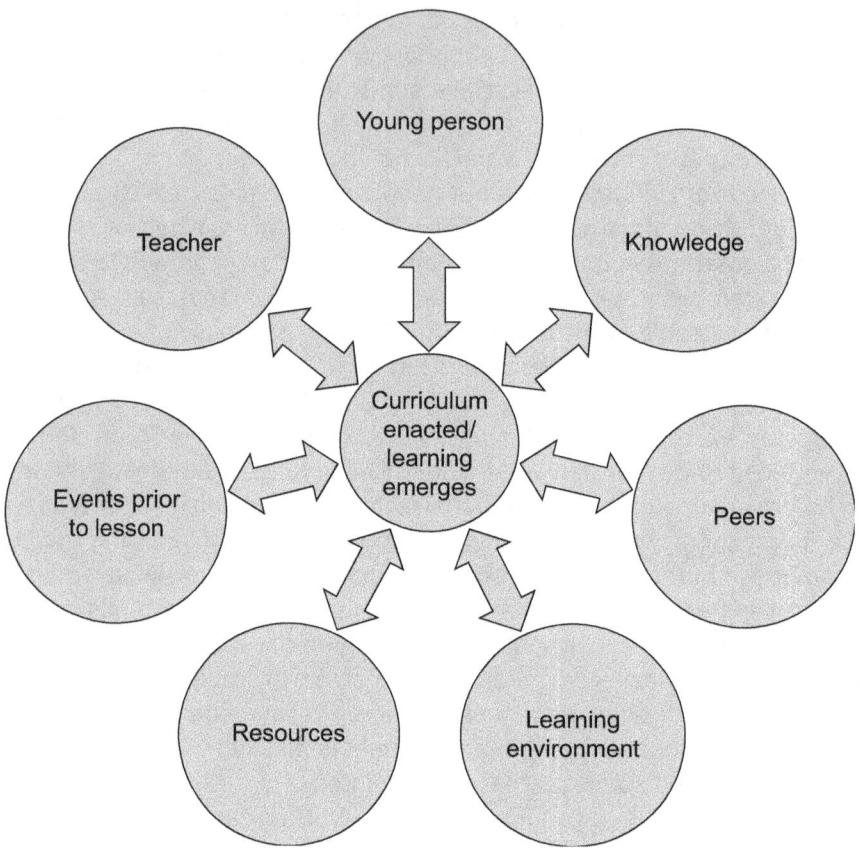

■ **Figure 7.2** Interactions leading to an emerging curriculum

their teacher, young people and their peers, and young people and the learning environment all involve the coming together of different perspectives. As Spruce (2015: 298) argues, each perspective brings with it particular historical, cultural, political, philosophical and experiential dimensions in a complex interplay, which is influenced by and itself influences the moment of interaction. Consequently, each interaction is unique to the individuals involved and to the moment in which it occurs. In other words, every individual, and every individual instance in which the music curriculum is enacted, will produce a different musical outcome or new musical learning unique to that moment, as it brings together a particular set of variables that are unlikely to be re-created in a different moment.

Doll uses the term "dancing curriculum" (Doll in Fenwick et al. 2011: 37). This term provides a useful metaphor to help us explain these ideas, where knowledge is constantly moving and interacting with resources, materials, the environment, each other and the teacher. Curriculum that is constantly under the influence of these interactions is never fixed or static, but always developing, creating new moments that can lead to new interactions and learning. This isn't to say that there is no place for teacher planning and preparation; indeed, the teacher role becomes vital in helping choreograph the dance, enabling new interactions to occur and providing the environment, resources and activities to stimulate the curriculum experience. As Beghetto (2012) argues, "moments of creative potential . . . emerge in everyday routines, practices and planned experiences" (134). What becomes the teacher's responsibility is ensuring that such routines, practices and planned activities provide rich and diverse interactions that enable young people's knowledge to emerge or develop from their lived experiences.

Recognising the central role young people have as co-creators of their own lived experiences through their interactions with teachers, each other, resources and the environment, and understanding their learning as *emerging from* these interactions challenges us to imagine a different way of planning, teaching and interacting. The final section of this chapter will explore the idea of an "emergent curriculum" and what it might involve in practice.

EMERGENT CURRICULUM

The idea of "emergent curriculum" has gained credence in curriculum literature (Osberg and Biesta 2008; Davis and Sumara 2006). While it is difficult to provide a comprehensive overview within the confines of this chapter, there are some key elements of emergent curriculum that resonate strongly with the previous discussion of music curriculum as a lived experience and are worth exploring in more detail. In an emergent curriculum,

- knowledge emerges as "human beings participate in the world" and therefore only exists "in our participatory actions" (Osberg and Biesta 2008: 313). In other words, knowledge is formed through interactions, either with peers, teachers, resources or other influences;
- we should be "concerned with the emergence of meaning [through these interactions] rather . . . than with the transfer of meaning from teacher to student" (Osberg and Biesta 2008: 314). The purpose of a curriculum is therefore no longer to facilitate the acquisition of knowledge *about* an abstract reality, but for young people to *find* their own reality;
- the aim is not to bring about "the convergence of individual perspectives . . . by attempting to initiate or socialize [young people] into a common way of being," but to maintain difference, enabling them "to become more unique" (Osberg and Biesta 2008: 324).
- we are less concerned with the content and presentation of a curriculum than with the idea "that content is *engaged* with and *responded* to." "The content that is engaged with is not pre-given, but emerges from the educative situation itself" (Osberg et al. 2008: 225; our italics).

Task 7.5 helps you to explore the implications of an emergent curriculum within a music education context.

> ## Task 7.5 Identifying interactions that lead to emergence
>
> Reflect on a music lesson you have taught or observed and answer the following questions:
>
> 1. What types of interaction (musical and non-musical) did young people experience during the lesson?
> 2. Who or what (peers, teachers, technologies, musical instruments, paper-based resources, learning environment) were the interactions between?
> 3. On the following spectrum between the transfer of someone else's knowledge and the emergence of young people's knowledge, mark where you feel each of these interactions best sits:
>
> ←—————————————————————————→
>
> Transfer of someone　　　　　　　　　　　Emergence of young
> else's knowledge or　　　　　　　　　　　people's own knowledge
> meanings　　　　　　　　　　　　　　　　or meanings
>
> 4. How far did the interactions in the lesson seek out, share and encourage differences of opinion, approach and outcomes?
> 5. To what extent was the lesson evaluated in terms of whether content was "covered"?

This view of curriculum as a constantly developing framework within which to facilitate young people's interactions, resulting in the emergence of their own knowledge and meanings, represents a significant shift in thinking from other conceptualisations of curriculum. In this view, curriculum is "dynamic, self-renewing and [engaged with] creatively" (Osberg et al. 2008: 225). As explored in Task 7.6, to achieve this involves an awareness as to how other conceptions of curriculum may limit such emergence.

> ## Task 7.6 Reviewing curriculum statements
>
> Spend a few minutes reviewing teachers' statements about curriculum in Box 7.1. In what ways would the views of curriculum in these statements limit young people's interactions and the emergence of their own musical knowledge and meanings?

As Tasks 7.4 and 7.5 demonstrate, an emergent curriculum raises significant challenges and opportunities for music teachers. These are examined in the following sections, which outline the principles that underpin an emergent curriculum, their implications for an emergent music curriculum and practical examples (Boxes 7.2 to 7.6) of what an emergent music curriculum might look and sound like.

WHAT IS A MUSIC CURRICULUM?

Conceptualising curriculum as a lived experience

As young people interact as musicians, both with each other and with their learning context, they will inevitably be drawing on their previous experiences, whether from school, home or the wider community. Therefore, the music curriculum as a lived experience is not constrained to young people's musical participation at school but embraces their wider musical experiences from across diverse contexts (Green 2005). This challenges music teachers to understand young people's musicianship in all its manifestations in order to create interactions that build on but also provide alternative perspectives to their existing experiences. As illustrated in Box 7.2, to do this effectively involves young people negotiating the next stages of the curriculum with their teacher, identifying what they want to explore, how they want to engage with it, what resources they will need and, most importantly, what experiences and ideas they already have in relation to the topic. This means that music curricula as designed and practised by music teachers will be diverse in formulation.

As well as responding to the needs of young people in their local contexts, music curricula will also demonstrate wide variety due to the richness of music teacher background, identity and experience (Anderson 2024). As such, they can be expected to be widely divergent in style, choice of topics and materials, and sequencing. Comparing school curricula across different settings is likely to reveal such differences, which indicate their moulding to young people's needs and music teachers' backgrounds, rather than a failure to conform to regimented pedagogical models.

Box 7.2 Curriculum as lived experience

Susie, a GCSE student, DJs at the weekends, so her class teacher has been working with her to explore how DJing links to the minimalism unit. By making some initial connections, Susie has started making all sorts of other links which are now coming through in her minimalist composition, which uses electronic samples and phasing. She has also become very interested in how the American minimalist composer Reich's work has been used in dance music.

Just learning about and practising the formulaic techniques of minimalism would have had such a superficial impact compared to the deep, integrated learning that Susie has generated with her teacher. It has also been an opportunity for her teacher to expand their knowledge and perspective on minimalist style and its impact upon other genres and practices.

Curriculum as a contextually connected experience

An emergent curriculum will inevitably be contextually connected by the particular influences and interactions that occur within the music classroom. With young people arriving with such varied musical identities, curriculum experiences will rarely be uniform. Every individual within a class will therefore respond to, interpret or take different things from their musical learning. Equally, the particular grouping of young people will create unique interactions with the teacher, leading to a diverse range of musical outcomes. This challenges the objective- and outcome-led planning on which many curricula are based and provides greater scope for teachers and young people to explore and discover new learning together. Box 7.3 offers an example of curriculum development in response to diverse learning contexts and experiences.

Box 7.3 Curriculum as contextually connected experience

In one secondary school, a medium-term planning document used to state that 13- to 14-year-olds studying the topic of the blues would compose using the twelve-bar blues chord sequence. But their teachers recognised that it became a very mechanical exercise, with the young people simply following regimented instructions. The teachers therefore changed the objective to, "working with musical features of the blues to compose their own piece," which meant the young people could go in many different directions, including into rock 'n' roll and blues-based jazz. The range of possibilities really engaged the young people, and their teachers enjoyed exploring a wider range of music to help their classes identify more blues connections to investigate further.

Interactions are core to curriculum decision-making

In an emergent curriculum, decisions about the nature, direction and detail of curriculum experiences are *negotiated*. At the centre of these negotiations are the musical and non-musical interactions that occur between the young people, their peers, the resources, the environment and the teacher. It is through these interactions that new directions, opportunities and possibilities are opened up to be explored together. But this presents a challenge to the teacher, as the direction of a particular unit with a particular class cannot be predicted but can only be anticipated. Therefore, the teacher has to be constantly open to alternatives and attentive to the musical decisions that the young people are making.

In many senses the curriculum decision-making process can be viewed a bit like improvising. There is a framework, but the young people and teacher are deciding together at every moment whether the framework is the right one, how it might be musically manipulated, and how to create something innovative and unique. To do this, it is necessary to make time for teachers and young people to reflect on the unit, the directions they have taken and whether they want to explore alternative routes. As discussed in Box 7.4, the teacher's role, therefore, is to guide young people as they decide which new ideas they might like to pursue.

WHAT IS A MUSIC CURRICULUM?

> ### Box 7.4 **Curriculum decision-making**
>
> The 12- and 13-year-olds in 8D started to compose a whole-class pop song but quickly found themselves disagreeing as there were so many different ideas. In the end, their teacher helped them to form four groups, each with compatible ideas, and set each group the same lyrics. The young people really enjoyed seeing the different results.
>
> Previously, the teachers in the music department would have made their classes stay together if the topic plan was to compose a whole-class song. But now, they allowed the curriculum to be owned by the young people, and they reported that they learnt much more from the experience.

Meaning, and therefore learning, emerges from interactions

If meaning, and therefore learning, emerges from interactions, it follows that *musical* meaning, and therefore *musical* learning, emerges from *musical* interactions. This means that, within the classroom, young people need to act as musicians, responding to the problems and opportunities that arise during musical interactions and learning as a result. To facilitate this, music teachers need to allow young people time to develop their own meanings—as in the scenario in Box 7.5—rather than imposing other meanings onto young people's musical experiences. Nonetheless, this is something that is easier said than done in a time-pressured, outcome-orientated environment.

> ### Box 7.5 **Musical learning and musical interactions**
>
> A group of music teachers analysed their use of questioning during their lessons and concluded that they needed to ask more questions to open up ideas and draw out understanding. After a few weeks of trying to ask such questions, they shared their experiences. In one class, a young person had asked to use the drum kit during a West African drumming unit. The teacher admitted that previously they would have told them that they were only using the West African drums. Instead, the teacher asked why he wanted to use the drum kit: what musical effect was he imagining as a result? The teacher and young person thought about what connections could be made between the different drums.
>
> For all the teachers, opening up their questioning made the curriculum far more exploratory, and they consequently expanded their planning and reworded objectives, outcomes and activities to make space for multiple interpretations.

Curriculum develops with young people's learning

As meaning emerges from interactions, curriculum constantly develops, moving with young people's learning. Although a curriculum will have structures that allow young people to engage with a wide range of musical resources and experiences (and therefore interactions), music teachers need constantly to be open to unexpected, creative meanings that lead young people in alternative directions. This involves expecting classes, groups and individuals to respond in different ways and ultimately to shape their own curriculum experiences (see Box 7.6).

> Box 7.6 **Young people as shapers of curriculum experiences**
>
> At the end of a topic on song-writing, a music teacher reflected on what he had originally planned that the 11- and 12-year-olds in his class would learn and what they had actually learnt—that is to say, how they had responded to the curriculum. His teaching had focused mainly on the technical aspects of composing and using appropriate technical musical terms. Most of the young people had understood these and had written melodies that began and ended on the tonic, used stepwise motion in a singable range, made use of repeated motifs and had words that fitted well. However, a significant minority of the class moved far beyond the teacher's expectations to consider aesthetic and expressive outcomes, such as using memorable rhythmic and melodic ideas and word-painting. In discussion with the class he found that they could confidently describe their compositional processes even though they didn't always know the appropriate technical language. The teacher felt he had learnt a lot about young people's song-writing, and crucially he saw what the young people had brought to the topic (how they had taken ownership of it) and what they had taken away from it.

PLANNING FOR AN EMERGENT CURRICULUM

Planning for an emergent view of a music curriculum does not provide a "template" for teaching and is not particularly disposed to being supported by commercial curriculum packages. Rather, it asks teachers to engage with fundamental *epistemological* questions around musical knowledge and understanding, and fundamental *pedagogical* questions of how such knowledge is best taught and assessed. Teachers must ask these questions in relation to the young people in the particular context in which they teach, recognising that this context includes musical learning that goes on beyond school. Task 7.7 provides an opportunity to explore how you might plan a lesson that allows for the principles of an emergent curriculum.

> Task 7.7 **Planning for an emergent curriculum**
>
> Choose a lesson you have taught or observed. Using the existing lesson plan or your observation notes, imagine an alternative lesson using the principles of an emergent curriculum as identified previously. Think about:
>
> - what would the learning environment look and sound like?
> - how would the young people be grouped?

WHAT IS A MUSIC CURRICULUM?

> - what activities would young people be involved in?
> - what would your role be as the teacher and how could you best prepare?
> - what resources would be needed?
> - would the routines of the lesson need to be altered?
>
> Prepare a plan for this new lesson. How would you structure and phrase the plan to make clear the emergent nature of the curriculum experience?

Most importantly, emergent music curricula require of teachers a willingness to initiate and engage in pedagogical discourse and knowledge construction with those they teach. It also entails critical reflection both before and after a lesson and—especially—"in-action" (in the moment) in response to this discourse and learning. In particular, an emergent curriculum challenges teachers to be more open to extemporising curriculum (both musically and non-musically) with their classes, allowing young people to take the lead, follow the teacher's lead or work together to develop new and exciting understandings. This does not mean that teachers aren't responsible for what goes on in the classroom, but rather that they come to the classroom not with fixed ideas about the what and how of learning, but with what Smith (2000) describes as "a proposal for action which sets out the essential features of the educational encounter" (15).

EVALUATING AN EMERGENT MUSIC CURRICULUM

As a music teacher, it is quite possible that you will work in a school with just one or two music specialists. It is therefore likely that you will have significant responsibility for, or many opportunities to influence, the music curriculum in your school. In this final section we want you to reflect on this responsibility.

If curriculum is emerging in the way we have described in this chapter, then frequently and critically evaluating it is of great importance. This will mean thinking about your curriculum philosophy (why you do what you do) as much as your curriculum activity (what you do). You will need to develop a rationale for why you are teaching particular topics to particular year groups in a particular sequence. This will enable you to articulate your curriculum thinking to young people, parents, colleagues, line managers and inspectors. Your curriculum thinking may change over time, particularly as the young people in your classes change and you reflect on their musical experiences and responses. Indeed, this is to be expected in an emergent curriculum. In this flexible and responsive approach, building in time to critically evaluate your curriculum is therefore important and should occur regularly throughout the year. Assessing your curriculum in this way will build your confidence as you think about the relationship between your approach to curriculum, young people's curriculum experiences and the development of musical learning.

Thinking about your music curriculum philosophy is especially important when you are engaged in wider school discussions about curriculum models or planning templates. Being sure of your own philosophy and the role of an emergent curriculum will help you to approach whole-school initiatives with an authentic understanding of your subject area. This will enable you to work within wider curriculum framings whilst consistently considering the musical outcomes and experiences you wish to embed through your programme of study. This can be a challenging negotiation if you have not developed a clear rationale for your own curriculum choices; Task 7.8 helps you consider evaluating your curriculum thinking as a beginning teacher.

Task 7.8 **Developing and evaluating curriculum thinking**

In order to develop your own curriculum thinking, complete the following tasks:

1. Articulate your curriculum philosophy in two sentences.
2. Discuss with another music teacher or mentor their curriculum design. What are the factors and issues they consider, and how do they ensure that the curriculum remains responsive to the young people's musical learning?
3. Informed by these conversations, either:

    a. tentatively plan your curriculum for one term. What might you include and how might you link your ideas together? Or,
    b. evaluate a curriculum you have been given to teach. What do you need to find out or put in place to create a curriculum experience for young people that is coherent and emergent?

4. Revisit the issues outlined in this chapter as well as your own initial curriculum philosophies. How are they evident in the way you have approached planning the music curriculum in Question 3?

SUMMARY

So, what is a music curriculum? As we noted at the beginning of the chapter, as a beginning music teacher you may well be faced with a curriculum document, comments about what it means to turn this document into practice and an expectation that this curriculum document will translate in similar ways for different teachers and classes. What we have outlined is a counterargument to this common focus on reified curriculum-as-content and curriculum-as-product approaches. However, it is vital to highlight that an emergent music curriculum approach does not necessarily rely on changing curriculum documents or others' curriculum discourse. Instead, an emergent curriculum relies on individual teachers developing pedagogies that enable them to work with young people in ways that allow lived experiences of the curriculum to have the greatest importance. In this way, our argument for an emergent curriculum empowers you—whether as a beginning or more experienced teacher—to develop responsive approaches within the context or career stage in which you are working.

In answer to the question, "what is a music curriculum?" we would argue that a music curriculum is how you use appropriate pedagogy to facilitate young people's exploration and co-creation of lived musical experiences from a "proposal for action" which allows their musical knowledge to emerge. But as illustrated in Task 7.9, it is an area which requires ongoing development.

> ### Task 7.9 **Reviewing your understanding of music curriculum**
>
> In Task 7.1, Question 2, you were asked to complete the following statements:
>
> a. "An effective music curriculum for teachers should . . ."
> b. "An effective music curriculum for young people should . . ."
>
> Revisit what you wrote and consider how—if at all—you might rewrite your statements to reflect any changes in your thinking. Consider how you would now answer the question, "what is a music curriculum?"

FURTHER READING

Anderson, A. (2026)
A music curriculum renewed: Classroom curriculum models of constraint or liberation?, in C. Philpott and G. Spruce (eds) *Debates in Music Teaching*, 2nd edn, Abingdon: Routledge, pp. 149-162.

Green, L. (2005)
'The music curriculum as lived experience: Children's "natural" music learning processes', *Music Educators' Journal*, 91, 4: 27-32.

Regelski, T. (2005)
'Curriculum: Implications of aesthetic versus praxial philosophies', in D.J. Elliott (ed) *Praxial Music Education: Reflections and Dialogues*, Oxford: Oxford University Press. pp. 219-249.

Smith, M.K. (2000)
Curriculum theory and practice, in M.K. Smith (ed) *The Encyclopaedia of Informal Education*. https://www.academia.edu/94785149/Curriculum_Theory_and_Practice_By

These readings will help you gain additional perspectives on different conceptions of curriculum, including ideas around informal learning and the curriculum as lived experience.

PLANNING FOR MUSICAL LEARNING

Elizabeth MacGregor and Gary Spruce with Vivienne John, James O'Neil and Alys Wilding

INTRODUCTION

Lesson planning has as its primary purpose two central and important questions:

1. *Learning outcomes*. What do I want young people to learn by the end of the lesson? What should they understand and be able to do when they leave the music classroom that they did not understand or could not do when they entered it?
2. *Teaching strategies*. What musical experiences do young people need to have in order to ensure that this learning takes place? How can these musical experiences be managed and structured?

Without addressing these two questions through planning, lessons will almost inevitably be much less effective than they might otherwise be. Unplanned lessons may well be full of activity, but if these activities are not directed towards some kind of planned learning outcomes, then learning (if it takes place at all) may be haphazard and you—and the young people—may not know what to do next in order to make progress.

Lesson planning in music is, however, about much more than responding to these questions—important though they may be. It is also about planning for how one will afford openings, opportunities, and departure points for young people's musical learning—including the kinds of musical learning that cannot necessarily be anticipated but that emerge from young people's responses to the musical stimuli, problems, and ideas that they encounter during a lesson. It is often these unexpected and surprising moments of music-making that are the most valuable to young people and reveal to the teacher young people's previously unrecognised musical understanding, knowledge, and skill.

The purpose of this chapter is to consider not only how these two central questions might be addressed during lesson planning, but also how you might plan to create a flexible framework that allows for the unexpected to happen and to flourish, and for young people to develop as confident and independent musicians. It will approach planning in terms of three key principles:

1. *Recognising musical knowledge*. Planning should take account of different types of musical knowledge, including the musical knowledge that young people bring into the classroom from their experiences beyond school.
2. *Immersive musical activities*. Planning should enable music to be taught musically through activities that immerse young people in musical engagement.
3. *Integrating musical experiences*. Planning should accommodate and connect different aspects of musical experience: appraising, improvising, composing, and performing.

Each of these principles will be addressed in turn and illustrated with examples from current teacher educators from across the United Kingdom. Afterwards, we will turn to the practical process of planning. There is a sense, of course, in which this entire book is about planning, and therefore some critically important issues—such as inclusion and adaptation (Chapter 4), behaviours for learning (Chapter 9), and assessment (Chapter 10)—are dealt with in detail elsewhere and only touched upon here.

Objectives

By the end of the chapter you will be able to:

- identify the key principles underpinning effective lesson planning;
- understand the key factors that need to be taken into account when planning;
- know how to apply these principles and factors to your planning for young people's musical learning.

THE PRINCIPLES OF PLANNING FOR MUSICAL LEARNING

1. Recognising musical knowledge

Many teachers and scholars have spent considerable time identifying and defining different kinds of musical knowledge. In Chapter 6 of this volume, Philpott draws on the work of Reid (1986) and Swanwick (1979, 1988) to propose three categories of musical knowledge: knowledge *about*, know *how*, and knowledge *of*. In contrast, Elliott (1995) differentiates between *formal*, taught knowledge and the *informal* knowledge resulting from musical enculturation, and *intuitive* knowledge of what feels "right" and *supervisory* knowledge of what is stylistically "right" (Spruce 2016).

In this chapter, we will consider four kinds of musical knowledge (Axtell et al. 2024) and the ways in which they can be integrated within effective and musical lesson planning. This typology has significant overlaps with Philpott's conceptualisation of musical knowledge in Chapter 6, but "knowledge about" is split into two discrete categories, "knowledge that" and "knowledge about." In the following list, the four types of musical knowledge are exemplified through reference to Bach's *Toccata and Fugue in D minor* (BWV 565). You can try applying this to other music in Task 8.1.

1. *Knowledge that* . . . conceptual, declarative knowledge such as key terminology relating to musical elements (e.g., melody, harmony, rhythm, texture) and musical devices (e.g., sequence, ostinato, drone, pedal). For example, *knowledge that* a toccata is a virtuosic piece of music designed to show off a performer's skills, and that a fugue is a contrapuntal composition in which voices enter one at a time with a subject and answer.
2. *Knowledge about* . . . contextual, abstract knowledge such as facts about the musical, historical, and social contexts of composers, performers, and audiences. For example, *knowledge about* Bach's life in Germany between 1685 and 1750 and his employment as a church musician.
3. *Knowing how* . . . embodied, procedural knowledge such as how to play an instrument or how to identify musical features through critical listening or reading notation. For example, *knowing how* to play the *Toccata and Fugue* on the organ, how to select appropriate registrations for the instrument and space, and how to programme the piece within a recital.
4. *Knowing of* . . . intuitive, tacit knowledge such as the feeling of how music should go resulting from immersion and enculturation within music-making. For example, *knowing of* the characteristic use of phrasing and ornamentation appropriate to the *Toccata and Fugue* and being able to improvise music in a complementary style.

Task 8.1 **Identifying musical knowledge**

Look at the examples of "knowledge that," "knowledge about," "knowing how," and "knowing of" in relation to Bach's *Toccata and Fugue in D minor*. Now choose a piece of music that you know well. Then consider:

1. What *knowledge that* do you have of the piece?
2. What *knowledge about* do you have of the piece?
3. What is your *knowing how* in relation to the piece?
4. What is your *knowing of* in relation to the piece?

PLANNING FOR MUSICAL LEARNING

This typology of four kinds of musical knowledge is particularly helpful in the way in which it distinguishes between "knowledge" and "knowing." Knowledge—as in "knowledge that" and "knowledge about"—can be thought of as existing externally to the knower. It often involves abstract facts that can be validated as true or false (Candy et al. 2021: 193). Knowing, on the other hand, is something internal and experiential. Knowing is unique to the knower and results from their personal practices. Different knowers, therefore, have different ways of knowing (Candy et al. 2021: 194).

Given that musical learning requires both "knowledge" and "knowing," we can only come to a deep understanding of music through immersion in diverse practices of music-making. Listening, appraising, and discussing music is vital for developing "knowledge that" and "knowledge about," while learning to perform and compose offers experiential "knowing how." Improvising and participating in group music-making is especially important for gaining a sense of "knowing of." But all of these practices—and their contemporary hybrids such as covering, remixing, and multitracking—are interrelated and contribute to multiple types of musical knowledge. It is therefore essential that they are integrated into lesson planning to introduce young people to different ways of musical knowing. The lesson plan in Box 8.1—and the activity that follows in Task 8.2—demonstrates how "knowledge that," "knowledge about," "knowing how," and "knowing of" can be incorporated during planning and teaching and their role in supporting young people's musical learning and development.

Box 8.1 Lesson planning for recognising musical knowledge (Vivienne John: Wales)

Context	Analysis
Ysgol Y Cwm is a comprehensive school in the South Wales Valleys, an area of significant social and financial deprivation but with a proud community and cultural history. In line with the requirements in the Curriculum for Wales (Welsh Government 2020), the music department is keen to draw from the area's local musical heritage to enable young people "to develop, shape and express [their] personal, social and cultural identities" as citizens of Wales (n.p.). The school has embraced the opportunities afforded by Curriculum for Wales to make "powerful connections" (Fautley and Savage 2011) with other subject disciplines to devise a unit of work that explores the "Cool Cymru" cultural movement from the late 1990s and early 2000s. In their history lessons,	The acquisition of **knowledge** **"that"** and **"about"** and **knowing** **"how"** and **"of"** is not unique to the subject of music. Young people are likely to develop similar ways of knowing in other subject disciplines. Whilst making connections with young people's knowledge gained elsewhere in the curriculum is mandatory for teachers in Wales (Welsh Government 2020), it is useful in any teacher's broader planning, in order to provide a holistic learning experience in the classroom.

(Continued)

(Continued)

Context	Analysis
young people learn that, following a period of severe hardship for the Valleys communities, Welsh devolution in the late 1990s sparked a period of positivity and a resurgence of interest in "Welshness," spearheaded in no small part by musicians and rock bands such as The Stereophonics, The Manic Street Preachers, and Catatonia. Music lessons, therefore, take the opportunity to harness and build on young people's learning of their local history and culture through musical activity that exemplifies the four kinds of knowledge outlined earlier.	
Lesson	**Analysis**
In this music lesson, young people learn the musical elements and devices that combine to create the song *Have a Nice Day* by The Stereophonics through appraising, performing, and improvising activities. They also develop a wider understanding of the role that The Stereophonics, a Welsh band that gained national and international recognition, had in the promotion and celebration of Welsh identity and aspiration.	The Curriculum for Wales (Welsh Government 2020) advocates for young people to understand and relate the relevance of their learning to the world beyond their school gates and encourages teachers to seek opportunities to forge links within and beyond the local community. Here, the teacher is maximising an opportunity to make relevant and authentic links between young people's musical learning and musicians who lived and worked in their locality.
Plan	**Analysis**
1. Whilst playing the song, the teacher reminds the class of the "Cool Cymru" movement and the role of The Stereophonics.	**Knowledge about** The Stereophonics and their impact is useful contextual information, but in and of itself it does very little to develop young people as musicians.
2. Using their aural perception skills and their prior knowledge, the teacher prompts the young people to listen out for a repeated pattern within the song. They are asked to clap and sing the repeated pattern as they listen to help with internalisation.	Here, the class develop musical **knowing how**: their aural skills are being utilised as they learn how to identify and join in with the repeated pattern in the song. Their **knowing of** music is also being developed as they engage in authentic musical activity.
3. The teacher introduces the term "riff" as a label for the repeated pattern and explains its function.	Young people are developing their conceptual or theoretical knowledge here. Through this activity they acquire **knowledge that** a riff is a musical device and that it serves a musical function.

(Continued)

■ ■ ■ ■ **PLANNING FOR MUSICAL LEARNING**

(Continued)

Plan	Analysis
4. On pitched instruments of their choice, young people are given the three pitches that comprise the riff and work collaboratively and aurally to work it out. As a scaffold, a recording of the song is played in the background so they can listen at any time to help with their explorations.	This immersive and integrated performing and appraising activity creates an intuitive and tacit **knowing of** music-making.
5. The teacher introduces the two bass notes of the song and explains the role of the bass line.	Through the teacher's activity, the young people gain **knowledge that** the bass line has a function within the song (and music generally).
6. Working in pairs or small groups, the class experiment with combining the riff and bass notes and aurally work out when and how they fit together. They are also encouraged to improvise a rhythm on the bass notes that they think works well with the riff.	Finally, the young people not only enhance their **knowing of** the component parts of the song through a practical and authentic musical experience but are also given the autonomy to make their own embodied musical decisions.

Task 8.2 **Identifying musical knowledge during lesson planning (Vivienne John: Wales)**

Look at a recent lesson plan you have created for a class of your choice or ask your tutor to source you an example lesson plan for a typical music lesson. Analyse the planned learning activities and teaching strategies and identify which types of knowledge each promotes. Consider the following questions:

1. Is there a presence of all types of knowledge within the plan? Label them clearly.
2. Why were these learning activities chosen in terms of knowledge acquisition? What knowledge is the class expected to gain? Justify why these activities are appropriate for acquiring this particular knowledge.
3. How do the learning activities and teaching strategies throughout the lesson differ as a result of the knowledge type that is being encouraged?
4. Are particular types of knowing privileged over others? Why? In your opinion, how might young people benefit as a result?
5. Reflecting on young people's ways of knowing, are there any improvements or missed opportunities you would consider if you were to teach (or repeat) this lesson?

2. Immersive musical activities

According to Swanwick (1979), the primary aim of music education–and therefore of lesson planning–should be to ensure that young people develop their "knowing of" music and consequently form a deepening relationship with it. This can occur only if young people are given the opportunity to become immersed in music: to be fully engaged in music as improvisers, composers, and performers, underpinned by a strong sense of "listenership." Immersion in music is complementary to recognising diverse forms of musical knowledge and fundamental to teaching music *musically*.

In particular, abstract and external forms of "knowledge that" and "knowledge about" must be rooted in, and proceed from, musical immersion. Attempting to learn formal musical knowledge about concepts and contexts without immersion in music itself may lead to young people developing negative attitudes towards music in the classroom, resulting in poor attainment.

One issue that is often subject to an overemphasis on formal "knowledge that" and "knowledge about" is that of western staff notation. For some teachers working with young people who do not have prior experience of reading notation, it is tempting to offer a series of abstract rules—disguised as well-known mnemonics such as "All Cows Eat Grass"—to help learn new concepts. This might give young people "knowledge that" the pitches in the "spaces" of the bass stave are A, C, E, and G. Other teachers might seek to contextualise their classes' understanding of the stave by explaining how, historically, the bass clef emerged from the F clef, which indicated where the pitch F was located on the stave. This might give young people "knowledge about" how clefs developed and their different forms. Yet even with this "knowledge that" or "knowledge about," young people might not "know how" to notate their own music or develop sufficient "knowing of" to be able to organise pitches along with other musical dimensions to form what Swanwick (1999) calls "expressive shapes" (47). These ways of knowing can only develop through immersion in listening, singing, playing, and creating music—since "if we always or even mostly insist on naming notes and intervals, identifying chords, reading rhythm patterns, and so on, we may get stuck at the level of materials" (47).

A second subject that is frequently taught without corresponding opportunities for "knowing how" and "knowing of" is listening to and evaluating music. When learning to appraise (especially as part of an examination course), young people are expected to have a huge breadth of "knowledge about" music in order to be able to recognise and identify the characteristics of different musical genres from across half a millennium. Teachers are forced into taking "short cuts" in order to cover the ground, drilling young people in the basic features of different musical styles in the hope that they will be able to apply their "knowledge that" and "knowledge about" during examination. But to be able to aurally recognise characteristics of musical subgenres (baroque dance or bebop jazz, for example), young people need to have been immersed in the music: to have listened to a wide range of examples, and, if possible, to have performed or composed in the style. Moore's (2005) description of the best way of acquiring wine-tasting skills could be applied equally well to identifying musical styles and genres:

> It's not such a difficult skill as you might think, although the only way to acquire it is by tasting until you know a wine's signature as instinctively as you might recognise a footballer—not by matching in your brain the words you would use to describe him to someone else (for example "heavy built

PLANNING FOR MUSICAL LEARNING

but fast, with black hair"), but because his gait across the pitch, that very particular way he leaps to head the ball, is a pattern you just *know*.

(65)

Box 8.2 and Task 8.3 both consider how immersion in local musical traditions, such as Scottish country dancing, can be mirrored through classroom activities and community partnerships that foster "knowing how" and "knowing of" through listening, improvising, composing, and performing.

Box 8.2 Lesson planning for immersive musical activities (James O'Neil: Scotland)

Context	Analysis
Argyle Academy is a rural island school with an established tradition of fiddle, highland bagpipes, and pipe band snare drumming within the school and the wider community. Scottish country social dancing is also explored in the Physical Education (PE) curriculum. Young people are familiar with the heritage of these instruments and dances and their use in local celebrations and ceremonies.	A typical Broad General Education music class at this school usually comprises a mix of learners receiving small groups lessons on fiddle, chanter, and drumming. Fiddlers and chanter players are familiar with the Scottish reel, and other players can play electronic keyboard or tuned percussion.
Unit objectives	**Analysis**
To explore and deepen knowledge of Scottish music through performing, composing, and listening by: ■ taking what we already know about Scottish music and learning new dance styles: reel, march, and waltz; ■ learning how to play in these dance styles whilst creating (composing) our own music in an improvised or planned way; ■ recording our compositions to be used in social dance in PE.	Before teaching a lesson on reels in this unit, the teacher can prepare to create immersive musical activities by: a. finding out what reels respective fiddle and chanter players **know how** to **perform** and asking them to bring their instruments to class; b. creating a simple, four-bar reel in A major pentatonic that the class can use as a basis to **improvise**. The Scottish Curriculum for Excellence (Education Scotland 2010) includes a focus upon interdisciplinary learning. Recording young people's compositions for social dance would open up further opportunities for project-based cross-curricular learning. This could include the use of digital technologies (a third curricular area) or collaboration with young people in another year group.

(Continued)

(Continued)

Lesson plan: Reels	Analysis
Starter task: Young people discuss what they know about Scottish music generally. e.g., ceilidh music can sound fast; music at remembrance events can be contemplative; bagpipers playing at weddings; street buskers; wider folk music (such as sea shanties) made famous by pop artists.	The teacher facilitates discussion, resulting in the sharing of young people's **knowledge that** Scottish music has distinctive musical characteristics and **knowledge about** specific styles such as dance musics and sea shanties. They may visually map out the class's ideas ready for the main task.
Main task—exposition: The teacher introduces the Scottish dance style **reel**. The teacher extends and builds upon informal knowledge explored in the lesson starter. e.g., Scottish music can sometimes sound fast, energetic, and good for dancing; this links to the purpose and rhythmic and melodic features of the reel. Young people listen to two styles of reel: one by a traditional Scottish country dance band and one by a Celtic rock band. The teacher prompts brief critical class discussion: ▪ Which sounds more energetic and why? ▪ Does the reel sound more energetic with or without drums and why?	The teacher could ask more experienced fiddle players or pipers to demonstrate their **know how** of relevant pieces, promoting active learning. As the young people listen to different examples of reels, the teacher could encourage them to explore their intuitive **knowing of** how reels might sound different with and without drums. How does the rhythmic drive change when it comes from the accompanying accordion vamp, melodic quaver figures, or a percussive drumbeat?
Main task—activity: Young people who have brought previously prepared music begin to practise their piece. Young people who do not play a native instrument begin to prepare an improvised two-bar reel melody using scaffolded rhythms and the A major pentatonic scale (A B C♯ E F♯): $\frac{4}{4}$ ♫ ♫ ♩ ♫ ♩ ♩ ♫ ♩ cof-fee cof-fee tea cof-fee tea tea cof-fee tea	This lesson immerses young people of all abilities and, if planned and taught effectively, will offer appropriate challenge and enjoyment for the class using the main elements of **performing**, **composing**, and **listening** in the reel style. The **improvisation** of a new melody can be used with young people who are both more and less experienced in playing an instrument to explore and develop their **knowing of** Scottish reels. The teacher can alternate between using notated music and playing short passages out loud to cater for different young people's preferred ways of **composing** and **performing**.

> **Task 8.3 Finding immersive musical learning through "border-walking" (James O'Neil: Scotland)**
>
> To plan immersive musical activities, it's important to reflexively adapt the musical content that you can leverage in your own school community's context. Consider "border-walking" using your own musical specialism and the local musical landscape, with which you may or may not be familiar (e.g., a rural Scottish school where fiddle and piping is part of the community tradition). How can your own "knowing how" and "knowing of" benefit your classes to deepen an immersive learning experience?
>
> 1. Which of your own specialisms can you leverage for your curriculum planning? Can you connect industry professionals who may be colleagues or acquaintances to help you develop more immersive experiences?
> 2. How could you connect local professionals, community musicians, or arts organisations with your school for partnership projects?
> 3. What class excursions or school trips could you arrange to local events to ignite young people's interest in a particular topic (e.g., a local music festival, a touring musical or opera)?
>
> In the Scottish Curriculum for Excellence (Education Scotland 2010), curriculum design should include a focus on partnership working (see Chapter 5), which involves helping young people to participate responsibly in social and cultural life. The preceding suggestions help to facilitate such opportunities in a meaningful and relevant way.

3. Integrating musical experiences

Integration can perhaps best be described as bringing together listening, improvising, composing, and performing activities to focus on common musical learning aims. A typical way in which integration might be employed is when teaching concepts such as triple time or syncopation. The teacher may ask their class to listen and respond to triple time or syncopated music from a range of traditions; perform simple pieces using triple time or syncopation; learn how such music can be represented using various notations; and improvise or compose a classical waltz or syncopated jazz melody. Through immersion in such music, the young people establish "knowledge that" triple time and syncopation have specific definitions in these specific contexts; "knowledge about" their use in different genres; as well as "knowing how" to recognise, read, write, and play them; and "knowing of" the way such music seems to feel and the expression it seems to evoke.

As shown in Box 8.3 and explored further in Task 8.4, lessons that integrate performing, composing, improvising, and appraising have the potential to provide young people with a rich musical learning experience and break down any artificial separation of performer, composer, and audience. Indeed, it can be argued that an integrated approach is fundamental to good classroom music teaching and, within formal education, is what gives curriculum music its distinctiveness. Young people learn to musically "problem-solve" by developing a multifaceted relationship with music as critic, improviser, composer, and performer.

Box 8.3 Lesson planning for integrating musical experiences (Alys Wilding: England)

Context	Analysis
This scheme of work or lesson could be adapted for classes aged 11 to 14 (Years 7 to 9 in England) in any secondary or high school.	The National Curriculum for Music in England requires young people to be able to: a. "understand and explore how music is created . . . through the inter-related dimensions of music" (or "musical elements"); b. "create and compose music on their own and with others" and "use technology appropriately"; c. "perform, listen to, review and evaluate music across a range of . . . genres, styles and traditions" (DfE 2013: 257).
Aims and objectives	**Analysis**
Scheme of work: For young people to develop an understanding of how music can be used in film to create tension and suspense. *Lesson:* ▪ To be able to identify musical features and devices which help to convey the feeling of tension and suspense; ▪ To play a part in a whole-class soundscape which creates a sense of tension and suspense; ▪ To begin composing using musical devices (e.g., drone, ostinato) which successfully help to convey a sense of tension and suspense.	These lesson aims and objectives should already be clearly setting out that during the course of the lesson young people will engage with **playing** and **singing**, **composing** and **improvising**, and **listening** and **appraising**. There does not need to be one discrete objective for each aspect, but overall there should be the sense that the lesson will encompass all of these features and immerse young people in the music.
Lesson	**Analysis**
1. Young people listen to a piece of film music that creates a sense of tension and suspense (such as "Like a Dog Chasing Cars" from *Batman*). They respond to this piece through drawing or writing a description of the images or emotions it conjures up in their minds.	Enabling young people to respond in a more informal way (through drawing or writing descriptions, words, or phrases) allows them to be able to start to express their relationship with and intuitive **knowing of** this kind of music, rather than a tick list of features to **know about**.

(Continued)

(Continued)

2. Young people's responses are then discussed and linked to previous learning and musical terminology. The class is introduced to some important musical features of this style such as ostinato and drones.	Talking about music can be tricky. Some young people will **know that** "ostinato" is a relevant key word, but it is more likely that they will use words such as "repeated" or "looped." These can be teased out through questioning and supported by **listening** to musical examples.
3. For each musical feature, the teacher leads a short musical activity that demonstrates the device. e.g., For ostinato, young people sing a repeated pattern over and over again (this could be as simple as their name). This may lead to a discussion of how the composer of "Like a Dog Chasing Cars" has used an ostinato to create a sense of tension (low pitched, driving, relentless quaver rhythms) and how young people perceived and described this in their drawings and writing.	"Show me, don't tell me!" Remembering this phrase can assist in ensuring lessons are musical and immersive. Young people will demonstrate their **know how** and develop as active **listeners** when this is a regular feature of lessons. Planning to model terms individually and involve young people in the process is key to going beyond **knowledge that** and **about** and developing **knowing how** and **of**. Consider whether you need to tell the class what a drone is (for example), or can you perform a piece without a drone to begin with, then add one and ask them what has changed? This allows young people to feel the devices and moves them from abstract **knowledge that** to embodied **knowing of**.
4. The class are each given a composer's notepad of different musical devices and ideas that could convey a sense of tension and suspense (such as drone, ostinato, string sounds, chromatic notes, chord cluster). The teacher models each idea to ensure the young people understand each element of the notepad.	This type of activity develops and builds on young people's **listening** skills—when they begin to use the ideas in the notepad to contribute to a whole-class soundscape, they need to listen to and **know how** their part fits and the impact that their contribution has on the overall effect of the mood they are trying to create. This is an opportunity for young people to work on the first two learning aims.

(Continued)

(Continued)

5. Using a variety of instruments (which could include their own) the young people use the ideas in their notepads to contribute to a whole-class soundscape. They are given free choice of which ideas they use and when. They can change ideas, play more than one at once, and drop in and out of the texture where they would like to. Record this soundscape.	Allowing young people to **improvise** as part of a whole-class soundscape can enable them to play around with ideas in a "lower stakes" environment where they are anonymous. Immersion in a soundscape also offers them time to come to **know of** the music and how they relate to it. This can then feed forward into more "formalised" **know how** as they develop skills to help them **compose**.
6. The class then listen back to the soundscape and consider what they liked, what worked, and what was maybe less successful and why. This constructive feedback can then feedforward into subsequent lessons.	Listening back to the piece created enables young people to be **performers**, **composers**, and **critics** all rolled into one!

Continuing the scheme of work

Following on from this lesson, the scheme of work could be developed in a variety of different ways depending on the class, context, and resources. One possible direction for subsequent lessons might involve:

1. Young people **composing** a soundtrack for a given video clip over several lessons. They can draw ideas from the composer's notepad used for the whole-class soundscape but should work on **knowing how** each idea can be adapted for the given film. While composing they could use acoustic instruments, Digital Audio Workstations, or mixing and multitracking.
2. During composing lessons young people **listen** to each other's work and offer feedback. They swap groups or workstations to give comments relating to their **knowledge about** the use of musical devices to create tension and suspense in different contexts. Peer feedback can be powerful and builds on young people's **listening** skills and critical **discussion** skills.

Task 8.4 **Evaluating the use of integrated musical activities (Alys Wilding: England)**

1. Consider a lesson that you have recently planned, taught, or observed. Reflect on whether the lesson enabled the young people to become immersed in the music. Detail and analyse the opportunities there were to:

    a. sing or play the music;
    b. compose or improvise with the music;
    c. listen to and appraise the music (both informally and formally).

■ ■ ■ ■ **PLANNING FOR MUSICAL LEARNING**

> 2. Plan two lessons that follow on from the lesson outlined in Box 8.3. Consider how you will use the lesson objectives, the sequencing of learning, and the resources available to you to integrate musical experiences and foster diverse kinds of musical knowledge.
> 3. Develop a sequence of three lessons on a topic of your choice. Focus on ensuring that singing and playing, composing and improvising, and listening and appraising are integrated throughout the lesson sequence.

Planning lessons that draw on and take account of different kinds of musical knowledge and knowing, that immerse young people in musical activity, and that integrate diverse musical experiences requires, on the part of the teacher, a high level of intellectual and creative energy and presupposes a deep and wide familiarity with music. It is a willingness and ability to make this creative and intellectual commitment that marks out the successful and innovative teacher from the one who is, perhaps, simply adequate. It is, moreover, what marks out the teacher as professional.

THE PROCESS OF PLANNING FOR MUSICAL LEARNING

As outlined in the previous section, the three key principles of lesson planning are that planning should:

1. take account of different types of musical knowledge, including that which young people bring into the classroom;
2. enable music to be taught musically through activities that immerse young people in musical experiences;
3. accommodate and connect different aspects of musical experience: appraising, improvising, composing, and performing.

Planning should also create a flexible framework within which unplanned and unexpected musical learning can take place.

However, these principles are *preconditions for* but not *guarantees of* effective teaching and learning. Effective teaching and learning can only be achieved through detailed and thought-through preparation, such as that illustrated in the following framework for lesson planning.

A framework for lesson planning

Figure 8.1 sets out a framework for planning lessons. It shows the sequence of planning and the ways in which various aspects of planning relate to one another. We now consider each of the central steps in turn and explore the issues addressed at each stage. Remember, however, that many of these issues are dealt with in much more detail in other chapters of this book.

LEARNING TO TEACH MUSIC IN THE SECONDARY SCHOOL

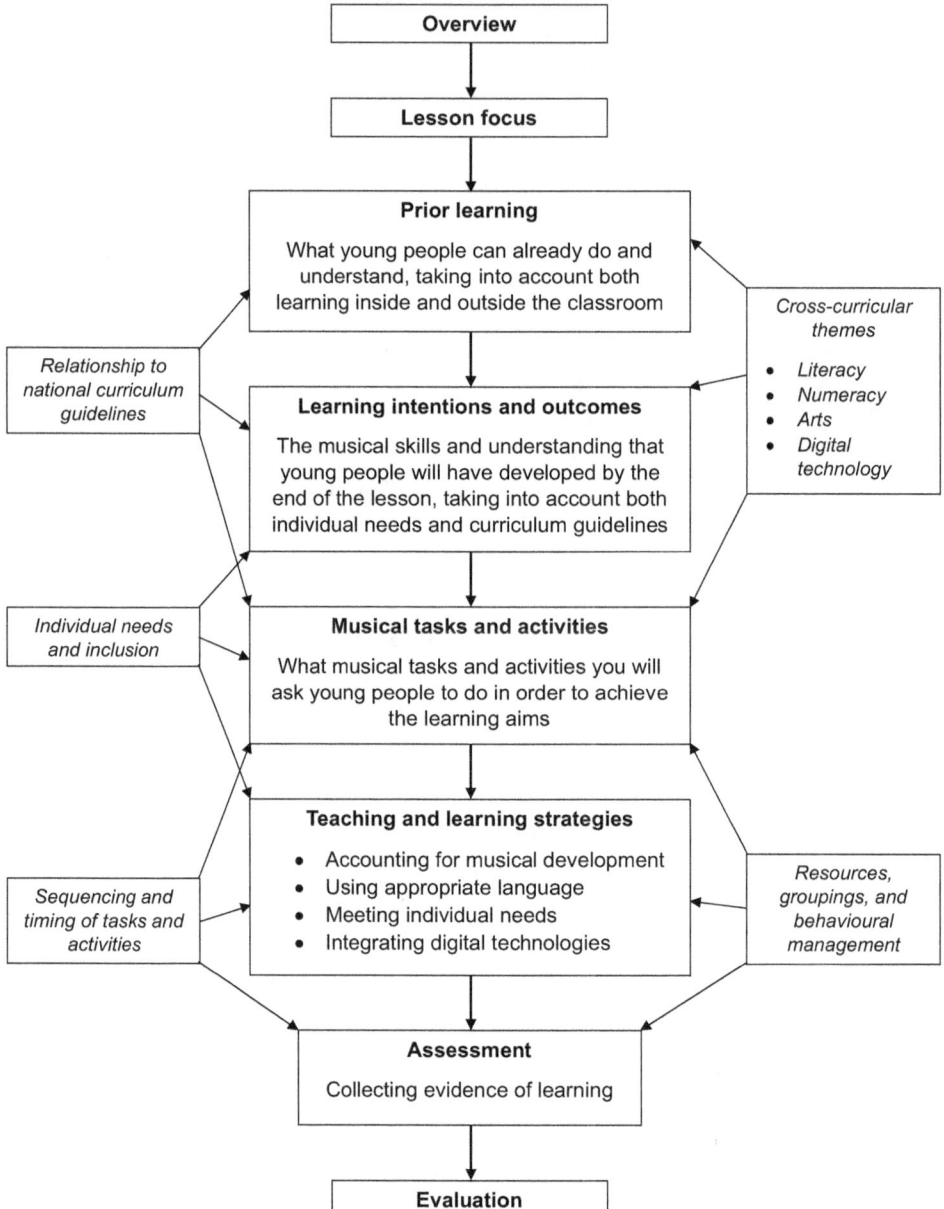

Figure 8.1 A framework for lesson planning

Overview

The overview is a brief statement concerning the focus of the sequence of lessons of which the planned lesson is a part. This statement is the same (or similar) for all lessons in the sequence and reflects the overall learning aim for the sequence identified in the scheme of work.

PLANNING FOR MUSICAL LEARNING

Lesson focus

This comprises a short and precise statement setting out in broad terms the purpose of the lesson, including the learning aims and musical activities. For example: "exploring musical change and variation through cover versions"; "developing compositions based around features of the Javanese gamelan"; "exploring the influence of social context on the form of the blues."

Prior learning

Prior learning should identify the past experiences and musical knowledge that young people may bring to the lesson. It should account for aspects formerly taught in the formal curriculum and for the learning that takes place informally, outside the classroom, as part of young people's enculturation. Young people bring into the classroom what Piaget (1952) described as "partial schemata"–understandings based on their previous experience–which they then bring to bear on their learning. In any one class, young people will have diverse experiences of playing, writing, or listening to music outside school, which–as illustrated in Task 8.5–will have a consequential impact on the planning that is needed to address individual knowledge and interests.

Task 8.5 **Accounting for prior learning**

As a beginning teacher planning lessons for the first time, you will need to gain as much information as possible about the musical interests of the young people in your classes. Note down the prior learning you are aware of for each of your classes through:

- talking to the young people themselves;
- talking to the class's previous teacher about their music-making;
- reading the scheme of work and noting the intended learning outcomes for previous sequences of lessons;
- scrutinising assessment information and young people's records (including noting down individual needs or disabilities).

Learning intentions and outcomes

Learning intentions and outcomes outline what you expect the young people in the class to have learnt by the end of the lesson. You may have several learning aims that accommodate the different prior experiences and musical knowledge of different groups of young people. For example, a learning outcome for one class might be, "to understand what an ostinato is and recognise one in a piece of music." Within the same class, for young people with greater experience of reading and writing staff notation, an additional learning outcome might be, "to listen to an ostinato and notate it by ear." All learning outcomes should be clearly linked to the overall sequence of lessons, proceeding from the previous lesson and preceding the one to follow.

There are two important issues to note about learning intentions and outcomes. First, it is critically important that learning outcomes are *musical*. "To be able to notate a pentatonic scale" may be a learning outcome but it is not a musical one. To understand the way in which the pentatonic scale is used in a range of different musics (including Balinese gamelan, Appalachian folk music, and French Impressionism) and then compose music based on the pentatonic scale provides a whole set of musical learning outcomes. Notating the scale may then become one activity (fostering "knowledge that") that supports progress towards these intentions.

Second, there needs to be clarity about the *distinction* between a learning outcome and a learning activity. To identify "performing 'On My Own' from *Les Misérables*" as a learning outcome is to misunderstand this distinction. The teacher should have a clear idea of why this song has been chosen in relation to the specific learning outcomes it could address. Learning occurs through using the song as a focus for a range of appraising, performing, and composing activities, which may result in, for example, "knowledge about" effective word-setting in musical theatre or "knowing how" to express different emotions through singing. Follow the instructions in Task 8.6 to reflect on learning outcomes that are both *musical outcomes* and *distinct outcomes*.

Task 8.6 **Planning learning intentions and outcomes**

Note down your answers to the following two questions and compare your answers to those of another beginning teacher.

1. *Musical outcomes.* Write an alternative learning outcome for "to be able to notate a pentatonic scale" that is musical.
2. *Distinct outcomes.* Write an alternative learning outcome for "performing 'On My Own' from *Les Misérables*" that is distinct from the learning activity.

Musical tasks and activities

This section identifies the musical tasks and activities that young people will undertake during the lesson in order to achieve the learning outcomes. It identifies the appraising, improvising, composing, and performing they will do and the musical repertories with which they will engage. As suggested in Task 8.7, it is always worth auditing a lesson plan to ensure that the musical tasks and activities are, indeed, musical. Ask the question, "would this activity be recognised as a musical activity outside the classroom?" If the answer is "no," you need to reconsider your planning.

PLANNING FOR MUSICAL LEARNING

> ### Task 8.7 **Auditing musical activities**
>
> Audit the lesson plan of a lesson you have recently taught or observed. Ask how the musical activities contributed to young people's musical experiences. Which activities were most "musical"? Which activities were least "musical"? What could be changed about the lesson to ensure the musicality of its content?

Teaching and learning strategies

Teaching and learning strategies are the ways you bring about learning. They should be sequenced in such a way as to optimise opportunities for developing new understanding. Planning teaching and learning strategies draws significantly upon your understanding of:

- musical learning and development (Chapter 6);
- musical learning and language (Chapter 11);
- meeting individual needs (Chapter 4);
- integrating digital technologies (Chapter 3).

Assessment

Assessment is discussed in detail in Chapter 10. Although Figure 8.1 places assessment near the end of the planning sequence, in practice, planning for assessment involves identifying opportunities for assessment that are integrated through lessons and sequences of lessons; choosing appropriate strategies for assessment, such as "no hands questioning" or peer assessment; and considering the place and purpose of formative and summative approaches to assessment. Effective assessment will, in turn, enable you to carry out lesson evaluation.

Lesson evaluation

Lesson evaluation involves evaluating the effectiveness of your teaching through assessing its impact on young people's learning. Evaluation addresses key questions such as:

1. Did the young people achieve the planned learning intention(s) or outcome(s)?
    a. If yes, what was the musical evidence for their learning?
    b. If no, what was the problem—the aims, the activities, the strategies, the assessment?

2. Did the young people achieve additional, unplanned learning intention(s) or outcome(s)?

    a. If yes, what did they learn and was it of musical value?
    b. If no, could I have made room for unplanned creativity if appropriate?

3. What can I change or try in future lessons to better support young people's musical learning and experience?

    a. How can I improve my teaching of this lesson or lesson sequence?
    b. How can I improve my teaching of the young people in this class?

Bringing planning to life in the classroom

Thorough and creative planning is an essential precursor to lessons in which young people learn *of* music *through* music. However, even the very best plans only become a reality in the classroom through the actions of teachers and responses of young people. Effective teaching that brings plans into action is key to successful, musical teaching and learning. For plans to be brought to fruition, teaching should:

- be well organised with a sense of pace and purpose;
- have high expectations of young people's music-making;
- provide opportunities for young people to engage in creative problem-solving;
- elicit and sustain interest;
- be relevant and challenging;
- account for the specific needs, interests, and experiences of the young people;
- consider the musical landscape of the local community and how it could be leveraged in the classroom;
- include a variety of tasks and activities;
- make clear the purpose of young people's participation;
- be transparent about the aims and modes of assessment.

Good teaching is also about being able to identify, accommodate, celebrate, and build upon those unanticipated instances of musical learning and manifestations of musical knowledge that evidence young people's musical personhood and development. But as a teacher, you will only be able to meet these challenges—and create a framework within which to react intelligently to unexpected occurrences in the classroom—if you have thought about and planned lessons that are comprehensive and musical. This is why planning is so important.

SUMMARY

In this chapter you have developed your understanding of the principles that underpin effective lesson planning, including:

1. taking account of different types of musical knowledge: "knowledge that," "knowledge about," "knowing how," and "knowing of";
2. enabling music to be taught musically through activities that immerse young people in musical experiences;
3. accommodating and connecting different aspects of musical experience: appraising, improvising, composing, and performing.

We have also examined the process of planning and the responsivity and creativity required to bring good planning to life within the music classroom.

FURTHER READING

DeLorenzo, L.C. and Silverman, M. (2022)
Music Lesson Plans for Social Justice: A Contemporary Approach for Secondary School Teachers, New York: Oxford University Press.

A selection of interesting and innovative example lesson plans on subjects such as protest, war, and climate change. Although this book is intended first and foremost for contexts in the United States, many of the principles and ideas are equally applicable to classrooms across the United Kingdom.

Fautley, M. and Savage, J. (2014)
Lesson Planning for Effective Learning, Maidenhead: The Open University.

A helpful generic guide to lesson planning for the music classroom.

Swanwick, K. (1999)
Teaching Music Musically, London: Routledge.

A seminal publication exploring how to teach music musically.

BEHAVIOUR FOR MUSICAL LEARNING

Carolyn Cooke

INTRODUCTION

Young people's behaviour is often cited as one the main concerns of beginning and newly qualified teachers (Welch et al. 2011), with poor behaviour often referred to as a reason many leave the profession. But do we have a common shared understanding of what we mean by learning behaviour in a music classroom, and how can beginning music teachers take a proactive approach to developing a positive learning environment? In many contexts, managing behaviour is concerned with how a teacher reacts to negative behaviour in the classroom. There is often an attempt to link behaviour to how teachers plan and facilitate learning, where emphasis is on maximising engagement and reducing opportunities for disruptive behaviour to occur (proactive steps) and to school-wide policies for rewards and sanctions (reactive steps).

However, this chapter will argue that this misses a vital step in learning about behaviour in the music classroom. While it is relatively easy to think of examples of "bad" behaviour (e.g., throwing a chair, pushing another child, breaking an instrument) and possible responses to these, it is far less common to consider the issue from the other perspective: "what behaviours do we want young people to demonstrate in order to learn effectively, and how can we create a learning environment in which they will do so?"

Understanding this alternative way of thinking about behaviour has led to a number of initiatives that adopt cross-curricular or whole-school approaches to thinking about learning behaviours. However, within the music education context, very little has been written to address specifically the question of what behaviours we want to promote and how to do this. Although generic learning behaviours (developed through a pastoral or cross-curricular programme) will, of course, complement and support musical learning, it is possible to argue that musical learning requires music-specific learning behaviours that may not be developed in other areas of the curriculum. Therefore, we need to be able to

BEHAVIOUR FOR MUSICAL LEARNING

articulate what these musical learning behaviours might be and consider how to develop them effectively.

This chapter will argue that facilitating learning behaviours in the music classroom requires us to:

- understand the complex relationships that underpin young people's learning behaviours in a music context;
- explore what it means to demonstrate learning behaviours in a music context and, as teachers, be able to recognise them;
- understand how to actively plan and facilitate musical learning behaviour.

It is through doing this that we can plan for all the young people in our classrooms, as they will have the learning behaviours to be able to access and co-create the curriculum successfully.

Objectives

By the end of the chapter you should be able to:

- justify why learning behaviour needs to be considered within a music-specific context;
- understand how developing learning behaviours underpins young people's relationships with the curriculum, with other people and with themselves as learners;
- understand what musical learning behaviours are and how they might be facilitated in the music classroom.

WHAT DO WE MEAN BY LEARNING BEHAVIOURS?

Ask two different teachers or schools what they consider to be learning behaviours and you may be surprised by the differences in their answers. Some may talk of skills such as teamwork, others may talk of organisation and independent learning, while some argue that learning behaviours should be about young people challenging assumptions or questioning their own learning processes. Identifying what we mean by learning behaviours—whether generic ones that might be useful across the school curriculum, or music-specific ones—is critical, as you will begin to explore in Task 9.1.

Task 9.1 Recognising musical learning behaviours

Consider a music lesson you can recall, either from when you were at school or from more recent school experiences. Think about the musical activities that were planned, and then:

- create a bullet-point list of the learning behaviours that were required (i.e., behaviours that the young people needed to understand and be able to enact to complete the tasks);

- look at your list and ask how many of these learning behaviours are specific to musical learning (e.g., analytical listening to how different parts fit together);
- was there any explicit support for developing these behaviours in class? If yes, how was this approached?

Generic educational research has explored the issues of learning behaviours, including the Teacher Effectiveness Enhancement Programme (TEEP) which explored areas such as collaboration, thinking, metacognition and communication (TEEP 2013), and the Project for Enhancing Effective Learning (PEEL) which developed a set of thirteen good learning behaviours (Box 9.1).

Box 9.1 Good learning behaviours (PEEL 2013)

1. Checks personal comprehension . . . requests further information . . . tells the teacher what they don't understand;
2. Seeks reasons for aspects of the work at hand;
3. Plans a general strategy before starting;
4. Anticipates and predicts possible outcomes;
5. Does not stay stuck, but proactively seeks to sort out what to do;
6. Checks teacher's work for errors; offers corrections;
7. Offers or seeks links between different activities and ideas, topics and subjects, schoolwork and personal life;
8. Searches for weaknesses in own understandings;
9. Suggests new activities and alternative procedures;
10. Challenges the text or an answer the teacher sanctions as correct;
11. Offers ideas, new insights and alternative explanations;
12. Justifies opinions;
13. Reacts and refers to comments of other students.

While these generic models and discussions are valuable to shift the conversation towards teachers being proactive in supporting learning behaviours, there is still a danger that good intentions are reduced and combined with more reactive procedures. As highlighted in Didau's (2012) article, "Children are at school to learn, not to behave," there is a risk that the term "learning behaviour" can get reduced at a practical level in schools to young people "being quiet and listening," which he argues gets distilled into or used to justify a set of classroom rules such as the ones listed in Box 9.2.

Box 9.2 Classroom rules (Didau 2012)

1. Listen when others are talking;
2. Follow directions;
3. Keep hands, feet and objects to yourself;
4. Work quietly, and do not disturb others;
5. Show respect for school and personal property;
6. Work and play in a safe manner.

BEHAVIOUR FOR MUSICAL LEARNING

As Didau (2012) goes on to argue, "these are great rules for instilling 'good' behaviour. . . . But they've got nothing at all to do with the types of behaviour required for learning" (n.p.). Didau is arguing here that although some of the listed rules might enable everyone in the room to engage and concentrate on learning, they don't in themselves help young people to understand *how* to learn. In fact, you could argue that some of the rules listed in Box 9.2 transmit messages about the type of learning that will occur which could be contrary to the type of behaviour needed for learning musically. This is explored further in Task 9.2.

Task 9.2 **Critiquing learning behaviours**

Consider the learning behaviours in Box 9.1 and the list of classroom rules in Box 9.2. Think critically about the type of learning that they promote and whether they work within a music context.

- Are there some that are inappropriate to a music context or would need rewording?
- Which do you feel are vital for effective *musical* learning?
- Are there any you would add?

School-wide rules or agreements and generic ideas about learning behaviours are important, but, as has been demonstrated, learning behaviour will be influenced by a range of factors, including the subject and pedagogy. For example, a 1950s history lesson delivered in a lecture style required young people to learn and therefore behave in a very different way from group composing and performing in a music classroom today. It is therefore crucial to consider what learning behaviour means within today's music education context.

Based on a systematic review into learning behaviour, Powell and Tod (2004) developed a model (Figure 9.1) to demonstrate that learning behaviours underpin, and in turn are a result of, a young person's relationship with three critical elements of education: the curriculum (cognitive wellbeing), other people (social wellbeing) and with themselves as learners (emotional wellbeing). This model acknowledges the complexity of external influences on an individual's behaviour (i.e., how the learning behaviour environment can impact their effectiveness as a learner) and the interdependent relationship between learning behaviours and a young person's relationships with curriculum, others and self. Put another way, the model recognises that to learn effectively and to build effective relationships (whether cognitive, social or self) requires young people to be able to behave in appropriate ways for the learning that specific situation requires. Task 9.3 asks you to reflect on this model.

Task 9.3 **Reflecting on Powell and Tod's (2004) model**

a. Using your own experience as a learner at school, consider how the model in Figure 9.1 reflects the development of your own learning behaviours as a musician.
b. If possible, discuss with other (beginning) music teachers the implications of this model for developing musical learning behaviours in the classroom.

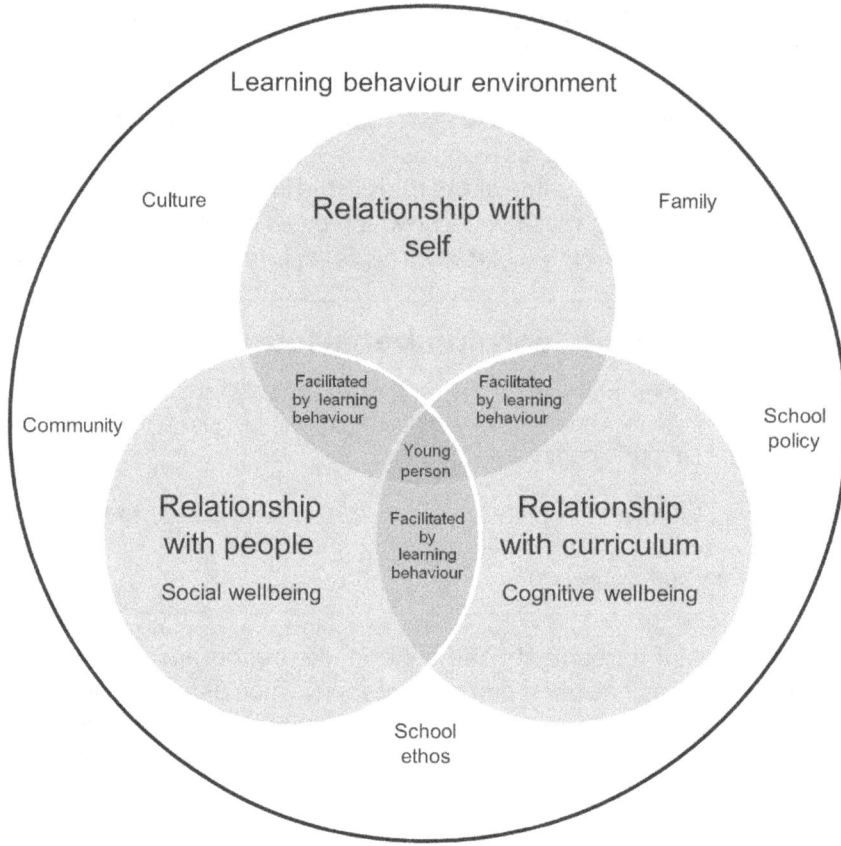

Figure 9.1 Learning behaviour conceptual framework

JUSTIFYING A MUSIC-SPECIFIC APPROACH

Although it wasn't designed for this purpose, Powell and Tod's (2004) model gives us a way of thinking critically about the relationships between the young people we teach and their cognitive, social and emotional wellbeing within a music-specific context. In doing so, we can justify why learning behaviours need to be considered within a music-specific context.

Musical learning behaviours and relationship with the curriculum

As discussed in Chapter 7, the concept of a music curriculum is complex. Part of this complexity stems from the range of prior music curriculum experiences young people bring with them and the relationships with music they have before they enter the classroom, whether as listeners, producers, composers or performers. This might be most obvious at points of transfer between schools, where young people within one class may have had very different past experiences, but equally might occur at transitions between different year groups or into examination classes. These previous experiences, if considered carefully during planning, may enhance young people's wellbeing as they are asked to draw on and extend learning behaviours that they have already begun to develop. For example, a class that has developed behaviours around effective group rehearsal (e.g., identifying for the teacher small sections that need rehearsing by themselves) could be asked to develop this further during a small-group project where they are expected to rehearse independently from the teacher and negotiate how best to rehearse as a group.

It is also important to consider that many young people will have developed musical learning behaviours independently from the school environment. Thinking about the range of musicians in a classroom demonstrates just how varied their learning behaviours might be: the young person who composes in their own bedroom; the group of friends who have formed a band; a young person who plays in the local youth orchestra; someone who learnt in a whole-class instrumental group at primary school; those who sing at church or learn and perform traditional folk instruments.

All of these young people will have developed quite different learning behaviours in relation to their experience, whether it be a high level of independent creative decision-making, carefully following instructions and etiquettes around particular types of group performance, questioning what is happening while playing or getting feedback on their performance or composition from virtual sources. Thus, asking young people to learn (and therefore behave) in a particular way may cause dissonance between what they know as musical learning behaviours and what is being promoted. For example, a girl may have taught herself a complex guitar accompaniment to a song aurally by listening, singing the bass note and then finding the chord through experimentation. In a project about pop songs, she may then be encouraged to read notated chord sequences (using only three chords) as the way of achieving the highest marks according to the success criteria, therefore undermining the more musical learning behaviour that she had developed.

Of course, no teacher would deliberately set out to cause such a stark dissonance between previously developed learning behaviours and the curriculum, but it is surprisingly easy to transmit a particular set of values about musical learning behaviours and what we as teachers consider valued knowledge—and difficult to identify young people's previous learning behaviours if they aren't given the opportunity to demonstrate and share them.

As well as the nature of the musical experiences young people bring to the classroom, there is also the issue of learning behaviours associated with different musical genres, cultures and traditions. A quick glance at how musicians learn in different musical cultures highlights the diversity of approaches to musical learning and therefore expectations of learning behaviours (e.g., in master-apprentice models, within community groups, through structured and progressive technical examinations). This raises some important questions which you can consider when reflecting on your practice:

- How do we as teachers know what musical learning behaviours our young people have already developed? These might relate to particular cultural

traditions and experiences but might also relate to the nature of the music activity.
- Do we allow spaces for young people to bring their own musical learning behaviours to a task?
- Do we prepare young people to understand that there are different musical learning behaviours, or do we make assumptions?

Musical learning behaviours and relationships with people

Powell and Tod (2004), in their systematic review of research into learning behaviours, identified that "social interaction is pivotal to cognitive development and influences the development of learning behaviours" (81). At a whole-school level, strategies to support young people's social wellbeing, such as mentoring, tutoring and social education sessions, all contribute to ensuring that they are able to be effective learners. This may involve helping young people work confidently in groups, communicate their ideas and present information. However, just as with cognitive wellbeing, there are some particular issues within a music learning context that may affect how young people behave as learners when working with others.

First, when working with peers, interactions about the nature of tasks, the processes for completing them and the musical learning behaviours needed for them can create tensions. This can often be seen during small-group work where the task requires negotiation about the direction it should take. It is in these circumstances that dominant views about musical styles, genres, processes or products (whether from peers or through the way the task has been scaffolded) might override valid and important minority views and musical learning behaviours. It is sometimes possible to see groups where capable individuals are less willing or able to contribute, or where those who may lack confidence in their musical learning behaviours are reluctant to get involved and may be seen as being passive.

Dominant voices or opinions can be related to young people's perceptions of hierarchies among peer groups. It is easy to bring to mind circumstances in which young people may feel that hierarchies exist within a group and how they then operate as a result. The most commonly referred to is the perception of young people who have instrumental or vocal tuition beyond the curriculum, their musicianship in relation to others in the class and their ability to succeed in curriculum music. Other hierarchies may also exist around perceived intelligence or resources to which young people have access beyond the classroom. These perceptions may influence social wellbeing and can lead to differences in levels of participation and engagement with tasks, within music learning contexts.

Equally, another influence on social wellbeing is the interactions that young people have with their teacher and the values and beliefs they promote (whether consciously or subconsciously). As has already been stated, it is surprisingly

BEHAVIOUR FOR MUSICAL LEARNING

easy for teachers to promote particular beliefs and values about music, musicianship or learning music through what they do or how they phrase something, which can have ramifications for social wellbeing. This leads to important questions to reflect on in your own teaching practices:

- How far do the tasks we set allow young people to share, develop and negotiate their musical learning behaviours in ways that allow equality in participation?
- How do we explicitly support young people to engage in tasks when their musical learning behaviours may be a limiting factor?
- How as teachers do we keep in check our own assumptions and beliefs about music and learning, to allow young people the openness to bring their own beliefs and experiences to the fore?

Musical learning behaviours and relationships with self

It is clear to anyone who has worked with young people within a music context that they either will have or will develop their own personal relationship with the music, musical activities or ways of learning. Of course, it is possible to argue that emotional wellbeing stems from cognitive and social wellbeing; however, there are a few more personal issues to consider within a music context. These include considering issues such as young people's reactions to the learning environment, their individual learning needs and the ability of individuals to manage their own learning and influence their experience within the music classroom.

The learning environment is a powerful, yet often underestimated ingredient in facilitating young people's learning. The layout, displays, accessibility of resources and instruments all send messages to young people about how they are expected to behave and learn. For example, a new class faced with lines of desks with computers and keyboards are likely to deduce a different message about musical learning from those faced with a circle of chairs and a variety of percussion and acoustic instruments in the centre of the classroom. Equally, a classroom filled with displays of photographs of young people working in groups on a variety of projects, with quotations, key words and reviews of projects, gives strong clues as to what the teacher considers to be valued ways of working, while a music history timeline displays something different. The impact of the learning environment on an individual's relationship with self cannot be underestimated. In an ideal situation it should make them feel safe to learn and experiment, supported in making musical decisions and choices and included as part of the classroom or even department community. At its least successful, it may turn young people off, making them feel that learning within school music bears little relationship to themselves as individuals.

As with any discussion of learning, the learning behaviours that need to be facilitated and supported by the teacher will vary from young person to young person. This is not just associated with the identifiable learning needs of certain individuals, but the learning needs of *all* young people, depending on their particular interests, backgrounds, ambitions and learning approaches. This requires of teachers a great deal of individual knowledge of, and commitment to, all young people as individuals at every opportunity.

Key to developing a sense of relationship to self is enabling young people to feel they can influence their own learning approach. It is through this process (often referred to as "pupil voice") that all young people can feel the curriculum is theirs, rather than something that is being done to them (see Chapter 7). Of course, running a busy department within the context of a school poses many challenges to the concept of a personalised, individualised curriculum experience. However, musical learning is characterised by personal interactions and experiences of music and a plethora of musical decision-making moments, all of which provide opportunity for young people to shape their experiences. At a larger scale, involvement in curriculum design and development, or developing young people's ability and confidence to take their learning in an alternative direction, gives greater scope for truly personalised experiences that may contribute to emotional wellbeing. Task 9.4 asks you to consider these issues in light of your own experiences.

> ### Task 9.4 **Young people's learning behaviours**
>
> Think of two young people you are working with, who were not learning effectively in a music context (remember this may not be that they were "misbehaving" but demonstrating little progress). Looking at the issues that have been raised in relation to cognitive, social and emotional wellbeing, which do you feel may impact (positively or negatively) these young people's learning behaviour in a music context?

MUSICAL LEARNING BEHAVIOURS

So far, we have discussed issues that impact on young people's learning behaviours within a music context and the justification as to why musical learning behaviours might need specific consideration. So, what do we mean by musical learning behaviours? Of course, the answer to this question will depend on the nature of the learning activity, the young people involved and the expected learning outcomes. However, we can start by considering what we mean by using three examples of learning behaviours during group composition tasks (Box 9.3).

In establishing what evidence there is of learning behaviours within these three vignettes, Claxton's (2002) research into learning power provides a useful framework. He argues that a supple learning mind, and therefore a powerful one, requires young people to develop four types of learning disposition: resilience, resourcefulness, reciprocity and reflectiveness. These four dispositions each have a number of capabilities, as set out in Table 9.1.

Box 9.3 Examples of learning behaviours

Vignette 1

Jack was asked to compose a pop song as part of a group of five. The group had already performed a range of pop songs, negotiating how different people in the group would contribute. This included some working aurally from a downloaded copy of the song, some teaching others in the group using imitation and call and response and some using a tab score. When it came to composing, the group decided that they would use a sequencing program to record their initial ideas in case they came up with something they couldn't then replicate. Two of the five also made some written notes about the chords. By the end of the first lesson, they had recorded a lot of material for a possible chorus. Jack, who was used to composing using a software package at home, volunteered to produce a draft version. In the next lesson they listened to the track and replicated it, although they found a more suitable drumbeat. They then repeated the process for composing the verse.

Vignette 2

During the first term in secondary school, Siobhan completed a unit of work on programme music, focusing specifically on writing melodies and using the musical elements to provide contrast. The unit was based around a children's story. When composing and refining their group composition, Siobhan was able to describe the composition process using phrases such as, "we used the first bit of the melody each time the main character came in," and "we thought the music for this bit of the story needed to be more dance-y and so we used some drums." In performance, the teacher identified that Siobhan was noticing when others in the group were out of time, out of tune or out of balance. Siobhan was able to negotiate with the others in the group how to stand in the space to make sure they could all see each other to improve the timing and balance.

Vignette 3

Ali knew that he didn't cope well with the hustle and bustle of a noisy music classroom when there was group work going on. He had an understanding with his teacher that his group would work in the corridor during group work or in the adjacent classroom if it was free. He was also aware that he was good at working on a specific problem or part of the composition independently rather than participating in group decision-making. This often meant that he found himself resources and asked for advice when he felt he needed it. This rarely involved the class teacher as he often involved his guitar teacher, who was usually in the music office during Ali's music lesson. Although the class teacher was fully aware that Ali asked the guitar teacher to listen to things during her lesson, she wasn't aware that these conversations and musical starting points continued during Ali's guitar lessons. Drawing on two different adult perspectives led to Ali having to make decisions about which opinions and ideas to take on board.

Table 9.1 Learning capabilities

Resilience	Resourcefulness	Reciprocity	Reflectiveness
Perseverance Staying with it. Dealing with uncertainty and disappointment.	**Making links** Seeing connections. Building patterns. Making meaning.	**Interdependence** Balancing self-reliance and sociability.	**Meta-learning** Knowing yourself as a learner and assessing possible learning gains.
Managing distractions Recognising, tolerating and reducing distractions.	**Questioning** Being curious. Asking questions. Playing with ideas.	**Collaboration** Sharing. Communicating effectively. Using appropriate roles.	**Planning** Planning ahead. Knowing what action to take. Using time well. Anticipating problems.
Absorption Being enrapt in learning.	**Capitalising** Looking out for and using materials and resources to support learning.	**Empathy and listening** Listening to understand. Putting yourself in others' shoes.	**Distilling** Drawing out points from a learning experience and applying them to further learning.
Noticing Perceiving and sensing the details in experiences.	**Imagining** Seeing how things might be. Visualising and using creative intuition.	**Imitation** Picking up habits, traits and values from those you admire.	**Revising** Adapting with flexibility. Thinking on your feet. Monitoring progress. Reviewing the situation.
	Reasoning Being logical and analytical.		

(adapted from Ellis and Tod 2009: 76)

BEHAVIOUR FOR MUSICAL LEARNING

Although many of these capabilities and their definitions are easily transferable to a music context, a few can be changed to make them subject relevant. For example, *imagining* talks of visualisation. Although there may be an element of visualisation, or seeing in your mind's eye, during a music task (e.g., the visual effect during performance or visualising a melodic shape), it may be helpful to add internalisation of musical sound to the definition. Equally, *listening* is defined as "listening for understanding" under the disposition of reciprocity. In a music context, listening has a far broader role and could therefore arguably sit across the dispositions of reciprocity, reflectiveness and resourcefulness (see Chapter 15). Finally, *noticing* within a music learning context could also be broader than Claxton's definition. Noticing details of experiences could arguably straddle resilience, resourcefulness, reflectiveness and reciprocity. The next Task 9.5 will help you consider how these dispositions relate to the vignettes in Box 9.3.

Task 9.5 **Identifying learning dispositions**

Using the four dispositions from Table 9.1 as sentence starters, note down what learning behaviours are evident in the vignettes in Box 9.3. You may feel that some dispositions are not explicitly mentioned but must have existed in order for the young people to be learning effectively.

FACILITATING EFFECTIVE LEARNING BEHAVIOURS

Throughout this chapter we have identified ways in which thinking about developing learning behaviours, instead of managing behaviour, can be used as an alternative, more proactive way to promote effective learning in the music classroom. It has been argued that through supporting young people's cognitive, social and emotional wellbeing and by being aware of exactly what learning behaviour looks and sounds like in a music classroom, we are more equipped to develop effective learners. However, it is arguably the teacher in the classroom who can make the most substantial contribution to ensuring this can happen. The question is how this might be achieved.

To answer this, the final sections of this chapter suggest there are four factors which can be considered key to developing young people's ability to be effective learners in a music classroom: knowledge of individuals as musicians and learners, planning for the development of musical learning behaviours, creating a musical learning environment and interactions with young people.

Young people as musicians and learners

Ensuring young people's social, emotional and cognitive wellbeing can only happen if we know individuals well. However, helping them to use and develop their learning behaviours in a music context requires us to know them as individuals with generic needs and personalities, as musicians with previous experiences, skills and understanding and as musical learners. This is daunting for any music teacher who may see hundreds of young people each week; however, much can be gained from ensuring that the following conditions exist:

- Young people have the opportunity to express and demonstrate how they learn best by influencing their approach to tasks and activities. This may be through choice of resources such as instruments or choosing how they approach a task rather than following a pre-set structure (i.e., allowing individuals to choose a different path to the end result rather than following what you would choose);
- Opportunities are provided to establish what previous musical learning young people have experienced and to demonstrate and draw on the learning behaviours that have been developed;
- Young people are made explicitly aware that they are co-creating the curriculum experience with you, and that with their help, you will try to find ways for them to learn effectively. It is through this partnership (using pupil voice) that you can begin to develop an understanding of them as individual learners.

Planning to develop musical learning behaviours

As with any learning, the question must be asked as to how we expect young people to know what we value as teachers. As has been argued, this is particularly important in a music context where the type of learning, and therefore learning behaviours, may be different from those experienced in other subjects. Planning for the development of this understanding and associated skills is not straightforward. For example, it is quite possible that a young person in their first year at secondary school may demonstrate more advanced noticing skills than an older peer, without the equivalent instrumental or vocal skill level. However, there are a number of points to consider in developing a young person's ability to learn effectively:

- They will need a range of opportunities to develop the learning behaviours that will help them. You may, for example, audit your units of work to see what learning behaviours you are expecting young people to demonstrate and think about whether you are making this explicit to them;
- In being aware of the perceived hierarchies that may impact on learning behaviour, you may need to explicitly plan ways of demonstrating and sharing the contributions that all young people can make. This may include suggesting alternative ways of tackling a task, being prepared to try something new, noticing connections between their musical learning and other experiences or reflecting on their learning process;
- Collaboration is key to effective musical learning. Planning how collaborative group work is introduced, and how those you are teaching know what

effective group learning can be like, is critical. This may involve modelling effective group work and decision-making (possibly in a whole-class activity) through to praising groups who demonstrate effective group learning and sharing their experiences with others in the class;

- Different young people will react to working in groups in different ways.

A musical learning environment

As highlighted by Claxton's (2002) research, resourcefulness is a key disposition to learning effectively. In a music classroom, this will often involve accessing a wide range of musical instruments and technologies but will also include having access to other people (e.g., the teacher, other young people). This is critical to planning the learning environment. How can you arrange the space and the resources within it to allow those in your classes to learn most effectively? Will you need to change the arrangement of the space for different types of learning? How can you plan space and time for young people to be able to work both independently and collaboratively?

As was highlighted in Vignette 3 about Ali in Box 9.3, managing distractions is also critical to successful musical learning. Thinking about other learning environments that young people might experience, there are very few that require this capability to such an extent. Discussing this issue openly with individuals and groups, noticing who finds it particularly difficult and organising spaces and groupings to maximise their ability to learn effectively will all help. This could be as simple as allowing young people to express when distractions are making learning difficult, organising resources to create enclosed circular working areas within the room or allowing young people to move into different spaces to complete certain parts of tasks (e.g., two boys want to listen carefully to a backing track they have composed and are allowed to listen to it in a practice room so that they can listen for the balance and timing accurately). In other words, it is imperative that the learning environment is a *musical* learning environment.

Interactions with young people

Developing behaviours for musical learning requires us as teachers to explicitly think about, plan for, model and discuss the behaviours we value. To this end, the interactions we have with individuals and classes will underpin how young people understand what we expect and what is effective in helping them to learn. These interactions may be verbal but may also often be musical, as young people begin to understand you as a musician and how you would approach musical learning tasks. This is, of course, a form of modelling and provides a strong argument for modelling musical learning processes (i.e., different approaches to a task or musical problem-solving) rather than just modelling the final musical outcome.

If the interactions are verbal, then using Claxton's (2002) research we can argue that open-ended, exploratory, questioning, reflective interactions are more likely to support the development of the behaviours we want young people to draw on. These might include, "what happens if . . .?" or "what other options did you experiment with?" or "why did you decide that . . . was the best option?"

Finally, viewing interactions from a learning behaviour standpoint may make us think about how we use praise to support the development of musical learning behaviours. Instead of praising musical outcomes (although this is of course vital), learning behaviours give us another reason to praise individuals (e.g., for noticing links between different units of work or persevering with a musical problem until a solution is found). This is important, not only for ensuring young people's cognitive, social and emotional wellbeing but also to reinforce what is valued behaviour.

The aforementioned factors support us in planning and facilitating music lessons in which we can promote and develop musical learning behaviours. In other words, *musical learning behaviours* can only occur and develop through *musical lessons* in which both teacher and young people are *acting musically*. Task 9.6 will help you consider how a music teacher's own behaviours can promote effective musical learning behaviours in young people.

Task 9.6 **Promoting effective learning behaviours**

Review the chapter (particularly the two models) and create a bullet-point list of teacher behaviours that will support young people in developing appropriate and effective learning behaviours in the music classroom.

Plan a lesson for a new class starting at the school. Think about how you could plan the learning environment, your dialogue with them, your musical interactions with them and the activities to promote the learning behaviours you feel are most important when introducing them to what it means to learn in music.

SUMMARY

This chapter has:

- discussed the importance of considering what learning behaviours we value and want to develop in young people;
- argued that to do this we must consider learning behaviours within a musical learning context, as the cognitive, social and emotional wellbeing of young people is underpinned by a number of music-specific issues.

It is in this complex web of factors, as demonstrated by Powell and Tod's (2004) model, that we as music teachers need to be able to articulate and facilitate the development of musical learning behaviours.

BEHAVIOUR FOR MUSICAL LEARNING

FURTHER READING

Capel, S.A., Leask, M., Younie, S., Hidson, E. and Lawrence, J. (eds) (2023)
Learning to Teach in the Secondary School: A Companion to School Experience, 9th edn, Abingdon: Routledge.

Chapter 3 specifically addresses behaviours for learning.

Claxton, G. (2002)
Building Learning Power: Helping Young People Become Better Learners, Bristol: The Learning Organisation. Online, available at: https://www.buildinglearningpower.com/

This website gives a comprehensive introduction to the principles and research underpinning Building Learning Power, including links to further publications.

ASSESSMENT IN CLASSROOM MUSIC—WHAT, HOW, AND WHY

Martin Fautley

INTRODUCTION

There are many views on assessment in education, and music education is no different! There are numerous opinions concerning how it should be done, what it should entail, and even why it needs to exist in the first place. Although it is undoubtedly complex, this chapter will help you navigate your way through its various difficulties, as well as hopefully providing you with some food for thought about assessment and its uses and purposes in the music classroom. We will focus particularly on what is going on with regards to assessment for young people aged between 11 and 14. The reason for this is that it is at this point of education that the majority of your teaching timetable is likely to be dedicated. It is also the part of the curriculum which is not (currently) subject to any statutory or external assessment regimes in most places in the United Kingdom. After age 14, when music is normally an optional subject, young people choose to take music leading to an externally validated qualification, such as GCSE, BTEC, or National 5, which have their own assessment and examination profiles.

It is also in the lower secondary school where music teachers are likely to have the most control over the curriculum and are often able to design their own assessment systems. This may not always be the case, however, as we know that some multi-academy trusts have both a common curriculum and a common assessment policy which operates across groups of schools. Nevertheless, even here there will have been some context-specific construction of learning and assessment undertaken. We are going to be making a number of observations, suggestions, and recommendations during the course of this chapter, but it is important to note at the outset that you will need to fit these alongside the systems in place in the school in which you are or will be teaching. To this end, in this chapter we will consider the well-worn terminologies of formative and summative assessment and also think about the audiences for various forms of assessment. In order to help with this, we will think about what is meant by the

ASSESSMENT IN CLASSROOM MUSIC

notion of assessment data, how assessment interlinks with marking and grading, and various ways this can help with musical teaching and learning.

> **Objectives**
>
> By the end of this chapter you should be able to:
>
> - describe and discuss the importance of formative assessment in the school music classroom;
> - know that there are different audiences for assessment;
> - understand that assessment is about more than just testing;
> - put day-to-day assessment ideas into practice in your music pedagogy.

ASSESSING MUSIC MUSICALLY

Swanwick (1999) wrote about "teaching music musically" in his book of the same title, and, building on his concept, it is useful to think about *assessing* music musically. In order to do this, let us think about some of the key assessment terminologies you will come across. One of these is the distinction that is frequently drawn between the ideas involved with *formative* assessment and *summative* assessment. There is much that has been written on this, and in music education it is very important to think about the distinction between the two. They do not necessarily represent different types of assessment but are more concerned with what you do, how you do it, and what happens to the information that is produced as a result.

Formative assessment is discussed in some detail by Booth (2022a) in the volume *Learning to Teach in the Secondary School*. In it he offers a helpful definition:

> In the United Kingdom, the term "formative assessment" tends to be built upon the work of Black and Wiliam (1998) as well as the Assessment Reform Group (ARG, 1999). Having researched the effects of formative assessment practice as an update of Natriello (1987) and Crooks' (1988) work, the oft-cited definition of "formative assessment" by Black and Wiliam (1998, pp. 7-8) is that it is "all those activities undertaken by teachers and/or their students, which provide information to be used as feedback to modify teaching and learning activities in which they are engaged".
>
> (423)

The important part of this definition is that formative assessment is concerned with *modifying* teaching and learning: it concerns itself with what is coming next by building on what has been learnt and done. What this means is that for formative assessment to take place, you, the teacher, need to do something with the information you have garnered. This active agency regarding assessment means that this is a thing that you *do with* young people. This distinguishes it from summative assessment, which, in many cases, is something which is *done to* young people. Summative assessment, in essence, sums up learning by giving a grade, mark, percentage, score, or level to a specific work of attainment. This is the sense in which popular understandings of assessment operate, and frequently allied to this are notions of any such grading arising from a test or examination. However, it is worth pointing out that whilst all examinations are assessments, not all assessments are examinations!

Within the context of music education, let us begin by considering what we might term the "traditional" instrumental music lesson. These have been taking place for many hundreds of years. The normal modality, wherever and whenever they take place, is for the young person to present themselves to their teacher, and play or sing whatever it is they have been working on. The teacher will then offer suggestions as to what the young person can do to improve, possibly discussing aspects of technique or interpretation, often demonstrating how to perform smaller sections or difficult passages within the piece, maybe slowing down sections to help with, say, fingering, and then reconstructing the performance as a whole. The teacher will then normally give the young person specific things to do before their next lesson, which the young person can work on by themselves in their own time. This way of working seems so normal in instrumental music lessons that it is often unquestioned, and its focus on what might be termed the "master-apprentice" modality is deeply rooted in many cultures around the world.

It is worthwhile at this stage pointing out that what the instrumental music teacher does *not* do is to listen to the performance of a young person and then say something like, "68%–next please!" Whilst this may seem a strange observation, nonetheless, in some instances classroom music lessons have been observed where this is the assessment regimen in operation. Clearly, this is of very little help or utility to the young person; they may have absolutely no idea as to what they need to do to improve, nor any clue as to what aspects of their music they need to work on, nor any knowledge of what to do next. You can explore this further in Task 10.1.

Task 10.1 **Exploring formative and summative assessment**

1. Talk to your mentors or music colleagues in school. How do they understand and use the terms *formative* and *summative* assessment?
2. Talk to teachers of other subjects too. Does their understanding of these terms tally with that of the music department?

What is being discussed here is the use of *assessment data*. Booth (2022b) introduces the notion of assessment data like this:

ASSESSMENT IN CLASSROOM MUSIC

> The term "data" can be considered one of the most common assessment-related words used in schools today. It covers a plethora of information for the classroom teacher ranging from scores, levels or grades from national examinations to ongoing conversations with and observations of pupils.
>
> (450)

The assessment data involved in awarding the learner 68% in the example above are of a very different order from those which arose in the instrumental music lesson we considered. However, both were established from the same performance, the first from an example of summative assessment—admittedly an ill-considered one—and the other from an example of formative assessment. This is important, as it shows the same performance (in both the musical and non-musical senses) can give rise to different forms of assessment data. The formative assessment example in the instrumental music lesson involved the teacher talking with the learner, explaining, modelling, exemplifying, and dealing with things in the moment. This form of assessment takes the form of a conversation, deals with specifics, and endeavours to give the learner involved a clear framework showing what to do to improve. The single percentage grade achieves none of these things!

KEY QUESTIONS REGARDING ASSESSMENT

Discussing the assessment data associated with formative and summative assessment leads us inexorably to some of the key questions we need to address when thinking about assessment in classroom music education. One of the first questions that teachers ask themselves, and, in many cases, each other, when thinking about assessment in the lower secondary school music class is often, "what am I going to assess?" However, it is more useful to think specifically about two slightly different questions shown in Box 10.1:

Box 10.1 Questions for thinking about assessment

1. Who is this assessment for?
2. Why am I assessing this?

Who is this assessment for?

It may seem an obvious question, but thinking about who will receive the results of an assessment is a helpful place to start. In one of the earlier examples we saw a young person being given a percentage grade for their musical performance. This sort of procedure can often be seen when the primary purpose of an assessment is to provide quantitative data, in many cases which can be entered onto a spreadsheet. This use of assessment data feeds what we can refer to as *systemic* purposes of assessment. It is not designed to help either the learner or the teacher; its primary purpose is to audit.

The systemic use of assessment data contrasts with occasions where teachers give learners very specific feedback about what they need to do as the very next steps in order to improve. The traditional notion of the instrumental teacher we discussed earlier is normally found to be working in this fashion. In this case, the purpose of the data arising from the assessment is to inform the young person with some specificity as to what they should be doing next. These data are not of the form that can be readily entered into a spreadsheet; instead the feedback is conversational, involves interaction with the learner, and can also use musical modelling and exemplification. The audience for these assessment data, then, is the young people themselves.

A third category of audience for assessment data will be you, the teacher. You may want, for example, to know how the young people in your classes are doing at learning a specific chord sequence on the ukulele. You have taught them the fingering for the chords, demonstrated what they should be doing, and provided a rhythmic element to the performances you are looking for. You then, maybe in a "show and play" session, or "on the hoof" as you walk around the classroom, listen to and observe what the class have been doing, and think about what it is that *you* need to do in order to progress their ukulele work. Do they, for instance, need to spend more time working at the fingering for the chords, or at changing from one specific chord to another, or maybe at their rhythmic accuracy? This is an assessment where the data are intended to be of use to the teacher in order to help the young people with their learning and attainment.

These three audiences for assessment data could arise from the same music-making, but they have very different utility. These three purposes for assessment data are represented in diagrammatic form in Figure 10.1. For the first audience—the young people themselves—the purpose of the assessment is to help them with learning and doing. Then there is an audience consisting of you, the teacher, as you will want to know how well (or otherwise!) the young people are doing, and what you may need to address in terms of any misconceptions, problematic aspects of technique, and so on. Finally, there are the systemic uses of assessment data for schools needing to keep track of young people's attainment across subjects.

Asking who assessment data are for will influence the type of assessment which is being done. For example, the assessment of young people's instrumental proficiency that you devise when working for systemic purposes (for example, when the school data manager wants your grades) is going to be of a different order than the assessment you use for yourself to see how well the class are working at their performances.

One of the quandaries that some beginning teachers find themselves in is when having to work within the strictures of whole-school assessment policies, especially as these can vary significantly between different establishments. Some schools have detailed documentation that goes into considerable specificity as to what assessment in that particular educational context should entail. In other places, assessment policies are simply marking procedures determining

■ ■ ■ ■ **ASSESSMENT IN CLASSROOM MUSIC**

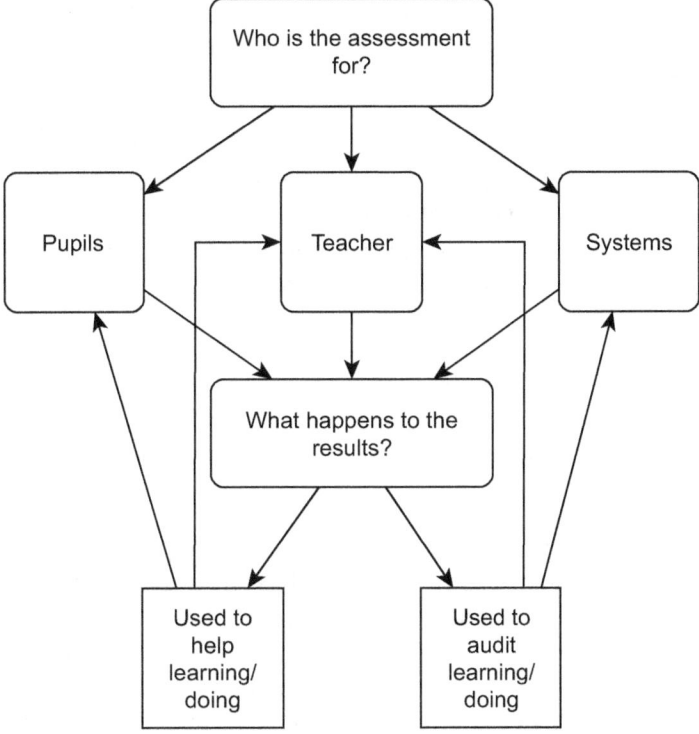

■ **Figure 10.1** Who is the assessment for?

(Fautley 2010: 70)

which rating scales to use (there is more on marking and grading later). Task 10.2 helps you to consider the different audiences for assessment in your own teaching context.

Task 10.2 **Exploring assessment in your context**

Ask your colleagues or mentors the following questions:

1. Who are the different audiences for the assessment data you work with? Are there any formal institutional requirements you have to conform to?
2. Is there a whole-school policy on assessment, and what does it entail? What emphasis does it place on assessment, marking, and grading?
3. Have there been any continuing professional development sessions on assessment for school staff? If so, what did these cover?
4. How do any whole-school assessment policies impact upon teaching and learning in music?

If your school has an assessment or data manager, ask them what sorts of assessment data they are interested in and what they do with them.

175

There are complex issues with thinking about the uses and purposes of assessment in schools generally, and there can be a lack of clarity concerning appropriate language. As Newton (2007) observed:

> (1) The term "assessment purpose" can be interpreted in a variety of different ways. (2) The uses to which assessment results are put are often categorized misleadingly. The fact that the term "assessment purpose" can be interpreted in a variety of different ways is, perhaps, the most basic point for an assessment professional to appreciate, to ensure that her advice is not misunderstood.
>
> (149)

This matters to us in music, and the three audiences for assessment identified in Figure 10.1–young people, teachers, and systems–should help you with thinking about *what* you want to know, and, importantly, *why* you want to know it.

Why am I assessing this?

The second key question asked in Box 10.1 has an answer which may be less straightforward than it at first seems. Assessment, particularly formative assessment, is integral to teaching and learning. Indeed, as Swanwick (1988) observed regarding music, "to teach is to assess" (149). We have already seen how the traditional model of instrumental music teaching involves formative assessment, and it is but a short leap to see that the same is true of classroom teaching. Music lessons should be inherently *musical*, and it is in this *being musical* that you will bring your pedagogic knowledge into play in order to respond to what you see and hear from the young people in your classes. Shulman (1986) wrote about the teacher's "pedagogic content knowledge" (PCK) (an area also considered in the context of digital learning in Chapter 3) and defined it as being one of the,

> Most useful forms of representation of these ideas, the most powerful analogies, illustrations, examples, explanations, and demonstrations–in a word, the ways of representing and formulating the subject that make it comprehensible to others.
>
> (6)

Using your own personal PCK–which you will be developing throughout your teaching career–you will be thinking about what to do to help with teaching and learning in your music classes. What this means is that addressing the question of *why* you are assessing should come directly from *what* you will be teaching.

This is an important aspect of developing teaching and learning: assessment arises from curriculum, or, as Colwell (2017) observes, "there must be a direct match between the curriculum and what the student is expected to know and do in the assessment" (371). What this means for music teaching and learning in the classroom is that deciding on the programme of study should precede deciding on the mode of assessment. To do otherwise is to fall into a trap, which Wiliam

(2001) pithily points out: "we start out with the aim of making the important measurable and end up making only the measurable important" (58). This may seem obvious, but as music educators we do need to be very careful with what we do and how we do it. As we discuss later, time in the classroom for lower secondary school music is often restricted, and there can be a lot of classes to teach and not much time in which to cover material. With the aim of being as musical as possible, for as much of the time as possible, we therefore need to be careful with our assessments.

But this takes us onto a deeper matter, which is what we think assessment actually is! We saw that Swanwick's (1988) oft-cited notion, "to teach is to assess" (149), is fundamental to teaching and learning in music, and so thinking this way means that you are assessing all the time, maybe even without realising it! As Fautley and Daubney (2025) note:

> Good formative assessment happens throughout lessons, including when you have conversations with pupils about their music making and musical learning, or even when you stand next to them during a group performance and, say, bring them back into time with the ensemble. It does not need to be written down, it can be verbal, involve musical modelling, or a combination of ways. It occurs in the moment, and is immediate. The importance of this should be recognised; formative, developmental assessment is fundamental in securing sound musical progress.
>
> (3)

What this means is that we may need to think about assessment afresh, and in a number of ways. There is day-to-day assessment, which we can think of being all-the-time-you-are-teaching assessment, and then there is assessment which takes place as a separate event. Returning to Newton's (2007: 149) observations, this can be a source of confusion in music education. What schools will often mean when they talk about assessment is for it to take place as a separate event. This is when your school will want your assessment data to be provided in a spreadsheet of grades. The all-the-time-you-are-teaching assessments are of no use or interest to senior leadership teams—it is the evental (Žižek 2009) use of assessment which will be of concern there. This notion of assessment as an event is not necessarily the terminology which will be commonplace in schools, but, as discussed in Task 10.3, it is appropriate for you as a beginning teacher to think about it in this way.

Task 10.3 Observing assessment in practice

Try to observe some lessons where mentors or colleagues have indicated that assessment will be taking place. Afterwards, talk to them about whether they think of assessment as being something which is done separately (as an assessment "event") or how else they are conceptualising and operationalising assessment. Aim to observe some assessment practices in other subject areas as well as in music.

WHAT IS THERE TO ASSESS IN MUSIC EDUCATION?

The essential components of classroom music which are taught and learned are normally defined as being *composing, performing,* and *listening* (see Chapters 13, 14, and 15). Whilst a holistic music education involving all three in equal balance is a *desideratum*, nonetheless many classroom teachers often separate out these three aspects for both teaching and assessment purposes. This makes sense, in many cases, as evental assessment is much more straightforward when dealing with a singular construct than when trying to combine multiple, sometimes unrelated, aspects. As Fautley and Daubney (2025) observe in this regard,

> When you come to write your own assessment criterion statements, it is worth pointing out that it is advisable to beware of statements which entail assessment by accretion. This occurs where criterion statements have lots of use of the word "and" in them. In other words, "the pupils can do this, and that, and something else too." This can make it difficult to effectively grade these sorts of statements, and you are advised to try and keep your statements to assessing a singularity, in other words focus in on one aspect of what you wish to assess, and if you need other areas of assessment, add those in as separate criterion statements. This is especially the case with some examples we have seen where the accretion statement covers multiple unrelated aspects of musical attainment, making grading ... problematic.
>
> (16)

Task 10.4 **Assessment statements**

1. Look at any assessment criterion statements you are currently using. Do these refer to a singularity, or do they have the word "and" in them?
2. If they do have an "and," how many separate things are being assessed in them? Can you re-write them so that perhaps you end up with more than one criterion statement?
3. If you do not have any assessment criterion statements at the moment, have a go at writing some that assess a singularity for something you will be teaching soon.

What all this means is that deciding what to assess should arise naturally from what it is that you want young people to learn. Assessment therefore arises from curriculum (Task 10.4)—the definition, design, and enactment of which is discussed in Chapter 7—and should be a mechanism whereby you can check that what you intend to be learnt, has actually been learnt!

ASSESSMENT—GRADING, RECORDING, AND REPORTING

As previously discussed, in some schools the assessment policy can primarily be concerned with marking and grading procedures. There are considerable

ASSESSMENT IN CLASSROOM MUSIC

differences in this aspect between schools, and there are far too many unique variables to be able to deal logically with these in a single chapter. However, the important thing to note is that you will need to fit with what is required of you, and that if you are on a training route that involves more than one placement, you will need to be flexible to accommodate varied practices between schools. Having said that, there are some general principles which it is useful for you to think about. Key amongst these is the issue of manageability.

It is very common for the secondary school music teacher to teach a large number of young people in a week, many of whom will only have a single weekly lesson of music; contrast this with the multiple maths or English lessons that the same classes will have. This means that when assessment data are required, the music teacher is likely to have to submit considerably more grades than teachers of some other subjects. Booth (2022a) cites from a 2016 publication by the Independent Teacher Workload Review Group (ITWRG 2016), observing that:

> As part of their published summary, the workload review group listed a range of ineffective marking practices, for example:
>
> - extensive written comments in different colour pens;
> - the use of "VF" on pupils' work to indicate when verbal feedback had been given;
> - marking which fails to help pupils improve their understanding; and
> - marking that fails to encourage motivation and resilience.
>
> (Booth 2022a: 429)

In order to deal with this, any marking and grading system that you employ needs to be manageable. You will not have time to deal with complex, multifaceted assessment procedures, so although you will need to work within your school's parameters, you will benefit from being able to do this in a manageable fashion.

Once you have produced any grades or marks you will then need to report these. Figure 10.1 highlighted three audiences for assessment data; for reporting, a fourth audience—that of parents—can be added to this already complex mix. How you report assessment data to these four audiences is likely to vary, as is the purpose of the assessments you have used. But parents are likely to want to know different things from assessment managers. Parents are normally focused on their child, whereas systemic uses of assessment data are typically concerned with overall trends and patterns. Task 10.5 presents some starting points for your thinking about how others think about assessment in school.

Task 10.5 **Others' marking and grading practices**

1. Talk to other beginning music teachers or colleagues in other schools. How do their experiences of marking and grading differ from yours? What policies and procedures do they have to do that you don't, and vice versa?
2. Talk to other beginning teachers or colleagues in other subjects at your school. Ask them about the marking they have to do; how does this compare with yours?

ASSESSMENT AND PROGRESS

Schools are rightly concerned with young people's progress, and one systemic use of summative assessment data that you submit to data managers is its input into complex progress tracking arrangements across different subjects. But progress in music is complicated, in part because of the complexities of the required learning materials. Another one of Swanwick's important contributions to thinking in music education was in drawing attention to the notion of the spiral curriculum (Swanwick and Tillman 1986; Anderson 2022), which had previously been presented more generally in education by Bruner (1960). The idea of development occurring in the form of a spiral is singularly apposite when thinking about music teaching and learning in the classroom. This is because young people's composing, performing, and listening skills do not necessarily develop at a uniform rate, and different units of work in curricular music are likely to prioritise different skills at different stages. Although the notion of curriculum music being taught and learned in a holistic fashion is an important one, this does not necessarily mean that the various components will progress uniformly. Indeed, one of the myths of learning more widely is that progression and development take place in a linear fashion.

> Real learning is developmental rather than linear. The acquisition of knowledge or the transmission of knowledge-content may be linear processes; the development of understanding certainly is not; it is a far more subtle process and much more likely to be brought about by some form of what Jerome Bruner has termed a "spiral curriculum," where one returns to concepts at ever higher levels of complexity and understanding, than by a ... linear and hierarchical set of offerings. Any view of the learning process that does not recognize this must be regarded as too simplistic to serve as a basis for any but the most unsophisticated of teaching activities.
> (Kelly 2009: 76)

In music education, this has significant ramifications for thinking about progression and how to track it with assessment. The multifarious nature of music curriculum content reveals the myth of linear progression: after all, composing and performing competences are unlikely to be directly linked in the ways in which they are treated in classroom music. A unit of work focusing on, say, singing extant repertoire, followed by one on composing a melody for keyboard is unlikely to develop the exact same skill set. It is improbable that progression made in singing will transfer isomorphically to composing, so tracking this in summative assessment may capture an overall upwards trend—we hope—but grades are likely to capture different stages on a spiral of attainment. This means that tracking progression needs to be thought about in the round, at macro- and meso-levels, rather than in micro-progression from one unit of work to the next. In other words, how has a young person progressed over the course of a term or a year? Does their music evidence sonic differences? Has their musical vocabulary become more sophisticated? What else has changed?

But this is not to say that assessment should not be used for tracking progression—far from it—merely that it takes careful handling and balancing over the longer term for such fine-grained assessment data to be of use at the school level for tracking individual young people. Since in some schools teacher performance is also monitored by close analysis of young people's assessment data, discussion at the departmental level may be warranted to work out how best to deal with this. Nevertheless, music is not alone in this: after all, in physical education we would not expect an individual pupil to have an equally linear trajectory in both rugby and gymnastics. This analogy may help with explanations, if required!

SUMMARY

In this chapter, a number of complex ideas with regard to assessment have been discussed. We have seen how important it is that assessment arises from curriculum, and that knowing what young people will be learning and doing needs to precede what you will be assessing. We have talked about audiences of assessment data—young people, teachers, parents, and school systems—and how data gathered for *systemic* purposes may not be of the best use to other audiences. We have also discussed how the pedagogic practices of instrumental music teachers can be of help in constructing classroom music assessments. Finally, we have thought about the role of assessment in tracking young people's progress and have shown how thinking about the non-linear ways in which learning progresses is an important component of thinking about teaching and learning in classroom music. Table 10.1 summarises many of these matters with headline terminologies, associated information, and impacts for professional practice.

Table 10.1 Summarising assessment in the music classroom

Assessing music musically	Building on Swanwick (1999). Is this what happens in your school?
Formative assessment	Formative assessment relates to modifying teaching and learning. It concerns itself with what is coming next by building on what has already been learnt.
Summative assessment	Summative assessment sums up learning by giving an attainment grade, mark, percentage, score, or level to a specific piece of work.
Assessment data	Assessment data cover "a plethora of information for the classroom teacher ranging from scores, levels or grades from national examinations to ongoing conversations with and observations of pupils" (Booth 2022b: 450).
Who is this assessment for?	Audiences include young people, teachers, parents and carers, and school systems.
Why am I assessing this?	"To teach is to assess" (Swanwick 1988: 149) (see also day-to-day assessment).

(Continued)

Table 10.1 (Continued)

Assessing music within whole-school structures	Data arising from what you assess for your own teaching and learning might not be those which are required by school data managers.
Assessment arises from curriculum	Deciding on the programme of study should precede deciding what any assessment might involve.
Day-to-day assessment versus assessment-as-event	Music often involves "all-the-time-you-are-teaching assessment," whereas what schools often mean when they talk about assessment is for it to take place as a separate event.
Assessment, marking, and grading	Any marking and grading system that you employ needs to be manageable. You will not have time to deal with complex, multifaceted procedures.
Assessment and progress (tracking)	How have young people progressed over the course of a term or a year? Does their music evidence sonic differences, for example?
Spiral curriculum	Young people's composing, performing, and listening skills do not necessarily develop at a uniform rate, and different units of work may emphasise different skills.
Non-linear attainment	The myth of linear progression can be readily seen in the multifarious nature of musical curriculum content.

There is no doubt that assessment is an important part of what you do as a teacher. We have seen that the notion of assessment covers a multitude of ideas and practices, and you will need to be thinking about what, how, and why you are assessing in the music classroom. Doubtless your ideas will change and develop as you progress in your career, but hopefully the ideas in this chapter have given you a helpful way of thinking about and operationalising things as you enter the profession. Whatever it is you do, please try to remember that it is music and being musical that is the whole point of assessing in the first place!

FURTHER READING

Brophy, T.S. (ed) (2019)
The Oxford Handbook of Assessment Policy and Practice in Music Education, New York: Oxford University Press.

In two volumes, this comprehensive survey of assessment in music education provides a huge amount of useful information and things to think about as you enter your career and beyond.

Colwell, R. (2017)
Assessment's potential in music education, in M.C. Moore (ed) *Critical Essays in Music Education*, Abingdon: Routledge, pp. 371-402.

This text, although written from an American perspective, raises a number of important issues and invites the reader to reflect on their practice.

Fautley, M. and Daubney, A. (2025)
A Framework for Curriculum, Pedagogy and Assessment in Lower Secondary School Music, London: Independent Society of Musicians.

These free materials contain helpful information for the classroom teacher in thinking about and constructing their own assessments.

Harlen, W. and James, M. (1997)
'Assessment and learning: Differences and relationships between formative and summative assessments', *Assessment in Education*, 4, 3: 365-379.

Written from a general education perspective, this article contains much useful information for thinking about the differences between formative and summative assessment.

PART 3

MUSICAL LEARNING

LANGUAGE AND LEARNING IN MUSIC

Chris Philpott with Keith Evans

INTRODUCTION

All teachers are charged with the development of young people's language, for it is inevitable that they will write and talk about music when composing, performing and responding. Indeed, all teachers can be considered as teachers of the English language and are committed to developing young people's speaking (oracy), reading and writing.

However, our primary concern in this chapter is how spoken and written language can be used to promote the development of musical learning. Language is one way (although by no means the only way) that we can develop our knowledge and understanding in music. There are three assumptions made in this chapter in relation to the use of language about music:

1. Intuitive, "literary" language *and* the language of conceptual, technical analysis are both important ways in which we can talk and write about music;
2. When learning to use language about music, there is a developmental shift from the intuitive to the technical;
3. These two assumptions are important factors for the way in which we plan and prepare for teaching and learning in music.

Intuitive language and technical language are not mutually exclusive. Indeed, much of this chapter explores the relationship between these two and the way in which each can be used to talk and write *about* music and thus extend our understanding *of* music.

> **Objectives**
>
> By the end of this chapter you should be able to:
>
> - understand the relationship between language and learning in music;
> - facilitate young people's use of both literary and technical language to make their musical understanding and learning explicit;
> - understand the sequence of learning implicit in the use of language about music;
> - understand the role of musical criticism in music teaching, learning and assessment.

USING LANGUAGE ABOUT MUSIC

The young people in your classes can talk and write about music! It is quite natural for them to do so, even though they may not have a technical vocabulary to describe what they hear. Furthermore, just because they cannot use a technical vocabulary does not mean that they have not *heard* or *understood* the content of the music. Young people intuitively understand and can describe the contrasting sections of *Chop Suey* by the Armenian-American band System of a Down. They can hear and sense the "build-up" in the opening of Strauss's *Also Sprach Zarathustra*. They know that much heavy metal has drive and raw energy. As a teacher you ignore these intuitive understandings at your peril, for they are responses to music itself and represent genuine musical understanding. Indeed, by the time young people reach secondary school they have much intuitive understanding and varying amounts of technical vocabulary to describe their musical experiences.

Young people need to be given opportunities to describe their intuitive musical experience. How can this be done? How can you help them to make their understandings explicit through language? At this stage we are not necessarily concerned with technical vocabulary, for analysis does not necessarily involve its use. It is also important to realise that intuitive responses to music are not somehow "lost" once we become technical or conceptual but are always the primordial source of our understanding when we respond to music. Task 11.1 will help you begin to explore these issues.

> ### Task 11.1 **Describing music**
>
> Choose a piece of music and try to describe it without the use of technical vocabulary. What is the music like? What happens in the music? How does the music sound?
>
> When a class or group are listening and responding to music in school, try asking these same questions of them or of other music teachers. Ask them to write down their responses. What sorts of language do they use?

■ ■ ■ ■ **LANGUAGE AND LEARNING IN MUSIC**

In relation to this primordial understanding, Swanwick (1979) helpfully distinguishes between music meaning something "for" us (our personal subjective response, likes, dislikes, conjured images, connotations and so on) and meaning "to" us (the objective existence of particular expressive gestures and structures in the music which have brought about this personal response). For example, a particular piece of music might mean little "for" us (in terms of personal response) but could mean plenty "to" us (in terms of identifying the musical gestures and structures used). When asking young people to respond to music, you can move them *from* the response "for" us, which is likely to be individual and subjective, *to* the recognition of what actually happens in the music, which might be common to many in the class. The ability to put technical, analytical "names" to this experience will vary from individual to individual but is not a necessary condition of describing the music. While naming can undoubtedly enrich musical experience, the names do not form the life blood of the experience itself. Young people can use "literary" language to describe their intuitive experience of meaning "for" and "to" them.

Supporting the use of "literary" language

One way in which the use of "literary" language about music can be encouraged is through the use of adjectives, either freely generated by the young people themselves or prompted through adjective groups provided by the teacher. These adjective groups can promote confidence in the use of language to describe music, which you will explore in Task 11.2. For example, in Table 11.1 later in this chapter (based on Queen's *Bohemian Rhapsody*), the voice-quality boxes might contain words such as *harsh*, *smooth*, *powerful*, *aggressive* and *crying*, and the class can be asked to circle the quality they hear in each section or add their own words.

Task 11.2 **Using adjective groups in worksheets**

Choose a piece of music with distinct sections and provide a range of adjectives for the class or group to choose from when describing the music. Try this out with a class or other music teachers.

Another way to unlock intuitive responses is to ask young people to compare pieces of music. As explored in Task 11.3, this approach can be a very fruitful way of getting them to talk or write about music. For example, a class could be tasked with comparing:

1. Two pieces of music in a similar style, e.g., Courtney Pine's version of *C Jam Blues* and Dave Brubeck's *Take Five*;
2. "Cover" versions of a pop song;

3. Different variations on a well-known theme;
4. Recordings of Balinese and Javanese gamelan;
5. Similar types of piece within the same work, e.g., choruses in Handel's *Messiah*.

> Task 11.3 **Comparing music**
>
> Develop a worksheet that asks young people to compare two pieces of music. You can scaffold responses through, for example, the use of adjective groups, or ask young people to undertake a free description of what they have heard.

While we are not yet explicitly concerned with the technical concepts of musical analysis, young people quite naturally talk about these when describing their intuitive experience. They will write and talk about pitch, structure, consonance and dissonance (even if they do not use these words), for they are natural sonic and expressive categories when describing the qualities of music. However, they will often use literary descriptions such as *dark, smooth then spikey* or *clashing* when engaging with these qualities. These intuitive understandings can be a gateway to more technical analysis and the introduction of musical vocabulary—when young people are ready.

LANGUAGE AND THE SEQUENCE OF MUSICAL LEARNING

Given some of the links we have made between music and language, it is important to reflect on the sequence of learning. When we learn our spoken and written language, there is a clear sequence in which we move from the sounds of the words to their meaning in the written form. The same might be said for music—that we need to internalise the sounds and meanings of music if the technical names or notations are to mean anything to us. The point here, in terms of the sequence of learning, is that sounds and intuitive musical meanings come before written notations and technical analysis. Indeed, the maxim of "sound before symbol" is now common to the philosophy of many music educators. In the same way, as part of the musical development of the young people in our classes, we can move *from* intuitive and literary responses *to* more technical understandings.

Language and the development of a musical activity

As musicians, it is easy to slip into the use of technical language and expect young people to understand these "shortcuts." One way round this is to provide, wherever possible, musical models of the things we are talking about, and also carefully audit and purge our own language of technical jargon. Most musical

LANGUAGE AND LEARNING IN MUSIC

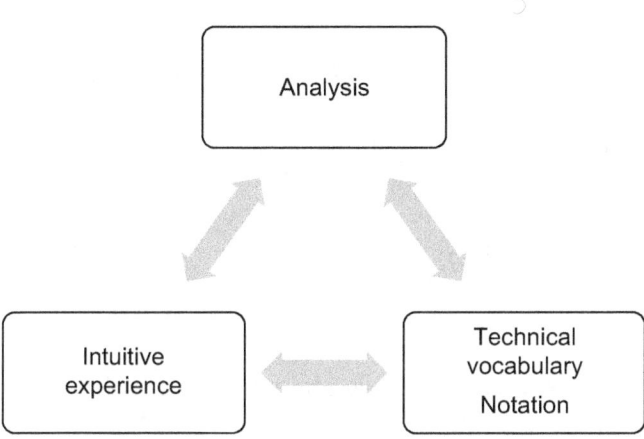

Figure 11.1 Intuition, analysis and technical vocabulary

phenomena can be described using literary, non-technical language, in much the same way that we can all use literary language to describe our musical experience. In a sense we must, as teachers, try to remember how we first learned to understand music if we are to help young people to progress.

Of course, as teachers we do have a duty to introduce musical vocabulary, although only after careful preparation, taking due account of the sequence of musical learning and making sure there has been significant exposure to a musical correlate for what we are introducing (such as a musical model for a "drone"). Technical and conceptual understandings can grow out of our intuitive relationships with music, both of which can contribute to analysis (see Figure 11.1). For example, a young person who is being taught to play in triple time needs to be immersed in the sense and feel of pulse and music in triple time before the "naming" makes any sense.

The implications of what we have said thus far for you as a music teacher are that you need:

- the ability to actively talk and write about music yourself. You must be good at what you are asking the young people to do, that is, the analysis of musical works using literary and technical language;
- the skills to be able to identify and describe important features in musical works for new learning and the reinforcing of past learning;
- the ability to break down your own responses into a form that can be readily understood, and to be able to talk about music in such a way that the language used is appropriate for the age and ability of the class. For example, a technical reference to "rising and falling scalic patterns followed by a perfect cadence" might mean little to young people, but they *are* able to hear and talk about such an event. They can hear music that rises and falls and comes to a solid ending, which amounts to the same thing but without the technical language. However, once the up and down patterns have been

assimilated, we *might* then talk of "scales" as a development of technical vocabulary, which can be reinforced later and over time;
- the awareness not to dismiss a particular response just because it did not use the "right" word. You need the sensitivity to ask and understand why young people have responded in a particular way;
- the ability to ask questions that help young people to develop musical vocabulary from intuitive understandings. For example, before asking, "what form is this piece in?" the question, "what happens in this music?" could be more appropriate.

Based on our observations thus far, we can recognise that the sequence of musical learning moves from intuitive musical experience to technical vocabulary and back to an enriched experience (see Figure 11.1). Music lessons that are informed by these observations are likely to engage with a musically led, as opposed to abstract, understanding of concepts when young people talk and write about their musical experience. You can explore this more in Task 11.4.

Task 11.4 Introducing concepts musically

The "naming" of concepts in technical analysis can be undertaken without suitable preparation for making connections between the name and the music. Choose a concept or feature of notation and design some classroom activities that will *prepare* the young people in your classes to be able to talk or write about music using the name. Bear in mind the links between intuitive experience and technical naming noted previously. Share your activities with a colleague or another beginning teacher.

CONFUSIONS AND MISCONCEPTIONS WHEN USING LANGUAGE ABOUT MUSIC

In developing a technical musical vocabulary, you need to be aware that there are some confusions and misconceptions over the use of certain names and concepts that are common to young people and teachers alike. Box 11.1 and Task 11.5 help you to consider these, for an appreciation of such misconceptions is important to how you respond to the learning needs of individuals.

Task 11.5 Confusions and misconceptions when using language about music

Read Box 11.1. Have you any experiences of such "confusions" thus far in your experience? Have any others caught your attention? Discuss your examples with colleagues, mentors or other beginning teachers.

LANGUAGE AND LEARNING IN MUSIC

> ### Box 11.1 Possible confusions when talking about musical "elements" or "dimensions"
>
> - **Pitch:** "high and low" needs care and clarification, as some young people think of these words as meaning high and low *volume* (and with good cause). Also, questions regarding pitch need to be targeted; for example, "can you name a high-pitched instrument in this piece?" Asking, "what is the pitch of this music?" will almost always elicit the answer, "high and low"!
> - **Dynamics:** "volume" or "loud and soft" needs careful separation from language used to describe pitch. Is the opposite of "loud" actually "quiet"? Also, in general usage, "soft" can relate more to texture.
> - **Texture:** there are several responses here, ranging from basic "thick or thin" (referring to the density of the sound) to more specific descriptions addressing the organisation of musical strands (e.g., monophonic, homophonic, polyphonic, heterophonic).
> - **Timbre:** while timbre refers to the quality of the individual sound or collection of sounds, it can get muddled with certain definitions of texture.
>
> Be sensitive to what young people say or write about music. They may not necessarily be "wrong" but merely using their words in a particular way. You should also clarify what you mean by your use of certain words. Do not assume that they, or indeed experienced musicians, know what you mean!

USING LANGUAGE ABOUT MUSIC IN WORKSHEETS

A worksheet is a useful tool for eliciting responses to music. It is possible to construct worksheets that offer young people the opportunity to use both literary and technical vocabulary. Indeed, this approach allows differentiated language to be used about the music, and this could be directed through a grid analysis. Table 11.1 exemplifies this structured approach when responding to Queen's *Bohemian Rhapsody*, although the grid can be easily adapted to cover other pieces or several pieces for comparison, as you are asked to do in Task 11.6.

- **Table 11.1** Worksheet idea: a grid analysis of music

Bohemian Rhapsody by Queen This piece falls naturally into five sections, A to E. However, the headings on the grid should be appropriate to the music being used and how you want to direct the responses.						
Section	Instruments	Voice quality	Speed	Volume	Mood or atmosphere	Other comments, for example special effects
A						
B						
C						
D						
E						

> **Task 11.6 Grid analysis of a piece of music**
>
> 1. Design a worksheet in grid form for a class of 11- to 12-year-olds to respond to a piece of music. Do not assume an understanding of technical vocabulary.
> 2. Then plan a similar exercise with a group aged 15 to 16, about to take a national qualification listening paper.
>
> What different approaches did you take for each year group? If you had a chance to use your worksheets in the classroom, what were the differences in responses from the young people?

USING LANGUAGE ABOUT MUSIC IN "STUDENT TALK"

Clearly, much of the language that takes place in the music classroom is between peers while making music, and we should not underestimate the value of this talk in the process of musical (and linguistic) learning. Auker (1991) makes the point that the most effective music teaching is that which allows young people to make music. However, he also recognises the importance of language to musical learning, especially the "exploratory talk" that takes place between young people. Barrett (1990) emphasises that the quality of "student talk" has important consequences for the process of learning and suggests that:

> Talk arises spontaneously from the creative music experience. Talk occurs when the child selects and organises information in order to ensure its transmission with clarity and accuracy. The child must assume responsibility by initiating talk while working co-operatively on a music task, by sustaining talk and where necessary, by concluding talk.
>
> (71)

Barrett (1990) feels that in such situations, student talk is quite natural, especially when they are engaged in "the musical challenge." She is concerned that the quality of both musical and linguistic experience is served by such talk. When responding to music, she maintains that the following categories of language are quite naturally used:

- investigative language;
- hypothetical language;
- imaginative language;
- descriptive language;
- analytical language;
- interpretative language;
- comparative language;
- reflective and evaluative language.

Try investigating student talk in your own classroom, using Barrett's (1990) classification to analyse your findings. Task 11.7 will help you to do this.

LANGUAGE AND LEARNING IN MUSIC

> ## Task 11.7 **Listening to student talk**
>
> Listen to some young people talking while they are composing or putting together a performance. Be sensitive to the effect that your presence will have on their talk. You might pick up only snatches of conversation from different groups. Use Barrett's (1990) categories of talk to analyse the language that you hear. Compare your observations with other music teachers.

Your role as a teacher is one of facilitator in creating the conditions for talk between peers to take place. Auker (1991) believes that the quality of talking here is fundamental to the quality of the musical product and maintains that:

> A better product will in fact emerge if we take seriously the role of language in the music lesson, because, lacking the musical vocabulary—it is through spoken language that children can begin to explore and share what they have to offer in terms of musical creativity.
>
> (166)

How is it possible for you to further facilitate student talk in your classes? One approach is to take the view that music education is musical criticism, both for you as teacher and for the young people you teach.

MUSIC EDUCATION, MUSICAL CRITICISM AND TEACHER TALK

The implication of much of what has been said so far is for music education as musical criticism, in which both the teacher and the young people act as music critics. Musical criticism does not necessarily involve making judgements about the value of a piece. The concepts of good and bad are not always useful constructs for the language of musical learning. The act of musical criticism at first invites us to describe (with or without technical language) and then perhaps suggest how things might be otherwise, to suggest further possibilities by posing and answering the question: "what would happen if . . .?" Authors such as Vygotsky (1962) have emphasised the importance of collaborative student and teacher talk in the development and scaffolding of all learning.

Swanwick (1991) finds that there are five dimensions or categories of musical criticism into which talk and writing (of young people and teachers) usually fall. These categories are:

- control of sonorities (the tone and quality of sound itself);
- expressive characterisation (the character of the music);
- structural relationships (how the piece hangs together, evolves and so on);
- personal evaluation;
- historical and technical context.

Indeed, Swanwick (1991) maintains that there is no critical comment about music that does not fit into one or other of these categories and that they fundamentally underpin our intuitive understanding of music even if we do not have the technical vocabulary to describe them. Engaging in music education as musical criticism for yourself is one of the first steps to encouraging the young people in your classes to become music critics, as you will begin to explore in Task 11.8.

> ### Task 11.8 **Musical education as musical criticism**
>
> When observing different teachers, use Swanwick's (1991) model of musical criticism to categorise how they discuss music with their classes. Note down comments that they make and try to place them into the categories provided by the model. Do comments fall into certain categories more often than others? What are the implications of this, and does it matter?
>
> Repeat the exercise to analyse any written worksheets that you have observed teachers using with their classes. Does the written language fall into certain categories more often than others? What are the implications of this, and does it matter?

Wrapped up in the notion of music education as musical criticism is the important role of teacher talk. For example, when engaging with Swanwick's (1991) five categories, music teachers will need to:

a. model critical comments about music;
b. ask questions;
c. scaffold critical comments through outlining possibilities for young people.

These strategies all have the aim of developing young people's increasing independence. In this context, teacher talk is especially important in assessment for learning in music (see Chapter 10).

Language and assessment

There are inevitable links between responses to music, language and assessment. Through young people's responses to music, in both formal and informal situations, you can come to know them and understand their learning and development. Their responses to music and the way they talk and write about it can become one of the foundations for your assessment practice. Young people's appraisals of music, their appraisal of themselves and your appraisal of their work can form the basis of assessment. In this sense there is a very close connection between assessment, appraisal and musical criticism. However, you should not rely only on young people's use of language in order to come to know

LANGUAGE AND LEARNING IN MUSIC

them and their work. Performances and compositions stand freely as the most important manifestations of musical understanding, without the need for words of description, analysis or explanation.

OTHER FORMS OF RESPONDING TO MUSIC

Much of this chapter has been about young people responding to music through language, such that they can make their understandings explicit. But the work of Flynn and Pratt (1995) suggests that "getting at" music through language is a limited vision of response and appraisal. There are other ways or "languages" through which we can access and develop understandings of music, such as through visual media, movement, drama and forms of notation. These are all important, for in relation to music there is nothing especially useful about verbal or written language that means it is superior to other forms, other than its convenience and dominance in our culture as a mode of communication. Other forms of response allow intuitive understandings to be made explicit in ways that are not limited to a musical vocabulary or even literary description. We suggest that you try out this approach through Task 11.9.

Task 11.9 **Responding to music in different ways**

Choose a piece of music that you know well and construct a sequence in which you challenge your class to respond to it through language and at least two other forms of response.

An example might be the opening of "Confutatis" from Mozart's *Requiem*. The initial ABAB structure is differentiated by, among other things, contrasting use of male and female voices, dynamics and melodic shape. You could ask your class to:

- draw a picture inspired by the music (what is it that the pictures and music share?);
- compose a piece inspired by the music or by the picture they have drawn in response;
- move in a theatrical or dance style in response to the various sections.

Learning how to notate music

Finally, it is worth a brief consideration of the learning and teaching of notation, based on our observations about the nature of and sequence of language and musical learning. While the case for teaching notation is well documented (and a curriculum requirement across the United Kingdom), there are many attendant problems for you as a music teacher. For example, what is the relationship of notation to a musical idea? When should notation be taught? How should notation be taught? What forms might notation take?

It must be emphasised that notation itself is *not* music itself but a written form of it. It is thus subject to our observations on the sequence of learning noted earlier—moving *from* the intuitive *to* the technical. To ignore this connection is to court the possibility of young people failing to learn anything at all and thus becoming demotivated and alienated from music lessons. In light of these observations, we must ask ourselves what comprises the "basics" in music education. In language, we seem to develop our sense of words before we learn how to write them down, as we have noted earlier. The process of learning appears to move from sounds and meanings to written signs, a principle that can also underpin musical learning. In relation to notation, the best way to learn how to understand and use written signs is by being immersed in relevant musical correlates and always moving from the intuitive to the technical (Task 11.10).

Task 11.10 **Notation**

1. List all forms of musical notation you are aware of. Which of these have you seen used and encouraged in school?
2. How is staff notation taught and reinforced in your school?
3. Devise a way of teaching a simple aspect of rhythmic notation (e.g., crotchets and quavers) in a way that is faithful to the notion of "sound before symbol."

SUMMARY

Connecting the learning of musical notation with the learning of the English language returns us to where we started in this chapter. Indeed, all of what we have suggested has implications for the dual role of the use of language in the music classroom: first to facilitate musical learning, and second to develop young people's use of the English language. In this chapter we have seen that:

- we need to recognise that we have an intuitive understanding of music that underpins any technical understanding;
- the process of musical learning is from intuitive experience to a more conceptual and technical understanding and back to an enriched musical experience, and the development of our use of language in response to music follows this sequence;
- as teachers, we support musical learning in the classroom through our own use of language and musical criticism in teaching, planning, developing resources and assessing;
- musical understanding can be expressed through diverse "languages" including notation, which is subject to the same sequential principles of learning as the relationship between intuitive and technical language used in response to music.

FURTHER READING

Auker, P. (1991)
'Pupil talk, musical learning and creativity', *British Journal of Music Education*, 8, 2: 161–166.

Barrett, M.S. (1990)
'Music and language in education', *British Journal of Music Education*, 7, 1: 67-73.

These two articles examine the role of talk and language about music in the mutual development of music and literacy skills.

Evans, N. and Fautley, M. (2024)
A Planning, Reflection and Progression Toolkit. Online, available at: https://www.bcmg.org.uk/listen-imagine-compose-primary-2

Although this resource is aimed at primary schools it is full of ideas that apply to all ages, especially the sections after "Listening and Responding."

CREATIVITY

Chris Philpott, Keith Evans and Victoria Kinsella

INTRODUCTION

Creativity is an important educational theme which has evolved through various ideological shifts over time. In the 1960s and 1970s, creativity was central to a progressive, child-centred ideology that emphasised holistic personal development. With the publication of *All Our Futures* in England at the turn of the century (NACCCE 1999), the focus on creativity became more instrumental, highlighting the need for creative individuals who could adapt to an ever-changing world and contribute to society and the economy. In recent years, the growing international importance of creativity in education has been underscored by the Organisation for Economic Co-operation and Development (OECD 2018), which identifies creativity and creative thinking as key skills for young people in its 2030 vision and in the Programme for International Student Assessment (PISA) test of creative thinking (OECD 2024). The inclusion of creativity in such assessments highlights its perceived significance in education practice.

These most recent developments signify that creativity is not exclusive to the arts. The popular notion of "two cultures" often portrays the sciences as rational and objective, while the arts are seen as inherently creative and subjective. However, creativity is a fundamental aspect of all human disciplines, including music. Music, like any other field, is deeply rooted in creative processes, and it plays a vital role in nurturing both general creativity and creativity specific to the musical domain. You can begin to explore personal and shared understandings of creativity through Task 12.1.

> Task 12.1 **Creativity and education**
>
> How would you justify the place of creativity in the music classroom? Think about the balance between three aspects of creativity: personal (such as self-expression),

practical (creativity as a skill for problem-solving), and subject-specific (the unique ways creativity manifests in music).

Which of these feels most important in your teaching? How do they connect and influence each other? How does your own experience of being creative shape the way you teach creativity?

Talk with other teachers and share ideas about how their creativity inspires their teaching. How do your approaches overlap or differ?

OBJECTIVES

By the end of this chapter, you should be able to:

- understand a variety of issues surrounding the nature of creativity;
- begin to develop a well-reasoned concept of creativity to underpin your classroom practice;
- understand how it is possible to develop creativity in the classroom;
- understand the role of creative teaching and teaching for creativity approaches;
- show your own creativity when planning for the classroom.

CREATIVITY AND THE CURRICULUM FOR MUSIC

Various iterations of the National Curriculum for Music in England have emphasised the importance of creativity, with one "Purpose of Study" statement noting that:

> Music . . . embodies one of the highest forms of creativity. A high-quality music education should engage and inspire pupils to develop a love of music and their talent as musicians, and so increase their self-confidence, creativity and sense of achievement.
>
> (DfE 2013: 257)

In the Curriculum for Wales (Welsh Government 2020), creativity is central to the Expressive Arts area of learning and experience and is seen not only as vital for personal growth and cultural identity, but also for interdisciplinary learning and global citizenship. This aligns with the curriculum's four purposes, which aim to nurture ambitious learners, creative contributors, ethical citizens, and healthy individuals.

In music, the concept of creativity is commonly associated with the acts of composing, improvising, and arranging. However, young people are also required to behave creatively when they perform and re-create music, which is always an act of interpretation and imagination. Creativity is also enacted when responding to a piece of music as an audience member and when communicating ideas and feelings about music. These dimensions to creativity are explored more fully in Chapters 13, 14, and 15. Having said this, there is little common consent about its nature or processes. For example, is creativity a gift or something that we can all learn? Most might agree that some level of creativity is needed to solve a problem (composers and performers are problem-solvers) and that the imagination needs to be applied in order for this to happen. These questions are where we begin.

WHAT IS CREATIVITY?

Box 12.1 contains some statements made about the nature of creativity, which exhibit a wide range of views. Read these quotations and then carry out Task 12.2 to explore your own views about creativity in music education.

Box 12.1 **Some ideas about creativity**

What possible virtue can there be in pretending that creativity, an attribute not possessed by towering geniuses until childhood is past, can and should be generated in the youngsters of primary schools . . . re-creation, that's the thing. But re-creation is surely also the apposite term for so many of the activities of that highly imitative being, the human child.

(Sherratt 1977: 34)

There is a continuum in the creative art which moves from the ordinary to the extraordinary, from daily perceptual vision to deep anological vision, to the rhythmic babblings and repetitions of pre-verbal utterance to the regular beat and syntactic echoing of epic and poetry.

(Abbs 1989: 8)

In contrast, on this approach (i.e. creativity = novelty), "true" creativity arrives when individuals break rules or invent new ones.

(Pateman 1991: 33–35)

Artistic activities which offer the greatest scope for the majority of youngsters to develop their innate sensitivity, inventiveness and imagination might have a strong claim for a place of importance in the curriculum.

(Paynter 1977: 5)

Composing is one of the most difficult things it is possible to undertake: there have been less than thirty composers over the past two hundred and fifty years in Europe who are generally remembered with any deep sense of gratitude now.

(Fletcher 1987: 41)

Martha Graham once said that it takes at least five years of training in the discipline to be spontaneous in dance, which brings out how misconceived is the notion that creativity is inhibited by learned technique. On the contrary, although of course technical competence does not necessarily give creative

CREATIVITY

> flair, it is a necessary precondition for such flair, in any subject discipline or activity.
>
> (Best 1992: 96)
>
> When the muse is upon him, he works frantically, without food or sleep, until the work has been produced. According to this view, creativity is mysterious, unconscious, irrational, and anything but ordinary.
>
> (Hargreaves 1986: 147)
>
> The painter Max Ernst claimed to exert no conscious control over his work . . . whereas the writer Edgar Allen Poe insisted that the creative involves no more than conscious planning and rational decision making.
>
> (Hargreaves 1986: 147)
>
> While some children prefer to work alone . . . others prefer to engage collaboratively, communally, collectively, technologically networked, where upon being a group member responsible for jointly authoring a piece that can be replayed across time, space and persons.
>
> (Burnard 2012: 279–280)
>
> In excessive moments of learning in the making, when bodies and pedagogies reach over and into each other, the pedagogical address and the learning self interfuse to become "more" than either intended or anticipated. The instability and fluidity of pedagogy hold the potential for an unknowable and unforeseeable "more," and the actualisation of that potential is what springs the experience of learning itself.
>
> (Ellsworth 2005: 55)

Task 12.2 **What is creativity?**

Use the ideas in Box 12.1 and any others from your reading or experience to answer the following questions:

1. What have you witnessed in the music classroom thus far as a teacher that you consider to be evidence of creativity (during listening and responding to music, composition, improvisation, and performance)?
2. Which of the preceding views have most resonance for you?
3. Come up with your own definition of creativity, or construct one with a colleague, mentor, or another beginning teacher.

Out of these quotations certain tensions arise in relation to the concept of creativity. These tensions are identified in Figure 12.1 and represent differing attitudes to the possibility of creativity and the conditions under which it can take

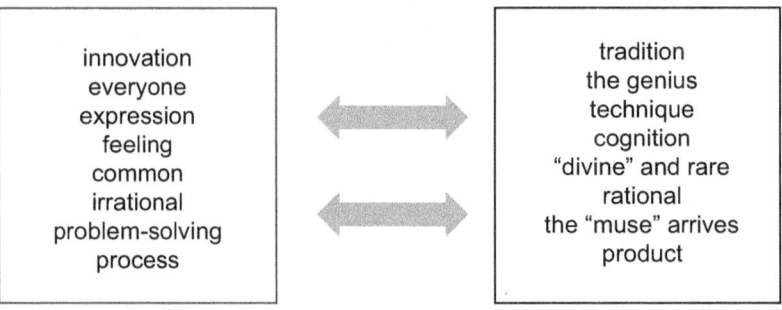

Figure 12.1 Some tensions in the concept of creativity

place. It is important for you to explore the tensions shown in Figure 12.1, for your attitudes to these determine the extent to which you believe creativity to be a possibility in the classroom.

For example, an important issue that arises out of studying creativity is its relationship to technique. Is it necessary to develop technique before we can become creative? If so, is creativity a state only achievable after a technical "apprenticeship"? Is it possible for technique to develop alongside the creative use of imagination? Can technique develop out of the problems posed by the creative process itself, where new technique becomes a means to solving the problem? The widespread use of music technology, as discussed in Chapter 3, creates an interesting perspective here and, arguably, "technique" in the traditional sense is no longer required at all for young people to be musically creative. In relation to such developments, Burnard (2012) argues that it makes more sense to talk of "creativities" as opposed to "creativity" in the singular, and that, in any case, technique is always being reinvented as a result of the interplay between music, society, and technology. Burnard maintains that:

> The notion of equally valued musical creativities is pertinent to the radical changes in the production and experience of music across the past 20 years. . . . The creativity from which music originates is evident in the interplay of myriad social and technological practices.
>
> (16)

To effectively incorporate creativity into classroom practice, it is important to first understand its definitions and implications. The *Durham Commission on Creativity and Education* (ACE 2019: 3) provides the following guidance:

- *Creativity*: the capacity to imagine, conceive, express, or make something that was not there before.
- *Creative thinking*: a process through which knowledge, intuition, and skills are applied to imagine, express, or make something novel or individual in its context. This process, present in all areas of life, may appear spontaneous but is often underpinned by perseverance, experimentation, critical thinking, and collaboration.

■ *Teaching for creativity*: explicitly using pedagogies and practices that cultivate creativity in young people.

These definitions offer a foundational understanding of creativity, which is essential when considering how to develop it in the classroom. Thinking about these definitions in the context of music education, creativity goes beyond teaching musical concepts and skills; it requires creating an environment that encourages young people to explore, experiment, and express themselves musically. You can use these definitions to guide the development of lessons and curricula that not only teach music but also foster creative thinking, problem-solving, and collaborative music-making.

Everyday creativity

The key concepts highlighted in the *Durham Commission* (ACE 2019) are important, but how do we, as teachers, begin to give value to the creative process in the classroom? Maslow (1970) stated that the creative individual is a fulfilled one whose life is characterised by agency. Others note that creativity brings joy, wonder, excitement, and pleasure into our lives (Baer 2017; Kaufman 2018). It also plays a significant role in individual wellbeing, self-expression, and identity formation (Robinson 2011). However, integrating creativity into the classroom poses unique challenges. To foster a creative environment, it is essential that both young people and teachers feel encouraged and supported when presenting new ideas, have the space and freedom to interact with others, and possess the ability to tolerate uncertainty and take risks (Amabile 1989). As educators, it is crucial to recognise and value the creative process as much as the final product. However, in subjects like music, identifying creativity can be challenging. For instance, when a learner creates a musical pattern, it might be something you have heard many times before. Yet, for that learner, it represents a new and creative response. As a teacher, it is therefore important to distinguish between everyday creativity and creativity of historical significance.

Boden (1990) provides a framework that makes the creative process more transparent, illustrating how creativity can be taught, learned, and valued. She approaches creativity from an everyday perspective, distinguishing between two forms of creative ideas. The first is psychological creativity, or "P-creativity," which refers to the ability to produce something novel from the perspective of the individual. P-creativity involves generating a surprising and valuable idea that is new to the person, regardless of whether others have had the idea before. Boden (1990) uses an example to explain this concept:

> If Mary Smith combines ideas in a way she's never done before, or if she has an idea which she could not have had before, her idea is P-creative—no matter how many people may have had the same idea already.

(43)

The second form is historical creativity, or "H-creativity," which occurs when an idea emerges for the first time in history, giving it societal prominence. Boden (1990) elaborates:

> Mary Smith's surprising idea is H-creative only if no one has had that idea before her. It may be an H-creative "combination", or it may be an H-creative "impossibility". But whichever type of creativity is involved, it's historically creative only if no one has had that thought before.
>
> (43)

While H-creativity represents the pinnacle of a creative idea, Boden (1990) emphasises the importance of understanding how an idea arises. Both P-creativity and H-creativity have significant implications for education. In the classroom, the concept of P-creativity is especially valuable, as it allows us to recognise the creative actions of a learner—even if they seem familiar to us as adults—as novel and meaningful for the young person concerned. This distinction also allows us to give value to creative *processes* rather than to a defined *outcome*. This is a more inclusive outlook that you can consider further through Task 12.3.

Task 12.3 **Recognising creativity and giving it value**

1. Reflect on a moment when a young person created something that seemed familiar or typical to you but was new and exciting for them. How did you, as a teacher, respond to this? In hindsight, how would you alter your response to better value the process of P-creativity?
2. How might you create an environment where young people feel encouraged to engage in the creative process without the pressure of achieving H-creativity?

Share your ideas with a colleague, mentor, or other beginning teacher.

WHAT IS THE PROCESS OF CREATIVITY?

Having briefly examined some of the issues surrounding the concept of creativity, we must also explore ideas around how it takes place—in other words, the process of creativity. Understanding the creative process further enhances our understanding of the concept of creativity itself. Three models of the creative process are presented in Box 12.2. These are not designed to be definitive but are introduced to illustrate a range of views to stimulate your own reflections on the creative process. Having read these models, carry out Task 12.4 to explore your own experiences of creative processes.

CREATIVITY

Box 12.2 **Models of creativity**

Model A: Wallas (1926) suggests that the creative process has four stages:

- Preparation: researching the problem;
- Incubation: when conscious attention is turned away from the problem and unconscious processes dominate; imagination plays a large role;
- Illumination: the "eureka" experience when a creative solution is defined;
- Verification: the formalisation of the solution, as it is refined and adapted to meet practical constraints.

Model B: Ross (1980) also proposes four stages to creativity:

- Initiating the creative impulse by exploring, doodling, and playing;
- Acquainting oneself with a particular medium, with its potential and possibilities for particular purposes, further playing around with ideas;
- Controlling the medium through the mastery of basic skills and techniques; understanding constraints and limitations;
- Structuring ideas into a satisfying and comprehensible whole, which can also involve reviewing.

Model C: Csikszentmihalyi (1996) views creativity as the interaction between three elements:

- The individual: who produces the creative work or ideas;
- The domain (e.g., music education): which includes the symbolic rules and knowledge base of the field;
- The field: the social environment that selects and validates the creative idea, including peers or teachers that evaluate whether the idea is valuable in the domain.

Task 12.4 **The process of creativity**

After examining the three models outlined in Box 12.2, answer the following questions:

1. What evidence have you seen of these processes at work in relation to composing, performing, and responding in your school or placement school?
2. Consider your own creativity in relation to music-making. Do you recognise any features of the creative process in your own work as composer, improviser, listener, or performer? Illustrate any comments you make.

HOW CAN WE FACILITATE THE DEVELOPMENT OF CREATIVITY IN THE MUSIC CLASSROOM?

Within the music classroom you can create the conditions for creativity to flourish, but, like any seedling, there is no guarantee it will grow as expected. Even in the most nurturing environments, creativity can sometimes falter, and both teachers and young people may encounter failures along the way. However, these setbacks are an integral part of the creative process and should be acknowledged and rewarded. Embracing the uncertainties and risks inherent in creativity is essential, as it is through experimenting with music in diverse ways that true creative opportunities emerge. It is only by making music in many ways that opportunities for creativity appear. In other words, a young person's entitlement to music is also an entitlement to be creative.

Dezuanni and Jetnikoff (2011) describe creative pedagogy as the imaginative and innovative arrangement of curricula and teaching strategies in school classrooms designed to foster creativity. In the context of music education, this approach can be further enriched by fostering creative habits of mind—such as inquisitiveness, persistence, imagination, collaboration, and discipline (Spencer et al. 2012; Lucas 2016). These five habits of mind offer valuable insights for creative pedagogy in music education. They align with pedagogical approaches that balance exploration with structure, encouraging young people to question and experiment (inquisitiveness), embrace challenges and iterative learning (persistence), generate and explore new ideas (imagination), work effectively in groups (collaboration), and apply technical precision (discipline):

- *Resources*: you can enhance potential for creativity by building up rich and stimulating resources which can be used to both initiate and support the creative process. These resources can be both musical (e.g., a variety of recordings) and extra-musical (e.g., images and video).
- *Structure*: it is appropriate to include various levels of structure when promoting creativity, depending on the class, the task, and the desired musical learning. For example, teachers might give young people:
    - a free choice about which problems to solve and how to solve them (self-directed creativity);
    - open-ended tasks that channel responses through particular stimuli, e.g., a verse-chorus song;
    - structured problem-solving in which the expressive and structural ingredients are limited to a specific set of conventions, e.g., creating a minimalist composition.
- *Challenge*: as a teacher, you can plan suitable challenges in relation to young people's developmental stages—challenges that stimulate them and present problems they have a realistic chance of solving.

- *Modelling*: you need to be a role model and set up opportunities for other role models to be seen and heard, such as peers and external musicians. This requires you to demonstrate your creativity by, for example, "jamming" with the class or composing with them yourself.
- *Space and time*: when solving problems, young people need "space" in which to demonstrate and develop their creativity. You need to be sensitive to this and flexibly adapt your expectations as the lesson or unit of work progresses.
- *Play*: create dedicated time and space for creative play. Play is essential in fostering creativity within music education. It provides young people with the freedom to explore, experiment, and engage with musical ideas in a low-pressure setting. Through play, young people can improvise, take creative risks, and discover new sounds and concepts without the fear of failure.
- *Support and intervention*: you should be prepared to provide the type of support your class needs to complete tasks, such as help with the technical skills that can enhance the work in progress. This support can also come in the form of assessment for learning, including feedback, questioning, prompting, and modelling
- *Creating a safe environment*: you should aim to establish an environment in which young people feel able to take risks, where all contributions are valued and mutually respected by all. This attitude can be modelled and encouraged through your exchanges with the class or group.

Use Task 12.5 to reflect upon these ideas based on your own experience.

Task 12.5 **Creating the conditions for creativity**

Can you think of any other conditions that will enhance creativity in the classroom? Consider an example of a lesson you have planned or observed in which you feel that creativity was promoted. How were the young people stimulated? What support was given to them? Describe and reflect upon the outcomes of the lesson.

Some practical strategies for stimulating and developing creativity in the classroom

There are many potential approaches and starting points for creativity in the music classroom, and what follows are some suggestions which may stimulate your own. While teaching in a way that promotes creativity and teaching creatively are not the same thing, it is the case that to facilitate creativity in the classroom, teachers must themselves be creative in their musicianship and the pedagogical strategies they employ.

Teaching and learning based around "expressive problems"

In this approach the "expressive problem" is seen as the essence of creative musical activity and a strategy for musical learning. The composer confronts themselves with expressive problems and must solve the problem of how the piece can be put together successfully. The performer needs to solve the problem of presenting the music coherently and address how the composer has solved a particular compositional problem. The listener is constantly interpreting in response to how the composer-performer (they might be the same person) has solved expressive problems. In all musical behaviours there is always, at the very least, an intuitive interpretation of particular creative solutions to particular expressive problems.

Box 12.3 **Expressive problems**

- **Factual notes on the history of the blues (knowledge about):** How does blues music reflect historical events? How do blues performers and composers solve the problems of creating meaningful music in this context? What expressive features and structures in blues music reflect its history? How can we perform a blues piece? How can we compose a blues piece?
- **Learning three chords on a ukulele (knowing how):** How can we effectively accomplish this skill in order to perform with confidence? Can we recognise the chords in different orders? What tunes can we now accompany? What are the expressive possibilities of these chords? Can we compose with them?
- **Learning about the concept of the semitone (knowledge that):** What is a semitone? How are tones structured on the keyboard? How can we play chromatic notes effectively and with confidence? How have composers used them? What would happen if . . .? How can we use them in our compositions? What expressive effects are possible?

The expressive problems approach may emerge from almost any starting point. If the expressive problem is framed around the fundamental activities of music-making, it is possible to turn even the driest and dustiest piece of "knowledge about" (Chapter 6) into a creative musical experience. Any starting point may lead us into the creative realm of solving musical problems, as we search for a means to express ourselves in the context of the traditions and styles that surround us (see Box 12.3). Starting points can be concepts, skills, features, factual knowledge, the so-called elements of music, or activities that immerse young people in creative music-making. All music-making can be viewed in terms of problem-solving, whether creative, re-creative, or receptive, and all musical knowledge can be used to set, solve, or seek solutions to problems. By setting expressive problems from a variety of starting points, we maintain direct

CREATIVITY

contact with real music and maximise the chance of young people's creative engagement with musical understanding (Task 12.6).

Task 12.6 **Using expressive problems to design a teaching activity**

Take any starting point (e.g., a specific example of any knowledge type; see Chapters 6 and 8) and develop a range of strategies based on the expressive problems that arise. Is it possible to cover all of the knowledge types? Design an outline of a unit of work to show your thinking.

Musical "features" as a stimulus for creativity

Swanwick (1988) suggests a different approach and argues that unless we plan for musical understanding and knowledge "of" music, we cannot expect it to happen except by accident. He suggests that one route to ensuring genuine musical experience is through creative engagement with real musical ideas in specific musical contexts—what he calls "features." For example, the opening four notes of Beethoven's *Fifth Symphony* are an expressive feature.

Using features as a stimulus for creativity might work in the following way. The figure from the opening of Siegfried's "Trauermusik" from *Gotterdamerung* by Wagner (see Figure 12.2) could form the basis for improvising, composing, performing, listening, and responding. You could explore the expressive and structural potential of this feature and possible transformations of it, by asking the question, "what would happen if . . . ?" For example:

- What would happen if it is played lightly like a whisper?
- What would happen if it is sped up and made into a more nervous feature?
- Can we experiment with playing the rhythm as an ostinato or riff?
- Can we use the rhythm as an accompaniment feature to a song such as the round *Old Ab'ram Brown*?
- Can we compose death music of our own by adding episodes to the Wagnerian feature?
- Can we base a class improvisation around the same process?
- Can we respond to the original music and talk or write about its expressive and structural qualities?
- Can we ask what expressive features other examples of funeral music have?

The point is that the primary emphasis is on "playing" creatively with the expressive qualities and possibilities of the musical feature. Swanwick (1988) is concerned that unless we engage with these qualities, musical experience and learning can become a barren and reductive experience (Task 12.7).

Figure 12.2 A musical "feature": Wagner's "Trauermusik"

> Task 12.7 **Musical features**
>
> Extract some "features" from a variety of different pieces of music. Choose one feature and suggest how you might use it to stimulate creativity. Design an outline for an integrated unit of work from this starting point and share with other music teachers or your mentor.

Musical creativity stimulated by extra-musical ideas

It is often the case that particular expressive problems are set for composers and performers based on ideas that are not musical at all. Music is by its very nature an abstract art in which meaning is notoriously difficult to pin down. It is common for us to attach feelings, emotions, and ideas to the music we are listening to, and this is an important way in which we can hold our knowledge "of" music. Extra-musical ideas are one way in which music can be "held," be known, and also act as a stimulus for creativity.

The following strategies might be employed when using extra-musical ideas in the teaching and learning of music:

- The use of a "programme" as an expressive problem—such as in Prokofiev's *Peter and the Wolf* or Dukas's *The Sorcerer's Apprentice*—is a perfect way of stimulating creativity;
- Extra-musical ideas that share shapes and structures with other aspects of our life—such as tension and release, ebb and flow, birth and death—can act as props and supports to our understanding of music. These props are important when we compose and discuss music;
- Artefacts, styles, and traditions from other art forms can be used to stimulate creativity. For example, sculpture can be used as a starting point for composition. Poems, pictures, plays, and film footage can be used in a similar way. Young people can also respond to music through drawing or painting and can use a common set of "concepts" to discuss the work (e.g., line, texture, colour, form). This approach can also highlight the different meanings of these concepts in each discipline.

While music can never definitively describe extra-musical concepts, these ideas clearly have an important role to play for professional musicians and thus inevitably for the music classroom. In young people's everyday experience, media are constantly being combined and used to mutually stimulate each other. As demonstrated in Task 12.8, as a music teacher you need to be sensitive to the ways in which extra-musical ideas can be used as a tool for learning, teaching, and creativity as well as their cross-curricular opportunities.

> Task 12.8 **Extra-musical ideas**
>
> Make two lists:
>
> 1. Pieces that have an explicit programme or that have been inspired by something extra-musical;
> 2. Pieces (or parts of pieces) that have a likeness to something external to music, such as a specific shape or feeling.
>
> Discuss with other teachers how these extra-musical features could stimulate creativity.

Creativity and improvisation

It is not always possible to distinguish between composition and improvisation (see Chapter 13). Improvisation is generally understood to mean "playing or singing with little or no preparation, inventing the music in whole or in part as it progresses," while composing is understood to mean "greater preparation . . . the fixing of ideas, refining, changing and thinking through ideas" (NAME 2000: 8).

However, composition might include improvisation in its process or as part of its performance. Furthermore, it is also the case that improvisation works within set parameters which allow us to prepare for it. Harvey suggests that we develop a wide series of musical ideas which we internalise through experience and draw upon when composing and improvising. He calls these musical ideas a "dynamic library" (NAME 2000: 9). The role of music education could be seen as developing the "dynamic library" of young people.

Improvisation is an important outlet for creativity, and for the aforementioned reasons it needs to be carefully and progressively developed in the classroom. All strategies for composition noted thus far can also be used to facilitate improvisation. The following strategies are intended to show how a young person's confidence and skills can be developed in improvisation and can be undertaken vocally, instrumentally, or using digital technology.

1. First attempts at improvisation can be approached through two-bar questions and answers, which at first can be practised with the teacher through clapping. Books such as Harvey's (1988) *Jazz in the Classroom* offer some useful advice on question-and-answer technique, and he encourages young people to intuitively "feel" the two-bar structure as opposed to reading it (see Figure 12.3).

Figure 12.3 Question and answer

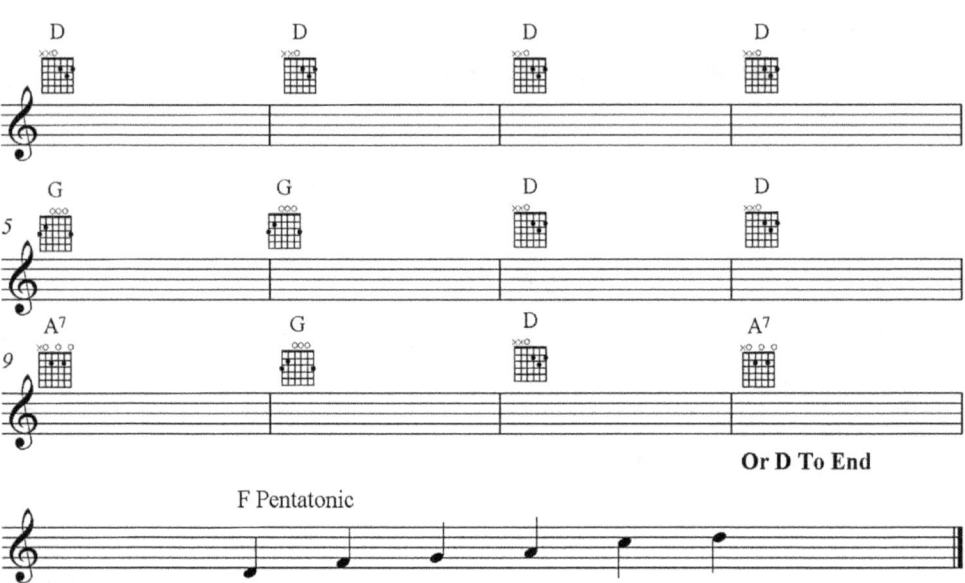

Figure 12.4 The blues in D with an F pentatonic improvisation

2. One of the main tasks of the music teacher, when encouraging first attempts at improvisation with young people, is to clear away some of the "technical" barriers. One way of approaching early attempts at melodic improvisation is to take away the issue of "wrong notes," that is, so that any note chosen will "work." This strategy engages young people in constructing melodic shape, yet provides them with the safety net of knowing that all notes "fit." For example, in blues in the key of D, melodic instruments can be set up for an F pentatonic scale (with Es and Bs taken off tuned percussion instruments, marked on keyboards, or muted in software) such that any improvisation "works" with the blues chord sequence played (see Figure 12.4).
3. Improvisation can also take place within the context of notated classroom ensemble pieces; for example, in the blues shown in Figure 12.4 you could model a simple riff in F pentatonic to be learnt by the whole class (see Figure 12.5). This could be interleaved with improvisations in the form of twelve-bar breaks (which might involve three questions and answers) or a two-bar answer to the riff itself. Other "white note" approaches can work in the same way and initially preclude the need for using chromatic instruments (see Figure 12.6). Each of these can provide easy access to improvisation as a whole class, in groups, or individually.

**CREATIVITY**

Figure 12.5 Riff and break

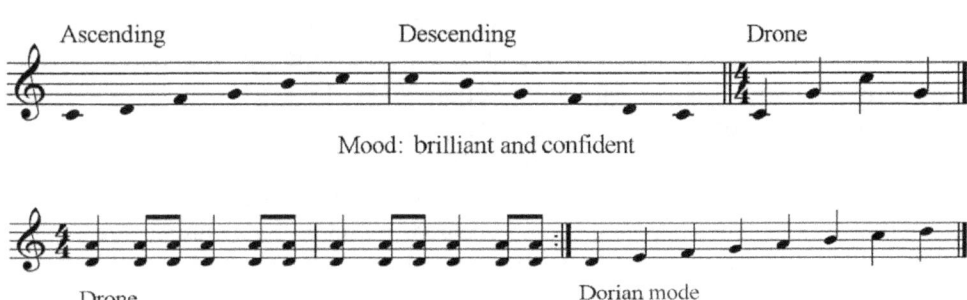

Figure 12.6 Some other ideas for improvisation

4. A more structured approach to improvisation can be made by paying attention to the underlying chord structures, by playing with motifs, or by using the conventions of different styles, genres, and traditions. Improvisation can also take a musical concept as a starting point, such as a strict metre (e.g., triple time) or "free" time like the *alap* used in Indian classical genres to improvise over a *tala* rhythm.
5. Other forms of improvisation can begin with extra-musical themes or ideas, for example "storm," "machines," or "the arch."

Above all, it is important to give young people the confidence to take part in improvisation, for making up music on the spur of the moment can be very daunting. Facilitating improvisation should clear away as many of the technical barriers as possible and seek to develop young people's dynamic libraries such that they can increasingly engage in creative musical dialogue (Task 12.9). Further explorations of improvising using music technology can be found in Chapter 3.

Task 12.9 **Developing and using improvision**

Beginning teachers need to build their own confidence in improvisation before trying it out in class. Take one of the ideas suggested earlier, such as using the two-bar question-and-answer technique or an extra-musical idea, and build up an improvisation either vocally or on your instrument. Try this exercise with a partner or small group of musicians. Finally, try this with a small group of young people by building their own confidence as suggested earlier.

Continuity and progression in creativity

Musical progression implies that knowledge, skills, and understanding develop over time from lesson to lesson, from week to week, and from year to year. But how can we build in continuity and progression when stimulating creativity? Imagine a scheme of work on the concept of musical variations. Lessons could be based around how composers have solved the problem of variation (there will be many solutions), how musical ideas have been employed and transformed in different examples of pieces, how we might employ successful variation techniques in our own compositions, and how to communicate these most effectively in performance. Continuity can then be achieved by formally revisiting the notion of variation over time. Bruner (1966) suggests that all concepts can be addressed through a spiral of progression at any age. Yet we should expect the nature of the engagement to change depending on developmental stage (see Chapter 6). The examples in Box 12.4 explore how Bruner's (1966) principles of continuity and progression might be managed over time in relation to a creative engagement with musical variations.

Box 12.4 An illustration of continuity and progression in the concept of "musical variations"

11- to 12-year-olds: With a composition or performance that young people are working on, ask, "what would happen if we . . .?" How can we make a single repetitive beat more interesting? Initiate compositions called "variations on one note" (or on a simple tune such as *Twinkle, Twinkle Little Star*). Listen to Ives's *America* variations and appraise the changes to the melody (and the appearance of the British National Anthem!). How can musical ideas be changed?

12- to 13-year-olds: Play a recording of *Variations on Frère Jacques* (arranged by Iveson for the Philip Jones Brass Ensemble). How is the melody changed? Sing the melody and ask, "what would happen if . . .?" to explore how variation can be achieved. Begin to learn *Frère Jacques* vocally or on instruments and then ask groups to compose variations, which might be performed and recorded in a class "set."

13- to 14-year-olds: Discuss the concept of "cover" versions while appraising various examples. How do cover versions work? Use motifs, phrases, or the whole melody (provided by the teacher or chosen by students) as the basis for a group arrangement and performance of a cover song.

14- to 16-year-olds: Compare more extended sets of variations—such as the Rachmaninov and Lloyd-Webber *Paganini* variations—and use these as the basis for composition, improvisation, and performance. For example, try using the underlying chord structure of the main theme for young people to construct their own variations.

Creativity in the music classroom can and should be at the heart of progression, and creative music-making can be central to musical learning at all levels of study. For example, when studying set works for post-16 examinations, creative

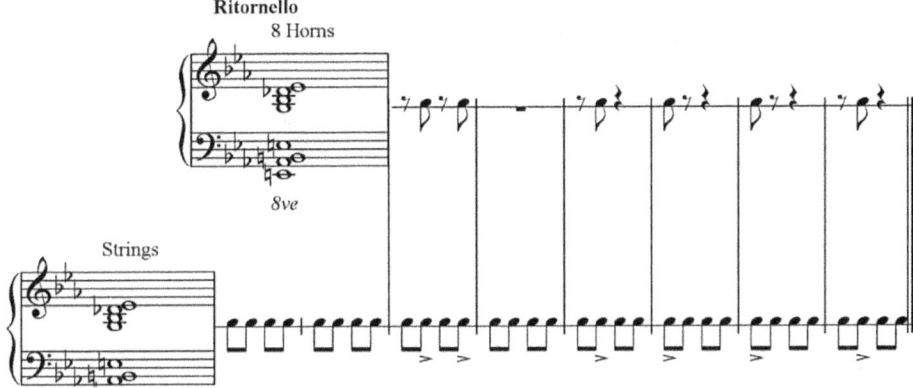

Figure 12.7 "Auguries of Spring": ritornello

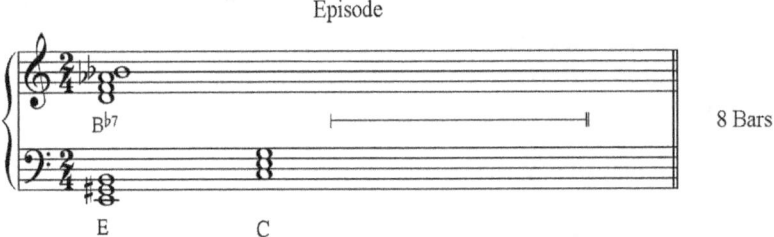

Figure 12.8 "Auguries of Spring": chord structure of episodes

exploration through composition, improvisation, and performance can be key to developing a rich musical understanding. This is modelled in Box 12.5 and Figures 12.7 and 12.8.

Box 12.5 *The Rite of Spring* (1913) by Stravinsky

Composition can bring about many gains in understanding through knowledge "of" the musical resources used in a particular expressive context.

1. Listen to "Auguries of Spring" from Part 1 of *The Rite of Spring* (although this could be saved until the end of the exercise);
2. This music has a pounding, percussive ritornello (see Figure 12.7), followed by a series of episodes;
3. The episodes use the chord structure found in Figure 12.8;
4. Teach the group the ritornello section (orally and aurally) and ask them to compose or improvise their own episodes based on the chords provided (the notes of each chord could be notated or simply listed).

Teaching points that may arise include the emancipation of dissonance, polytonality, expansion of tonality, primitivism, elemental pounding, dark register of strings, percussive chords hurled out by the horns on the rhythmically dislocated accent, hypnotic insistence of ostinato (a favoured "folk" device for Stravinsky), and so on.

> Task 12.10 **Creative musical approaches to teach at post-16 level**
>
> Many qualifications in the later years of secondary school expect young people to study prescribed texts. How might you develop the necessary analytical, technical, and stylistic understanding through creative approaches to singing, performing, composing, and improvising? Devise a lesson based on some of the practical strategies suggested earlier and share with colleagues or a mentor for comment.

In the preceding examples, we have tried to establish some principles of working that encourage you to look for creative approaches to musical learning, even where the syllabus or curriculum does not explicitly require you to do so. Creativity is at the heart of what it means to behave musically and so should also be at the heart of a pedagogy for developing a rich musical understanding. Think about this further as you complete Task 12.10.

SUMMARY

In this chapter we have seen that:

- creativity is an important theme in music education and that creativity underpins many of the expectations in music curricula, syllabi, national policies, and examination requirements;
- it is important for teachers to have a well-reasoned concept of creativity and the creative process to underpin their practice;
- creativity is complex and there are many ideological issues surrounding the conditions under which it is assumed that it can manifest;
- whatever the rationale for creativity in the classroom, the teacher needs much sensitivity to create the pedagogical conditions for it to flourish;
- this requires that the teacher exercise their own creativity when designing musical strategies for responding, performing, improvising, and composing;
- finally, continuity and progression in creativity can be achieved by carefully sequencing the depth and demand in the tasks and strategies used and should be underpinned by a "musical" pedagogy.

The ideas and principles outlined in this chapter are universally relevant to all phases and ages of music education. By embedding creativity at the heart of music lessons, you can nurture deeper engagement and reflect the essential, expressive nature of music itself.

FURTHER READING

These publications are full of ideas for stimulating and managing creativity in the classroom:

Arts Council England (ACE) (2019)
Durham Commission on Creativity and Education. Online, available at: https://www.artscouncil.org.uk/durham-commission-creativity-and-education

Burnard, P. (2012)
Musical Creativities in Practice, Oxford: Oxford University Press.

Odena, O. (ed) (2012)
Musical Creativity: Insights from Music Education Research, Farnham: Ashgate.

Savage, J. and Fautley, M. (2007)
Creativity in Secondary Education, Exeter: Learning Matters.

Snepvangers, K., Thomson, P. and Harris, A. (eds) (2018)
Creative Policy, Partnership and Practice in Education, Cham: Palgrave MacMillan.

13 COMPOSING

Kirsty Devaney and Kelly Davey Nicklin

INTRODUCTION

Composing and the justification for its place within a high-quality music curriculum has been well researched and appears in literature spanning centuries. In 1762, Genevan philosopher, writer and composer Rosseau (2013) argued that "to learn music thoroughly we must make songs as well as sing them and the two processes must be studied together, or we shall never have any real knowledge of music" (206). While Rosseau was making this argument more than 250 years ago, the value of composing in the secondary school curriculum is still a contested issue today.

Over the last century, writers and researchers in music education have continued to advocate the importance of composing as part of a rich music education. British composer and music educator Paynter (1997) believed composing to be "the surest way for pupils to develop musical judgement and to come to understand the notion of 'thinking' in music" (18). Meanwhile, Odam (2000) explained that "acquiring the language of music requires immediate experience of it and the chance to use and experiment with it, finding out what it says and how it works by using it" (125). The common theme here is that composing supports musical learning as it enables young people to actively engage with and understand how music works from the inside out.

Thanks to the championing of some of these music educators, it is now widely accepted that composing is and should be a key part of any music curriculum. The Model Music Curriculum published in England in 2021 makes several references to composing, including the aim for all young people to "start to find their own compositional voice towards the end of Year 9 [aged 13 to 14]" (DfE 2021: 38). Likewise, the National Plan for Music Education in Wales states one of its priorities to be "promoting equality by ensuring access for all learners to play, sing, take part, progress and create music" (Welsh Government 2022: 4). It is worth noting too that young people's engagement with composing has developed in recent years, particularly following the COVID-19 pandemic. Nevertheless, the challenge faced by music educators today is in recognising and understanding how composing can be taught so that young people benefit from high-quality and musical learning experiences.

> **Objectives**
>
> By the end of this chapter you should know:
>
> - that composing is part of a rich, broad, and balanced music curriculum;
> - some of the barriers to composing in the classroom and how to overcome these barriers;
> - that to support musical learning, the process of composing is as important as the end-product;
> - ways in which you can support young people to become better at composing;
> - how feedback can be used to support young people as part of the composing process.

BUILDING CONFIDENCE TO TEACH COMPOSING

Although composing has become a normalised part of music-making in the classroom (Task 13.1), its adoption into the curriculum has not been without challenges. Composing is often an area of a music syllabus that teachers feel uncertain about. Paynter (2000) wrote that, "whilst we enthusiastically encourage [young people] to be musically creative, we are far less sure of ourselves when it comes to helping them get *better* at composing" (2). Traditionally, in western art music, there is often a division between those who perform and those who compose (see Chapter 14). This has contributed to viewing composing as a separate, specialist activity, with many music teachers believing they do not have adequate skills or experience to teach composing. As a result, there is a danger that units or schemes of work in a secondary school music department may be heavily weighted towards performing, with composing only making a brief appearance as a tokenistic part of the curriculum. However, it is important to note that across history, cultures, and different genres of music, this separation of "composer" and "performer" is less clear, with music-making often being more holistic and integrating aspects of performing, composing, improvising, and listening.

> **Task 13.1 Composing in the curriculum**
>
> Review the nationally published music curriculum guidance for the country in which you are or will be teaching:

1. Where does composing appear within the published curriculum?
   a. Is it called "composing" or are other terms used?
   b. How is composing integrated into the curriculum?
2. What does the published curriculum indicate to you about the value that is placed upon composing?

Despite past reports of teachers feeling low in confidence regarding teaching composing, recent research has in fact found that music teachers come to teaching with a diverse range of composing experiences, such as songwriting, media-music composing, electronic production, improvisation, arranging, and working collaboratively across different art forms (Devaney 2024). Although your confidence to teach composing may take time to develop, use Task 13.2 to consider where creative music-making, in all its forms, has happened during your own musical life. This may help to raise your confidence and encourage the next generation to enjoy composing as a normalised part of music-making.

Task 13.2 **Reflecting on your own experiences of composing**

Reflect upon your own experiences of composing both inside and outside the classroom (e.g., being part of a band, using a Digital Audio Workstation, improvising on your instrument). How have these experiences shaped what you believe composing to be? What skills and experience can you bring into the classroom when teaching composing?

It is important to remember that there is not one universally recognised composing pedagogy (Fautley 2014) and how we teach will vary depending on the young people we are working with, the resources we have, the genres of music we are exploring, and much more. Finding continuing professional development that focuses on composing can be a great way to gather ideas for how to teach composing, as well as talking to and sharing resources with other teachers. It might also be possible to reach out to local music organisations who run creative music-making projects and enquire about forming a partnership or shadowing some sessions. The principal recommendation here is to keep an open mind, continue to learn, take risks, and try new things, which is what composing is all about!

■ ■ ■ ■ COMPOSING

COMPOSING IN THE CURRICULUM

Music teachers have to think carefully about how they will teach the published curriculum. Whilst the content of the curriculum might be outlined in policy documents, the approach to teaching the content is not usually specified. Your pedagogical understanding will underpin how you plan and teach music lessons that enable young people to make progress in all aspects of their musical learning. Chapter 8 explains how immersing young people in music can be achieved through an integrated approach to planning music lessons.

In order to ensure that young people have a rich musical learning experience, opportunities for composing and responding creatively should be considered at the planning stage in all units or schemes of work. For example, samba is a common topic in music curricula and lends itself well to a focus on performing. Young people can learn about the features of samba music (e.g., rhythm, structure, texture) through performing on a percussion instrument as part of an ensemble and listening to musical examples. But where are the opportunities for young people to be creative with their knowledge of samba by composing or responding creatively? An integrated approach to planning a unit of work around samba music might include opportunities for young people to compose and arrange with syncopated polyrhythms, use call-and-response features, and structure their own piece of music in the genre's style. Consider this further using Task 13.3.

Task 13.3 **Opportunities for composing**

Consider the units or schemes of work that you are currently teaching or supporting in your school or during your school placement:

1. Does every unit or scheme of work have the opportunity for young people to compose or to respond creatively to a given stimulus?
2. If you have encountered any units or schemes of work that do not have the opportunity for young people to compose, consider how you might plan a similar topic using an integrated approach. Where might there be opportunities for young people to compose or respond creatively to enhance their musical learning?

DISMANTLING MYTHS ABOUT COMPOSERS

While music teachers may feel uncertain or underconfident about integrating composing into their teaching, young people can also feel quite anxious when composing for the first time; the phrase "I can't compose" is, unfortunately, a common phrase in the music classroom. Why do young people have this visceral reaction to composing, and what can we do to empower them to see themselves as composers?

Despite researchers and composer-educators fiercely advocating composing as something all young people can learn and experience, it is still a commonly held belief that composing is only for the extraordinarily musically "talented"–either something you *can* do, or you *can't* do. Well-known classical composers are often elevated to "greatness," something French sociologist Bourdieu (1993) found was commonplace within the arts.

> Task 13.4 **Composing myths**
>
> List some of the stereotypes and myths that surround composers. How have these influenced your own beliefs about composers and the process of composing? How might these beliefs help or hinder young people? How might you break down some of these misconceptions in your classroom?

As illustrated in Task 13.4, we may have heard romanticised tales of child prodigies or famous composers dreaming up whole symphonies in their heads. Imagined in this way, composing almost appears to be a passive process, with music seemingly flowing through the composer. However, this perception is particularly unhelpful as it reinforces potentially harmful narratives and falsehoods about the real working practices of composers:

> The celebration of the composer's genius and of the music's transcendent greatness . . . is misleading when viewed in the light of the working practices of many composers.
>
> (Green 1997: 82–83)

Composing is in fact an active (and sometimes messy!) process involving trial and error, exploration, collaboration, improvisation, self-reflection, editing, and refining ideas . . . and the list goes on.

REDEFINING COMPOSING

Recognising that the words "composer" and "composing" carry social, historical, and cultural baggage, it is important to take some time to consider how we might define or redefine composing, ensuring it is perceived as an inclusive practice with which everyone can engage (Task 13.5).

> Task 13.5 **Defining composing**
>
> Create your own definition of the word "composing." Now consider if the following activities meet your definition of composing, and why or why not:
>
> - Looping and layering samples;
> - Bach chorale or four-part harmony exercises;
> - Free improvisation;
> - Creating a graphic score.

It can be worthwhile identifying the differences between the acts of composing and improvising. Although both are related activities and many composers use improvisation as a tool for composing, a commonly recognised difference between the two is that an end-product of composing (a "composition") can be reproduced time and time again, whereas an end-product of improvising (an "improvisation") exists in the moment and will vary between performances. But these boundaries are not clear cut: for example, composers may write music that involves improvisatory elements, but the end-product is still classified as a composition.

Some definitions tie composing with the act of writing music down. In fact, the term "writing music" is often used interchangeably with composing. But it is crucial to question why composing is so commonly tied to the act of writing. By writing music down (such as through graphics, staff notation, or text), we are fixing certain elements of the music (harmony, rhythm, structure, and so on). The notation acts as a set of instructions for performers to follow. But what if the performers are also the composers and the intention is to record the music for an album? Is notation still essential in composing? Notation can be a tool to help edit and remember ideas, but there are also music creators who convey their ideas without the use of notation, such as through audio-recording. The increasing availability of digital technologies continues to reshape what composing looks and sounds like, enabling more young people to engage with the act of composing without notation and to create music that feels culturally relevant to them.

Composing within the classroom can sometimes over-emphasise getting to the final end-product or "composition":

> There is a long-standing dichotomy in music education as to whether the process of composing is assessed, or whether assessment is that of the product which results.
>
> (Savage and Fautley 2011: 146)

Interestingly, although most examination boards require a score to be submitted alongside a recording for the assessment of composing, they are often open to a diverse range of notational approaches, emphasising the relevance of notation to the style of music being created. Despite examinations focusing on the finished *product* (such as a recording and score), there are many ways to support young people through the *process* of composing which will be discussed later in the chapter.

Although it might detract from the mystery of composing, it can be beneficial to view composing as a set of decisions. Some decisions might be consciously situated within a genre-specific framework: for example, the harmony of the twelve-bar blues, the structure of a pop song, the use of an Alberti bass, or the choice of *rāga* in Indian classical music. Some composers use processes (such as twelve-tone serialism) to make the decisions for them. Other decisions may be more internalised or exploratory, allowing for a unique compositional voice to emerge. Understanding a composer's intention is important, and, over time, young people may progress to make more complex, independent decisions of their own.

So why does all this matter? Well, the language we use can influence young people's perceptions and understanding of composing. A simple switch from asking a young person what they have "written" to asking what they have "created" can help to dismantle the idea that composing is primarily about writing music down. It could even be argued that the term "composing" is in fact outdated and terms such as "songwriting" and "producing" are more relevant. However, we believe that composing–when viewed not just as the writing of western art music but in the broadest sense of the word–is still a relevant, exciting, and creative mode of expression that all young people can access. We can work with young people to redefine what composing is and who composers are, empowering them to take ownership of the word.

SUPPORTING THE COMPOSING PROCESS

How do composers go from a blank page or screen to a finished piece of music? The process of composing can seem to be shrouded in mystery, but there is now a wealth of research investigating how composers create music. It can be helpful to draw upon research that models creativity as a staged process, such as that described in Chapter 12. By breaking composing down into possible stages–as shown in Task 13.6–we can start to demystify composing for young people and identify how to support them at different stages of the process.

Task 13.6 **Identifying the different stages of composing**

Reflect on the last piece of music you composed; this could be when you were in school. List the different activities or steps that you went through when composing. Using your own list, or the list that follows, arrange the activities into the order in which you did them (e.g., start, middle, end).

- Add accompaniment;
- Listen and make changes;
- Share with a friend for feedback;
- Develop the melody line;
- Listen to other pieces of music for inspiration;
- Improvise chords with friends;
- Come up with a title;
- Decide instruments;
- Add a contrasting section.

Compare your list with other beginning teachers and note any similarities or differences.

COMPOSING

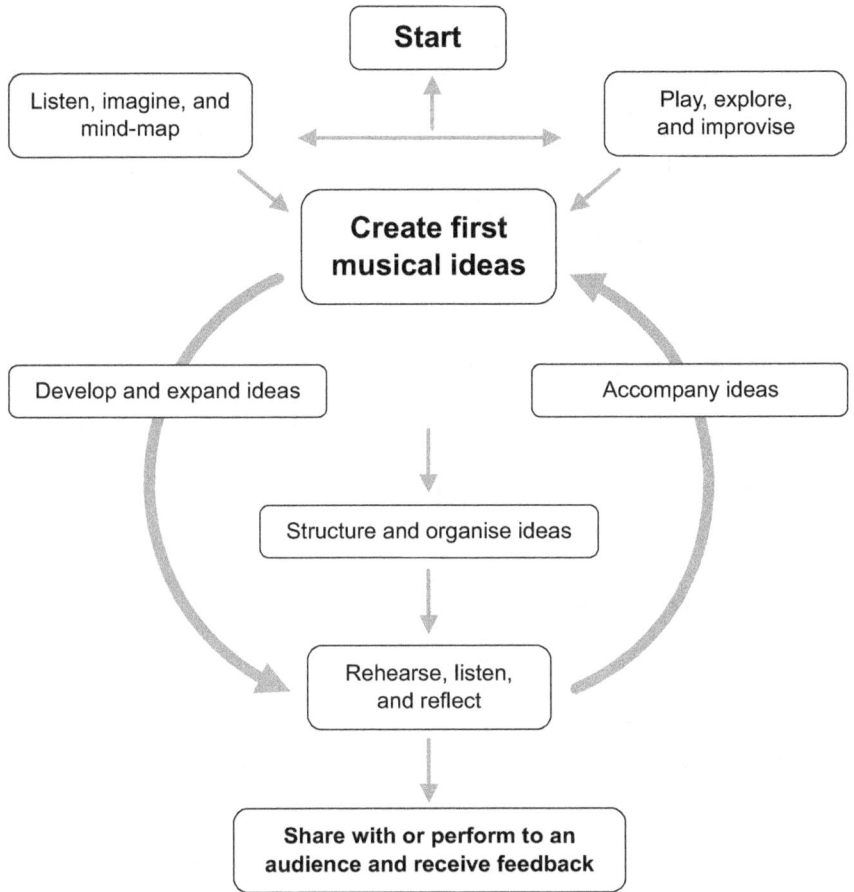

Figure 13.1 A composing process flow chart
Reproduced with permission of the authors (Evans and Fautley 2024: 18)

By reflecting on your own composing processes, or observing how young people compose, you might come to realise that composing does not look the same for everyone. In addition, composing rarely takes place in clearly defined, linear stages but instead might be complex, messy, or even cyclical. Figure 13.1 (Evans and Fautley 2024) shows a composing flow chart and offers a great starting point for thinking about the different stages of composing in Task 13.7. This may also be a useful tool for young people to reflect on their own composing.

Task 13.7 **Supporting the composing process**

Look at the composing process flow chart presented in Figure 13.1. Drawing upon your own experiences of supporting young people composing—are there any stages that they appear to find most difficult? Why do you think this is? Which stages might get missed out when teaching composing in the secondary school? Which stages take most time in the classroom?

Consider your role as a teacher and the different types and levels of support that might be needed at different stages. What sort of feedback do you think would be most useful for the different stages of composing? How might feedback change depending on the progress being made?

Starting points for composing

The following examples may help you to support a class of young people through the creative and messy process of composing. These are not intended as "how to guides" but as stimuli for you to critique and develop your own composing pedagogies.

1. Composing to a visual stimulus

For topics that relate to composing for film and media, using a video or still image as a stimulus can be an effective starting point for young people to compose. This first example uses a visual stimulus as a starting point for a group composing task, where prior learning might have included an exploration of the use of musical elements (including harmony) and musical devices (such as motif) to portray a specific film scene or visual image.

Prior to the group composing task, the teacher can model the creative process by choosing an image to share with the class and inviting them to contribute their thoughts about what they can see and how this makes them feel. After this discussion, invite the class to choose musical instruments to explore what they saw and felt. Offer prompts if they need support. What instruments could be used quietly to represent apprehension or fear? What instruments could use high pitches to represent excitement and anticipation? After collecting ideas together, you can then support the class in creating a soundscape in which they all contribute sounds in response to the visual stimulus. This will prepare the young people for responding to a visual stimulus in smaller groups and promote discussion around the emotive use of symbolic discourse (rather than sound effects) and musical elements and devices (rather than set structures).

Next, each small group is shown their image (covertly, so that the other groups cannot see) and given some starting points on a worksheet. Example stimuli might include:

- a haunted house;
- a police car chase;
- a boxing champion celebrating a victory;
- a desert landscape with pyramids.

COMPOSING

Prompts for the groups could include:

- discussing what they can *see* in the image;
- discussing how the image makes them *feel*;
- evaluating how to use the *musical elements* to portray the image;
- a *scale* or *chord progression* that could help represent the image.

Figure 13.2 and Figure 13.3 show two examples of worksheets with prompts for a haunted house image (recommending the use of a chromatic scale) and for a police car chase image (recommending the use of a minor scale).

Your knowledge of the class and their prior learning and experience will enable you to assign a visual stimulus that will help them to be successful. For example, the use of the chromatic scale in Figure 13.2 might be suitable for a group with less experience in notation and harmony but will enable a creative output through "noodling" around the chromatic scale. You can scaffold the level of support offered to each group–you may have some groups who need no prompting at all but others who need more structured support. The use of the prompt worksheet will provide this structure and a starting point whilst enabling the young people to be creatively and musically responsive.

It is important to be clear about the expectations for all composing activities so that young people can plan and prepare accordingly. In this activity, the expected outcome is that all groups will compose a piece of music to play to the rest of the class and for their peers to try to work out what their original visual stimulus might have been. Make this expectation clear to all groups before they begin to compose.

Recording each group's performance so that they can listen back to it provides important opportunities for reflection. In addition, inviting the class to reflect, feed back, and contribute ideas about the original visual stimulus–while encouraging them to explain their answers using musical terminology–can offer important insights for you as the teacher and the composing group. Questions to ask might include, did they manage to convey the intended image? What was successful in their composing that conveyed the intended image? How could they have further manipulated musical elements or devices to convey their image even more vividly?

2. Composing in the style of Balinese gamelan

In a topic that explores Balinese gamelan music, there are many opportunities for composing and young people will benefit from the chance to perform as part of a whole-class ensemble using a mixture of tuned and untuned classroom percussion instruments. Using an existing piece of Balinese gamelan music, the class can be introduced to the role of each instrument, the textural layering of melodies, the use of cyclical rhythmic patterns, and the specific Indonesian scales.

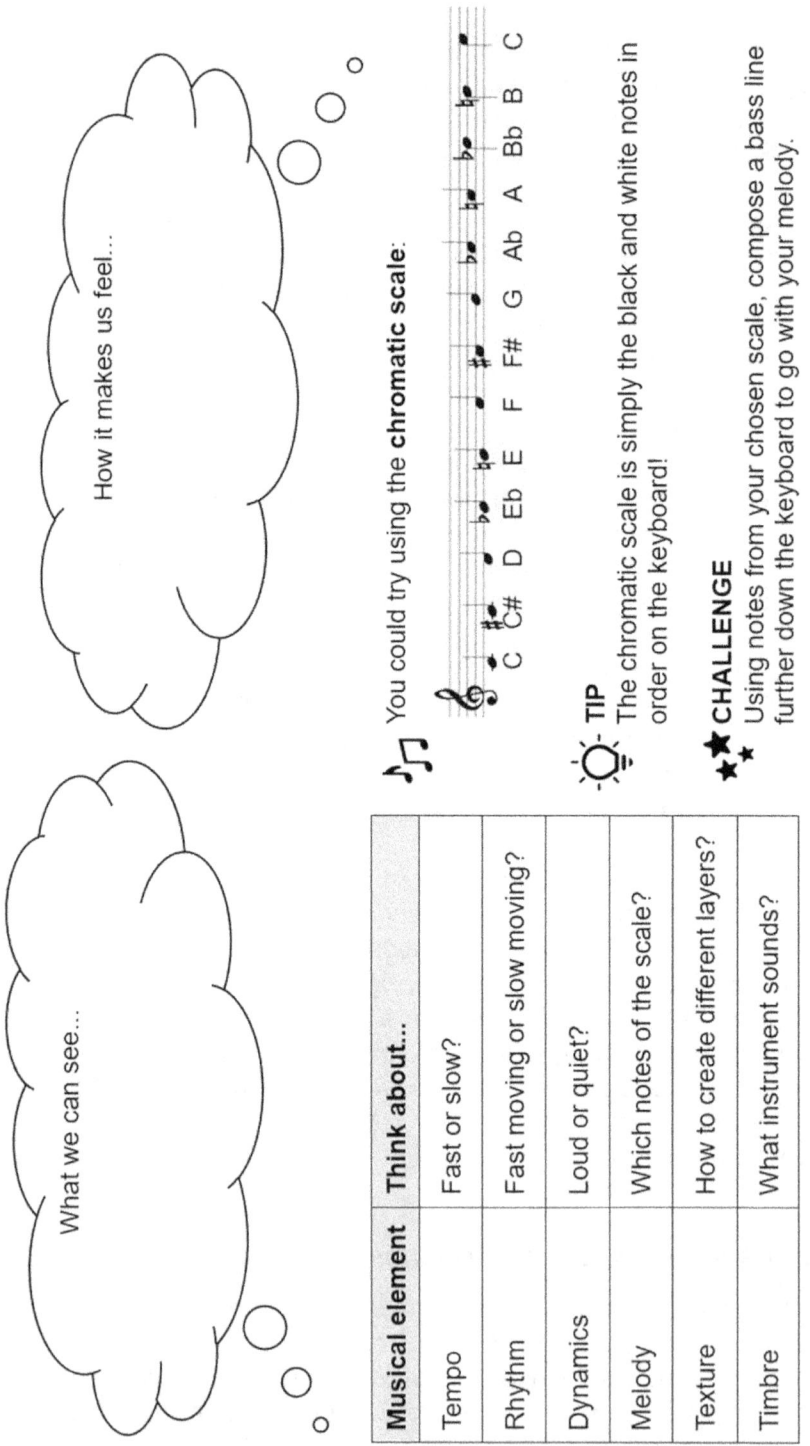

Figure 13.2 A worksheet for a group composition beginning with an image of a haunted house

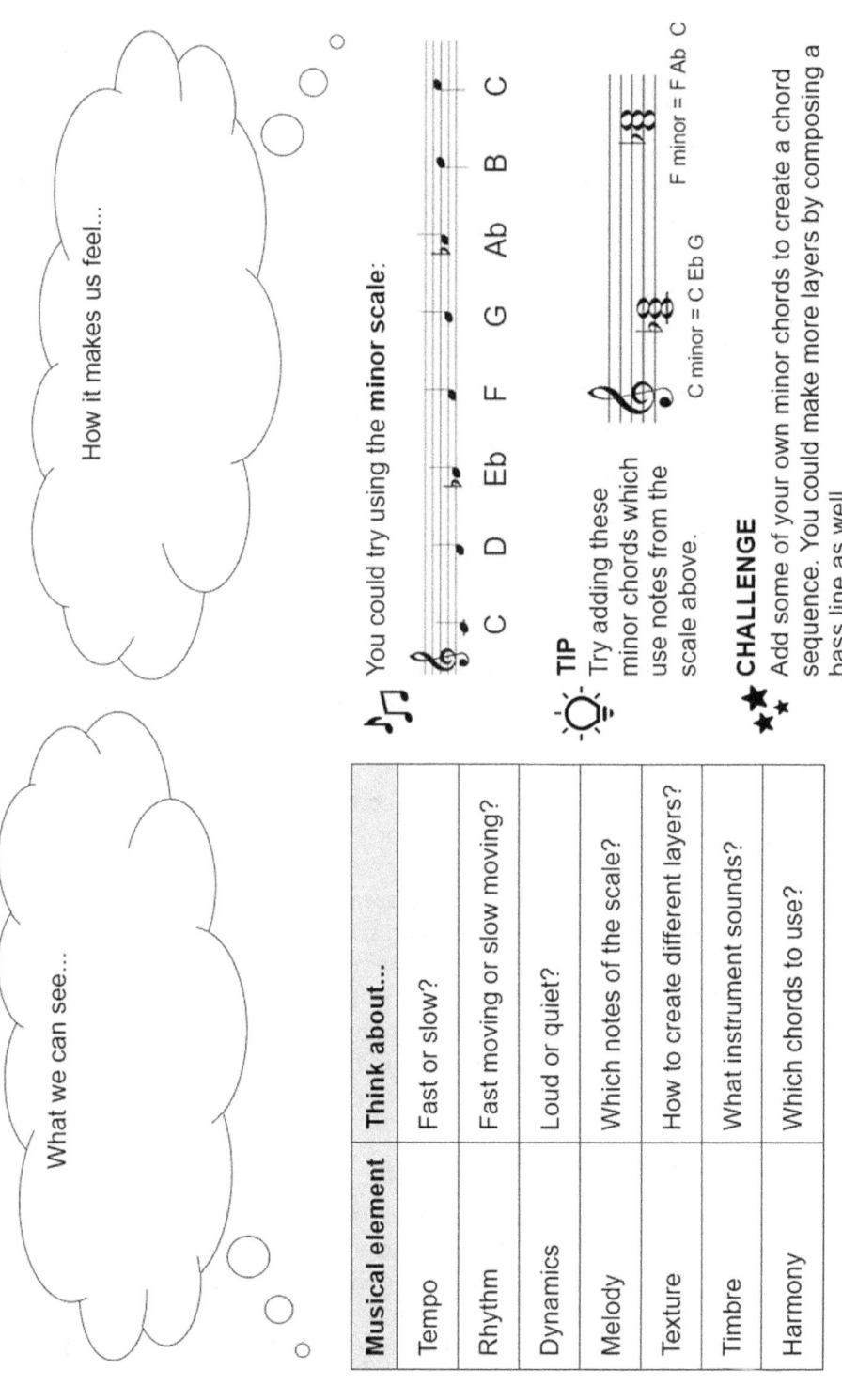

Figure 13.3 A worksheet for a group composition beginning with an image of a police car chase

With this knowledge, young people can work in groups to compose a melody using a tuning system such as *slendro* or *pelog*. Once groups have composed a melody, they can use their knowledge of rhythmic expectations in gamelan to compose parts for specific instruments such as:

- the *katilan*–which doubles the melody an octave higher;
- the *pemade*–which plays the main melody with one note per beat;
- the *bonang*–which plays the melody an octave lower on the off-beat.

You can scaffold this process for each group by providing a template–such as the one shown in Figure 13.4–for them to notate their *slendro* or *pelog* melody and compose the other parts for their gamelan ensemble.

Each group can then develop their composing further by considering other percussion parts that might accompany their piece. Composing with the intention of the music being performed for a special occasion is a helpful way in which to consider the culture and roots of the music that the young people are learning about.

3. Using music technology

There are a range of ways in which young people can use technology to support the composing process, some of which are explored further in Chapter 3. One specific example would be using sequencing software (e.g., GarageBand) for songwriting. Sequencers can provide an effective way to differentiate the composing process for songwriting. For example, as the teacher you can pre-record a bassline for the class to compose an accompanying chord sequence or pre-record a chord sequence for the class to compose an accompanying melody. Some young people will be able to use sequencing software to record their own loops from scratch, while some may need a more scaffolded approach with suggestions for harmony and structure.

The visual layout of sequencers can also be helpful in supporting young people to understand the textural layers of songwriting as well as its structural elements (e.g., verse, chorus, middle-eight). Many sequencers come pre-populated with loops which young people could use to explore texture and structure before composing their own.

Cross-curricular ideas for composing

Integrating composing with subjects across the curriculum can be a powerful stimulus. By drawing on topics from other disciplines, young people will find that they have pre-existing knowledge and experience (even if not explicitly musical) that they can bring to their composing. For example, if they are writing a protest song about climate crisis, they might be able to create lyrics using what they have learnt about global warming in science. Or if they are writing music in a specific historical style, they may be able to imagine how it would have

COMPOSING

Instrument	1	2	3	4	5	6	7	8
Katilan (doubles the melody an octave higher)								
Pemade (main melody, one note per beat)								
Bonang (plays the off-beat melody an octave lower)								

Figure 13.4 A template for notating a *slendro* or *pelog* melody

been performed in different settings, such as music played by minstrels during performances at the Globe Theatre, or music sung by choirs at different sacred celebrations.

You can explore further opportunities to make links with the wider school curriculum through composing in Task 13.8. Examples might include:

- links with the English curriculum through composing with poetry;
- links with the physical education curriculum through composing for dance;
- links with modern foreign languages through composing songs with lyrics in other languages;
- links with computer science through composing using technology;
- links with personal, social, and health education and history through political song-writing;
- links with geography and religious education through composing that is inspired by non-western music.

Task 13.8 **Cross-curricular composing opportunities**

In addition to the aforementioned examples, what other cross-curricular opportunities with composing exist within your school? How could you collaborate directly with teachers in other subject departments to create projects that allow young people to draw on their knowledge and experience from across school? How might this impact the composing process?

Composing in groups

Although traditional western notions of a "composer" might lead us to believe that composing is a solitary act, in reality many music creators of all genres create music collectively and collaboratively. Even composers whose practice is mostly independent will likely have an open dialogue with musicians. It can be fascinating to watch footage of songwriters (such as Taylor Swift and Billie Eilish with Finneas O'Connell) collaborating with others and constructing new songs in their studios, moving between doodling on their instrument, creating lyrics and melodies, recording ideas, and inputting layers into software programmes. Through the process of working with others, what is commonly an "internal process" becomes a "social activity" (Biasutti 2012: 351) where ideas, decisions, revisions, and thoughts are externalised and voices outload through conversations and discussions.

Composing in groups is a great way for young people to start uncovering the different stages of composing and the decisions they might make about their music. The previous examples in this chapter relating to composing to a visual stimulus and composing in the style of Balinese gamelan provide some ideas as to how groups can compose together.

Although composing for national examinations typically requires young people to compose individually, it is still worthwhile to include some group work to support young people as they continue to develop their composing skills and approaches. Group work may foster confidence in young people who feel uncertain about composing individually for the first time, encouraging them to think about the practicalities of performance as well as offering a safe space to try out ideas and take risks with others in a low-stakes environment. When young people then come to compose individually for examinations, they can draw on their experience and learning as a group around how to generate, revise, structure, and develop ideas. Task 13.9 encourages you to try this out with an examination class.

Task 13.9 **Group planning**

Select a past national examination brief for composing or set a defined composing task. In groups of five, ask young people in your class to mind-map ideas for how to approach this brief. Allow them a couple of lessons to work as a group on composing and performing their work before letting them work individually or as pairs to develop their initial ideas.

It is important to note that collaborative composing is a valued practice in and of itself in the professional world. Therefore, the purpose of group composing does not need to be solely to prepare young people to compose individually. Offering young people a diverse range of methods and processes to create music can help to break down some of the myths and preconceptions about composers and composing discussed earlier in the chapter.

Dealing with creative blocks

By presenting composing to young people as a musical activity just like any other—and therefore as something that requires practice, patience, and hard work—young people might not instantly feel they "can't compose," but still give up as soon as they hit their first "creative block." It is essential to recognise composers of all ages, styles, and stages experience creative blocks and it is often a normal, albeit frustrating, part of the creative process. However, Task 13.10 demonstrates that there are things that we can do as teachers to support young people through such issues.

> Task 13.10 **Creative blocks**
>
> Create an inspiration board for young people to use when they get stuck while composing. Ask them what they have done in the past to get over their "creative blocks." The following examples might be a useful starting point.
>
> - Listen to music of a similar style or using a similar ensemble;
> - Get feedback from the teacher or a friend;
> - Listen to your composition with the score or screen off;
> - Take some time away and focus on a different task;
> - Print off your music, lay it out on the floor, and try to hear it in your head;
> - Imagine the venue you'd like your music to be showcased or performed (e.g., festival, concert hall, place of worship, art gallery, theatre).
>
> Display your inspiration board in your classroom for the young people to come back to when they get stuck.

If we view composing as a series of decisions, we can support young people by scaffolding these decisions so that they don't feel overwhelmed by the blank page or screen. One way might be by narrowing down some of their options: we could, for example, give young people a choice of chords to order, ask them to follow a predetermined structure, or provide them with a series of rhythms or loops to layer. The examples shared previously in Figures 13.2, 13.3, and 13.4 scaffolded the processes of compositional decision-making by including suggested scales, harmonies, or rhythmic structures.

Nevertheless, in specifying boundaries for young people to adhere to when composing, we must consider how such limitations might influence their learning and whether they are in fact allowed to "break the rules"! Evans and Spruce (2023) explore this debate in more detail in the series companion, *A Practical Guide to Teaching Music*. They highlight how different composing briefs (such as open versus closed) have different positive and negative attributes which need to be considered when designing a composing task for young people. This is because,

> There can be a tendency in teaching composing to gravitate to the extremes of the spectrum where, at one end, composing is reduced to a painting by numbers exercise, and at the other, little guidance or intervention from the teacher takes place. Operating at both extremes can cause a disconnect with pupils.
>
> (Evans and Fautley 2024: 26)

In our experience of teaching composing, we have found that although some young people enjoy working within parameters, others may feel confined with their creativity restricted. Therefore, offering a range of composing briefs

COMPOSING

throughout the curriculum helps to ensure that no one type is overly prioritised. Keep in mind that we want young people to gradually become more independent and able to make their own creative decisions over time.

CREATING A SAFE ENVIRONMENT

Music plays a significant part in many young people's identities, and composing might be one way for a young person to express who they are. However, for some young people, composing can be quite a daunting prospect; they are being asked to create and share their own original ideas, perhaps in such a way that never happens elsewhere in school. This can be especially the case for young people who might be used to replicating music through presentational performance (see Chapter 14) and focused on getting things "right." Therefore, composing–which often involves a lot of trial and error, as well as sharing ideas that are not "finished"–can seem far outside some young people's comfort zones. Likewise, for other young people who might have been engaged in creating their own music for years on their laptops or instruments, being asked to share their music with others and receive feedback might provoke anxiety. Some might even use composing privately as a tool to help them to understand or come to terms with issues that are personal to them. As teachers, we therefore have a responsibility to foster an environment where young people feel safe to experiment with new ideas and share work-in-progress without fear of harsh judgement or mockery.

Young people's voices

Engaging with composing can feel like a very personal endeavour for young people, and it is important that they feel comfortable in the environment of the music classroom so that they can be confident in being creative. All teachers should consider asking young people about what they feel they need to create a safe environment for composing, as suggested in Task 13.11. Even if you feel sure that your classroom is an inclusive and safe environment, you may be surprised by some of the answers from your classes.

Task 13.11 **Creating class guidelines for composing**

Before beginning a composing activity or unit, start a class discussion about what young people feel they need to be creative. Create a class set of guidelines that everyone agrees to when composing. For example:

1. Keep an open mind;
2. Give constructive and kind feedback;
3. Challenge myself to do the best I can;
4. Ask for help when I am feeling stuck;
5. Be inspired by each other.

Positive role models

As previously discussed in this chapter, there are many preconceptions about who composers are and how they compose. It is entirely possible for young people not even to realise that composers are real, living people. These perceptions can lead to the exclusion of certain groups, especially young women (Partti and Devaney 2023). Therefore, providing diverse examples of composers, songwriters, producers, and music creators from all cultural and social backgrounds, genders, and styles of music can help to empower young people to see themselves as composers (Task 13.12).

> Task 13.12 **Role models**
>
> Examine the composers, songwriters, or producers that you use as examples in your lessons. Do they reflect a wide range of music creators from diverse musical and cultural backgrounds? Are different genders, ethnicities, and disabilities represented? How might you include examples of positive role models for all young people?

Conversations around equality, diversity, inclusion, and access in western art music have been increasing. For example, in 2015, after noticing that there were no female composers in her A-level music syllabus, Jessy McCabe campaigned to have the syllabus changed. Similar campaigns have taken place, including those exhorting the Associated Board of the Royal Schools of Music to include more pieces by composers of colour in their graded instrumental examinations. However, such campaigns are not just about replacing or adding female composers or composers of colour but about understanding some of the structural, societal, and cultural inequalities and how we as music educators play a role in reinforcing or changing the dominant narrative.

The process of diversifying the music curriculum is complex, but there are fantastic, supportive resources now widely available (e.g., Holder 2020). Although it might feel uncomfortable to explore these issues, remember that it is an ongoing process of self-reflection, unlearning, and re-learning, as well as continual professional development. Nevertheless, such processes must also be supported and viewed as strategic priorities from within school leadership and wider education policy. As long as you are open-minded and willing to recognise that there may be different ways of thinking about music education, you will gradually be equipped to integrate new ideas and approaches into teaching composing.

Formative feedback

Regular formative feedback is an essential part of the learning process in composing; therefore, how we give feedback to young people plays a central role in creating an environment of support and trust. However, it can at times feel like a difficult balancing act, as a negative remark may accidentally damage a young person's confidence—but equally, offering no feedback at all can raise

COMPOSING

their anxiety as they might not know what to do next or how to improve (Hickey 2012).

It is important to consider what sort of feedback we might offer to young people at different stages in their composing experiences. At times, it can be easy to fall into only giving feedback on the technical or notational aspects of a composition (e.g., harmony, rhythm, or performability), over feedback that encourages young people to explore and develop the creative potential of a piece. This might be due to the tight time constraints on classroom composing, as well as the pressure to show progress and ensure task completion (Fautley and Kinsella 2017). However, as Eisner (2002) argues: "not everything that matters can be measured, and not everything that is measured matters" (178). As illustrated in Figure 13.1, progress in creative work might not be linear or clearly visible (it may even seem to go backwards).

A useful tool when considering feedback (see Chapter 10) is to view it in two ways: the "micro" and "macro" (Barrett 2006). "Micro" feedback focuses on specific parts of the music, offering precise and focused suggestions such as on the shape of a melody line, the voicing of a chord, or the structure and flow of a section. The "macro" zooms out to the bigger picture of a whole composition and tends to focus on the overarching structure, the meaning behind the music, the aims of the composer, and considerations about how or where the music might be performed or shared. This is also where we might consider the music in the context of the wider sociocultural field, perhaps comparing it to other composers or genres of music.

As explored in Task 13.13, questioning is an important tool for supporting young people's composing. Asking questions helps the teacher to uncover "important insights about the musical workings of each child's mind" (Webster 2003: 245) and discover their creative intentions. Instead of telling young people what to add or change, we can develop their own ability to evaluate and reflect on their music independently. The sorts of questions we ask young people are ultimately the types of questions they will ask themselves in the future.

Task 13.13 **Asking questions**

Create a list of questions you might ask young people about their composing. For example:

- Do you have a favourite part of your piece?
- Are there any bits that you are struggling with?
- What might happen next?
- How might you develop the melody?

Peer feedback is another way to boost young people's confidence and for them to develop their own listening and evaluation skills. Facilitating a space where peer feedback is a positive, normalised practice can have numerous benefits. For example, you could ask young people to feed back on one aspect they liked about a peer's composition and one thing of which they wanted to hear more. It is important to acknowledge that music is personal and feedback is potentially subjective; therefore, encourage young people to view feedback not as definitive or true, but as something they can evaluate and from which they can take what they need.

SUMMARY

In this chapter we have encouraged you to reflect upon your own experiences as a composer so that you can consider how they shape and inform your pedagogical approaches to composing in the classroom. We have shared some practical examples that will help you to think about how composing can be an integral part of musical learning across a range of topics within the music curriculum in your school. We have suggested that composing can be understood as a process rather than as an end-product and have provided some practical ways to support young people in becoming better at composing.

In addition to the tasks within this chapter we encourage you to discuss some of the key points about composing with mentors and colleagues in your own school setting. We leave you with one final—and pertinent—question:

> The question we should be asking is not "how much do children need to know before they can start composing", but rather "how little do children need to be taught before they can start composing?"
>
> (Fautley 2024: n.p.)

FURTHER READING

Evans, N. and Fautley, M. (2024)
A Planning, Reflection and Progression Toolkit. Online, available at: https://www.bcmg.org.uk/listen-imagine-compose-primary-2

A very useful toolkit for composing with young people of any age.

Evans, N. and Spruce, G. (2023)
Exploring composing, in C. Cooke and C. Philpott (eds) *A Practical Guide to Teaching Music in the Secondary School*, 2nd edn, Abingdon: Routledge, pp. 65-76.

This chapter further explores concepts of practical composing and music-making.

Paynter, J. (2000)
'Making progress with composing', *British Journal of Music Education*, 17, 1: 5-31.

A very useful read for thoughts from a significant writer in the field of school-based composing.

Shapey, R. (2021)
How to Teach Composition in the Secondary Classroom: Fifty Inspiring Ideas, London: Collins Music.

This publication provides lots of useful starting points for composing with young people.

PERFORMING
Elizabeth MacGregor

INTRODUCTION

On the face of it, performing is what musicians do. Aspects of performance—whether formal or informal, individual or collective, or deliberate or spontaneous—are often interwoven with music-making of all kinds, not least the responsive, creative, collaborative, inclusive, and digital music-making discussed in this book. Performing is a fundamental means of engaging with music and developing musical understanding, ultimately leading to the "knowing how" and "knowing of" that captures the rich creative and expressive possibilities at the heart of musical practice (see Chapters 6 and 8).

While a curriculum that promotes musicianship through the interrelated skills of performing, composing, and listening has been the common understanding of music education in the United Kingdom for almost half a century, within many classrooms performance remains a standalone skill focusing upon technical control and instrumental fluency. It is often far-removed from the kinds of music-making that young people most regularly encounter in their communities outside school, which seamlessly integrate creating, improvising, and performing. These musics, which emphasise inclusivity and sociality over technique and mastery, are what can be called "participatory"—clapping games, jam sessions, and dance parties—and are often "the most frequent means by which ordinary citizens derive the musical and social benefits of performing" (Regelski 2014: 79).

Both inside and outside the classroom, performing enables young people not only to develop their expertise and fluency with their voice or instrument but also to come to know the processes and relationships inherent to music-making. Technical mastery is merely a means to an end, since "skills allow us to find our way into music but they can also divert us from further musical understanding if they become ends in themselves" (Swanwick 1994: 17). This chapter will therefore interrogate the role of performing in the classroom, comparing the technical and "presentational" forms of performing that typically characterise music-making inside the school, to the diverse, "participatory" cultures of music-making that often take place within young people's communities outside the school. Drawing on Evans's (2016b) valuable contribution on performing in the previous edition of *Learning to Teach Music in the Secondary School*, it will exemplify ways in which young people could become more closely acquainted with music-making in the classroom through fostering participatory, inclusive, and engaging opportunities for performing.

> **Objectives**
>
> By the end of the chapter, you should be able to:
>
> - define your own beliefs about the value and purpose of performing in the classroom in relation to performing in the wider community;
> - establish and critically reflect upon different classroom pedagogies that prioritise "presentational performance";
> - establish and critically reflect upon different classroom pedagogies that prioritise "participatory performance."

PERFORMING IN THE COMMUNITY

For many young people, their interaction with music-making outside the classroom is complex and varied. Although some might have attended performances in traditional settings—whether a local pantomime or a Taylor Swift concert—they are usually more likely to come across performances in casual settings such as playgrounds and youth clubs or through digital platforms and social media (Bunch and Bickford 2022). In these spaces, conventional performance is mediated through dynamic processes of arranging, covering, and remixing. Music may be reshaped within multimodal forms of performance, such as the short videos popularised by the platform TikTok (www.tiktok.com), or garner additional layers of meaning through real-time commentary, such as in the mash-ups of Korean popular music posted to the Asian streaming service Bilibili (bilibili.com).

At their heart, these kinds of performance are "participatory." Ethnomusicologist Turino (2008) defines "participatory performance" as:

> A special type of artistic practice in which there are no artist-audience distinctions, only participants and potential participants performing different roles, and the primary goal is to involve the maximum number of people in some performance role.
>
> (26)

Even when performing individually, online and offline spaces alike offer young people opportunities to share their music with others, initiate immediate collaboration, and seek support from more experienced performers (Task 14.1). The success of the music-making is determined by the engagement of the participants rather than the status of the end-product, and maximum participation is ensured through accessible opportunities for adding new parts, remixing existing parts, and fusing different parts (Turino 2008).

> Task 14.1 **Participatory performing in the community**
>
> As you are getting to know young people during your lessons, ask them how they engage with musical performance outside school.
>
> - When and where do they see or hear music being performed?
> - When and where do they take part in music being performed?
>
> In your opinion, how should musical performance inside the classroom relate to young people's experiences of musical performance outside the classroom?

Individual performing in the community

Although some young people have experience of individual performance through instrumental or vocal tuition, graded examinations, or solo recitals, for many the traditional modes of performance associated with western art music can seem far-removed from their daily experience. Even at gigs and festivals the boundaries between participation and non-participation are blurry. Audiences are often expected to join in with artists through singing and dancing.

For most young people who engage with individual performing outside the classroom, they are much more likely to use informal ways of learning that foreground listening, experimenting, and trial-and-error. Streaming video tutorials, downloading backing tracks, and sharing clips of their music-making ensure that such experiences are inherently participatory and that the process is valued as much as (if not more than) the end-product (Smolarczyk et al. 2024).

Small-group performing in the community

Increasingly, digital means of creating and sharing music have bridged the divide between individual and small-group performing. Although the casual after-school "garage band" may have been superseded by the use of GarageBand (Väkevä 2010), forms of online and offline collaboration have ensured that participatory performance has continued to take place across communities. Digital production platforms, web-based collaboration programmes, and hardware such as laptops and tablets have the potential to enhance small-group performing through helping young people experience enjoyment and belonging (Hanrahan et al. 2019).

Nevertheless, in some communities, traditional ways of small-group music-making remain an important part of young people's cultures. Practices such as American old-time music, Malian djembe and konkoni drumming, and English change-ringing often cross multiple art forms, ensuring that a range of participants can take part through song, dance, or worship, regardless of pre-existing musical experience or ability. In many societies, young people's socialisation into these kinds of participatory practices remains essential for honouring cultural traditions (Campbell and Wiggins 2012).

Large-group performing in the community

Larger-scale participatory forms of performance can also be at the heart of communities. In some instances, these may be formalised practices such as community choirs or brass bands. More often, participatory music-making is most prevalent in gatherings where music serves a secondary purpose, such as at sporting events, during protests and riots, and in congregational worship. It is during such occasions that the potential for music-making to transmit emotion across large groups—and thereby stimulate excitement, express solidarity, or even incite violence—is most obvious. For these reasons, the role of participatory performance within communities must not be underestimated. Not only does it build social networks and create cultural meaning, but it also offers an alternative model of citizenship that values sociality and acceptance over competition and mastery (Turino 2016). Use Task 14.2 to reflect on how this could impact teaching and learning in the music classroom.

Task 14.2 **Bringing the community into the classroom**

As you get to know the kinds of musical performance that the young people in your classes engage with outside school, explore how you could acknowledge these experiences inside school. An example might be introducing an activity like "Song of the Week":

- Each week, one young person brings in a song that they have performed outside school. This could be a recording of something they've been learning on an instrument, work-in-progress on a Digital Audio Workstation, or some sheet music they've worked on during a choir or ensemble.
- They can choose to perform to the class, play a recording, or talk about how they came across it. The class might want to ask questions or reflect on how it links to what they're learning in school.

PERFORMING IN THE CLASSROOM

While participatory and informal cultures of performance are integral to many young people's everyday music-making, performing in the secondary music classroom often revolves around a small range of uniform practices. These are typically characterised by an emphasis on the high-stakes assessment of instrumental technique and a polished end-product. For example, individual keyboard playing may result in an end-of-year test of keyboard skills; progress in small-group performing may be tracked through playing work-in-progress to peers at the end of each lesson; a term of whole-class singing may culminate in a competition or talent show staged in front of the rest of the school; and whole-class workshopping or composing may finish with compiling a digital recording to send to family and friends.

This focus upon a tangible accomplishment that can be captured and measured is typical of "presentational performance." Turino (2008) defines presentational performance as that which is specially prepared for performance by a designated "performer" to a discrete "audience." This mode of performance is "the easiest to commodify through the sale of tickets, merchandise, and recordings" (Turino 2016: 301) and the easiest to codify through learning objectives, progression targets, and standardised grades. As illustrated in Task 14.3, it is therefore commonly found in music education policies from across the United Kingdom.

Task 14.3 **Policy context for performing in the classroom**

Performance is a key component of music education across the four nations of the United Kingdom and beyond. For each of the following curriculum extracts, or for a curriculum you work with, consider:

1. What modes of performance are given value?
2. How do these modes of performance reflect the reality of musical practice outside the classroom?

England: National Curriculum for Music, Key Stage 3 (DfE 2013: 259)

Pupils should be taught to:

- play and perform confidently in a range of solo and ensemble contexts using their voice, playing instruments musically, fluently and with accuracy and expression;
- improvise and compose; and extend and develop musical ideas by drawing on a range of musical structures, styles, genres and traditions;
- use staff and other relevant notations appropriately and accurately in a range of musical styles, genres and traditions;
- identify and use the inter-related dimensions of music expressively and with increasing sophistication . . . and listen with increasing discrimination to a wide range of music.

Scotland: Curriculum for Excellence, Expressive Arts: Experiences and Outcomes (Education Scotland 2010: 9)

Through music, learners have rich opportunities to be creative and to experience inspiration and enjoyment. Performing and creating music will be the prominent activities for all learners. Through these activities they develop their vocal and instrumental skills, explore sounds and musical concepts, and use their imagination and skills to create musical ideas and compositions. They can further develop their understanding and capacity to enjoy music through listening to musical performances and commenting on them. They use ICT to realise or enhance their composition and performance, and to promote their understanding of how music works.

Wales: Curriculum for Wales, Discipline-Specific Considerations (Welsh Government 2020: n.p.)

Music includes performing, improvising and composing, listening and appreciation. You should consider . . . performing (including vocal, instrumental, technology e.g. DJ-ing), improvising and composing (including vocal, instrumental, acoustic, electric and digital, editing/production), listening (including analysing, evaluating, and appreciating a range of musical forms and styles across genres and periods of time).

Northern Ireland: Statutory Curriculum for Music, Key Stage 3 (CCEA 2007b: 8–9)

Pupils should develop their musical potential by having opportunities . . . to:

- improvise, compose and perform music in a range of styles;
- explore and combine the elements of music (pitch, rhythm, dynamics, timbre, texture) to create structure and style when improvising and composing;
- perform individually and in groups, and discuss and decide on points of interpretation in the music;
- use existing and emerging music technology resources when composing and performing;
- listen to and appraise their own music and that of others.

Individual performing in the classroom

Individual performing in the classroom is often the most explicitly presentational, especially when focused on western art music and its associated skills. Through promoting exclusive, high-status knowledge, an emphasis upon instrumental mastery can seem far-removed from young people's lives outside the classroom (Regelski 2014). Take, for example, classroom performance on keyboards. Since the late 1980s, many secondary music classrooms have been equipped with keyboards and for some young people these become the mainstay of their opportunities for performing in school. Although there are benefits of young people working individually at keyboards, wearing headphones, and not disturbing each other, often space is restricted and instruments have to be shared. Then, even when young people's capacity to work at their own pace or use both hands is constrained, they may still be rigorously assessed on their proficiency in traditional keyboard skills, such as the use of correct fingerings, understanding of clefs, and the performance of a set melody and accompaniment. Such skills are often considered essential aspects of performing, despite the fact that the classroom setting—in which keyboards have neither the range, articulation, or dynamic expressivity of conventional pianos—feels inauthentic and far-removed from "real" musical performance (Wright 2008). Use Task 14.4 to consider how classroom keyboards are typically used for assessing presentational performance and how else they could be utilised for inclusive and musical learning.

Task 14.4 **Individual performing on keyboards**

Playing keyboards in the classroom often focuses on mastering the skills of presentational performance, but keyboards can also be used effectively to foster accessible, participatory performance. Use the following table to plan two contrasting lesson activities: one focusing on presentational skills and one focusing on participatory skills.

Using keyboards for presentational performance	Using keyboards for participatory performance

---

Small-group performing in the classroom

Organising young people to work in small groups has been a common strategy for creative work in music lessons since the 1970s. The reasons for this are both educational and pragmatic: socio-constructivist theories suggest that young people learn more effectively working collaboratively with others, and dividing a class into five or six smaller groups allows young people more space and greater agency to share diverse musical ideas. Small groups also allow for the integration of learning that includes appraising, improvising, composing, and performing.

Since the 2010s, small-group performing has often followed the informal learning model promoted by Musical Futures (www.musicalfutures.org), based on research by Green (2008) (see Chapter 6). As shown in Task 14.5, Green's approach builds small-group performing around five principles: starting with music chosen by the group; predominantly learning by ear; working alongside friends in self- and peer-directed learning; progressing haphazardly and without a formal plan; and integrating diverse and creative ways of listening and responding. Within such instances, the teacher's role becomes primarily one of facilitator and observer.

However, as Musical Futures has become more embedded within classroom practice, notable tensions have seen its pedagogical realisation shift over recent years. Some teachers have perceived informal learning to be in conflict with the linear progression expected by formal assessment and have therefore increased their own oversight and decreased young people's autonomy (Mariguddi 2022). Furthermore, young people's increasingly varied musical preferences and participation—mediated by networking and interconnection across new media platforms (Bickford 2017)—are not necessarily accommodated by the original approach as conceptualised for the performance of pop and rock music of the early 2000s. Given the marketisation of Musical Futures (Mariguddi 2022), its signature opportunities for informal, small-group performing have therefore become more likely to be aligned with standardised presentational practices, in which young people closely emulate recordings to prepare high-quality, high-stakes performances.

Task 14.5 Using informal, small-group approaches for performing in the classroom

Using the diagram shown in Figure 14.1, consider the five principles of Green's (2008) conceptualisation of informal learning in Musical Futures. How could you incorporate each feature into performing in the classroom, either alone or in combination with other aspects? Try planning and teaching one lesson or unit which incorporates all five features.

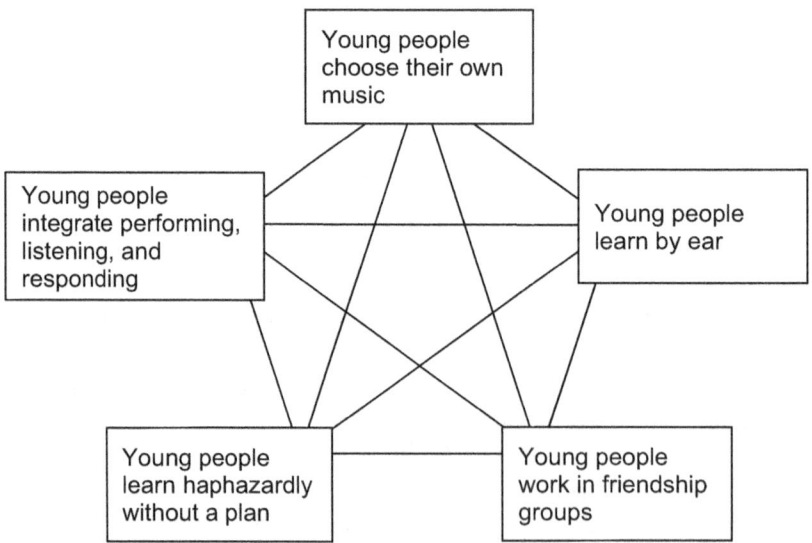

Figure 14.1 The interconnection between the five principles of Green's (2008) informal learning

PERFORMING

Large-group performing in the classroom

Within the secondary school, it is quite surprising how little performing takes place as a whole-class activity. Given the popularity of whole-class ensemble teaching as an approach to "first access" or "first experience" in the primary phase (Fautley et al. 2019), it can be an underutilised aspect of musical performance for young people at the secondary stage. When it is incorporated, it sometimes capitalises on the popularity of instruments such as the ukulele. Typically, a class will learn three or four chords and then be led by their teacher in a performance of a song as they accompany themselves. Although such an approach to large-group performing can be effective for re-engaging disaffected learners (Rusinek 2008; Thibeault 2015), it is worth stopping to consider the intended outcome. Is there any goal other than a polished end-product? Are there opportunities for different ways of participating? And is the emphasis on instrumental mastery to the detriment of other musical skills?

Nevertheless, within the large-group context there are rich opportunities to transcend presentational modes of performance to foster inclusivity, unity, and flexibility. Whole-class workshopping—in which the teacher initiates the activity, but the young people determine the outcomes—can provide chances for accessible and low-stakes performing. Workshopping can incorporate different instruments, digital interfaces, voices, and body percussion to explore varied timbres, dynamics, articulations, and techniques. Using simple repeating patterns to create a sense of constancy and dense heterophonic textures to mask individual contributions within the collective whole, it can offer a valuable way for young people to experience participatory performance practices (MacGregor 2020, 2023) (Task 14.6).

Large-group or whole-class workshopping can take place either using existing compositions such as Riley's *In C* (see Figure 14.2) or material devised by the teacher (see Figure 14.3). In both instances, the musical ideas fit diatonic tuned percussion and the white keys of a keyboard, so can be played on instruments readily available in the classroom. The motifs vary from the simplest repeated patterns to more complex disjunct, syncopated parts but are generally characterised by their basic scalic nature or sequential repetition. They can be learnt individually, supported by peer learning, or taught by the teacher using call-and-response. For some young people staff notation might be helpful, while others might prefer to learn by ear. The teacher can initiate some attempts at performance, setting the tempo and directing the initial entries before joining in as the music-making becomes more collaborative. The young people can then be encouraged to drop out and re-enter the performance at will—or, in time, to improvise their own parts—allowing different melodic fragments to emerge over time.

Such performances evolve organically as a result of the young people's "in the moment" decisions. Therefore, no two performances are the same, other than having similar repetitive and hypnotic momentum. The music-making is determined by the class, rather than by the teacher's intentions. Within the given framework, the young people have the opportunity to improvise, compose,

Figure 14.2 Extract from Riley's *In C*

Figure 14.3 Extract from devised material in the Aeolian mode

and make creative decisions in real time. In doing so, they progress beyond the presentational mastery of technical expertise, through music-making that is "homing in . . . from different angles in order to become aware of its richness of possibilities" (Swanwick 1979: 42).

PERFORMING

> ## Task 14.6 **Large-group performing**
>
> Here are some comments from beginning teachers who have been experimenting with creative workshop practice:
>
> - "You're there to enable them to do something rather than to teach them something."
> - "With this very live, very reactive model, if you're attentive to what's going on in the room, you should always get some sort of result."
> - "There's no possibility of them getting it wrong because they're always working at their own level. You (the teacher) are always looking for what's good about it and you're really measuring success in terms of participation rather than in terms of outcome."
> - "It's about getting everyone involved, no matter what their ability is."
> - "It's making music accessible to everyone. . . . Every single individual can get something out of that way of working, and it's not exclusive."
>
> What are the main themes to come out of these quotations? These comments are all positive about this way of working. You might be more circumspect. What would be your concerns? What do you see as the musical and organisational challenges you would face in exploring creative work in a large-group context?

CREATING PARTICIPATORY COMMUNITIES WHEN PERFORMING IN THE CLASSROOM

As demonstrated by the examples of large-group workshopping in the previous section, performing in the classroom can be a valuable opportunity to foster the inclusive and supportive values of participatory music-making that define young people's communities outside school. This is not to say that there is no place for presentational performance—indeed, the mastery of a voice or instrument is central to art music cultures from across the world—but that participatory performance offers alternative ways to encourage social collaboration and collective achievement.

Therefore, to conclude, this chapter offers four examples of performing in the classroom—individual performing, small-group performing, large-group performing, and whole-class singing—accompanied by teachers' accounts of young people's engagement and participation. It hopes to demonstrate that simple adaptations to everyday classroom music-making practices can make it possible to move closer towards inclusive and equitable participatory cultures.

Individual performing

Despite its prevalence in the secondary music classroom, individual performing can often provoke fear and anxiety, especially among young people who might be self-conscious or embarrassed about making music in front of others

(MacGregor 2025). Yet small changes to pedagogical approaches can have big impacts on young people's classroom experiences. In Box 14.1,[1] a secondary teacher describes how adopting a popular app for digital music-making allowed her class to curate their own individual performances without the pressure of being observed by others. As considered further in Task 14.7, the potential to record, re-record, and multitrack their own singing offered the security of a participatory practice while resulting in a polished presentational outcome demonstrating their individual achievements.

Box 14.1 **Individual performing using multitracking**

I did a lesson where we'd had a go at singing *The Lion Sleeps Tonight*. They'd enjoyed all of that, so in a later lesson I gave them the iPads with the Acapella app on it. And they had to see what they could do in thirty seconds of multitracking themselves. This one girl, who's so shy and down on herself—but a lovely musician—she'd done this fantastic, four-part multitracking of herself doing the harmonies to *The Lion Sleeps Tonight*, adding the thirds and a little descant over the top. It was just me and her in the room as I listened to it, and I just went, "Wow! This is, this is absolutely fantastic! I would like to be able to use that as an example to the others when we come back next time. I've never heard you sing this beautifully." And she went red and stammered, "Oh, no, no, no, it was, it's, it's nothing." But she didn't stop me—she allowed it to be used as an example to the others, when usually she's like, "It's no good, I need to do it again, I need to delete it." That was the one time when she had accepted that it was OK.

Task 14.7 **Individual performing and digital technology**

a. Reflect on the vignette in Box 14.1. How did the use of multitracking technology change the young people's experience of individual performance on this occasion?
b. Drawing on the vignette in Box 14.1, how could you incorporate digital technologies to support young people's experience of individual performance in your classroom? Choose an individual performance task you're planning to use in the classroom and consider:

- How could digital technology be used to help the young people learn performance skills in an accessible way (e.g., online tutorials, educational apps)?
- How could digital technology be used to help the young people extend their existing performance skills (e.g., recording, mixing, multitracking)?

Small-group performing

Small-group performing like that used in Musical Futures (Green 2008) can be a valuable way of introducing low-stakes opportunities for participatory music-making in the classroom. It can also be beneficial for fostering skills such as collaboration, cooperation, and compromise—but only when young people are suitably equipped to work through any conflicts that may arise (MacGregor 2020). Box 14.2 illustrates how accommodating young people's diverse musical preferences—and the unconventional and idiomatic modes of music-making sometimes associated with them—enabled one secondary teacher to support engaging and fruitful small-group performing. As you read the vignette, use Task 14.8 to consider how the young people's experimentation with grime challenged the boundaries and conventions of small-group performing in the music classroom.

Box 14.2 **Exploring grime through small-group performing**

Last year I said to my class, "What do you want to learn about?" And they all said grime. It's got bad language and gang culture in it, but I was like, "OK." There'd happened to be a recent documentary on where it came from, and I thought, "I can get my teeth into this." So we bolted it onto protest music because it's got that kind of message. We had some ground rules, but then I was almost giving them free license. I was like, "Well, I'm going to come in and check on you and I want to hear what you've done, but there's no expectation that you'll have finished it." So I went into one room, and there was this bunch of boys who'd taken a bass drum apart and put their iPad in there so they could record from inside it. They were playing a bassline on the piano, and making their own distortion basically. They were really proud of this—maybe because they got to take apart school equipment. But I was like, "Yes, that's exactly what I want! That's how people discover stuff!" and when they listened back to their recording they were like, "This is really good, this is fantastic!" From then on there was a trust built: they trusted that I got what they thought, and that I wouldn't make them do anything that they couldn't relate to.

Task 14.8 **Experimenting with small-group performing**

Reflect on Box 14.2.

- What genres of music would best facilitate young people's small-group performing in your classroom?
- What presentational performance skills would the young people need to develop to perform in this genre (e.g., mastering a specific instrument, singing in a particular style)?
- What opportunities does this genre offer for the young people to work in ways that are participatory and inclusive?

Large-group performing

Through facilitating exploration of timbre, dynamics, articulation, and technique, large-group performing with diverse musical instruments can create myriad opportunities for musical learning. In doing so, it can also be of great value for adaptive teaching that differentiates according to young people's unique needs. Box 14.3 demonstrates how large-group performing has the potential to transform a secondary classroom into an accessible and inclusive space—in this case for an autistic boy who had not previously been able to engage in music-making. Through carefully choosing an instrument well-suited to his preferences and capabilities, his teacher enabled his full participation in whole-class performance and witnessed his resulting joy and satisfaction (Task 14.9).

Box 14.3 **Adaptation and inclusion in large-group performing**

There was a time where I had a very autistic youngster who had extreme learning difficulties. He hadn't been in any of his class's first lessons because he'd been refusing to come into the classroom. So, he came in when we started the gamelan project. We started off by learning the *balungan*, and he really struggled with that because it's quite a lot of coordination. So the first additional instrument I added in was the *kethuk*. I said, "OK Stephen, you've been trying really, really hard. Why don't you have a go at this?" He really took to it. He had a good sense of timing and he managed it really quickly. He was just excited to come in every lesson and get his *kethuk*. I was able to help him learn different techniques, and he responded well to praise. He was obviously paying attention to the fact that his part fitted in really nicely with the others, and he got a lot of sensory gratification from the way the beater bounces in a very satisfying way.

Task 14.9 **Accessible opportunities for large-group performing**

1. Reflect on Stephen's experience recounted in Box 14.3. How did incorporating a variety of gamelan instruments allow his teacher to accommodate Stephen's strengths and skills so that he could fully participate in large-group performing?
2. Using Box 14.3 as a starting point, think about what variety of instruments you could include in large-group performing in your classroom to accommodate young people's varied strengths and skills. Consider the following questions:
    a. Do the young people have existing instrumental skills that could be used?
    b. If you are using classroom instruments and digital tools, such as untuned percussion or Digital Audio Workstations, how could you use them in creative and engaging ways?

In contexts where you have limited access to instruments, experiment with making music with everyday objects, such as through body percussion, chair drumming, or creating boomwhackers from recycled materials.

Whole-class singing

Although singing has often been highlighted as a weakness within secondary music provision (e.g., Ofsted 2023), it can offer some of the most inclusive music-making in the classroom. Nevertheless, teachers who lack confidence in singing tend to avoid it altogether, and therefore their classes miss out on what is undoubtedly an important way to internalise sound and make music with others. Singing is possibly the most accessible form of music-making, because the musical resources are the young people themselves. Successful teachers recognise young people's inherent interest in song and are aware of the culture of singing to which they aspire. Rather than passing judgement on the success of popular vocalists and competitions such as *X Factor*, they capitalise on their popularity to "normalise" the act of singing as both a social and educational activity. As shown in Box 14.4[2]–in which a secondary teacher describes the preparation for an end-of-year singing competition at an all-girls school–a vibrant singing culture can be established once young people recognise that the classroom is a safe and non-judgemental space for singing, and when they know what to expect around what, when, why, and how singing will take place (Task 14.10). In this instance, the class customarily began every music lesson with ten minutes of class singing, and so were excited about the opportunity to develop their skills further ahead of a competitive performance in front of the rest of their year group.

> ### Box 14.4 **Performing and competing through whole-class singing**
>
> When I first announced the end-of-year singing competition to the class there was a real buzz of excitement. There was so much enthusiasm, in fact, that our rehearsals were a little chaotic: so many students wanted to share their ideas and get involved that they were not listening very well to me or to each other, and a few students remained hesitant about taking part. We discussed the fact that in order to put on a fantastic performance we needed to work as a team and every single person needed to give 100%. As the performance approached the quality of the singing improved; we even managed to add in a harmony part, which took some practice, but by the week of the performance sounded great. More than half the class put themselves forward for a solo line and showed courage in auditioning in front of the whole class—it was very difficult choosing only a few. Even though the class didn't win the competition, their performance was an overwhelming success, and all the young people performed with enthusiasm and comradery.

> ### Task 14.10 **Creating cultures and structures for whole-class singing**
>
> Whenever you start teaching at a new school or in a new academic year, think about how you could develop cultures and structures in your classroom that facilitate positive experiences of whole-class singing. Singing with young people right from the first time you meet them helps normalise it as an inclusive, fun, and low-stakes opportunity for performing together.

SUMMARY

This chapter has asked you to explore your own beliefs about the value and purpose of performing in the classroom and to compare them to young people's experiences of performing within their local and global, cultural and familial, and online and offline communities. It is important to recognise that there is no "right" or "wrong" way of incorporating performance in the classroom, but that, often, participatory, multimodal ways of performing that are integrated with improvising, composing, and appraising are more closely aligned with young people's musical meaning-making than technical, presentational performance. Even as young people's musical cultures and communities continue to shift over time (Bunch and Bickford 2022), it is likely that participatory practices will remain those that are most equitable and inclusive, accommodating and adaptable, and therefore beneficial for teaching and learning.

NOTES

1. The vignettes in Boxes 14.1, 14.2, and 14.3 are taken from *Musical Vulnerability: Receptivity, Susceptibility, and Care in the Music Classroom* (MacGregor 2025). All names and locations have been pseudonymised for confidentiality.
2. Personal communication with Elizabeth MacGregor, 24 September 2024.

FURTHER READING

D'Amore, A. (ed) (2009)
Musical Futures: An Approach to Teaching and Learning, Resource Pack, 2nd edn, London: Paul Hamlyn Foundation.

This includes useful resources for a range of classroom performing activities, including whole-class workshopping and small-group informal learning.

MacGregor, E.H. (2023)
Exploring performing, in C. Cooke and C. Philpott (eds) *A Practical Guide to Teaching Music in the Secondary School*, 2nd edn, Abingdon: Routledge, pp. 77–88.

This chapter offers more detail on participatory performing cultures and examples of using Riley's *In C* in the classroom.

Regelski, T.A. (2014)
'Resisting elephants lurking in the music education classroom', *Music Educators Journal*, 100, 4: 77–86.

Regelski makes a persuasive case for the importance of integrating participatory performance alongside presentational performance in the music classroom.

Thibeault, M.D. (2012)
Music education in the postperformance world, in G.E. McPherson and G.F. Welch (eds) *The Oxford Handbook of Music Education, Volume 2*. New York: Oxford University Press, pp. 516–530.

A valuable exploration of how interaction with musical performance has changed as a result of new media.

LISTENING
Gary Spruce

INTRODUCTION

There is a paradox at the heart of school music education, which is that listening, the musical activity that many young people involve themselves in most frequently outside school, is often the aspect of the music curriculum they find least attractive and, in the way in which it is sometimes taught and assessed, the one in which they achieve least well. In the course of this chapter, we try to identify some of the reasons for, and strategies to address, young people's negative attitudes towards listening and their consequent underachievement in this area of the music curriculum.

Significantly less research has taken place into how young people's musical understanding can be developed through listening than through composing and performing, and fewer resources have been developed to support its teaching. This relative neglect is perhaps symptomatic of a belief that the way in which listening is best taught is essentially straightforward: young people listen to music and through analysing the way in which the "musical elements" fit together, and sometimes informed by historical and stylistic knowledge, they gain an understanding of its meaning. Their understanding is then most effectively articulated through verbal and written responses.

This unproblematic perception of the pedagogy of listening is rooted in assumptions about the nature of music and the relationship between "the music" and "the listener" that, although seemingly universal and self-evident, have developed in tandem with, and in order to reflect and support, the traditions and protocols of western art music–constituting what we refer to in this chapter as the ideology of "aesthetic listening." This ideology has then influenced the way in which listening is taught.

In this chapter we explore the assumptions and beliefs that underpin aesthetic listening. We then go on to explore the impact of aesthetic listening on music teaching and learning through analysing three hypothetical examples of the way in which listening is taught in the music classroom. Following this, issues associated with the personal construction of musical meaning and responses to listening other than verbal and written are considered. Finally, we suggest ways in which listening can be taught through its integration with composing and performing.

The main argument of this chapter is that a much richer relationship exists (or can exist) between music and the listener than that which is often promoted in formal music education, and that this richer relationship can lead to young people engaging more positively and more successfully with listening and responding activities. Such a relationship acknowledges and values:

- responses that go beyond the verbal and written;
- the role of the listener in constructing musical meaning;
- the diversity and plurality of musical practices beyond the school;
- integrating listening with composing and performing.

Objectives

By the end of this chapter you should be able to:

- identify the strengths and limitations of "aesthetic listening" in music education;
- understand the assumptions underpinning the way in which listening has traditionally been taught in the music classroom;
- identify ways in which listening activities can be expanded to reflect and develop a wider range of musical learning, understanding and experience and thus become more inclusive.

WHAT IS MEANT BY THE "IDEOLOGY OF AESTHETIC LISTENING"?

Task 15.1 Your own experience of listening and responding in school

Note down the kinds of listening activities you were asked to do at school. Structure your notes under the following headings:

- The types of music you listened to;
- How you were asked to respond to the music;
- The musical skills and knowledge that were intended to be taught through listening and responding activities;
- What you actually learnt.

It is likely that the listening activities you have identified in Task 15.1 are one of two types (or perhaps a combination of both):

1. Music appreciation: you might have been asked to suggest what it is that the composer is trying to express through the music—say, in terms of a particular emotion, place or narrative—referring perhaps to the use of the "musical elements" to support your answer. In other words, what message or meaning is being communicated by the composer through the music?
2. Aural analysis: you might have analysed the music in terms of its structure and elements—its pitch, rhythm, harmony, timbre and texture and how these fit together.

Both these kinds of listening activities and the responses to them that are expected reflect the ideology of aesthetic listening, which is predicated upon a number of beliefs about the nature of "good" music and the way in which it makes and communicates its meaning. These beliefs are that:

- the meaning of a piece of music is what the composer intends it to be (or what we are told by "experts" it is intended to be);
- musical meaning is articulated through the interplay of the musical materials, and that consequently . . .
- musical meaning is fixed and independent of social context or function. In other words, good music is *autonomous* music.

From these beliefs it follows that:

- musical meaning flows in one direction: *from* the composer via their music *to* the listener (the music is a conduit for communicating the composer's meaning);
- the role of the listener is to listen "knowledgeably" and thereby gain understanding of the "true" meaning contained within the music;
- the role of the teacher is to teach this knowledge and understanding.

The role of the listener in aesthetic listening

It is not the intention of this chapter to suggest that aesthetic listening is an inappropriate way of engaging with music *per se*, but rather, as Dibben puts it, to recognise that "'contemplative' listening, the act of listening afforded to audience members by Western classical concert music is just one of a number of ways of listening" (Dibben in Clayton 2003: 201)—and consequently just one way in which young people can respond to music.

The argument here is that aesthetic listening assumes that only one relationship can exist between the music and listener, that of "listener-as-audience." Listener-as-audience is predicated upon the belief that listening is an essentially discrete and individual activity, distinct and separate from composing and performing. The sonic materials of music are cognitively processed "in the head" and musical meaning construed. The degree of success with which the listener construes the "correct" musical meaning is taken as an indicator of that person's musical understanding. The "correct" meaning is what the composer intends it to be, and such meaning is uncovered through detailed analysis of the musical materials.

The ideology of aesthetic listening is located in the wider concept of "objective knowledge." In *The Courage to Teach*, Palmer (1998) argues that there is a myth that sees truth as a set of propositions about objects; education as a system for delivering those propositions to young people; and an educated person as one who can remember and repeat the experts' propositions.

> *Objects* of knowledge . . . reside "out there" somewhere, pristine in physical or conceptual space, as described by the "facts" in a given field.
>
> *Experts* [teachers] are people trained to know these objects in their pristine form without allowing their own subjectivity to slop over onto the purity of the objects themselves.
>
> *Amateurs* [students] are those who do not presently possess these objects. They must depend on experts for objective or pure knowledge of the pristine objects.
>
> *Baffles* allow objective knowledge to flow downstream while preventing the subjectivity of the amateurs to flow back up—possibly contaminating the intellectual purity of the *objects*.
>
> (Palmer 1998: 100-101)

The common characteristic of objective knowledge and aesthetic listening is that neither concept recognises the role of the listener in constructing meaning and understanding.

THE IMPACT OF AESTHETIC LISTENING ON THE MUSIC CURRICULUM

In this section we are going to consider the strengths and limitations of aesthetic listening in terms of developing young people's musical understanding and providing them with valuable and rich musical experiences. To this end, we critically analyse three hypothetical scenarios of the teaching of listening, each of which exemplifies a particular aspect of aesthetic listening: that musical meaning is what the composer intends it to be; that musical meaning is articulated exclusively through musical materials; and that good music is autonomous music. Consider this further through Task 15.2.

■ ■ ■ ■ **LISTENING**

Musical meaning is what the composer intends it to be

Task 15.2 Musical meaning and "high-status" musical knowledge

Read Box 15.1 and note down what you think it tells you about:

- the types of musical knowledge and understanding the teacher values and rewards;
- the musical understanding and perception of each of the three young people involved;
- what the teacher understands as the relationship between the musical work, the composer and the listener.

Box 15.1 Valuing musical knowledge and understanding

A class of 11-year-olds enters the classroom whilst a recording of "Mars" from Holst's *Planets Suite* is being played. They sit behind their desks, and the teacher plays the music once more. She then asks them what they think the music is "about." They respond enthusiastically. Marcus says that it reminds him of a storm and refers to the loud dynamics and the use of brass and percussion instruments. Phyllis remarks how the "rhythmic ostinato" (she uses this term) makes her think of machinery in a factory. The teacher makes encouraging noises of the, "good but not quite right . . ." kind. At the back of the class, Samuel has his hand raised and is giving every indication that he will burst if not given an opportunity to answer. To avoid this catastrophe, the teacher asks him for his response, which is, "It's 'Mars, the Bringer of War', Miss." "Excellent," says the teacher, "how do you know that?" "My father told me. He plays it in the car all the time," says Samuel. "Well, *well* done," says the teacher and gives him three merit points. She then moves on to the next part of the lesson.

There are many positive things the teacher is doing here, particularly the way in which the lesson begins with music and how young people's responses are actively sought. However, the teacher is deeply committed to the idea that although personal responses to the music are to be encouraged, they are to be more greatly valued (and rewarded) the closer these responses accord with the intentions of the composer. So, however much musical understanding and perception a listener might bring to bear on the music, it will be never be more valued than simply possessing the knowledge of what the composer intended (or what we think they intended) the meaning of the music to be. In this scenario the teacher is happy to move on once she has the "correct" answer. She does not explore the extent to which Samuel's answer is indicative of his musical understanding. She is content that he has got the answer "right." It is a pedagogical approach rooted in the assumption that the meaning of a piece of music is what the composer desires it to be, that this is not open to negotiation and that the role of the listener is, as Small (1998) says, "simply to contemplate the work, to try to understand it and to respond to it, but that she or he has nothing to contribute to its meaning. That is the composer's business" (6). Musical meaning is seen as flowing in one direction: from the composer via the musical object to the passive listener.

Musical meaning is articulated exclusively through the relationship and interplay of the musical materials

> Task 15.3 **Musical meaning and musical materials**
>
> Read Box 15.2 and make notes on:
>
> - the knowledge that is considered to be important in developing musical understanding;
> - the extent to which the task given to the young people reflects the way in which they (or you) listen to music outside the music classroom.

> Box 15.2 **Analysing musical elements and structures**
>
> A class of 13-year-olds are studying the "March" from *Star Wars*. The young people are given a worksheet divided into five sections, each one headed by a different musical element: pitch, rhythm, harmony, texture and timbre. They are asked to respond to the music under each of these headings, and their responses form the basis of a class discussion into how the composer achieves particular musical effects. The class are then asked to listen to the music again, this time identifying its structure.

In the scenario outlined in Box 15.2, teaching is predicated upon an understanding that—as meaning is what the composer intends it to be—it follows that such meaning must be encoded within the musical materials and therefore can be understood through the atomistic and "distanced" analysis of the elements and structure. Musical knowledge and understanding are understood here as the ability to aurally deconstruct the music into its discrete elements, explore the character of these elements separate from the musical whole and finally "reconstruct" the work to see how the musical elements "fit together."

Clearly there are benefits to be gained from being able to analyse the component elements of a musical work in order to understand how they fit together. It enables young people to consider the ways in which musical elements are organised to create the sonic *lingua franca* of, in this case, film music. There are then opportunities to transfer learning to their own composing activities. However, as a musical experience *in its own right*, such an approach has significant limitations.

One problem with this approach is that the music is being thought of as akin to a painting in a gallery—as an object. Consequently, the relationship between the music and the listener is understood as being similar to that of the viewer and the painting. Both the listener and the viewer study the art object in a distanced, objective way, contemplating how its formal properties contribute to an aesthetically complete whole. However, is the experience of looking at a picture really similar to the experience of listening and responding to music? A painting in a gallery is by its very nature an object. Its framed presentation is fixed in time and space and distanced from the viewer—it is "out there." Consequently, thinking of music as an object leads to the idea that music is, or can be, experienced in a similar, "distanced" way. However, both Handel and Bowman argue that there is a qualitative difference between listening and looking (Elliott 1995: 126). Handel argues, "listening is centripetal; it pulls you into the world. Looking is centrifugal; it separates you from the world . . . looking makes each of us a focused observer, listening makes each of us a surrounded participant." Bowman makes the critical point that experiencing music is not static (like observing a painting), "but temporal and, therefore, full of ambiguity . . . a moment-by-moment renewal. . . . We see the world as a noun and hear it as a verb" (Elliott 1995: 127).

The metaphor of noun and verb is a potent one in that it challenges the deeply rooted idea of music as object. Thinking of art objects (such as paintings and sculptures) as nouns means that they are fixed and unchanging. One can contemplate them both holistically and atomistically, moving at will from the object as a whole to contemplating the way in which its elements contribute to that whole. The totality can be observed in a single moment. The idea of talking about these objects in a distanced way—analysing the relationship between the whole and its parts—is arguably legitimate. However, the reality of musical experience as a "verb"—as an active, fluctuating, temporal, moment-by-moment experience—throws into question the distanced, analytical approach, at least as an exclusive way of understanding the way in which one constructs and construes musical meaning. Indeed, research by Smith (1973) and Cook (1990) suggests that whereas people *can* listen to music atomistically in terms of the musical elements or musical structure if required or guided to do so, few (even "trained" musicians) do so naturally as a matter of course. Use Task 15.4 to explore your own ideas about holistic listening.

> **Task 15.4 Adopting a holistic approach to traditional listening and responding tasks**
>
> Develop a listening activity and accompanying questions based on a holistic approach to musical responses and music as an active, fluctuating, temporal, moment-by-moment experience. Examples of questions might be:
>
> - What are your first thoughts about the music?
> - What happens during the course of the music?
> - Where do you feel the climax of the music occurs?
> - What point in the music do you find most exciting, moving or effective?
> - What aspects of the music do you find least effective?
> - Where did you feel that there was a really interesting use of rhythm, instrumentation or harmony?
>
> Now create a sequence of more atomistic-type questions (those typically used in listening tests) to help young people analyse how these effects were achieved. Think about how you can make strong links between these two sets of questions.

Good music is autonomous music

If the meaning of a piece of music must be what the composer intends it to be, and if musical meaning is articulated exclusively through the musical materials, it follows that musical meaning is fixed and remains the same in whatever context the music is heard. Such music can then be said to enjoy an autonomous existence. The notion of musical autonomy is a key aspect of the ideology of aesthetic listening and is reinforced through the way in which people typically engage with western art music in the concert hall or through recordings. This paradigm of musical engagement is then often mapped onto the classroom, where young people sit in neat rows behind desks (a kind of surrogate concert hall), listening to recordings of music respectfully, in a detached manner and informed by knowledge.

Kivy makes the point that recordings, which play an important part in listening activities, reinforce the ideology of aesthetic listening by creating "the false allusion that listening is private and passive" and "that music is a collection of autonomous sounds alone" (Kivy in Elliott 1995: 102). In fact, as Elliott (1995) points out, for most people in the world (and consequently most musical practices), listening is far from private and passive but is an activity where "people join together in the communal and ritual actions of listening, watching and participating empathetically as music makers bring forth unique musical events and experiences" (102).

Young people's negative reactions to listening in the music classroom can result as a consequence of them being asked to engage with music which they have experienced as part of these "communal and ritual actions" outside the

■ ■ ■ ■ **LISTENING**

classroom, in a way that to them seems (and indeed *is*) alien: through the ideology of aesthetic listening. Now read Box 15.3.

Box 15.3 **Managing emotive and embodied responses to music**

Simon is a beginning teacher. On Friday afternoon he takes 9A for their "listening lesson." They are a class with a "reputation." Simon decides that the best way of surviving his encounter with 9A is to base the lesson on some music that they know and like. He chats with some of the young people and identifies a song that is particularly popular with many of them. He downloads the track and creates a "listening worksheet," which asks the young people to listen to the music in terms of the musical "bits" (harmony, melody, rhythm and so on) and to write down their responses. He adopts the school's policy for behaviour management, requiring the young people to sit in rows behind desks in boy–girl–boy formation. At first the lesson goes well. The class are pleased that they are being asked to listen to music they know and like. However, they show little enthusiasm for "analysing" the music and even less for writing down their responses. Instead, they begin to react to the music in the way they would in the youth club—they begin to move to it (albeit within the confines of the physical limitations of the classroom) and to talk over it. The teacher tries to quell what he perceives as indiscipline. The young people comply, but the lesson quickly becomes characterised by sullen acquiescence.

As in all the scenarios, there are positive things in what the teacher is doing in the scenario in Box 15.3, particularly in the way he is trying to break down barriers between curriculum music and music outside school. However, the lesson is less than successful because Simon assumes that young people's alienation from listening activities in the music classroom can be addressed simply through changing the musical focus to something to which they can more easily relate. In fact, the issue lies in the *way* in which they are being asked to respond to the music. Such is the assumed universality of aesthetic listening that he can conceive of only one way of musical meaning being construed: through distanced, objective analysis, with the young people in the role of listener-as-audience. He doesn't recognise that responses to music need not be exclusively distanced and cognitive but can also be physical and emotional. Moreover, whatever the mode of response, the opportunity to construct personal meaning is critical to an authentic and meaningful engagement with music. You will begin to think about this in Task 15.5.

Task 15.5 **Thinking about different ways in which people respond to music**

Choose a piece of music from a tradition other than western art music. Make notes about the music in terms of the following:

> - The way in which the music is created;
> - How the music is communicated to "the listeners" and the way in which they respond and relate to it.
>
> Note down some ideas of how this music might be used in the classroom in a way that is similar to how it is experienced in its original context.

PERSONAL CONSTRUCTION OF MEANING

The ideology of aesthetic listening is located within the concept of "objective knowledge"–an understanding of knowledge as being somehow "out there," waiting to be engaged with and understood. However, as Small (1999) has written,

> Knowledge . . . is the relationship between the knower and the thing known. . . . There can be no such thing as completely objective knowledge, knowledge of the external world exactly as it is, since everything we can possibly know about it is mediated by the way we, the knowers, work on the stimuli to convert them to usable knowledge.
>
> (14)

It follows from this that, as Carey (2005) says, "emotions and ideas do not reside in artworks but in the people responding to them [and] their responses display infinite variation" (78). Consequently, "musical meanings are negotiated not absorbed; constructed not given; appropriated not bestowed. The processes and experiences we call musical, then, never reside in a hermetically-insular 'aesthetic' realm, but are part of our lived, social reality" (Elliott 1995: 125). This lived social reality includes responses to music that go far beyond the purely distanced verbal and written ones.

Emotional and physical responses to music

Young people attending a Bruce Springsteen concert described their experience of the music in the following way: "it gets you physically, because you're dancing, you're moving around, you're waving your arms, you're clapping your hands. . . . It's just an energizing experience and it's a spiritual experience. So, it gets your *mind, body and soul*" (Cavicchi quoted by Finnegan in Clayton 2003: 185; my emphasis). Clearly the holistic (mind, body, soul) response to music is very important to these young people. It is not difficult, then, to imagine how responses to music that are restricted to the written and verbal may seem to them limiting and impoverished. Indeed, Philpott suggests that, within the classroom, "part of the reason for the alienation of some older pupils is that the needs of the body are severed from the mind" and that "connections need to be constantly reinforced between cognition and our bodily sense" (Philpott and Plummeridge 2001: 89).

LISTENING

What Philpott and the young people are doing is rejecting the mind-body split explicit within Cartesian dualism. In a telling passage, Small (1998) argues that:

> Properly understood, all art is *action*–performance art, if you like, and its meaning lies not in creating objects but in acts of creating, displaying and *perceiving*. It is an activity in which humans take part in order that they may come to understand their relationships–with one another and with the great pattern which connects. In all these activities we call the arts, *we think with our bodies*. They negate with every gesture the Cartesian split between mind and body.
>
> (40, my emphasis)

Small's (1998) notion that "we think with our bodies" is supported by Elliott (1995), who argues that a young person's musical understanding, and what he describes as their "listenership," are best developed and assessed through "thinking" and "knowing" "in action" (97). In other words, musical understanding is demonstrated through the "physical doing" of music. It follows, therefore, that young people's responses to music are likely to be most authentic and illuminating if such responses take place through musical activity. So, one listens to music and responds to it, demonstrating one's knowledge, understanding and perception through composing, improvising and performing; that is, through the integration of musical activities.

Implications for the teaching of listening

Where young people are enabled to respond to and appraise music in a range of ways, where personal construction of meaning is valued and where listening is integrated with composing and performing, there is created a context in which they have ownership over rich musical learning.

Box 15.4 **Interpreting and rehearsing a cover song**

Suki, Jennifer, David and Gerry are 15-year-old music students who have formed a rock group to meet the requirements for the performing aspect of the national music qualification they are working towards. Most of their repertoire is cover versions. Having selected the music they want to perform, they learn their parts individually through repeated listening to recordings. When listening to the recordings, they focus not just on the building bricks of rhythm, pitch and harmony but also on the nuances of the recording. They then rehearse collectively, and once the piece is "hanging together" they work on the "interpretation," collectively informed by their personal reflections on the music gained during their individual study of the recording. They decide which aspects of the recorded performance to keep and which of their own ideas to include in order to make the performance their own.

LEARNING TO TEACH MUSIC IN THE SECONDARY SCHOOL

One of the key aspects of the scenario in Box 15.4 is that the musical decision-making emerges from immersion in the music. However, neither the recording nor any notated form of the music is treated as fixed (as encapsulating definitive musical meaning). The construction of meaning occurs not just through verbal discussion but as "thinking-in-action"—as an ongoing, individual and collective process; musical meaning is constructed as the interpretation develops. Different ways of shaping a phrase, bending a note, swinging a rhythm, and different guitar and drum effects are all tried out, listened to, responded to and then accepted or rejected. The young people are engaged in making informed, artistic and intelligent decisions about their music-making. This thinking-in-action is also holistic, as physical as it is cognitive—what feels right is what feels right bodily, emotionally and intellectually. Task 15.6 asks you to consider this in relation to young people's music-making in pop or rock bands.

> Task 15.6 **Finding out how young people use listening to support performing and composing**
>
> Speak with some young people who play in a pop or rock band about the ways in which they learn the music. Focus your questions particularly on the listening and responding skills they deploy in creating the performance they want. If possible, observe them working together.

PLANNING AN INTEGRATED APPROACH TO LISTENING AND RESPONDING

In the final section of this chapter, we look at a skeletal plan of a sequence of three music lessons based upon the song *Strange Fruit*, which refers to the lynching of Black Americans during the first part of the last century (see Table 15.1). These lessons show how:

- performing and composing might be used as the means by which young people respond to their listening;
- curriculum requirements for music might be met through an integrated approach to listening;
- young people can demonstrate their listening and responding skills and musical understanding through responses other than written;
- opportunities might be created for young people to be involved in the construction of musical meaning.

Now use Task 15.7 to consider how you might apply the principles in these example lessons to your own planning.

Task 15.7 **Applying the principles of this chapter**

Read carefully through the lesson plans in Table 15.1. Then, using a template of your own devising, plan a lesson or sequence of lessons that meets the four criteria listed before this task and focuses on developing young people's understanding of music through listening and responding. Make the lesson:

- specific to a class that you know and are likely to teach;
- build on young people's prior learning;
- link into your school's scheme of work and any national curriculum requirements within which you are working.

Table 15.1 Applying the principles: an example

Learning and teaching activities	National Curriculum for Music (England) (DfE 2013)	Commentary
Lesson 1		
A recording of Billie Holiday singing *Strange Fruit* is playing as the class enter the room. They are asked to identify the style of the music and most are able to identify it as jazz. The teacher asks about their reactions to it. Where might they expect to hear such music? Why does it sound like jazz? The young people have clear ideas about where such music is likely to be heard but only a few can really describe *verbally* what it is about the music that makes it sound like jazz.	To understand and explore how music is created, produced and communicated.	The lesson begins with musical activity. Clear links are made between the music and the contexts in which it is likely to be heard. Young people's "knowledge of the external world" (Small 1999: 14) is used to enable them to create appropriate meaning. The teacher identifies those able to appraise music verbally.
The teacher asks the class to identify one short phrase that, for them, really sounds jazz-like. They do this and listen to it a few times. They divide into groups, some working on keyboards, others vocally and others using digital technologies. The teacher asks them to compose a short phrase which sounds like jazz and is similar to the one to which they have been listening.	To understand musical structures, styles, genres and traditions, identifying the expressive use of musical dimensions.	Activities are set up to enable young people to demonstrate their understanding of jazz through composing, improvising and performing. The exploration of musical ideas means that musical meaning emerges from the young people rather than being imposed upon them.

(Continued)

Table 15.1 (Continued)

They explore musical ideas and motifs for ten minutes. Some young people are able to produce musical ideas that are typically jazzy and reflect the phrase they have heard; others struggle. The class discuss why some ideas are more successful than others in reflecting a jazz style. Some of the keyboard players refer to their use of "black notes" and some of the singers talk about "bending the notes." They exemplify what they are saying with musical examples. The teacher talks briefly about the idea of "blue" notes (referring back to a previous topic on the blues), swung rhythm and "bent" notes. The young people spend five more minutes working on their phrases in the light of their learning and then perform them to each other.		From this activity—rather than from verbal descriptions—the teacher is able to assess those young people whose listening has enabled them to understand jazz characteristics. Musical understanding developed in previous lessons is used to inform their understanding of jazz and their ability to construct their own meaning.
Lesson 2		
Young people now compare the Billie Holiday version of *Strange Fruit* with a version sung by Sting. They discuss differences in the performance, listening particularly to the extent to which the performances conform to their expectations of what jazz should be like.	To listen with discrimination to the best in the musical canon.	Listening and responding skills are now used to compare different performances of the same music, drawing on learning from the previous lesson.
Young people listen to a jazz number performed or recorded "straight" by the teacher. They are given the lyrics and chord symbols for one verse but no staff notation. They are asked to work on a "jazz performance" of this verse, drawing on	To improvise and compose, extend and develop musical ideas by drawing on a range of musical structures, styles, genres and traditions.	Responding skills are now strongly linked to young people's performing skills and interpretative understanding.

(Continued)

Table 15.1 (Continued)

their understanding of jazz style to create a convincing interpretation. The class then perform their versions to each other, discussing the perceived strengths and weaknesses of each interpretation informed by their learning.		
Lesson 3		
The class discuss with the teacher the meaning that lies behind the words of *Strange Fruit* and explore the role of jazz and blues in Black American culture. They are given the lyrics of a Black American protest song and compose music for it—not notated, but created and learnt aurally, drawing on their listening and responding through previous lessons.	To develop a deep understanding of the music that they perform and to which they listen.	Here, listening and responding from previous lessons are used to inform critical reflection and creative composition.

SUMMARY

In this chapter we have considered approaches to listening and responding in the classroom curriculum that

- embrace and acknowledge a much wider range of musical responses than formal "aesthetic listening";
- recognise the different ways in which young people learn musically;
- integrate listening and responding more fully with performing and composing.

In other words, we have developed and discussed an approach to listening and responding that is characterised by its musical inclusivity, diversity and criticality.

FURTHER READING

Cooke, C. (2023)
Exploring responding, in C. Cooke and C. Philpott (eds) *A Practical Guide to Teaching Music in the Secondary School*, 2nd edn, Abingdon: Routledge, pp. 16-25.

Fautley, M. (2014)
Listen, Imagine, Compose Research Report, Birmingham: Birmingham City University. Online, available at: https://www.open-access.bcu.ac.uk/7818/1/LIC%20Final%20Report%20web%20version.pdf

Vigl, J., Ojell-Järventausta, M., Sipola, H. and Saarikallio, S. (2023)
'Melody for the mind: Enhancing mood, motivation, concentration, and learning through music listening in the classroom', *Music and Science*, 6.

These publications address the issue of listening and responding in the music classroom. Cooke makes explicit reference to this chapter in outlining an approach to responding to listening through composing, improvising, performing or through the use of digital technologies. The research report "Listen, Imagine, Compose" provides a rich resource for understanding, first, how listening, composing and performing can be addressed in an integrated way, and second, effective ways of working in partnership with composers and other professional musicians. Finally, Vigl and colleagues explore the impact of listening to self-selected music on young people's emotional state, concentration and motivation in the classroom.

REFERENCES

Abbs, P. (1989) *A Is for Aesthetic: Essays on the Creative and Aesthetic*, London: Falmer.

Abie, S. (2014) 'Curriculum models: Product versus process', *Journal of Education and Practice*, 5, 35: 152-155. https://core.ac.uk/reader/234636681

Abrahams, F. (2005) 'The application of critical pedagogy to music teaching and learning: A literature review', *Update: Applications of Research in Music Education*, 23, 2: 12-22. https://doi.org/10.1177/87551233050230020103

Additional Learning Needs and Education Tribunal (Wales) Act 2018. Online, available at: https://www.legislation.gov.uk/anaw/2018/2/contents (accessed 28 March 2025).

Allsup, R.E. (2003) 'Transformational education and critical music pedagogy: Examining the link between culture and learning', *Music Education Research*, 5, 1: 5-12. https://doi.org/10.1080/14613800307104

Allsup, R.E. (2016) *Remixing the Classroom: Toward an Open Philosophy of Music Education*, Bloomington: Indiana University Press.

Amabile, T.M. (1989) *Growing Up Creative: Nurturing a Lifetime of Creativity*, Norwalk, CT: Crown House Publishing Limited.

Anderson, A. (2021) 'Topic choices: Revealing concealed processes of curriculum sequencing in English secondary school music classrooms', *The Curriculum Journal*, 32, 4: 722-740. https://doi.org/10.1002/curj.118

Anderson, A. (ed) (2022) 'Special issue—The Swanwick/Tillman spiral of musical development: Impacts and influences', *British Journal of Music Education*, 39, 1: 1-140. Online, available at: https://www.cambridge.org/core/journals/british-journal-of-music-education/issue/F8AB63AE70BD5F5F6FC2F21B59A76D6A (accessed 27 March 2025).

Anderson, A. (2024) 'Curriculum power positioning in classroom music education: Music curriculum design in the secondary music classroom in England', *Arts Education Policy Review*, 125, 2: 94-107. https://doi.org/10.1080/10632913.2021.2023060

Arts Council England (ACE) (2019) *Durham Commission on Creativity and Education*. Online, available at: https://www.artscouncil.org.uk/durham-commission-creativity-and-education (accessed 24 March 2025).

Assessment Reform Group (1999) *Assessment for Learning: Beyond the Black Box*, Cambridge: University of Cambridge School of Education.

Auker, P. (1991) 'Pupil talk, musical learning and creativity', *British Journal of Music Education*, 8, 2: 161-166. https://doi.org/10.1017/S0265051700008263

Axtell, I.J., Anderson, A., MacGregor, E., Nenadic, E., Fautley, M. and Evans, N. (2024) 'Beowulf opera scenes: Classroom music pedagogy and knowledge when composing an opera with primary-school children', *Research Studies in Music Education*, 47, 2: 297-315. https://doi.org/10.1177/1321103X241285560

REFERENCES

Baer, J. (2017) Content matters: Why nurturing creativity is so different in different domains, in R.A. Beghetto and B. Sriraman (eds) *Creative Contradictions in Education*, Cham: Springer, pp. 129-140.

Bain, V. (2019) *Counting the Music Industry: The Gender Gap*. Online, available at: www.vbain.co.uk (accessed 28 March 2025).

Barnes, J. (2011) *Cross-Curricular Learning 3-14*, 2nd edn, London: SAGE.

Barnes, J. (2023) Exploring music within cross-curricular learning, in C. Cooke and C. Philpott (eds) *A Practical Guide to Teaching Music in the Secondary School*, 2nd edn, Abingdon: Routledge, pp. 89-100.

Barrett, M.S. (1990) 'Music and language in education', *British Journal of Music Education*, 7, 1: 67-73. https://doi.org/10.1017/S0265051700007518

Barrett, M.S. (2006) 'Creative collaboration: An "eminence" study of teaching and learning in music composition', *Psychology of Music*, 34, 2: 195-218. https://doi.org/10.1177/0305735606061852

Barrett, M.S. (2014) Collaborative creativity and creative collaboration: Troubling the creative imaginary, in M.S. Barrett (ed) *Collaborative Creative Thought and Practice in Music*, Farnham: Ashgate, pp. 3-14.

Bate, E.H. (2020) 'Justifying music in the national curriculum: The habit concept and the question of social justice and academic rigour', *British Journal of Music Education*, 37, 1: 3-15. https://doi.org/10.1017/S0265051718000098

Beghetto, R.A. (2012) Expect the unexpected: Teaching for creativity in the micromoments, in M.B. Gregerson, H.T. Snyder and J.C. Kaufman (eds) *Teaching Creatively and Teaching Creativity*, New York: Springer, pp. 133-149.

Benedict, C., Schmidt, P., Spruce, G. and Woodford, P. (eds) (2015) *The Oxford Handbook of Social Justice in Music Education*, New York: Oxford University Press.

Bernstein, B. (2000) *Pedagogy, Symbolic Control and Identity: Theory, Research, Critique*, rev. edn, New York: Bowman and Littlefield Publishers.

Best, D. (1992) *The Rationality of Feeling*, London: Falmer Press.

Biasutti, M. (2012) 'Group music composing strategies: A case study within a rock band', *British Journal of Music Education*, 29, 3: 343-357. https://doi.org/10.1017/S0265051712000289

Bickford, T. (2017) *Schooling New Media: Music, Language, and Technology in Children's Culture*, New York: Oxford University Press.

Black, P. and Wiliam, D. (1998) 'Assessment and classroom learning', *Assessment in Education: Principles, Policy and Practice*, 5, 1: 7-74.

Blacking, J. (1987) *A Commonsense View of All Music*, Cambridge: Cambridge University Press.

Board of Education (1927) *Handbook of Suggestions for Teachers*, London: His Majesty's Stationary Office.

Boden, M. (1990) *The Creative Mind: Myths and Mechanisms*, London: Weidenfeld and Nicolson.

Booth, N. (2022a) Developing formative assessment practice for high-impact teaching, in S.A. Capel, M. Leask, S. Younie, E. Hidson and J. Lawrence (eds) *Learning to Teach in the Secondary School: A Companion to School Experience*, 9th edn, Abingdon: Routledge, pp. 421-437.

Booth, N. (2022b) Using assessment data effectively, in S.A. Capel, M. Leask, S. Younie, E. Hidson and J. Lawrence (eds) *Learning to Teach in the Secondary School: A Companion to School Experience*, 9th edn, Abingdon: Routledge, pp. 450-461.

Bourdieu, P. (1977) *Outline of a Theory of Practice*, Cambridge: Cambridge University Press.

Bourdieu, P. (1993) *The Field of Cultural Production: Essays on Art and Literature*, Cambridge: Polity Press.

REFERENCES

Bowman, W.D. (2014) 'The ethical significance of music-making', *Music Mark Magazine*, Winter, 3. Online, available at: https://jfin107.wordpress.com/scholarly-paper-the-ethical-significance-of-music-making-by-wayne-bowman/ (accessed 9 October 2024).

Bresler, L. (2018) Collaborative journeys across pedagogical cultures: Attunement and the interplay of knowing and unknowing, in C. Christophersen and A. Kenny (eds) *Musician-Teacher Collaborations: Altering the Chord*, Abingdon: Routledge, pp. ix-xv.

Brewer, J. (1997) *The Pleasures of the Imagination: English Culture in the Eighteenth Century*, London: HarperCollins.

Bruner, J.S. (1960) *The Process of Education*, Cambridge, MA: Harvard University Press.

Bruner, J.S. (1966) *Towards a Theory of Instruction*, Cambridge, MA: Harvard University Press.

Bull, A. (2015) *The Musical Body: How Gender and Class Are Reproduced among Young People Playing Classical Music in England*. Doctoral thesis, Goldsmiths, University of London. Online, available at: https://research.gold.ac.uk/12299/ (accessed 7 March 2025).

Bull, A. (2019) *Class, Control, and Classical Music*, New York: Oxford University Press.

Bull, A., Bhachu, D., Blier-Carruthers, A., Bradley, A. and James, S. (2022) *Slow Train Coming? Equality, Diversity and Inclusion in UK Music Higher Education*. Online, available at: https://edims.network/report/slowtraincoming/ (accessed 28 March 2025).

Bunch, R. and Bickford, T. (2022) Children's musical cultures: Industries and audiences, in D. Lemish (ed) *The Routledge International Handbook of Children, Adolescents, and Media*, 2nd edn, Abingdon: Routledge, pp. 135-143.

Burnard, P. (2012) *Musical Creativities in Practice*, Oxford: Oxford University Press.

Cain, T. (2013) 'Passing it on: Beyond formal or informal pedagogies', *Music Education Research*, 15, 1: 74-91. https://doi.org/10.1080/14613808.2012.752803

Campbell, P.S. (2018) *Music, Education, and Diversity: Bridging Cultures and Communities*, New York: Teachers College Press.

Campbell, P.S. and Wiggins, T. (2012) Giving voice to children, in P.S. Campbell and T. Wiggins (eds) *The Oxford Handbook of Children's Musical Cultures*, New York: Oxford University Press, pp. 1-24.

Candy, L., Edmonds, E. and Vear, C. (2021) Knowledge, in C. Vear (ed) *The Routledge International Handbook of Practice-Based Research*, Abingdon: Routledge, pp. 193-204.

Capel, S.A., Leask, M., Younie, S., Hidson, E. and Lawrence, J. (eds) (2022) *Learning to Teach in the Secondary School: A Companion to School Experience*, 9th edn, Abingdon: Routledge.

Carey, J. (2005) *What Good Are the Arts?*, London: Faber and Faber.

Center for Applied Special Technology (CAST) (2018) *Universal Design for Learning Guidelines Version 2.2 [Graphic Organizer]*, Wakefield, MA: CAST. Online, available at: https://udlguidelines.cast.org (accessed 5 March 2025).

Chapin, C.M. (2020) *Adapting Instruments, Not Students: A Study of Adaptive Musical Instruments*. Honors Program Thesis, Northern University, Iowa. Online, available at: https://scholarworks.uni.edu/hpt/430 (accessed 27 March 2025).

Children and Families Act 2014. Online, available at: https://www.legislation.gov.uk/ukpga/2014/6/contents/enacted (accessed 12 January 2025).

Claxton, G. (2002) *Building Learning Power: Helping Young People Become Better Learners*, Bristol: The Learning Organisation. Online, available at: https://www.buildinglearningpower.com/ (accessed 29 January 2025).

Colwell, R. (2017) Assessment's potential in music education, in M.C. Moore (ed) *Critical Essays in Music Education*, Abingdon: Routledge, pp. 371-402.

Cook, N. (1990) *Music, Imagination and Culture*, Oxford: Clarendon Press.

Cooke, C. and Philpott, C. (eds) (2023) *A Practical Guide to Teaching Music in the Secondary School*, 2nd edn, Abingdon: Routledge.

REFERENCES

Cornbleth, C. (1990) *Curriculum in Context*, Basingstoke: Falmer Press.
Council for the Curriculum, Examinations and Assessment (CCEA) (2007a) *The Statutory Curriculum at Key Stage 3: Rationale and Detail*. Online, available at: https://ccea.org.uk/downloads/docs/ccea-asset/Curriculum/The%20Statutory%20Curriculum%20at%20Key%20Stage%203.pdf (accessed 9 October 2024).
Council for the Curriculum, Examinations and Assessment (CCEA) (2007b) *Music: Key Stage 3 Non-Statutory Guidance for Music*. Online, available at: https://ccea.org.uk/downloads/docs/ccea-asset/Curriculum/Key%20Stage%203%20Non-Statutory%20Guidance%20for%20Music.pdf (accessed 9 October 2024).
Creative United (2020) *Guide to Buying Adaptive Musical Instruments*. Online, available at: https://takeitaway.org.uk/wp-content/uploads/2020/06/Guide-to-Buying-Adaptive-Musical-Instruments.pdf (accessed 27 February 2025).
Cringen, A.T. (1889) *The Teacher's Handbook of the Tonic Sol-fa System*, Hungerford: Legare Street Press.
Crooks, T.J. (1988) 'The impact of classroom evaluation practices on students', *Review of Educational Research*, 58, 4: 438–481.
Crowe, J. (1996) 'The better class of music', paper presented at *Canada: Past Present and Future: A Cross-Disciplinary Conference*, University of Calgary, October. Online, available at: http://www.mcwetboy.net/useful_music/better_class/ (accessed 27 March 2025).
Csikszentmihalyi, M. (1996) *Creativity: Flow and the Psychology of Discovery and Invention*, New York: Harper Collins.
Csikszentmihalyi, M. (2002) *Flow: The Classic Work on How to Achieve Happiness*, London: Random House.
Davis, B. and Sumara, D. (2006) *Complexity and Education: Inquiries into Learning, Teaching and Research*, Mahwah, NJ: Lawrence Erlbaum Associates.
Deci, E.L. and Ryan, R.M. (2017) *Self-Determination Theory: Basic Psychological Needs in Motivation, Development, and Wellness*, New York: Guilford Press.
DeNora, T. (1996) *Beethoven and the Construction of Genius*, Berkeley, CA: University of California Press.
DeNora, T. (2000) *Music in Everyday Life*, Cambridge: Cambridge University Press.
Department for Education (DfE) (2013) *The National Curriculum in England: Framework Document*. Online, available at: https://www.gov.uk/government/publications/national-curriculum-in-england-framework-for-key-stages-1-to-4 (accessed 25 February 2025).
Department for Education (DfE) (2021) *Model Music Curriculum: Key Stages 1 to 3*. Online, available at: https://assets.publishing.service.gov.uk/media/6061f833d3bf7f5ce1060a90/Model_Music_Curriculum_Full.pdf (accessed 1 November 2024).
Department for Education (DfE) (2024) *Working Definition of Trauma-Informed Practice*. Online, available at: https://www.gov.uk/government/publications/working-definition-of-trauma-informed-practice/working-definition-of-trauma-informed-practice#:~:text=Trauma%2Dinformed%20practice%20is%20an,biological%2C%20psychological%20and%20social%20development (accessed 12 January 2025).
Department for Education (DfE) and Department for Culture, Media and Sport (DCMS) (2011) *The Importance of Music: A National Plan for Music Education*. Online, available at: https://www.gov.uk/government/publications/the-importance-of-music-a-national-plan-for-music-education (accessed 15 September 2015).
Department for Education (DfE) and Department for Culture, Media and Sport (DCMS) (2022) *The Power of Music to Change Lives: A National Plan for Music Education*. Online, available at: https://www.gov.uk/government/publications/the-power-of-music-to-change-lives-a-national-plan-for-music-education (accessed 30 October 2024).
Department for Education (DfE) and Department of Health and Social Care (DHSC) (2015) *Special Educational Needs and Disability Code of Practice: 0 to 25 Years*. Online,

REFERENCES

available at: https://www.gov.uk/government/publications/send-code-of-practice-0-to-25 (accessed 12 January 2025).

Devaney, K. (2024) Teaching and assessing composing in English secondary schools: An investigation into music teacher confidence, in A. Ziegenwyer, J. Grow, M. Fautley and K. Devaney (eds) *The Routledge Companion to Teaching Music Composition in Schools: International Perspectives*, Abingdon: Routledge, pp. 444-451.

Dezuanni, M. and Jetnikoff, A. (2011) Creative pedagogies and the contemporary school classroom, in J. Sefton-Green, P. Thompson, L. Bresler and K. Jones (eds) *The Routledge International Handbook of Creative Learning*, Abingdon: Routledge, pp. 264-272.

Dibben, N. (2003) Musical materials, perception and listening, in M. Clayton, T. Herbert and R. Middleton (eds) *The Cultural Study of Music: A Critical Introduction*, Abingdon: Routledge, pp. 193-203.

Dickinson, C. and Wright, J. (1993) *Differentiation: A Practical Handbook of Classroom Strategies*, Coventry: National Council for Educational Technology.

Didau, D. (2012) 'Children are at school to learn, not to behave', *The Guardian, Teacher Network*. Online, available at: https://www.theguardian.com/teacher-network/2012/feb/13/learning-behaviour-teaching (accessed 27 March 2025).

Education (Additional Support for Learning) (Scotland) Act 2004. Online, available at: https://www.legislation.gov.uk/asp/2004/4/contents (accessed 27 February 2025).

Education Scotland (2010) *Curriculum for Excellence: Expressive Arts, Experiences and Outcomes*. Online, available at: https://education.gov.scot/media/ogyjyehk/expressive-arts-eo.pdf (accessed 9 October 2024).

Eisner, E. (2002) *The Arts and the Creation of Mind*, New Haven: Yale University Press.

Elliott, D.J. (1995) *Music Matters: A New Philosophy of Music Education*, 1st edn, Oxford: Oxford University Press.

Elliott, D.J. and Silverman, M. (2015) *Music Matters: A Philosophy of Music Education*, 2nd edn, New York: Oxford University Press.

Ellis, S. and Tod, J. (2009) *Behaviour for Learning: Proactive Approaches to Behaviour Management*, 1st edn, Abingdon: Routledge, https://doi.org/10.4324/9781315811819

Ellsworth, E. (2005) *Places of Learning: Media, Architecture, Pedagogy*, Abingdon: Routledge.

Equality Act 2010. Online, available at: https://www.legislation.gov.uk/ukpga/2010/15/contents (accessed 27 February 2025).

Evans, J. (2016a) Collaboration, in C. Cooke, K. Evans, C. Philpott and G. Spruce (eds) *Learning to Teach Music in the Secondary School: A Companion to School Experience*, 3rd edn, Abingdon: Routledge, pp. 210-225.

Evans, K. (2016b) Performing for musical understanding, in C. Cooke, K. Evans, C. Philpott and G. Spruce (eds) *Learning to Teach Music in the Secondary School: A Companion to School Experience*, 3rd edn, Abingdon: Routledge, pp. 128-142.

Evans, K. and Philpott, C. (2023) Exploring musical literacy, in C. Cooke and C. Philpott (eds) *A Practical Guide to Teaching Music in the Secondary School*, 2nd edn, Abingdon: Routledge, pp. 26-38.

Evans, N. and Fautley, M. (2024) *A Planning, Reflection and Progression Toolkit*. Online, available at: https://www.bcmg.org.uk/listen-imagine-compose-primary-2 (accessed 24 March 2025).

Evans, N. and Spruce, G. (2023) Exploring composing, in C. Cooke and C. Philpott (eds) *A Practical Guide to Teaching Music in the Secondary School*, 2nd edn, Abingdon: Routledge, pp. 65-76.

Everitt, A. (1997) *Joining In: An Investigation into Participatory Music*, London: Calouste Gulbenkian Foundation.

Fancourt, D. and Finn, S. (2019) *What Is the Evidence on the Role of the Arts in Improving Health and Well-Being? A Scoping Review*, Health Evidence Network Synthesis Report, 67.

REFERENCES

Fautley, M. (2010) *Assessment in Music Education*, Oxford: Oxford University Press.

Fautley, M. (2013) *Teaching and Learning Notation*. Online, available at: https://drfautley.wordpress.com/ (accessed 31 October 2024).

Fautley, M. (2014) *Listen, Imagine, Compose Research Report*, Birmingham: Birmingham City University. Online, available at: https://www.open-access.bcu.ac.uk/7818/1/LIC%20Final%20Report%20web%20version.pdf (accessed 27 March 2025).

Fautley, M. (2024) Composing in schools: Thoughts on revisiting John Paynter. *I Can Compose Blog*, 19 November. Online, available at: https://www.icancompose.com/composing-in-schools-thoughts-on-revisiting-john-paynter/ (accessed 19 November 2024).

Fautley, M. and Daubney, A. (2025) *A Framework for Curriculum, Pedagogy and Assessment in Lower Secondary School Music*, London: Independent Society of Musicians.

Fautley, M. and Kinsella, V. (2017) The use of activity theory as an analytical tool for the music learning processes, in J. Bugos (ed) *Contemporary Research in Music Learning across the Lifespan: Music Education and Human Development*, Abingdon: Routledge, pp. 26-38.

Fautley, M., Kinsella, V. and Whittaker, A. (2019) 'Models of teaching and learning identified in whole class ensemble tuition', *British Journal of Music Education*, 36, 3: 243-252. https://doi.org/10.1017/S0265051719000354

Fautley, M. and Savage, J. (2011) *Cross-curricular Teaching and Learning in the Secondary School*, Abingdon: Routledge.

Fenwick, T., Edwards, R. and Sawchuk, P. (2011) *Emerging Approaches to Educational Research: Tracing the Sociomaterial*, Abingdon: Routledge.

Finnegan, R. (2003) Music, experience and the anthropology of emotion, in M. Clayton, T. Herbert and R. Middleton (eds) *The Cultural Study of Music: A Critical Introduction*, Abingdon: Routledge, pp. 181-192.

Finney, J. (2011) *Music Education in England, 1950-2010: The Child-Centred Progressive Tradition*, Abingdon: Routledge.

Finney, J. and Philpott, C. (2010) 'Informal learning and meta-pedagogy in initial teacher education in England', *British Journal of Music Education*, 27, 1: 7-19. https://doi.org/10.1017/S0265051709990167

Fletcher, P. (1987) *Education and Music*, Oxford: Oxford University Press.

Florian, L. and Black-Hawkins, K. (2011) 'Exploring inclusive pedagogy', *British Educational Research Journal*, 37, 5: 813-828. https://doi.org/10.1080/01411926.2010.501096

Florian, L. and Spratt, J. (2015) 'Inclusive pedagogy: From learning to action: Supporting each individual in the context of "everybody"', *Teaching and Teacher Education*, 49: 89-96. https://doi.org/10.1016/j.tate.2015.03.006

Flynn, G. and Pratt, G. (1995) 'Developing an understanding of appraising music with practising primary teachers', *British Journal of Music Education*, 12, 2: 127-158. https://doi.org/10.1017/S0265051700002576

Folkestad, G. (2005) 'Here, there and everywhere: Music education research in a globalised world', *Music Education Research*, 7, 3: 279-287. https://doi.org/10.1080/14613800500324390

Folkestad, G. (2006) 'Formal and informal learning situations or practices vs formal and informal ways of learning', *British Journal of Music Education*, 23, 2: 135-145. https://doi.org/10.1017/S0265051706006887

Francis, B. (2000) *Boys, Girls and Achievement: Addressing the Classroom Issues*, London: RoutledgeFalmer.

Freire, P. and Macedo, D. (1987) *Literacy: Reading the Word and the World*, London: Routledge.

Gaines, J. (2004) *Evening in the Palace of Reason*, London: Fourth Estate.

Gall, M. (2016) 'TPACK and music teacher education', in A. King, E. Himonides and A. Ruthman (eds) *The Routledge Companion to Music, Technology and Education*, Abingdon: Routledge, pp. 305-318.

REFERENCES

Gaunt, H. and Westerlund, H. (2013) The case for collaborative learning in higher music education, in H. Gaunt and H. Westerlund (eds) *Collaborative Learning in Higher Music Education*, Surrey: Ashgate, pp. 1–9.

Gibson, R. (1986) *Critical Theory and Education*, London: Hodder and Stoughton.

Goehr, L. (2007) *The Imaginary Museum of Musical Works: An Essay in the Philosophy of Music*, 2nd edn, New York: Oxford University Press.

Green, L. (1995) Gender, musical meaning and education, in G. Spruce (ed) *Teaching Music*, London: Routledge, pp. 123–131.

Green, L. (1996) The emergence of gender as an issue in music education, in C. Plummeridge (ed) *Music Education: Trends and Issues*, London: Institute of Education, pp. 41–58.

Green, L. (1997) *Music, Gender, Education*, Cambridge: Cambridge University Press.

Green, L. (2002) *How Popular Musicians Learn: A Way Ahead for Music Education*, Aldershot: Ashgate.

Green, L. (2005) 'The music curriculum as lived experience: Children's "natural" music learning processes', *Music Educators' Journal*, 91, 4: 27–32. http://eprints.ioe.ac.uk/1104

Green, L. (2008) *Music, Informal Learning and the School: A New Classroom Pedagogy*, Aldershot: Ashgate.

Green, L. and O'Neill, S. (2001) Social groups and learning in music education, in G. Welch, S. Hallam, A. Lamont, K. Swanwick, L. Green, S. Hennessy, G. Cox, S. O'Neill and G. Farrell (eds) *Mapping Music Education Research in the UK*, Southwell: British Educational Research Association, pp. 26–31.

Hallam, R. (2011) 'Effective partnership working in music education: Principles and practice', *International Journal of Music Education*, 29, 2: 155–171. https://doi.org/10.1177/0255761410396963

Hallam, S. (1998) *Instrumental Teaching: A Practical Guide to Better Teaching and Learning*, London: Heinemann.

Hallam, S. (2001) Learning in music: Complexity and diversity, in C. Philpott and C. Plummeridge (eds) *Issues in the Teaching of Music*, London: RoutledgeFalmer, pp. 61–75.

Hallam, S. and Himonides, E. (2022) *The Power of Music: An Exploration of the Evidence*, Cambridge: Open Book Publishers. Online, available at: https://www.openbookpublishers.com/books/10.11647/obp.0292 (accessed 6 March 2025).

Hanrahan, F., Hughes, E., Banerjee, R., Eldridge, A. and Kiefer, C. (2019) 'Psychological benefits of networking technologies in children's experience of ensemble music making', *International Journal of Music Education*, 37, 1: 59–77. https://doi.org/10.1177/0255761418796864.

Hargreaves, D.J. (1986) *The Developmental Psychology of Music*, Cambridge: Cambridge University Press.

Hargreaves, D.J. and Marshall, N.A. (2003) 'Developing identities in music education', *Music Education Research*, 5, 3: 263–273. https://doi.org/10.1080/1461380032000126355

Harland, J., Kinder, K., Lord, P., Stott, A., Schagen, I. and MacDonald, J. (2000) *Arts Education in Secondary Schools: Effects and Effectiveness*, Slough: National Foundation for Educational Research.

Harvey, E. (1988) *Jazz in the Classroom*, London: Boosey and Hawkes.

Henley, J. (2021) *Listen, Explore, Do: Five Years of Musicate*, Manchester: Royal Northern College of Music. Online, available at: https://www.rncm.ac.uk/uploads/Full-Report.pdf (accessed 31 October 2024).

Henley, J. and Barton, D. (2022) 'Time for change? Recurrent barriers to music education', *British Journal of Music Education*, 39, 2: 203–217. https://doi.org/10.1017/S026505172200016X

REFERENCES

Hess, J. (2015) 'Decolonizing music education: Moving beyond tokenism', *International Journal of Music Education*, 33, 3: 336-347. https://doi.org/10.1177/0255761415581283

Hess, J. (2019) *Music Education for Social Change*, Abingdon: Routledge

Hess, J. (2020) 'Finding the "both/and": Balancing informal and formal music learning', *International Journal of Music Education*, 38, 3: 441-455. https://doi.org/10.1177/0255761420917226

Hewitt, G. (2013) Why technology with hard to reach kids? in P. Mullen and C. Harrison (eds) *Reaching Out: Music Education with 'Hard to Reach' Children and Young People*, London: Music Mark, pp. 104-112.

Hickey, M. (2012) *Music Outside the Lines: Ideas for Composing in K-12 Music Classrooms*, New York: Oxford University Press.

Holder, N. (2020) *Where Are All the Black Female Composers?*, Holders Hill.

Independent Society of Musicians (ISM) (2022) *Music: A Subject in Peril? Ten Years on from the First National Plan for Music Education*. Online, available at: https://www.ism.org/music-in-peril/ (accessed 30 October 2024).

Independent Teacher Workload Review Group (ITWRG) (2016) *Eliminating Unnecessary Workload Associated with Data Management*. Online, available at: https://assets.publishing.service.gov.uk/media/5a8014c5e5274a2e8ab4e12a/Eliminating-unnecessary-workload-associated-with-data-management.pdf (accessed 1 December 2024).

Jorgensen, E. (2003) *Transforming Music Education*, Bloomington: Indiana University Press.

Kassner, K. (1988) 'Rx for technophobia', *Music Educators Journal*, 75, 3: 18-21. https://doi.org/10.2307/3398070

Kaufman, J. (2018) 'Creativity as a stepping stone toward a brighter future', *Journal of Intelligence*, 6, 2: 1-7. https://doi.org/10.3390/jintelligence6020021

Kelly, A.V. (2009) *The Curriculum: Theory and Practice*, 6th edn, London: SAGE.

Kendall, I. (1977) The role of literacy in the school music curriculum, in M. Burnett (ed) *Music Education Review: A Handbook for Music Teachers, Volume 1*, London: Chappell, pp. 29-44.

Kenny, A. (2016) *Communities of Musical Practice*, Abingdon: Routledge.

Kenny, A. and Christophersen, C. (2018) Musical alterations: Possibilities for musician-teacher collaborations, in C. Christophersen and A. Kenny (eds) *Musician-Teacher Collaborations: Altering the Chord*, Abingdon: Routledge, pp. 3-12.

Kinsella, V., Fautley, M. and Whittaker, A. (2019) *Exchanging Notes Research Report*, Birmingham: Birmingham City University. Online, available at: https://bcuassets.blob.core.windows.net/docs/FULL%20research%20report%20ExN.pdf (accessed 30 October 2024).

Kinsella, V., Fautley, M. and Whittaker, A. (2022) 'Re-thinking music education partnerships through intra-actions', *Music Education Research*, 24, 3: 299-311. https://doi.org/10.1080/14613808.2022.2053510.

Kokotsaki, D. (2017) 'Pupil voice and attitudes to music during the transition to secondary school', *British Journal of Music Education*, 34, 1: 5-39. https://doi.org/10.1017/S0265051716000279

Kwami, R.M. (2000) *Non-Western Musics: PGCE Knowledge Development Materials*, Milton Keynes: Open University (no longer available).

Kwami, R.M. (2001) Music education in and for a pluralist society, in C. Philpott and C. Plummeridge (eds) *Issues in Music Teaching*, London: RoutledgeFalmer, pp. 142-155.

Lamont, A., Hargreaves, D.J., Marshall, N.A. and Tarrant, M. (2003) 'Young people's music in and out of school', *British Journal of Music Education*, 20, 3: 229-241. https://doi.org/10.1017/S0265051703005412

REFERENCES

Laughey, D. (2006) *Music and Youth Culture*, Edinburgh: Edinburgh University Press.

Leppert, R. and McClary, S. (1987) *Music and Society: The Politics of Composition, Performance and Reception*, Cambridge: Cambridge University Press.

Lucas, B. (2016) 'A five-dimensional model of creativity and its assessment in schools', *Applied Measurement in Education*, 29, 4: 278–290. https://doi.org/10.1080/08957347.2016.1209206

MacGregor, E.H. (2020) 'Participatory performance in the secondary music classroom and the paradox of belonging', *Music Education Research*, 22, 2: 229–241. https://doi.org/10.1080/14613808.2020.1737927

MacGregor, E.H. (2022) 'Conceptualizing musical vulnerability', *Philosophy of Music Education Review*, 30, 1: 24–43. https://doi.org/10.2979/philmusieducrevi.30.1.03

MacGregor, E.H. (2023) Exploring performing, in C. Cooke and C. Philpott (eds) *A Practical Guide to Teaching Music in the Secondary School*, 2nd edn, Abingdon: Routledge, pp. 77–88.

MacGregor, E.H. (2025) *Musical Vulnerability: Receptivity, Susceptibility, and Care in the Music Classroom*, Abingdon: Routledge.

Mariguddi, A. (2021) 'Perceptions of the informal learning branch of Musical Futures', *British Journal of Music Education*, 38, 1: 31–42. https://doi.org/10.1017/S0265051720000303

Mariguddi, A. (2022) 'Tensions, issues and strengths of Professor Lucy Green's model of informal learning', *Music Education Research*, 24, 4: 442–454. https://doi.org/10.1080/14613808.2022.2074383

Mariguddi, A. (2026) The professional journeys of music teachers, in C. Philpott and G. Spruce (eds) *Debates in Music Teaching*, 2nd edn, Abingdon: Routledge, pp. 328–343.

Martin, P.J. (1995) *Sounds and Society*, Manchester: Manchester University Press.

Maslow, A.H.A. (1970) *Motivation and Personality*, New York: Harper and Row.

Maté, G. (1999) *Scattered Minds: The Origins and Healing of Attention Deficit Disorder*, New York: Avery.

McCarthy, B. (2000) *About Teaching: 4MAT in the Classroom*, Wauconda, IL: About Learning.

McClary, S. (1987) The blasphemy of talking politics in Bach year, in R. Leppert and S. McClary (eds) *Music and Society: The Politics of Composition, Performance and Reception*, Cambridge: Cambridge University Press, pp. 13–62.

McLachlan, J. (2016) *Music Therapy and Autism*. Online, available at: https://www.autism.org.uk/advice-and-guidance/professional-practice/music-therapy (accessed 27 February 2025).

McPhail, G. (2022) *Knowledge and Music Education: A Social Realist Account*, Abingdon: Routledge.

Metcalfe, M. (1987) Towards the condition of music, in P. Abbs (ed) *Living Powers*, London: Falmer, pp. 97–118.

Mills, J. and McPherson, G. (2015) Musical literacy: Reading traditional staff notation, in G. McPherson (ed) *The Child as Musician*, Oxford: Oxford University Press, pp. 177–191.

Mishra, P. and Koehler, M. (2006) 'Technological pedagogical content knowledge: A framework for teacher knowledge', *The Teachers College Record*, 108, 6: 1017–1054. https://doi.org/10.1111/j.1467-9620.2006.00684.x

Moore, V. (2005) 'One for the rack', *The Guardian Weekend*, 20 August, London: The Guardian.

Musical Futures (2022) *Transition Projects: Wellerman Collection*. Online, available at: https://www.musicalfuturesonline.org/resource-type/transition-projects/wellerman-collection/ (accessed 29 October 2024).

National Advisory Committee on Creative and Cultural Education (NACCCE) (1999) *All Our Futures: Creativity, Culture and Education*, London: Department for Education and Employment.

REFERENCES

National Association of Music Educators (NAME) (2000) *Composing in the Classroom: The Creative Dream*, London: NAME.

Natriello, G. (1987) 'The impact of evaluation processes on students', *Educational Psychologist*, 22, 2: 155-175.

Newton, P.E. (2007) 'Clarifying the purposes of educational assessment', *Assessment in Education*, 14, 2: 149-170. https://doi.org/10.1080/09695940701478321

NHS Digital (2021) *Mental Health of Children and Young People in England, 2021: Wave Two Follow up to the 2017 Survey*. Online, available at: https://digital.nhs.uk/data-and-information/publications/statistical/mental-health-of-children-and-young-people-in-england/2021-follow-up-to-the-2017-survey (accessed 6 March 2025).

North, A., Hargreaves, D.J. and O'Neill, S. (2000) 'The importance of music to adolescents', *British Journal of Educational Psychology*, 70, 2: 255-272. https://doi.org/10.1348/000709900158083

O'Brien, T. (1998) *Promoting Positive Behaviour*, London: David Fulton.

Ockelford, A. (2013) *Music, Language and Autism: Exceptional Strategies for Exceptional Minds*, London: Jessica Kingsley.

Odam, G. (2000) 'Teaching composing in secondary schools: The creative dream', *British Journal of Music Education*, 17, 2: 109-127. https://doi.org/10.1017/S0265051700000218

Office for Standards in Education, Children's Services and Skills (Ofsted) (2012) *Music in Schools: Wider Still, and Wider: Quality and Inequality in Music Education 2008-11*, London: Ofsted Publications. Online, available at: https://www.gov.uk/government/publications/music-in-schools (accessed 7 October 2015).

Office for Standards in Education, Children's Services and Skills (Ofsted) (2013) *Music Education in Schools: What Hubs Must Do*, London: Ofsted Publications. Online, available at: https://assets.publishing.service.gov.uk/media/5a8039f7ed915d74e622d370/Music_in_schools_what_hubs_must_do.pdf (accessed 1 September 2025).

Office for Standards in Education, Children's Services and Skills (Ofsted) (2023) *Striking the Right Note: The Music Subject Report*, London: Ofsted Publications. Online, available at: https://www.gov.uk/government/publications/subject-report-series-music/striking-the-right-note-the-music-subject-report (accessed 7 October 2024).

Organisation for Economic Co-Operation and Development (OECD) (2018) *The Future of Education and Skills: Education 2030*, Paris: OECD Publishing.

Organisation for Economic Co-Operation and Development (OECD) (2024) 'New PISA results on creative thinking: Can students think outside the box?' *PISA in Focus, Volume 125*, Paris: OECD Publishing. https://doi.org/10.1787/b3a46696-en

Osberg, D. and Biesta, G. (2008) 'The emergent curriculum: Navigating a complex course between unguided learning and planned enculturation', *Journal of Curriculum Studies*, 40, 3: 313-328. https://doi.org/10.1080/00220270701610746

Osberg, D., Biesta, G. and Cilliers, P. (2008) 'From representation to emergence: Complexity's challenge to the epistemology of schooling', *Educational Philosophy and Theory*, 40, 1: 213-227. https://doi.org/10.1111/j.1469-5812.2007.00407.x

Palmer, P. (1998) *The Courage to Teach*, San Francisco, CA: Jossey-Bass.

Parsons, M., Johnston, M. and Durham, R. (1978) 'Developmental stages in children's aesthetic responses', *Journal of Aesthetic Education*, 12, 1: 83-104. https://doi.org/10.2307/3331850

Partti, H. and Devaney, K. (2023) 'Addressing gender inequality in and through music composing studies', *Nordic Research in Music Education*, 4: 48-66. https://doi.org/10.23865/nrme.v4.5456

Pateman, T. (1991) *Key Concepts: A Guide to Aesthetics, Criticism, and the Arts in Education*, London: Falmer.

Paynter, J. (1977) The role of creativity in the school music curriculum, in M. Burnett (ed) *Music Education Review: A Handbook for Music Teachers, Volume 1*, London: Chappell, pp. 3-28.

Paynter, J. (1982) *Music in the Secondary School Curriculum: Trends and Developments in Classroom Teaching*, Cambridge: Cambridge University Press.

Paynter, J. (1997) 'The form of finality', *British Journal of Music Education*, 14, 3: 5-16. https://doi.org/10.1017/S0265051700003405

Paynter, J. (2000) 'Making progress with composing', *British Journal of Music Education*, 17, 1: 5-31. https://doi.org/10.1017/S0265051700000115

Paynter, J. and Aston, P. (1970) *Sound and Silence: Classroom Projects in Creative Music*, Cambridge: Cambridge University Press.

Philpott, C. (2009) Swanwick, musical development and assessment for learning in the 21st century, in H. Coll and A. Lamont (eds) *Sound Progress: Exploring Musical Development*, Matlock: National Association for Music Education, pp. 67-72.

Philpott, C. (2010) The sociological critique of curriculum music in England: Is radical change really possible? in R. Wright (ed) *Sociology and Music Education*, Farnham: Ashgate, pp. 81-92.

Philpott, C. (2012a) Assessment for self-directed learning in music education, in C. Philpott and G. Spruce (eds) *Debates in Music Teaching*, 1st edn, Abingdon: Routledge, pp. 153-168.

Philpott, C. (2012b) The justification for music in the curriculum: Music can be bad for you, in C. Philpott and G. Spruce (eds) *Debates in Music Teaching*, 1st edn, Abingdon: Routledge, pp. 48-63.

Philpott, C. (2022) 'What does it mean to decolonise the school music curriculum?' *London Review of Education*, 20, 1: 7. https://doi.org/10.14324/LRE.20.1.07

Philpott, C. and Plummeridge, C. (eds) (2001) *Issues in Music Teaching*, London: Routledge Falmer.

Piaget, J. (1952) *Construction of Reality in the Child*, London: Routledge and Kegan Paul.

Pitts, S.E. (2014) 'Exploring musical expectations: Understanding the impact of a year-long primary school music project in the context of school, home and prior learning', *Research Studies in Music Education*, 36, 2: 129-146. https://doi.org/10.1177/1321103X14556576

Plato (1982) *The Laws*, London: Penguin.

Plummeridge, C. (1991) *Music Education in Theory and Practice*, London: Falmer.

Pollard, A. and Triggs, P. (1997) *Reflective Teaching in Secondary Education*, London: Continuum.

Powell, S. and Tod, J. (2004) *A Systematic Review of How Theories Explain Learning Behaviour in School Contexts*, London: EPPI-Centre.

Project for Enhancing Effective Learning (PEEL) (2013) *Good Learning Behaviours*. Online, available at: https://peelweb.org/good-learning-behaviours-3/ (accessed 29 January 2025).

Rainbow, B. and Cox, G. (2006) *Music in Educational Thought and Practice: A Survey from 800BC*, Woodbridge: Boydell Press.

Regelski, T.A. (2005) Curriculum: Implications of aesthetic versus praxial philosophies, in D.J. Elliott (ed) *Praxial Music Education: Reflections and Dialogues*, Oxford: Oxford University Press, pp. 219-249.

Regelski, T.A. (2014) 'Resisting elephants lurking in the music education classroom', *Music Educators Journal*, 100, 4: 77-86. https://doi.org/10.1177/0027432114531798

Regelski, T.A. (2015) *A Brief Introduction to a Philosophy of Music and Music Education as Social Praxis*, Abingdon: Routledge.

Reid, L.A. (1986) *Ways of Understanding and Education*, London: Heinemann.

Reimer, B. (1989) *A Philosophy of Music Education*, 2nd edn, Englewood Cliffs, NJ: Prentice Hall.

Reimer, B. (2003) *A Philosophy of Music Education: Advancing the Vision*, 3rd edn, Albany: State University of New York Press.

Robinson, K. (2011) *Out of Our Minds: Learning to Be Creative*, Mankato, MN: Capstone.

REFERENCES

Ross, M. (1980) *The Arts and Personal Growth*, London: Pergamon.
Ross, M. (1995) 'What's wrong with school music?' *British Journal of Music Education*, 12, 3: 185-201. https://doi.org/10.1017/S0265051700002692
Ross, M. (eds) (1982) *The Development of Aesthetic Experience*, Oxford: Pergamon.
Rousseau, J.-J. (2013) *Emile*, Mineola, NY: Dover Publications.
Rusinek, G. (2008) 'Disaffected learners and school musical culture: An opportunity for inclusion', *Research Studies in Music Education*, 30, 1: 9-23. https://doi.org/10.1177/1321103X08089887
Russell, D. (1987/97) *Popular Music in England 1840-1914*, Manchester: Manchester University Press.
Savage, J. (2013) *The Guided Reader to Teaching and Learning in Music*, Abingdon: Routledge.
Savage, J. (2020) 'The policy and practice of music education in England, 2010-2020', *British Educational Research Journal*, 47, 2: 469-483. https://doi.org/10.1002/berj.3672
Savage, J. and Fautley, M. (2011) 'The organisation and assessment of composing at Key Stage 4 in English secondary schools', *British Journal of Music Education*, 28, 2: 135-157. https://doi.org/10.1017/S0265051711000040
Schmidt, P. (2005) 'Music education as transformative practice: Creating new frameworks for learning through a Freirean perspective', *Visions of Research in Music Education*, 6, 1: 2. https://digitalcommons.lib.uconn.edu/vrme/vol6/iss1/2
Schmidt, P. and Colwell, R. (2017) *Policy and the Political Life of Music Education*, New York: Oxford University Press.
Schools Council (1968) *Enquiry One: Music and the Young School Leaver*, London: Her Majesty's Stationary Office.
Schools Council (1971) *Music and the Young School Leaver: Problems and Opportunities*, Schools Council Working Paper 35, London: Methuen Educational.
Scope (2024) *Social Model of Disability*. Online, available at: https://www.scope.org.uk/about-us/social-model-of-disability/ (accessed 1 December 2024).
Scottish Education Department (1955) *Junior Secondary Education*, Edinburgh: Her Majesty's Stationary Office.
Sefton, H.F. (1868) *Three-Part Songs for the Use of the Pupils of the Public Schools of Canada*, Toronto: James Campbell and Son.
Shepherd, J. (1991) *Music as Social Text*, Cambridge: Polity Press.
Sherratt, R.G.A. (1977) Who's for creativity? in C. Cox and R. Boyson (eds) *Black Paper*, London: Temple Smith, pp. 34-37.
Shulman, L.S. (1986) 'Those who understand: Knowledge growth in teaching', *Educational Researcher*, 15, 2: 4-14. http://www.jstor.org/stable/1175860
Shulman, L.S. (2004) Just in case: Reflections on learning from experience, in L.S. Shulman, *The Wisdom of Practice: Essays on Teaching, Learning and Learning to Teach*, San Francisco: Jossey-Bass, pp. 462-482.
Shuter-Dyson, R. and Gabriel, C. (1981) *The Psychology of Musical Ability*, London: Methuen.
Slater, J. (2010) Introduction: The meme of collaboration, in J.J. Slater and R. Ravid (eds) *Collaboration in Education*, Abingdon: Routledge, pp. 1-13.
Sloboda, J. (1985) *The Musical Mind: The Cognitive Psychology of Musical Ability*, London: Methuen.
Small, C. (1977) *Music, Society, Education*, London: John Calder.
Small, C. (1998) *Musicking: The Meanings of Performing and Listening*, Middletown, CT: Wesleyan University Press.
Small, C. (1999) 'Musicking—the meanings of performance and listening: A lecture', *Music Education Research*, 1, 1: 9-22. https://doi.org/10.1080/1461380990010102
Smith, A. (1973) 'Feasibility of tracking musical form as cognitive listening objective', *Journal of Research in Music Education*, 4: 373-391.

REFERENCES

Smith, M.K. (2000) Curriculum theory and practice, in M.K. Smith (ed) *The Encyclopaedia of Informal Education*. Online, available at: https://infed.org/mobi/curriculum-theory-and-practice/ (accessed 25 March 2025).

Smolarczyk, K., Birnbaum, L., Christ, A. and Kröner, S. (2024) 'Children's and adolescents' engagement with music and the potential for (digital) empowerment processes: A text-mining-supported scoping review', *Psychology of Music*, 53, 2: 275-297. https://doi.org/10.1177/03057356241241535

Snedeker, J.P. (2005) 'Adaptive engineering for musical instruments', *Medical Problems of Performing Artists*, 20, 2: 89-98. https://doi.org/10.21091/mppa.2005.2017

Sounds of Intent (2015) *Assessment Framework*. Online, available at: https://soundsofintent.org/en/sounds-of-intent-framework/assessment/index (accessed 27 February 2025).

Special Educational Needs and Disability Act (Northern Ireland) 2016. Online, available at: https://www.legislation.gov.uk/nia/2016/8/contents/enacted (accessed 27 February 2025).

Spencer, E., Lucas, B. and Claxton, G. (2012) *Progression in Creativity: Developing New Forms of Assessment–Final Research Report*, Newcastle: Creativity, Culture and Education.

Spruce, G. (2012) Musical knowledge, critical consciousness and critical thinking, in C. Philpott and G. Spruce (eds) *Debates in Music Teaching*, 1st edn, Abingdon: Routledge, pp. 185-196.

Spruce, G. (2015) Music education, social justice, and the 'student voice': Addressing student alienation through a dialogical conception of music education, in Benedict, C., Schmidt, P., Spruce, G. and Woodford, P. (eds) *The Oxford Handbook of Social Justice in Music Education*, New York: Oxford University Press, pp. 287-301.

Spruce, G. (2016) An integrated approach to lesson planning, in C. Cooke, K. Evans, C. Philpott and G. Spruce (eds) *Learning to Teach Music in the Secondary School: A Companion to School Experience*, 3rd edn, Abingdon: Routledge, pp. 80-93.

Spruce, G. and Matthews, F. (2012) Musical ideologies, practices and pedagogies: Addressing pupil alienation through a praxial approach to the music curriculum, in C. Philpott and G. Spruce (eds) *Debates in Music Teaching*, 1st edn, Abingdon: Routledge, pp. 118-134.

Stakelum, M. (2024) 'Music literacy and the instrumental teacher', *Music Education Research*, 26, 1: 47-57. https://doi.org/10.1080/14613808.2024.2309547

Street, J. (2012) *Music and Politics*, Cambridge: Polity Press.

Style, E. (1996) 'Curriculum as window and mirror', *Social Science Record*, Fall. Online, available at: https://www.nationalseedproject.org/images/documents/Curriculum_As_Window_and_Mirror.pdf (accessed 1 September 2025).

Swanwick, K. (1979) *A Basis for Music Education*, Windsor: NFER-Nelson.

Swanwick, K. (1988) *Music, Mind and Education*, London: Routledge.

Swanwick, K. (1991) 'Musical criticism and musical development', *British Journal of Music Education*, 8, 2: 139-148. https://doi.org/10.1017/S026505170000824X

Swanwick, K. (1994) *Musical Knowledge: Intuition, Analysis and Music Education*, London: Routledge.

Swanwick, K. (1997) 'Editorial', *British Journal of Music Education*, 14, 1: 3-4. https://doi.org/10.1017/S0265051700003399

Swanwick, K. (1999) *Teaching Music Musically*, London: Routledge.

Swanwick, K. and Tillman, J. (1986) 'The sequence of musical development: A study of children's compositions', *British Journal of Music Education*, 3, 3: 305-309. https://doi.org/10.1017/S0265051700000814

Teacher Effectiveness Enhancement Programme (TEEP) (2013) *Teacher Effectiveness Enhancement Programme: A Summary of the TEEP Framework*. Online, available at:

REFERENCES

https://webcontent.ssatuk.co.uk/wp-content/uploads/2013/11/TEEP-Overview-document-Oct-20131.pdf (accessed 29 January 2025).

Thibeault, M.D. (2015) 'Music education for all through participatory ensembles', *Music Educators Journal*, 102, 2: 54–61. https://doi.org/10.1177/0027432115610170.

Turino, T. (2008) *Music as Social Life: The Politics of Participation*, Chicago: University of Chicago Press.

Turino, T. (2016) Music, social change, and alternative forms of citizenship, in D.J. Elliott, M. Silverman and W.D. Bowman (eds) *Artistic Citizenship: Artistry, Social Responsibility, and Ethical Praxis*, New York: Oxford University Press, pp. 297–312.

United Nations Educational, Scientific and Cultural Organization (UNESCO) (1994) *The Salamanca Statement and Framework for Action on Special Needs Education*. Online, available at: https://unesdoc.unesco.org/ark:/48223/pf0000098427 (accessed 25 March 2025).

United Nations Educational, Scientific and Cultural Organization (UNESCO) (2009) *Policy Guidelines on Inclusion in Education*, Paris: UNESCO. Online, available at: https://unesdoc.unesco.org/ark:/48223/pf0000177849 (accessed 27 February 2025).

Väkevä, L. (2010) 'Garage band or GarageBand®? Remixing Musical Futures', *British Journal of Music Education*, 27, 1: 59–70. https://doi.org/10.1017/S0265051709990209

Van Klompenberg, A. (2022) 'Trauma-informed practices in the music classroom', *NAfME Blog*. Online, available at: https://nafme.org/blog/trauma-informed-practices-in-the-music-classroom/ (accessed 6 March 2025).

Vulliamy, G. (1978) What counts as school music?, in G. Whitty and M.F.D. Young (eds) *Explorations in the Politics of School Knowledge*, Driffield: Nafferton, pp. 19–34.

Vygotsky, L.S. (1962) *Thought and Language*, Cambridge, MA: MIT Press.

Walker, N. (2021) *Neuroqueer Heresies: Notes on the Neurodiversity Paradigm, Autistic Empowerment, and Postnormal Possibilities*, Fort Worth: Autonomous Press.

Walker, R. (2005) 'A worthy function for music in education', *International Journal of Music Education*, 23, 2: 135–137. https://doi.org/10.1177/0255761405052408

Wallas, G. (1926) *The Art of Thought*, London: Watts.

Webster, P.R. (2003) 'Conference keynotes—Asking music students to reflect on their creative work: Encouraging the revision process', *Music Education Research*, 5, 3: 243–249. https://doi.org/10.1080/1461380032000126337

Welch, G., Purves, R., Hargreaves, D. and Marshall, N. (2011) 'Early career challenges in secondary school music teaching', *British Educational Research Journal*, 37, 2: 285–315. https://doi.org/10.1080/01411921003596903

Welsh Government (2020) *Curriculum for Wales*. Online, available at: https://hwb.gov.wales/curriculum-for-wales (accessed 27 March 2025).

Welsh Government (2022) *National Plan for Music Education*. Online, available at: https://www.gov.wales/sites/default/files/publications/2022-05/national-plan-for-music-education.pdf (accessed 9 October 2024).

Westerlund, H., Karlsen, S. and Partti, H. (2020) 'Introduction', in H. Westerlund, S. Karlsen, and H. Partti (eds) *Visions for Intercultural Music Teacher Education*, Cham: Springer, pp. 1–12.

Whittaker, W.G. (1925) *Class-Singing*, Oxford: Oxford University Press.

Wiliam, D. (2001) 'What is wrong with our educational assessments and what can be done about it?', *Education Review*, 15, 1: 57–62.

Woodford, P. (2005) *Democracy and Music Education*, Bloomington: Indiana University Press.

Woodford, P. (2012) 'Music education and social justice: Towards a radical political history and vision', in C. Philpott and G. Spruce (eds) *Debates in Music Teaching*, 1st edn, Abingdon: Routledge, pp. 85–101.

REFERENCES

Wright, R. (2001) 'Gender and achievement: The view from the classroom', *British Journal of Music Education*, 18, 3: 275-291. https://doi.org/10.1017/S0265051701000365

Wright, R. (2008) 'Kicking the habitus: Power, culture and pedagogy in the secondary school music curriculum', *Music Education Research*, 10, 3: 389-402. https://doi.org/10.1080/14613800802280134

Wright, R., Johansen, G., Kanellopoulos, P. and Schmidt, P. (eds) (2021) *The Routledge Handbook to Sociology of Music Education*, Abingdon: Routledge.

Young, S. (2023) 'Where neoliberalism and neoconservatism meet: The inception and reception of a Model Music Curriculum for English schools', *British Journal of Music Education*, 40, 2: 147-157. https://doi.org/10.1017/S0265051723000074

Younger, M. and Warrington, M. (1996) 'Differential achievement of girls and boys at GCSE', *British Journal of Sociology of Education*, 17, 3: 299-313. https://www.jstor.org/stable/1393405

Zeserson, K. (2012) Partnerships in music education, in C. Philpott and G. Spruce (eds) *Debates in Music Teaching*, 1st edn, Abingdon: Routledge, pp. 209-220.

Žižek, S. (2009) *First as Tragedy, Then as Farce*, London: Verso.

INDEX

Page locators in **bold** represent a table
Page locators in *italics* represent a figure

adaptation 48, 59, 135, 251, 254; *see also* differentiation
adaptive instruments 65-66
advocacy 7, 17, 21, 80, 112, 138, 220
aesthetic ideology *see* philosophy
aesthetic listening 257-260, 264, 266
agency 50, 70, 90, 172, 205, 247
anxiety 47, 49, 237, 251
assessment: context 175; data 173-175, 177, 179-181; examination 24, 115, 119, 140, 170-173, 216-217, 225, 235; formative 110, 171-173, 176-177; grading 178-179; observation 177; summative 110, 170-173, 180
attention deficit hyperactivity disorder (ADHD) 68-69; *see also* Special Educational Needs and Disabilities (SEND)
aural: analysis 159, 163, 259, 262, 271; perception 17, 112-113, 139-140
autism spectrum condition (ASC) 65, 67; *see also* Special Educational Needs and Disabilities (SEND)
autonomy 23, 29, 70-71, 79-81, 248, 264
awareness: critical 26, 31, 34, 58, 65, 192; cultural 36-37, 59

Bach, J. S. 10, 35-36, 136, 224
bands: brass 102, 106, **108**, 244; dance 35, 142; garage 243; heavy metal 188; rock 33, 138, 142, 268
Beethoven, L. van 10, 23, 27, 211
behaviour 68-69; and curriculum 158-160; environment 157-158, 167-168; learning 154-157; management 17, 68, 104, *148*, 154; musical 158-165; proactive 154, 156, 165; Project for Enhancing Effective Learning (PEEL) 156; reactive 154; and relationships 160-162; Teacher Effectiveness Enhancement Programme (TEEP) 156
blues music 34, 128, 149, 210, 214

charities 66, 76
choirs 83, 102, 106, 234, 244; *see also* singing
collaboration: benefits of 78; challenges of 74, 79, 90; with colleagues 81; in higher education 87-89; with instrumental teachers 85; interdisciplinary 81-82; model of *82*, 83-85, *86*, 88-89; with musicians 86; policy 78; with primary schools 83-84
community: local 138, 152; performing in the 242-244; of practitioners 2, 9
composing 178; creative 20, 35; cross-curricular 232-234; experiences of 130, 221-222, 237; feedback 238-239; in groups 162-163, *230-231*, 234; myths 223-224, 235; opportunities for 223, 229; processes 221, 224-226, 228; stages of 226-228, 234; style 229; visual stimuli 228
concert 13, 23, 29, 82, 236, 242, 259, 264
confidence 12, 41, 47, 70, 160, 221
constructivist perspective *see* philosophy
COVID-19 69, 221

INDEX

creativity: blocks to 235-236; concept of 201, 203, *204*, 206, 218; development of 208; the Durham Commission 204-205; models of 207; in the Programme for International Student Assessment (PISA) 200; process of 206-207; progression in 216
critical pedagogy 42-44, *45*, 50
cross-curricular learning 4, 113, 141; see also interdisciplinary learning
curriculum: as content 31, 60, 118-119, 122, 132; as contextually connected 127-128; decision-making 128-129; emergent 125-128, 130-132; interactions 123, *124*, 124-126; as lived experience 120, 127; philosophy 131-132; as product 118, 122, 132; reification 118-120; syllabus 2, 115, 218, 221, 238; see also National Curriculum for Music
Curriculum for Excellence see National Curriculum for Music
Curriculum for Wales see National Curriculum for Music

dialogic pedagogy 72-73, 123-124
differentiation 56, 63-64, 67, 72-73; see also adaptation
digital: Digital Audio Workstation (DAW) 47-51; identity 44; Musical Instrument Digital Interface (MIDI) 47-48, 51; social media 102, 106, 242; technology 40-44, *45*, 49, 52-54, 241, 252; tools 45-48, 50-51, 254
Digital Audio Workstation (DAW) see digital
disabilities see Special Educational Needs and Disabilities (SEND)
diversity: cultural 36-37, 159; musical 33, 59-60, 74, 238, 258, 271

emotion 8, 13, 17, 25, 58, 68-70, 111, 157-162, 165, 212, 265-267
enculturation 25, 27, 99-103, 106, **111**, 135-136, 149
examination see assessment
expressive arts 13, 18-19, 201, 203
expressive problems 210-212
extra-curricular 81-82

feedback: formative 46, 238; peer 146, 239; verbal 46, 179; see also assessment
film music 115, 263
formal learning 100-102, 104-105, *107*, **108**, 114

gamelan music 24, 37, 149, 150, 190, 229, 235, 254
gender: representation 22, 60-62, 93, 238; stereotypes 26, 59; underachievement 60-61
group work 12, 70-71, 160-163, 166-167, 228-232, 235, 243-244, 247-251, 253-255

Handel, G. F. 190, 263
Holiday, B. 269-270

improvising 12, 20, 34, 37, 203, 213-217, 224
inclusive education 55-56, 63, 70, 73; concept of 55-57, 67; engagement 224, 237, 242, 251, 255-256; pedagogy 58, 64; technology 53, 252; see also Special Educational Needs and Disabilities (SEND)
Indian music 60, 215, 225
informal learning 24, 79-80, 103-106, *107*, 108, **108**, 24**7**
interdisciplinary learning 113, 141, 201; see also cross-curricular learning
intuitive: language 187; learning **100**, 114, **164**, *191*, 204; understanding 96, 99, 188, 190, 192, 196-198

jazz music 34, 128, 140, 143, **269-271**

knowledge see musical knowledge

language: and assessment 196; explicit 188, 197; misconceptions 177, 192-193; about music 187-190; student talk 194-195; teacher talk 195-196; see also literacy
lesson planning 134-135, 147-153, 269-271; for emergent curriculum 130-131; evaluation 151-152; for immersive activities 139-143; for integrated experiences 143-147; for musical knowledge 135-139
listener: active 145; role of 258-250, 262
listening 31, 258, 259, 263
literacy: musical 4, 32-34; skills 13, 17, 112; see also language

mathematics 8-9, 16, 47, 112, 179
minimalist music 37, 115, 127
music education: aim 98, 102, 139; history 16, 98, 103; philosophy 3, 14-15, 20, 23-24, 32, 37-38, 99

289

INDEX

musical criticism 188, 195-196, 198
musical development 8, 18, 65, 109-110, **111**, 202
musical elements 49, 115, 210, 246
Musical Futures 83, 103, 247-248, 253
Musical Instrument Digital Interface (MIDI) see digital
musical identity 44, 53, 71, 77, 120, 127
musical knowledge 20, 44, 93-99, 106, 109, 114, 130, 135-139, 141-142, 147, 149, 152-153; about 95-97, 136-139, 141-142; high-status 8, 246, 261; how 95-97, 136-139, 141-142; of 95-97, 136-139, 141-142; recognising 93-94, 96, 109, 135-137, 149, 153, 261; that 136-139, 141-142; transfer of 112-114
musical meaning 20, 23, 27-28, 31-32, 35, 190, 259, 261-262
musical notation 12-13, 15, 32-34, 51, 95, 140, 150, 190, *191*, 197-198, 225, 249

National Curriculum for Music 18, 106, 119; England 18, 31, 57, 144, 201, 245, 269-271; Model Music Curriculum 19-20, 220; Northern Ireland 18-20, 246; Scotland 18, 115, 141-143, 245-246; Wales 18-19, 137-139, 201, 246; National Plan for Music Education: England 18-19, 78, 220; Wales 18, 78, 220
neurodiversity 67; see also Special Educational Needs and Disabilities (SEND)
non-formal learning 33, 106-107, *107*, **108**
notation see musical notation

Pedagogical Content Knowledge (PCK) 43, *45*, 176; Technological Pedagogical Content Knowledge (TPCK) 43-45, *45*
peer: assessment 151; collaboration 77; feedback 239; interaction 90; support 70-71
performing: in the classroom 241, 246; in the community 242-244; large-group 249, 251, 254; participatory 242, 247, 250; presentational 237, 242, 245, 251, 253, 256; small-group 243-244, 247-248, 251, 253
philosophy: aestheticism 13-14, 23-24, 257-260, 264, 266; constructivism 101, 104-105; praxialism 14-15, 20, 23-24, 37-38, 99; social realism 99; sociocultural 22-24, 32, 39
planning see lesson planning
policy 3, 7, 10-12, 22, 31, 55, 78, 115-117, 120-121, 123, 178-179, 245-246; see also National Curriculum for Music
praxial philosophy see philosophy
professional: development 45, 175, 222, 238; obligation 2; practitioners 4
progression 81, 83, 180-182, 216, 218, 229
Prokofiev, S. 212

reciprocity 162, 165
reflection 2, 41, 63, 229
rehearsal 27-28, 41, 82, 87, **108**, 159, 267
reification 28, 31-32, 118-119; see also curriculum
resilience 69, 90, 165, 179
resourcefulness 162, 165, 167
response to music **111**, 134, 188-190, 196, 198, 265-267
role models 80, 209, 238

self-determination theory (SDT) 70-71
set works 35-36, 216-217
singing: culture 8, 255; whole-class 245, 251, 255; see also choirs
social development 16, 21, 51, 67, 72, 123, 160
social justice 21-22
social realism see philosophy
sociocultural perspective see philosophy
sonic material 23, 51, 180, **182**, 190, 260, 263
Sounds of Intent 65
Special Educational Needs and Disabilities (SEND) 56-57, 64, 67, 69, 72-73; Education, Health, and Care Plan (EHCP) 56; social, emotional, and mental health difficulties (SEMHD) 69; Universal Design for Learning (UDL) 58-59, 63
Stravinsky, I. 217
student talk see language

teacher talk see language
Technological Pedagogical Content Knowledge (TPCK) see Pedagogical Content Knowledge (PCK)
technology see digital
technophobia 49-50

theme and variations 149, 190, 216
theory and practice 2, 21
trauma-informed practice 69-70

Universal Design for Learning (UDL) see Special Educational Needs and Disabilities (SEND)

Wagner, R. 211, *212*
wellbeing 157, *158*, 160-162, 165, 168

western art music 34, 36-37, 60, 221, 225, 259
workshopping 245, 249, 251

young people: engaging with 25, 60, 70, 72, 123, 130, 160, 220, 251, 265; identities 44, 71-72, 77, 127-128; interests 76, 149; language 187, 190, 195; as musicians 62-63, 66-67, 127, 138, 165-166, 201; voices 77, 83, 160, 234, 237

For Product Safety Concerns and Information please contact our EU representative GPSR@taylorandfrancis.com
Taylor & Francis Verlag GmbH, Kaufingerstraße 24, 80331 München, Germany